Music in Special Education

Mary S. Adamek, PhD, MT-BC
Alice-Ann Darrow, PhD, MT-BC

The American Music Therapy Association is a non-profit association dedicated to increasing access to quality music therapy services for individuals with disabilities or illnesses or for those who are interested in personal growth and wellness. AMTA provides extensive educational and research information about the music therapy profession. Referrals for qualified music therapists are also provided to consumers and parents. AMTA holds an annual conference every autumn and its eight regions hold conferences every spring. For up-to-date information, please access the AMTA website at www.musictherapy.org

ISBN: 978-1-884914-26-3

The American Music Therapy Association, Inc.
8455 Colesville Rd., Suite 1000
Silver Spring, MD 20910

Phone: (301) 589-3300
Fax: (301) 589-5175
Email: info@musictherapy.org
Website: www.musictherapy.org

Cover design – GrassT Designs
Technical assistance — Wordsetters, Inc.
Layout design and formatting — Angie K Elkins

Printed in the United States of America

Music in Special Education

Mary S. Adamek, PhD, MT-BC
Alice-Ann Darrow, PhD, MT-BC

Music in Special Education

Mary S. Adamek, PhD, MT-BC
Alice-Ann Darrow, PhD, MT-BC

MARY ADAMEK is Clinical Professor of Music Therapy at The University of Iowa. She specializes in music therapy and music education with special populations, in particular, students with behavior disorders and students with autism. She has published several clinical articles and book chapters on these topics and has offered music in special education workshops around the country. She has received a Collegiate Teaching Award from The University of Iowa and a Service Award from the American Music Therapy Association. She presently serves on the editorial boards of the Journal of Music Therapy and Music Therapy Perspectives, and is a former president of the American Music Therapy Association.

ALICE-ANN DARROW is Irvin Cooper Professor of Music at Florida State University. Her teaching and research interests are teaching music to special populations, nonverbal communication, and the role of music in deaf culture. Related to these topics, she has been the recipient of eighteen federal, university, or corporate grants, and has published numerous monographs, research articles, and book chapters. She is editor of the text Introduction to Approaches in Music Therapy. She presently serves on the editorial boards of the Bulletin for the Council on Research in Music Education, Update: Applications of Research in Music Education, and Music Therapy Perspectives, and has been the recipient of research and clinical practice awards from the American Music Therapy Association.

Published by the American Music Therapy Association, Inc.

Dedications

To my family who nurtures me,
my colleagues who believe in me,
and my students who teach me;
Thank you for providing such a positive environment
for my personal and professional endeavors.

—MSA

To my students, both with and without disabilities,
Thank you for all that you have taught me,
and for making my life abundantly rich.

—AAD

Preface

The passage of Public Law 94-142 in 1975, the Education for All Handicapped Children Act, was a landmark in American public education. With this book, we wish to celebrate the 35th anniversary of this historic law, now currently enacted as the Individuals with Disabilities Education Act (IDEA 2004), as amended in 2004. The purpose of P.L. 94-142 was to support states in protecting the rights of and meeting the educational needs of children and youth with disabilities. Before this law was passed, public schools educated only 1 in 5 children with disabilities. Most children with disabilities were denied access to their neighborhood schools and were educated in segregated institutions, if at all. In the years since the passage of P.L. 94-142, significant progress has been made toward meeting national goals for developing and implementing educational programs and services for infants to students 21 years of age. Many of these students now receive music education and music therapy as a part of their educational experience. Our own careers as music educators and therapists began in the public schools over 30 years ago. We are privileged and proud to have been a part of these early efforts on behalf of children with disabilities.

We have observed important changes in the field of special education over these past three decades. Throughout this time, music educators and therapists have adapted to each new change, especially in regard to the movement toward inclusive practices. As a result of inclusion, the role of many music educators and therapists in schools has changed. *Music in Special Education* provides perspective on the history of music in special education and an introduction to the current role of music education and music therapy in the field.

Music educators and music therapists today carry greater accountability than ever before in the education of their students. They work with students whose abilities range from gifted to those with severe disabilities. The knowledge base required to work effectively with such a broad range of student abilities increases with the passage of each new amendment to the Individuals with Disabilities Education Act; consequently, continued education and training for professionals is a necessity.

Music in Special Education explains essential features of special education that are important for interdisciplinary communication and effective teaching. *Music in Special Education* answers the following questions:

♦ Who are the students who have special needs in the music setting? What are the characteristics of the disabling conditions?

♦ What legislation is at the foundation of the movement to include students with disabilities in general education? What does the current legislation mandate and how does that affect the music educator and music therapist?

♦ What role does the music educator play in the education of students with disabilities in the school? What role does the music therapist play in the education of students with disabilities in the school?

♦ What is the purpose of a music therapy eligibility assessment? What is involved in this type of assessment? How can music educators assess the skills of students with disabilities?

♦ What are the characteristics of students with specific disabilities? What are appropriate music education and music therapy goals and interventions for students with specific disabilities?

♦ What are appropriate accommodations and adaptations for students with disabilities in the music setting? How can students with disabilities be included successfully in music education classrooms?

♦ What does the research literature tell us about music therapy with school-aged clients? What types of interventions and procedures are used in the research? What does the research tell us about effectiveness of the music therapy services?

♦ How can students with disabilities be included in the beginning band class? What instructional strategies can be utilized to support the student's success in band?

♦ What is the impact of disability on the family? What roles can music education and music therapy play within the culture of the family?

In this 2nd edition of *Music in Special Education*, we have updated and enhanced all of the information from the previous edition, and we have added four new chapters (Chapter 10, Students with Autism Spectrum Disorders (ASD); Chapter 14, A Content Analysis of the Research Literature on Music Therapy with School-Aged Clients; Chapter 15, Including Students with Disabilities in Beginning Band; and Chapter 16, Family and Disability). We are pleased to include the contributions of two guest authors, Sarah B. Klein, MM, MT-BC (Chapter 14), and Kristin Webster, MA, MT-BC (Chapter 15). We are grateful to these young professionals who helped us broaden the scope of this 2nd edition with new topics and information.

Part I introduces the reader to the historical and instructional foundations of music in special education. Major topics and developments in the field of special education, important terminology, and curricular issues are covered in Part I. Part II describes the characteristics of students with specific disabilities, the educational effects of these disabilities, appropriate adaptations, as well as music education and music therapy approaches used with students who have these disabilities. New to this 2nd edition of *Music in Special Education*, Part III extends the information from Parts I and II to address music therapy research in the schools, including students with disabilities in beginning band, and issues related to the family of students with disabilities.

It seems appropriate to pay homage to individuals whose work guided us through our early years as music teachers and therapists in special education. In 1980, Richard M. Graham and Alice S. Beer wrote the first text related to P.L. 94-142, *A Handbook for Mainstreaming: Teaching Music to the Exceptional Child*, and 10 years later, in 1990, Betty W. Atterbury wrote, *Mainstreaming Exceptional Learners in Music*. We hope that our text, *Music in Special Education* (2nd edition), will be as useful to readers today as their texts were to us.

Resources

The following products and services from the American Music Therapy Association may be helpful in using this book.

Music Therapy & Family Quality of Life - DVD

In this plenary session presented at the 2003 AMTA Conference, Professors Rud and Ann Turnbull talk about their first-hand experience with the effect music therapy had on their son, J.T. The Turnbulls are co-directors of the Beach Center on Family and Disability at The University of Kansas and their consistent advocacy for music therapy has reached far and wide. They are joined in this presentation by their son, J.T., who received music therapy services for most of his life. J.T. was a great teacher to the many music therapy students who had the honor of working with him! Enjoy this heartfelt, intimate look at the role of music therapy in their lives and an uplifting message for all.

Music in Special Education - DVD

Music in Special Education DVD includes segments on various music classrooms that include students with sensory disabilities (vision and hearing), cognitive disabilities, behavior disorders, multiple disabilities, and physical disabilities. Included in these segments are illustrations of classroom instruction as well as interviews with the music teachers and their students. Also included in the DVD are two segments on music teachers with disabilities.

Teacher Materials to Support Music in Special Education

Supportive teaching materials such as chapter outlines, model syllabi, and sample test questions are available in digital format for purchase by professors using this textbook. All files on this resource are created in Microsoft Word so they can be adapted to the specific needs of each teacher and class.

For more information on ordering these and other helpful products, please contact:
American Music Therapy Association
8455 Colesville Road, Suite 1000
Silver Spring, Maryland, USA
(301) 589-3300
info@musictherapy.org
www.musictherapy.org

Table of Contents

Part I

Historical and Current Issues Related to
Music in Special Education

Chapter 1

Current Profile of Students with Disabilities in Public Schools with Implications for Music Professionals

CHAPTER OVERVIEW

Schools in the U.S. are mandated to educate all children, regardless of their abilities and disabilities. This means that music educators and music therapists who work in schools are responsible for providing educational services for students with disabilities in the general music class, performance groups, special music classes, and music therapy sessions. This chapter answers the questions: (a) Who are the students who receive special education services in the school? and (b) How does the role of the music professional change when working with students who have special needs?

This chapter includes information on the following topics:
 ♦ Overview of students receiving educational services under the Individuals with Disabilities Education Act (IDEA)
 ♦ Limited English proficiency (LEP)/English language learners (ELL) and poverty: Other factors that can affect students' ability to learn
 ♦ Identifying with labels/person-first language
 ♦ The changing role for music educators and music therapists in schools

Overview of Students Receiving Educational Services under the Individuals with Disabilities Education Act (IDEA)

During the fall of 2007, over 6 million students ages 3 through 21 received special education services under the Individuals with Disabilities Education Act (IDEA). This breaks down into two categories, students ages 3–5 (710,310 students) and students ages 6–21 (6,007,832 students). Approximately 10% of students ages 6 through 21 received special education services that year. The number of students served under IDEA increased by over 600,000 students from 1998 to 2007. This is a steady increase of close to 80,000 students per year who received special education services (Data Accountability Center, 2007).

There are many possible reasons for such a striking increase in numbers. Over this time period, IDEA was reauthorized and amended several times and, in addition, a new regulation in 1997 gave states the option to provide service to students ages 3 through 9 under a "developmental delay" category. Over the years more states have begun to utilize this optional category. Some specific disability categories such as "autism" and "other health impaired" (OHI) have increased significantly, which could be due to an increase in diagnosis for ADHD (under OHI category) and autism seen nationwide. These factors could explain the dramatic increase in the number of students served under IDEA over that time period.

Students Served by Disability Category (Ages 6–21)

IDEA lists 13 disability categories under which students could be eligible for special education services, which include specific learning disability, speech or language impairment, mental retardation, emotional disturbance, multiple disabilities, hearing impairment, orthopedic impairment, other health impairment, visual impairment, autism, deaf-blindness, traumatic brain injury, and developmental delay. The nonspecific "developmental delay" category may be used only for students ages 3 through 9.

As presented in Table 1.1 on the previous page, almost half of the students with disabilities served under IDEA in 2007 had specific learning disabilities, which was the most prevalent disability served (2.6 million students, 44% of students with disabilities served). The next most prevalent categories were speech and language impairments (19%), other health impairments (11%), mental retardation (8%), and emotional disturbance (7%). Of all students ages 6 through 21, 89% were classified under one of these five disability categories. Although developmental delay and autism are relatively small categories, they have experienced large growth over the past decade (Data Accountability Center, 2007).

Table 1.1 Students with Disabilities Served under IDEA in 2007, by Disability Category, Ages 6–21

Disability	Number of Students Served under IDEA	Percentage of Students Served under IDEA
Specific Learning Disability	2,620,240	44
Speech or Language Impairment	1,154,165	19
Other Health Impairments	631,188	11
Mental Retardation	498,159	8
Emotional Disturbance	440,202	7

Disability	Number of Students Served under IDEA	Percentage of Students Served under IDEA
Autism	258,305	4.3
Multiple Disabilities	132,594	2
Developmental Delay	88,629	1.5
Hearing Impairments	72,160	1.2
Orthopedic Impairments	60,523	1
Visual Impairments	26,423	< 1
Traumatic Brain Injury	23,864	< 1
Deaf-Blindness	1,380	< 1
Total Disabilities	6,007,832	

(Data Accountability Center, 2007)

Age Groups of Students Served Under IDEA 2007 (Ages 6–21)

Students served under IDEA ages 6 through 21 are typically divided into three age groups: 6–11 year olds (elementary age), 12–17 year olds, (junior/senior high school age), and 18–21 year olds (post high school age). The majority of students served under IDEA are within the 6–11 and 12–17 year-old groups, with only about 5% of the students served from the 18–21 year-old group.

Speech and language impairments and specific learning disabilities were the most prevalent disabilities in the 6–11 age group. The largest percentage of students in the 12–17 age group had specific learning disabilities; the next most prevalent disability was other health impairments. The largest group of students in the 18–21 age group served under IDEA had specific learning disabilities, followed by mental retardation (see Table 1.2).

Table 1.2 Students with Disabilities Served under IDEA in 2007 by Age Group

Age Group	Two Most Prevalent Disabilities
Ages 6–11	Speech or language disabilities; specific learning disability
Ages 12–17	Specific learning disability; other health impairment
Ages 18–21	Specific learning disability; mental retardation

(Data Accountability Center, 2007)

Students having the most prevalent disabilities, such as specific learning disabilities or speech and language disabilities, may or may not have problems functioning in the music setting. In fact, music educators may not even be aware that a student has one of these disabilities if it is a mild form of the disorder. Students with mild disabilities may not require any additional adaptations by the music educator to participate and succeed at the same level as the other students in the class, especially if the teacher is utilizing principles of Universal Design for Learning (UDL). (See Chapter 4 for more information about UDL.) Students with moderate to severe disabilities may require significant instructional adaptations in music. In addition, students with emotional disorders, autism, multiple disabilities, and hearing impairments can prove to be more challenging for music educators than students who have the more prevalent learning disabilities and speech and language disabilities.

Age Groups of Students Served under IDEA 2007 (Preschool Aged, 3–5 Years Old)

Specific IDEA funds are earmarked for states to provide services to children with disabilities ages 3 through 5. In order to receive these funds, states must have policies and procedures in place to provide a free and appropriate education for all children with disabilities in this age group. During the fall of 2007, over 700,000 preschool children with disabilities were served under IDEA. Although enrollment of preschoolers in special education varies by state, the national average for preschool students with disabilities receiving special education services is approximately 5% of the total number of preschool students (see Table 1.3). Some states service a higher percentage (more than 8%), and some states service a much lower percentage (less than 4%).

States may use the IDEA disability categories to identify preschool children who are eligible for services, or they may use the less specific "developmental delay" category for children who are ages 3 through 9. Schools may use this nonspecific classification to document eligibility for special education services, since it is sometimes difficult to identify the specific nature of a very young child's disability.

Table 1.3   Students with Disabilities Served under IDEA in 2007, Ages 3–5, Most Prevalent Disability Categories

Disability	Number of Students Served under IDEA	Percentage of Students Served under IDEA
Speech or Language Impairment	328,375	46
Developmental Delay	269,821	38
Autism	39,434	5

(Data Accountability Center, 2007)

Age Groups of Students Served under IDEA in 2007 (Early Intervention, Children Ages Birth Through 2 Years, and Families)

Part C of IDEA provides for early intervention services for children ages birth through 2 and their families. During the fall of 2007, over 300,000 children of this age group and their families received services. This number is approximately double the number of children in this age group served 10 years prior in 1997. The children in this age group are quite diverse in terms of disability and service needs. Most infants and toddlers who are eligible for services have some sort of a developmental delay. Many children who begin early intervention before 12 months of age have problems related to prenatal/perinatal abnormalities, which can cause physical or cognitive disabilities. For children who are older than 12 months, the most prevalent need for services is related to speech or communication difficulties. A small proportion of children ages birth through 2 have difficulty with hearing, vision, the use of their arms and hands, or the use of their legs and feet. In addition, some children may have behaviors that are more challenging than those of a typically developing young child (Data Accountability Center, 2007).

Limited English Proficiency and Poverty: Other Factors that Can Affect Students' Ability to Learn

In addition to specific, identified disabilities, there are other factors that can negatively affect a student's ability to achieve educational benefits in school. Students' cultural, linguistic, and socioeconomic characteristics may play a role in how a student learns and how professionals work with students to accommodate their needs.

The demographics of the U.S. have been changing dramatically over the past 30 years due to rapid increases in immigration and changes in immigration patterns. English is not the primary language for many people who immigrate to this country, which means that greater numbers of students in schools have limited English proficiency (LEP). Another term used to identify these students is English language learner (ELL).

Approximately 10% of the total student population in U.S. public schools has limited English proficiency (Government Accountability Office [GAO], 2006). According to the Elementary and Secondary Education Act, the definition of a student who has LEP is one who is age 3–21 and enrolled or preparing to enroll in school; who has sufficient difficulty speaking, reading, writing, or understanding the English language; and whose difficulties may deny such individual the opportunity to learn successfully in classrooms where the language of instruction is English or to participate fully in our society due to one or more of the following:

- was not born in the United States or whose native language is a language other than English and comes from an environment where a language other than English is dominant
- is a Native American or Alaska Native or who is a native resident of the Outlying Areas
- comes from an environment where a language other than English has had significant impact on such individual's level of English language proficiency
- is migratory and whose native language is other than English and comes from an environment where language other than English is dominant (Abedi, 2007)

Limited English proficiency alone is not sufficient for special education eligibility; however, many students with limited English are assessed and placed in special education inappropriately due to poor performance on culturally or linguistically biased assessment procedures. Other students with limited English may also have disabilities that qualify them for special education and related services under IDEA. Although estimates vary on the number of students with LEP, in 2006 there were more than 5 million students with limited English proficiency in the U. S. (U.S. Department of Education, 2008).

Students with limited English, whether receiving LEP services, special education and related services, or a combination, will be a part of the regular education inclusive music classroom, adapted music classroom, or music therapy services. All professionals need to be aware of the student's specific needs in order to help that student fully participate, contribute, and benefit from the music experience. Music educators and music therapists may have to adapt instruction to help students who have limited English succeed in music. In addition to the limitations that these students might have in school, they frequently bring with them rich cultural diversity that can enhance the music experience for all students. Creative music professionals can augment the music curriculum with musical experiences based on the varied cultures of the students in the school. In doing so, they recognize the many contributions that all students bring to the class and they highlight the important individual differences that make the U.S. a rich cultural mosaic.

Music professionals might ask the following questions in order to more effectively teach students with limited English:

- What is the student's first language?
- What functional words in English does the child understand?
- Is there someone on staff or available outside of school to translate some basic music terms? Can a translator assist the teaching staff in any way?
- How does the classroom teacher communicate lessons to the students? Can I use some of these techniques in my music class?
- What are some key cultural issues that the teachers should be aware of in order to be respectful and be culturally sensitive?

Poverty is another factor that can negatively affect a child's ability to learn in school. According to the Children's Defense Fund (2009), nearly 18% of children in the U.S. are poor and almost 8 % of children in the U.S. live in extreme poverty. Low socioeconomic status (SES), family poverty, and living in an economically disadvantaged neighborhood are factors that can contribute to lower academic achievement and an increase in socioemotional problems in school. Inner city schools are now educating large numbers of students who are poor and/or are immigrants, come from unstable homes, and tend to have problems in school. Children who live in persistent poverty have an even greater risk of suffering detrimental effects on academic achievement and socioemotional functioning than students who experience occasional poverty (Gottlieb, Atler, Gottlieb, & Wishner, 1994; McLoyd, 1998). There is also an increased risk for disability among children who live in poverty. According to a national database analysis looking at children with disabilities and children without disabilities, researchers found that

> (a) the proportion of American children living in poverty increased significantly in the past decade, (b) the greatest concentration of poverty is found among single-parent households, and (c) each of these trends is exacerbated in households with a child with a disability. (Fujiura & Yamaki, 2000, p. 191)

It is not difficult to see why a child who does not have enough food to eat, who is homeless or transient, or who must take responsibility for younger children when the parent is working late may have difficulty in school academically and socially. Children who live in poverty may or may not have a disability that qualifies for special education services; however, these children still might need special consideration or accommodations in class in order to be successful. In music classes, these children might exhibit behavioral or social/emotional problems, such as limited participation and interaction with other children, isolative behaviors, or acting out in order to receive attention from peers or adults. Students who live in poverty might have academic difficulties, such as problems with reading or understanding concepts. Adaptations recommended for students with behavior, emotional, or cognitive problems can also be used with students who are not identified as having a specific disability but who struggle with the academic and social demands of school.

Identifying with Labels/Person-First Language

This chapter has focused on the different disability labels that qualify a student for special education and related services, along with other factors such as LEP or poverty that may cause limited academic and social success in school. Students are given labels based on standardized diagnostic criteria that characterize deficits and limitations of the individual student. When students are found to have an intellectual disability, a specific learning disability, autism, or other IDEA-listed disability, they may be eligible for additional educational support to enhance progress in school. This function might be considered to be the advantage of giving labels to students. Labels can also segregate students with disabilities from students without disabilities and can override any other attributes of the individual student. Labels can affect the expectations that a teacher has for a student, since teachers are more likely to have lower expectations for students who have a disability label than for those who do not.

For instance, the music teacher knows that Joanne is a student with autism who will be joining the third grade class today. The label of autism might alert the teacher to some of the disabling characteristics, like communication disorders, social withdrawal, and possible cognitive difficulties. She also might wonder if Joanne will have inappropriate classroom behaviors or if she will be able to follow the directions for the music activities. The label of autism does not tell the teacher anything about what Joanne can do in music. Maybe she loves to sing and knows more songs than any of the other students in the third grade class. Maybe she has exceptional beat competency and can provide a strong, solid foundation for the bass xylophone part in today's lesson. It is possible for Joanne to have these positive characteristics that can make her highly successful in music class; however, it is likely that these abilities will go unnoticed unless the teacher goes beyond the label of autism to discover Joanne's capacity and promise.

The language that professionals use to describe a disability has changed dramatically over the years, reflecting the changes in how society views people with disabilities. In the past, terms like *idiot, moron, feeble-minded,* or *educable or trainable mentally retarded* were used as labels for persons with intellectual disabilities. A person who was deaf might have been considered to be "deaf and dumb," and a person with a physical disability might have been called "a cripple" or "physically handicapped" (Vergason & Anderegg, 1997). This language is demeaning and carries a stigma that can contribute to separation and segregation based on what is valued in society.

Educators are encouraged to use "person-first" language, which is just as it sounds—putting the person first before the disability. Rather than seeing the person as the disability first, person-first language demonstrates that the person has many characteristics and qualities of which a disability might be one. So rather than referring to a student as the "mentally retarded student" or the "autistic student," using person-first language, the students would be called the "student with mental retardation [intellectual disabilities]" or the "student with autism." Better yet, teachers should consider just referring to all students in the same way, by using their names. The purpose of this approach is not to minimize or deny a disability, but to affirm that the student is more than the disability and that the disability does not supersede all of the other human attributes that the child possesses (Darrow & White, 1998; Turnbull, Turnbull, & Wehmeyer, 2010).

The disability labels of autism or mental retardation/intellectual disabilities do not really tell us much information about a student. We might know some general characteristics that are true for people with that label, but we do not know exactly what that individual student can and cannot do in class. Rather than focusing on the disability label, educators are encouraged to view first the student's instructional needs, characteristics, and abilities. Then, one can balance this information along with what are known to be general characteristics of people with the specific disability. This approach will assist in developing appropriate interventions to meet the specific needs of the student and will help the music professional build on the abilities that the student brings to the music setting. When it is necessary to use disability labels, person-first language is preferred. However, going beyond the language, teachers who see the student as a unique individual who has abilities and challenges, rather than as a label, will promote inclusive practices over exclusionary practices. Disability labels are one category of terminology used in special education. As a professional working in schools, it is important to know and use appropriate terminology when communicating with other professionals, parents, and school administrators. Using labels and other terminology unique to special education demonstrates an understanding of related laws, school culture, and recent developments in the field. There are few fields as jargon-laden as special education. Appendix A provides a list of useful terminology related to special education and schools.

The Changing Role for Music Educators and
Music Therapists in the Schools

The percentage of students with disabilities educated in regular education schools and regular education classrooms continues to increase steadily. Schools are required by law to educate students with disabilities in the least restrictive environment with children who do not have disabilities to the greatest extent possible. Currently, more than half of students with disabilities are educated in the regular education classroom for at least 80% of the school day. Nearly all students with disabilities (96%) are educated in regular education or inclusive schools, with the remaining 4% of students educated in segregated settings (Data Accountability Center, 2007). These segregated settings could be special schools for students with behavior disorders or learning disabilities, or residential settings for students with severe intellectual disabilities, physical disabilities, or brain injuries. There is no question that the school population in the U.S. today is extremely diverse, with students' skills ranging from significantly below average for the age group to significantly above average. Each child presents certain characteristics that may affect that child's ability to learn. From the child with obvious disabilities, such as severe physical disabilities or severe mental retardation, to the child with limited English proficiency or mild disabilities, teachers must create the best educational environment to help all children succeed to the best of their abilities.

What does this mean for the music educator and music therapist in the schools? The role of the music educator and music therapist in the schools has changed dramatically over the past 30 years. Congruent with this role change comes the need for additional skills designing interventions based on Universal Design for Learning principles and creating adaptations to accommodate the needs of students with varying abilities. Music educators are trained to teach music knowledge and skills to students in the general school population. Music education may be provided through general music classes for elementary grades, music appreciation and music theory for upper grades, and music performance classes such as band, orchestra, and chorus. Prior to legislation such as IDEA, music educators did not typically work with students with moderate or severe disabilities on a regular basis, but the school milieu has changed. The music class today usually consists of students who are typically developing and are at grade level or above for academic and social skills, along with students who are not typically developing and are at risk for academic or social problems, or who have disabilities ranging from mild to severe.

Teachers are faced with the job of educating a diverse group of students with a variety of needs and abilities. In many instances, the music educator may not be aware that a student has a specific disability, but he or she is likely to see that the student's ability to learn makes it necessary for accommodations to be made in the music class. Some music educators are assigned to teach music in special classrooms for students with severe disabilities. This role can be especially challenging for the music educator who does not have adequate education, training, and supervised experience working with students who have significant disabilities. Many performing groups in the middle school/junior high and high school levels enroll students from across the continuum of needs and abilities who are eager to participate in vocal and instrumental music. Music educators from preschool through high school need to understand their roles in implementing inclusion and learn methods for making appropriate accommodations so that all children can benefit from participation in music experiences.

Chapters 4, 5, and 6 address some important ways that music educators can be better prepared to meet the challenges of the inclusive music class. Some issues to consider include:

- Understanding your role in the school, along with the expectations and rationale for teaching students with disabilities in an inclusive music class or a self-contained music class
    - » Why is this student placed in the music class? What are the expectations of the team for the student's participation? What are the goals for the student and how can they be met in music?
- Obtaining information from classroom teachers concerning the needs of specific students with disabilities and appropriate ways to work with the students
    - » What are the primary learning methods for this student? How does this student function in the non-music classroom? Are there special interventions that can be used in music that are also used in the non-music classroom? What are the student's strengths as well as limitations?
- Designing and adapting instructional methods, expectations, materials, or the environment to support the students' learning
    - » In what ways should the lessons be designed or adapted to ensure optimal participation and learning? Should the student be expected to complete all of the same assignments/activities as the rest of the class? What are the expectations for behavior and how are they structured?
- Seeking support from other professionals, including music therapists, classroom teachers, special education teachers, or paraprofessionals to create the best possible music experiences for the students

> » Is there a paraprofessional assigned to work with the student who should also come to music class? Is there an opportunity for the music professional to observe the student in the regular classroom in order to link intervention strategies? Can there be an email dialogue with other teachers who work with this student to share successful teaching techniques?

The role of the music therapist in the schools has also expanded with inclusive education models. The music therapist may work individually with a student who has music therapy as a related service listed on the IEP to help that student make progress on program goals and objectives. The music therapist might also work in special self-contained classrooms with students who have disabilities to help the students improve social, cognitive, language and communication, physical, academic, and music skills. In addition, the music therapist might consult with classroom teachers to help them utilize music in the classroom to benefit the students, or with music educators to help them create positive educational environments to increase the success of students with disabilities in the music class. The issues for music educators in the bulleted list above are also relevant for music therapists working in schools. Understanding their role, obtaining information, designing appropriate interventions, making adaptations, and seeking support from others will help all music professionals in their efforts to meet the needs of challenging students and challenging situations. More specific information about the various roles for music educators and music therapists in schools can be found in Chapter 6.

Summary

Schools in the U.S. today are required to provide free and appropriate public education for all students, no matter what their abilities or disabilities. Music educators and music therapists who work in schools will most likely have some role in educating students with disabilities in the inclusive classroom, performing group, self-contained classroom, or individual music therapy sessions.

KEY POINTS FROM THE CHAPTER

Current profile of students with disabilities in schools today:

- ♦ Over 6 million students received special education services under the Individuals with Disabilities Education Act (IDEA) during the fall of 2007. This amounts to approximately 10% of the total student population during that year.
- ♦ IDEA lists 13 disability categories for special education services eligibility.

♦ The most prevalent disabilities are specific learning disability and speech or language impairment, followed by other health impairments, mental retardation, and emotional disturbance.
♦ The role of the music educator and music therapist in the schools includes servicing the educational needs of students with disabilities in the general education/full inclusion music classroom, self-contained classroom, or individual sessions.

Other factors that affect students' ability to learn in school:
♦ *Limited English Proficiency (LEP)* can negatively affect a student's ability to learn and progress in school. Approximately 5 million students in U.S. schools have limited English proficiency.
  » In addition to language differences, teachers should also keep in mind the cultural differences in order to be respectful and culturally sensitive when working with students from varied backgrounds.
♦ *Poverty* is another factor that can negatively affect a student's ability to learn and progress in school. Currently, 18% of children in the U.S. are poor, and almost 8% are living in extreme poverty;
  » Students who live in poverty are at risk for lowered academic achievement and increased social/emotional problems in school.
  » There is also an increased risk for disability among children who live in poverty.

Use of labels and person-first language:
♦ Services are provided for students who meet eligibility criteria for a particular disability category. However, labels can serve to segregate students and lower teachers' expectations for students' achievements.
♦ Language related to disabilities has changed dramatically throughout history, and the current practice is to use person-first language. Person-first language places the focus on the individual first, not the disability first.

Changing roles for music educators and music therapists in the schools:
♦ All music educators can expect to teach students who have various skills and abilities, including students with disabilities (sometimes severe disabilities) in their classes.
♦ Music experiences for students with disabilities may occur in the general education music class or performance group, a self-contained music class or music therapy session, or in one-to-one music therapy sessions as a related service. Music educators and music therapists can work together to develop the most beneficial plan of service for a student with disabilities.
♦ Inclusive education necessitates that music professionals understand the students' needs, gather information on effective interventions, adapt instruction, and seek support from other professionals.

REFERENCES

Abedi, J. (2007). English language proficiency assessment and accountability under NCLB Title III: An overview. In J. Abedi (Ed.), *English language proficiency assessment in the nation: Current status and future practice.* Davis, CA: University of California, School of Education.

Children's Defense Fund. (2009). *Children in the states factsheets.* Retrieved April 6, 2010, from http://www. childrensdefense.org/child-research-data-publications/data/state-data-repository/children-in-the-states-factsheets.html

Darrow, A. A., & White, G. W. (1998). Sticks and stones... and words CAN hurt: Eliminating handicapping language. *Music Therapy Perspectives, 16,* 81–83.

Data Accountability Center. (2007). *Individuals with Disabilities Education Act (IDEA) data: Part B data and notes.* Retrieved April 6, 2010, from https://www.ideadata.org/PartBData.asp

Fujiura, G. T., & Yamaki, K. (2000). Trends in demography of childhood poverty and disability. *Exceptional Children, 66*(2), 187–199.

Gottlieb, J., Atler, M., Gottlieb, B. W., & Wishner, J. (1994). Special education in urban America: It's not justifiable for many. *Journal of Special Education, 27*(4), 453–465.

Government Accountability Office. (2006). *No Child Left Behind Act: Assistance from education could help states better measure progress of students with limited English proficiency.* Report GAO-06-815 (July). Washington, DC: Author.

McLoyd, V. (1998). Socioeconomic disadvantage and child development. *American Psychologist, 53,* 185–204.

Turnbull, A., Turnbull, R., & Wehmeyer, M. (2010). *Exceptional lives: Special education in today's schools* (6th ed.). Upper Saddle River, NJ: Merrill.

U.S. Department of Education. (2008). *2004–2006 biennial evaluation report to Congress on the implementation of the state formula grant program.* Retrieved April 6, 2010, from http://www.ed.gov/offices/oela

Vergason, G. A., & Anderegg, M. L. (1997). The ins and outs of special education terminology. *Teaching Exceptional Children, 29*(5), 35–39.

Chapter 2

History of Special Education and the Impact on Music Programs

---

CHAPTER OVERVIEW

Many events throughout history contributed to the current laws that ensure quality educational services for students with disabilities. Education for students with disabilities has moved from an exclusion model, with limited access to educational services, to an inclusion model, where students with disabilities have the right to a free and appropriate public education in the least restrictive environment. This chapter traces some of the important historical, legal, and legislative events that helped change the way students with disabilities are educated. These events provide a foundation for current principles and practice in education that affect the roles of music educators and music therapists in U.S. schools.

This chapter includes information on the following topics:
- ♦ Brief history of public education for students with disabilities
- ♦ Historical roots of music in special education
- ♦ History of litigation and legislative events affecting special education
- ♦ Six principles of IDEA 2004
- ♦ Comparison between IDEA and Section 504

Brief History of Public Education for Students with Disabilities

There have been significant changes in the educational services available to students with disabilities over the past 200 years. During most of the 1800s, students with disabilities were not even considered eligible for public education. Later, when these students were offered educational services, these services were provided in separate and segregated schools and classrooms. Education for students with disabilities has moved from no services or limited, segregated services, to an inclusive educational services model that is based on the requirements of federal legislation titled the Individuals with Disabilities Education Improvement Act 2004 (or IDEA 2004).

One of the first educational programs for children with disabilities was the American Asylum for the Education and Instruction of the Deaf and Dumb, established by Thomas Gallaudet in 1817 in Connecticut (Stainback, Stainback, & Bunch, 1989). Other institutions providing education for students who were deaf or blind or who had mental disabilities were established later in various cities across the U.S. However, there were few educational options for most students with disabilities at this time in our history.

By the early 1900s, schooling was the norm for children without disabilities in the United States, and while there were some programs for students with disabilities, most of these students received limited or no public school education. Although the educational opportunities for students with disabilities increased throughout the 1900s, the majority of these students were educated in residential institutions and asylums throughout the first half of the century. This was especially true for students having severe disabilities who were primarily housed in under-funded and sometimes inhumane institutions.

By the 1950s, parent groups started to advocate for improved educational services for children with disabilities, federal legislation affecting this education expanded, and educators were considering the special educational needs of children with disabilities. Increased federal and state support for special educational services promoted additional expansion in the 1960s. Although most children with severe behavior problems or severe mental retardation continued to be serviced in institutions, students with less severe disabilities began to have more options for public school education. While opportunities for educational services increased during this time, classes for students with disabilities tended to be separate, segregated environments with limited contact with students in general education (Adamek, 2002).

Public demands for better living conditions and treatment of people in institutions brought about significant societal changes in the 1970s. A movement towards deinstitutionalization and normalization for people with disabilities began throughout the country. Institutions that previously housed hundreds of residents were scaled back or closed, and the residents were placed in smaller, more normalized settings in the community. Normalization practices were built on the belief that all students have individual differences and that all members of the community should respect those differences. This concept of normalization was evident in the schools with the advent of mainstreaming. Students who were mainstreamed spent much of their school day in a segregated, special education classroom, but joined students in a regular education classroom or other setting for part of the day. Students with disabilities were mainstreamed to the greatest extent appropriate, which was frequently during a social time such as lunch or recess. At this time, educational practices began to shift from educating students with disabilities solely in segregated settings, to educating these students in the general education setting with support from special education services (Winzer, 1993). Great progress was made throughout the 20th century in providing educational services for students with disabilities. However, by 1975 there were approximately 8 million children with disabilities in the United States, and only about half were receiving appropriate educational opportunities. Approximately 3 million children received inadequate education, and one million students with disabilities were totally excluded from public education (Rothstein, 2000).

The early 1980s brought increased pressure to provide more integrated educational experiences for students with disabilities, limiting the need for segregated special education placements. From this time to the present, different educational models have been developed to provide normalized, inclusive experiences for students with disabilities. In the mid 1980s, the Regular Education Initiative (REI) was introduced as a model to improve educational services for students with disabilities. Proponents of the REI called for a dismantling of the dual system of education (general education and special education) in favor of a unified system (Will, 1986). The new unified system would be developed to meet the unique learning needs of all students. This movement challenged educators to re-evaluate current educational practices related to at-risk students as well as students with disabilities. The REI served as a catalyst for change, moving education from a segregated system to a more inclusive and integrated system.

Special education reform at this time in history was anchored in the themes of inclusion and collaboration. Inclusion was based on the legislative mandates for equal opportunities and least restrictive environment placement. In order for inclusion to be successful, collaboration between general education teachers and special education teachers was seen to be essential. It is still true today that all members of the team, including general education teachers, special education teachers, administrators, related service providers, and other school personnel, must work together to provide an appropriate education for the student with disabilities. Collaborative teaching can result in greater feelings of competency for the teachers who are working together to enhance learning and expectations for students (Villa, Thousand, Meyers, & Nevin, 1996).

The reauthorization of IDEA in 1997 placed a strong emphasis on giving all students access to the general curriculum, while the reauthorization of IDEA in 2004 as the Individuals with Disabilities Education Improvement Act 2004 continued to promote accountability and high standards for students, increased parental involvement, and use of research-based practices and materials. Special education is now seen as a service rather than as a place where students are sent to be educated. Given that premise, most students begin in the general education classroom, with additional supports when necessary, and are removed only when the student is unable to benefit from that placement. As the least restrictive environment varies for different students, the students' placements in the continuum of services offered by the schools will also vary. See Chapter 6 for more information about the continuum of placement options.

Educational reform is an ongoing issue; however, implementation of practices can be difficult at best. Many schools struggle with meeting the mandates of the law, providing appropriate educational opportunities for all students, and providing adequate professional and paraprofessional staff to meet the demands on a limited budget. These factors, along with differences in backgrounds, educational experience, professional training, and varied interpretations of the laws, create differences in inclusive education and services across the country. While all states are mandated to follow the requirements of IDEA, the state's and district's interpretation of the law and the financial resources of the area may dictate how educational services are actually provided to all students. Many schools continue to struggle to meet the various needs of students with disabilities and the needs of all of the students in the school, according to legal, fiscal, and educationally appropriate parameters.

Historical Roots of Music in Special Education

Music has been a component of some special education programs as far back as the early 1800s, when people like Jean-Marc-Gaspard Itard (1775–1838) and others utilized music in the diagnosis and treatment of speech and hearing problems. In addition, music was found to be effective to teach auditory and speech skills to students with cognitive impairments (Solomon, 1980). The early use of music in special education settings was with children who were blind, hard of hearing, deaf, or mentally retarded. Music was used as a way to facilitate learning and to reinforce students' achievements. Based on a review of the early literature related to music in special education, four themes emerged: (a) music was used to train or educate students with disabilities; (b) singing was used to improve speech, breathing, and articulation abilities; (c) music activities were used as diagnostic tools prior to the development of diagnostic audiology equipment; and (d) music was used in the education of deaf and hard of hearing students since the early 1800s (Solomon, 1980).

Throughout the early history of music education in the U.S., music was an important part of the curriculum in schools for students with disabilities. Some schools for children who were deaf or blind included singing, rhythm activities, instrument playing, and other music activities to enhance the students' education. Music was also a part of the programming in institutions for children who had mental retardation. Music activities were used to meet the current educational needs of the students and to prepare the students for interactions in their communities (Adamek, 2002).

Opportunities for students with disabilities to participate in music experiences increased concurrent with the growth in overall educational opportunities for these students. Jellison (2000) compiled an extensive review of the music in special education research from 1975–1999. This review documents the increase in services and the effectiveness of music as therapy for students with disabilities in a variety of educational settings.

History of Litigation and Legislative Events Affecting Special Education

Throughout the history of public school education in the U.S., children with disabilities were denied access to services that were appropriate to their educational needs. These exclusionary practices took one of two different forms: total exclusion or functional exclusion. Total exclusion occurs when a school denies access to education by refusing to admit a child. Functional exclusion occurs when, although a child is admitted to the school, the educational program is inappropriate or inadequate for the child's specific learning needs. When functional exclusion occurs, the students cannot substantially benefit from their education, and they gain little or none of the intended benefits of their educational program. Exclusion is just one of the many practices that denied the rights of children with disabilities to an appropriate education. Frequently children were misclassified through the use of biased and discriminatory evaluation procedures. This misclassification particularly affected children from minority races who tended to perform poorly on tests that were focused on English and knowledge based on majority culture. Once students were placed in special education, there were rarely ever opportunities for re-evaluation. Limited availability of funds, architectural barriers, and limited accountability were additional issues that limited equal access to education for students with disabilities. Special education was a terminal, permanent placement, with little hope of re-evaluation or integration with students without disabilities. Parental input was rare and not required, and systematic due process procedures were unavailable (Turnbull & Turnbull, 2000).

Many factors contributed to the changes in special education that led to the right-to-education reform movement in the late 1960s and early 1970s. This movement was based in the ideas of civil rights and equal protection under the law, egalitarianism, and normalization. Individuals with disabilities who might be "less able" were no longer to be considered less worthy. The scientific community provided evidence that even the most severely disabled persons were able to learn, even if just the most basic of skills. And one of the most important factors for special education reform was the involvement of family members as advocates for appropriate educational services. Politicians also championed the rights of people with disabilities, especially those who had first-hand experience with family members who had disabilities. One key political figure, John F. Kennedy, whose sister had mental retardation, established the President's Committee on Mental Retardation. Another contemporary political figure, Senator Tom Harkin from Iowa, whose brother was deaf from birth, championed the rights of individuals with disabilities by authoring the Americans with Disabilities Act. Societal changes, political changes, and strong leadership led the way for legislative activity to support equal access and appropriate education for all students (Winzer, 2007).

Prior to the 1970s, there was no body of special education law in the United States. Education was not mentioned in the Constitution, and public education in the U.S. typically was thought to be the responsibility of state and local governments. Before the 1954 landmark U.S. Supreme Court school desegregation decision, *Brown v. Board of Education*, there was little general school law. In many ways, the courts did not recognize the rights of students and teachers, which we now take for granted, until recent decades. There were no court decisions prohibiting discrimination based on disability, race, or gender, nor any decisions ensuring free speech rights of students and teachers. The desegregation decision from Brown made it clear that individual rights guaranteed in the U.S. Constitution (specifically, the Bill of Rights and the Fourteenth Amendment) applied to teachers and students in schools (Huefner, 2000). The rights of students with disabilities in schools expanded over the decade due to (a) increased involvement in educational issues by the federal court, (b) increased focus on the larger civil rights movement, and (c) the movement toward deinstitutionalization of people with disabilities. The issues addressed by the courts and lawmakers dealt not only with the rights of students and teachers, but also with the responsibilities of school personnel to work together with parents to provide a beneficial educational experience for the student who has special needs.

Selected Court Cases and Legislation Affecting Special Education

Brown v. Board of Education (1954)

The original school desegregation case, *Brown v. Board of Education*, was a landmark civil rights case that laid the groundwork for the future of integrated educational settings. The Brown case dealt with the issue of educating black children in separate settings from white students. These segregated schools were developed under the principle that the schools for black students and the schools for white students were "separate but equal." The Supreme Court ruled that this model did not provide an equal educational experience for the minority students and that this segregation had a detrimental effect on minority children. By educating children separately, the court determined that students were denied opportunities to interact with children from different backgrounds, and that this system promoted the stigma that minority students were inferior to white students (Hulett, 2009; Turnbull & Turnbull, 2000). *Brown* was a civil rights case dealing with discrimination due to race that subsequently had a great impact on the civil rights of students with disabilities. This important decision brought an end to exclusionary educational practices based on race, and it was the legal foundation for the elimination of exclusionary educational practices for students with disabilities.

Education of the Handicapped Act (1970)

In 1970, Congress enacted the Education of the Handicapped Act (EHA), which expanded previous federal grant programs and funded state and local pilot projects for special education. Funds were made available to higher education institutions for the development of special education teacher training programs, and to regional centers to provide technical assistance to school districts in the states (Huefner, 2000).

Pennsylvania Association of Retarded Citizens (PARC) v. Commonwealth of Pennsylvania (1971)

PARC v. Commonwealth established the right for a free and appropriate education for children who were mentally retarded. In this case, the federal district court in Philadelphia overturned a state law that allowed schools to exclude students who had the diagnosis of mental retardation. The court decision was based on evidence that these students could benefit from educational services provided in public schools, and that by denying them a public education, the state was denying them due process and equal protection (Boyle & Weishaar, 2001). The *PARC* decision mandated that students with mental retardation could not be excluded from schools based on their label, that due process must be followed, and that students should be educated in less restrictive settings when possible, favoring integration over segregation (Hulett, 2009; Weiner, 1985).

Mills v. Board of Education of the District of Columbia (1972)

The year following the *PARC* decision, *Mills v. Board of Education* expanded on the previous PARC ruling to solidify the educational rights of students with disabilities. The *Mills* decision mandated that "due process include procedures relating to the labeling, placement, and exclusionary stages of decision making" (Rothstein, 2000, p. 13). In addition, the court ruled that students with disabilities must be educated even when finances in the district were limited, and that these students should not suffer any more than students in general education when the district was experiencing financial difficulties. While the *PARC* decision acknowledged the rights of students with mental retardation to a free and appropriate education, the *Mills* decision established educational rights for children with other disabilities besides mental retardation. Going back to the *Brown v. Board of Education* decision, the judge in the *Mills* decision found that, since segregation on the basis of race was unconstitutional, exclusion from education on the basis of disabilities was unconstitutional as well (Huefner, 2000). Based on the decisions in the *PARC* and *Mills* cases, schools were required to provide access to a public education for students with disabilities and to provide basic procedural due process rights before placing a student in a program that was separate from regular education. These decisions established the framework for P.L. 94-142 in 1975, which later became known as the Individuals with Disabilities Education Act (IDEA) (Hulett, 2009; Yell & Drasgow, 2005).

Section 504 of the Rehabilitation Act of 1973

Section 504 of the Rehabilitation Act of 1973 provides important protections for students who have disabilities. This federal antidiscrimination law prohibits any state, local, or private organization that receives federal funds from discriminating against an otherwise qualified person solely on the basis of a disabling condition. Since all public schools receive federal funds, they are mandated to abide by this law.

Section 504 uses a functional approach when defining eligibility for accommodations, addressing how the disability impacts the individual's major life activities. According to Section 504, a person is protected if there is a physical or mental impairment that substantially limits one or more major life activities, such as walking, seeing, hearing, and learning (Boyle & Weishaar, 2001; Guernsey & Klare, 2001; Hulett, 2009). This law has a very broad definition for eligibility, and many students who are not eligible for services under IDEA are protected under Section 504. For example, students who are potentially eligible for accommodations under Section 504 may have the following disorders:

- permanent or temporary medical conditions, such as asthma, HIV, diabetes, cancer, broken leg
- behavior problems
- attention deficit hyperactivity disorder (ADHD)
- addiction to drugs or alcohol

A student may qualify under Section 504 due to a medical condition such as HIV and may not be eligible for special education. In this situation, a student may be discriminated against by being denied access to educational programs or participation in extracurricular activities, or even total exclusion from the school setting. Section 504 protects the student from discrimination and requires that the school make appropriate accommodations for the student, providing opportunities similar to those students who do not have disabilities, in the least restrictive environment (Turnbull & Turnbull, 2000). Students must have an equal opportunity to participate in nonacademic services and extracurricular activities. While equal participation is not required in these types of activities, students with disabilities must have an equal opportunity to participate. In regard to music programs, if a school has an elite choir that is chosen by audition, students must be given the opportunity to audition (and possibly participate) in the choir. The student does not automatically have the right to participate in the choir if he or she does not meet the standards of the audition selection process. If the school has a nonselective choir, then students of all abilities would be given the opportunity to participate. The school would then need to make accommodations for a student with a disability to participate in the choir, if necessary. There are many similarities and differences between Section 504 and IDEA. A comparison of Section 504 and IDEA can be found later in this chapter.

P.L. 94-142 – Education for All Handicapped Children Act (EAHCA) (1975), later renamed Individuals with Disabilities Education Act (IDEA) (1990), and revised and reauthorized as Individuals with Disabilities Education Improvement Act 2004 (IDEA 2004)

With the *Brown, Mills,* and *PARC* decisions, the EHA, and Section 504, courts and Congress laid the groundwork for significant special education legislation. In 1975, Congress passed the Education for All Handicapped Children Act (P.L. 94-142), which in 1990 became known as the Individuals with Disabilities Education Act (IDEA). This law amended the EHA and provided grants to states for special education services. Based on this law, no child could be denied a free and appropriate public education, and that education must take place in the most integrated, least segregated setting as possible. Six basic underlying principles for special education services in public education were established through this important legislation (Hallahan, Kauffman, & Pullen, 2009; Hulett, 2009; Rothstein, 2000; Turnbull & Turnbull, 2000):

- Zero reject, free and appropriate public education (FAPE) must be provided for all children with disabilities.
- Nondiscriminatory evaluations must be used to determine eligibility and need for services.
- Services must be individualized to meet the needs of the student (Individualized Education Program, IEP).
- Educational services must be provided in the least restrictive environment (LRE).
- Parents have the right to be included and involved in the development of their child's educational program.
- Procedural protections must ensure that the requirements of the law are met (due process).

At this point in the history of education, all children were considered to be educable, using a broader definition of the term than had been used in the past. This definition centered on the view that education involved systematic instruction on necessary life skills. The individual needs of the student were to be considered, and systematic instruction based on their needs was to be planned and facilitated. If through this systematic instruction a child could develop basic skills such as language and communication skills, social skills, or daily living skills such as dressing and hygiene, then the child was educable. With this broader definition of educability, the school was now responsible for the education of all children under the law.

IDEA is a comprehensive law that is divided into four sections: Part A, Part B, Part C, and Part D (see Table 2.1). Part A describes the definitions, purposes, and policies upon which IDEA is based, including the goals of equal opportunity, inclusion, and full participation, independence, and productivity. Part B provides federal funding for direct services to individual students (ages 3–21 years) with disabilities listed in the law. Part C provides services for children under age 3 who need early intervention services due to developmental delays/risk of developmental delays or who have a diagnosed physical or mental disability. Part D provides funding for discretionary grant programs (Turnbull, Turnbull, & Wehmeyer, 2010).

Table 2.1 Sections of IDEA

Section	Elements of Each Section
Part A	General definitions, purposes, and provisions of the law
Part B	Federal financial assistance to states for special education and related services for children with disabilities ages 3–21
Part C	Early intervention programs for children with developmental delays/at risk of delays, or with diagnosed disability, ages birth–2.
Part D	Discretionary grant programs

This law was a milestone in the education of children with disabilities. For the first time, the federal government was engaged as a partner with the states by offering grants to states to pay for direct services to students in special education. Federal funding was authorized at that time to reach 40% of the average national expenditure per student but in reality it has not yet reached that level (Guernsey & Klare, 2001; Huefner, 2000). Although federal funds assist the states in funding special education services, these funds have been found to be inadequate to meet the expectations of the law. The states must make up the difference to cover the total costs of special education.

Amendments to EAHCA and IDEA (1980–2004)

During the 1980s, Congress enacted various additional amendments to the EAHCA in order to secure the rights of a free and appropriate public education for students with disabilities. The most significant changes to the law were made in 1986, 1990, and 1997 (Boyle & Weishaar, 2001; Huefner, 2000).

1986 Amendments:
- Rights and protection of the law were extended to preschool children who were disabled or had developmental delays (ages 3–5).
- Funding incentives were provided for early intervention programs (ages birth–2) for children who were experiencing developmental delay or were at risk of developmental delays.
- Parents who prevailed in a due process hearing or lawsuit could recover attorneys' fees from the school district.

1990 Amendments:

- The name of the law was changed to Individuals with Disabilities Education Act (IDEA).
- The term *handicap* was eliminated, and the term *disability* was substituted. Person-first language was preferred to indicate that all individuals were persons first and also have various characteristics that may include a disability. For example, "student with a disability" or "child with development delays" would replace language such as "handicapped student" or "developmentally delayed child." (See Chapter 1 for more information about person-first language.)
- Autism and traumatic brain injury were added to the list of eligible disabling conditions.
- Assistive technology and rehabilitative services were added to the list of possible related services. Definitions of these services were also clarified.
- Transition planning was required for all students served under IDEA by the age of 16.

1997 Amendments:

IDEA amendments in 1997 were numerous and significant. Changes were made to parallel the educational reform goals evident in the federal *Goals 2000: Educate America Act and the Improving America's Schools Act.* Goals reflected by the 1997 amendments included increasing school readiness, improving the safety of the school setting, improving teaching skills, increasing graduation rates, and promoting better partnerships with parents. Specific changes addressed the following areas:

- Annual goals, educational benchmarks, and IEP objectives must be measurable.
- A general education teacher must be a member of the IEP team.
- Students with disabilities must be included in state and district-wide assessments, with accommodations made when necessary. Alternate assessments must be developed for students who are unable to participate in the general assessment due to the profound nature of their disability.
- Mediation must be offered as a voluntary option for parents.
- Specific disciplinary procedures were added to uphold the rights of students with disabilities and to maintain the safety and security of the school setting.

2004 Amendments:

The Individuals with Disabilities Education Improvement Act 2004 (IDEA 2004) is the current law under which states must operate. Changes were made to the 1997 law to coincide with No Child Left Behind (Hulett, 2009; U.S. Department of Education, 2003); to promote additional accountability, high standards, and parental involvement; and to reduce paperwork burdens on teachers. Specific changes addressed the following areas:

- Specific criteria were included to define "highly qualified" special education teachers.
- The use of research-based techniques and materials was mandated.
- The terms *benchmarks* and *short-term objectives* were deleted from IEP requirements, leaving the requirement that the IEP includes measurable annual goals.

Current Purpose of the Law

Congress initially passed IDEA to enforce the equal protection clause of the federal constitution, since state and local practice had been to misclassify and exclude students with disabilities from public education. Since schools were treating students with disabilities differently than students without disabilities, they were in violation of the equal protection clause. The law was originally passed to ensure the rights for children with disabilities to a free and appropriate education, to protect students' and parents' rights related to that education, to provide financial assistance to the states for that education, and to assess state and local effectiveness in educating students with disabilities. When IDEA was reauthorized in 1997, these original purposes were restated, with further objectives added to clarify the purpose of the law. One important area of concern in 1997 was that of pervasive low expectations in schools regarding the capabilities of students with disabilities. Another area of concern was the schools' "insufficient focus on applying replicable research on proven methods of teaching and learning for children with disabilities" [20 U.S.C. Sec. 1401(c)(4)]. These were seen as barriers to effective special education and areas that needed to be addressed. In order to deal with these problems, legislators proposed that schools

- have higher expectations for students with disabilities;
- increase access to general education curriculum as much as possible;
- strengthen the role of the parents in the education of the children;
- redefine special education as a service for eligible students, rather than a place where eligible students are educated; and
- support effective professional development for all school personnel. [20 U.S.C. Sec. 1401(c)(5)]

In addition to the problems of low expectations and insufficient use of research-based teaching methods, many students with disabilities either did not pass classes or dropped out of school completely. A current function of IDEA is to alleviate these problems by promoting outcome-based education and linking student outcomes to necessary school reforms. IDEA continues to reaffirm that FAPE is based on the constitutional rights of equal protection. As a result of their education, students with disabilities should have the skills and supports to lead independent lives as adults, including employment options congruent with the individual's abilities.

Eligibility for Special Education and Related Services

The *Mills* and *PARC* decisions were the first to list specific disability categories for special education eligibility. When P.L. 94-142 was passed in 1975, a major cause of concern was exclusion of students from education, and misclassification of school-aged children between the ages of 6 and 18. Over the years, IDEA was amended to provide early education for younger students, ages 3 through 5, transition services for students ages 16 through 21, and early intervention for children ages birth through 2 (Turnbull et al., 2010).

Part B of IDEA focuses on the needs of students ages 3 through 21 and delineates a categorical approach to defining eligibility for special education services. Students who have a disability that adversely affects their ability to learn in the general education setting may be eligible for special education and related services. Disability categories are defined according to the student's age. IDEA regulations provide operational definitions for the disability categories listed in the law, which can by addressed as three broad groups: physical impairments; mental, emotional, and cognitive impairments; and the nonspecific catch-all group (Bartlett, Etscheidt, & Weisenstein, 2007; Guernsey & Klare, 2001). The following IDEA categories are for students age 6 through 21 (inclusive):

Related to physical impairment/functioning:
- Deaf-blindness
- Hearing impairment, including deafness
- Orthopedic impairment
- Speech or language impairment
- Visual impairment, including blindness

Related to mental, emotional, or cognitive impairment/functioning:
- Autism
- Emotional disturbance
- Mental retardation
- Specific learning disability
- Traumatic brain injury

Catch-all categories:
- Developmental delay
- Multiple disabilities
- Other health impairment

Developmental delay is the most recently added disability category, and it is applicable only to children ages 3 through 9. State and local education agencies have the option of using this category to provide services under IDEA to children ages 3 through 9, and many states are now using this option.

Attention deficit hyperactivity disorder (ADHD) is not listed as an eligible disability in the categories specified above. In amendments made to federal regulations in 1999, the category of "other health impaired" was expanded to include ADHD. If a student has ADHD and does not qualify for special education and related services, that student may qualify for accommodations under Section 504.

The early education needs of students ages 3 through 9 (inclusive) are also addressed in IDEA. The categories listed above apply to this age group, but, in addition, each state may also include children who
- are experiencing developmental delays in social, cognitive, physical, communication, emotional, or adaptive areas; and,
- need special education and related services due to these developmental delays (Boyle & Weishaar, 2001; Turnbull & Turnbull, 2000).

When a child is very young, it can be difficult to determine the cause of delays or learning problems. By using the "noncategorical" developmental delay category for identifying young children who might need special education services, the states are allowed to address the needs of students who may have delays, but the exact nature of a disability may not yet be determined. This option for the states to provide early intervention services can help lessen the effects of the disability on later learning and, in some cases, can eliminate the need for subsequent special education services.

Part C of IDEA gives states the opportunity to provide early intervention services to students ages birth through 2. According to this section of the law, services can be provided for a child under age 3 who
- has a developmental delay in one or more areas including cognitive, physical, communication, social, emotional, or adaptive development; or
- has been diagnosed as having a mental or physical disability that puts the child at high risk of developmental delays.

An Individual Family Service Plan (IFSP) must be developed for each child and family to structure the individualized program for the child and family. Qualified personnel must provide educational interventions and appropriate related services in as natural environment as possible according to the needs of the child (Bartlett et al., 2007; Turnbull et al., 2010).

Six Principles of IDEA

IDEA specifies who is entitled to services and the nature of those services under this special education law. IDEA also specifies the benefits to students through six principles that describe what students with disabilities and their parents can expect from the schools. The principles of IDEA are *zero reject, nondiscriminatory evaluation, appropriate education, least restrictive environment, procedural due process,* and *parent and student participation.* These six principles govern the education of children with disabilities and guarantee their access for educational services.

Zero Reject

Individuals with disabilities of school age (ages 3–21) have the right to receive a free and appropriate public education (FAPE). Students may not be excluded from educational services because of a disability, no matter how severe the disability. Schools are required to provide services for students with disabilities, even if it is to help the students develop the most basic of skills. Zero reject applies to public and private schools, psychiatric hospitals, and residential facilities for people with severe disabilities. Schools may not expel or suspend students if their behavior is caused by their disabilities, and schools may not exclude students who have contagious diseases. This rule guarantees access to education for all students with disabilities.

Nondiscriminatory Evaluation

Students are entitled to a nondiscriminatory, nonbiased evaluation to determine first if the student has a disability. If the student is found to have a disability, then the evaluation process continues to determine if that disability negatively affects the student's ability to benefit from his or her education (and thus needs special education and related services), and then to determine what special education and related services the student needs. Some standardized tests have been found to be culturally and linguistically biased against minority students. Only standardized tests that are not discriminatory may be used in the evaluation process, and evaluators must consider potential cultural differences when assessing culturally diverse students. Other nonstandardized evaluation tools may also be used; however, education professionals must guard against cultural or linguistic bias.

In order to uphold this principle, the team must gather functional and developmental information about the student using a variety of assessment tools and approaches. Information is gathered through formal assessments and through background information about the student, student preferences, teaching styles encountered by the student, or other informal assessment strategies (Turnbull et al., 2010). The team must look at the whole child in terms of cognitive, behavioral, physical, or other developmental factors, and identify not only the student's deficit areas but also areas of strength and ability.

A member of the IEP team might request a music therapy assessment to determine if music therapy as a related service should be provided for a student. This request may come from a teacher, parent, or any other member of the team. If the team agrees to a music therapy assessment, a qualified music therapist would facilitate an assessment to determine if music therapy is necessary for the student to make progress on IEP goals and to benefit from special education. More specific information about the music therapy assessment process can be found in Chapter 6.

Appropriate Education

Education for students with disabilities must be appropriate, designed for the individual child, and at no cost to the parents. IDEA mandates two different types of plans for students who are eligible for special education and related services: the Individualized Education Program (IEP) for students ages 3 through 21, and the Individualized Family Services Plan (IFSP) for students ages birth through 2. According to the interpretation of IDEA, students who qualify are entitled to an *appropriate* education, not the *best* possible education. This is sometimes called the "benefit standard." An appropriate education is one where the student is making progress and is benefiting from special education.

If an IEP team requests a music therapy eligibility assessment, based on the outcome of that assessment, the team may decide that music therapy is a necessary service for a student to benefit from special education. Music therapy will then be added to the student's IEP as a related service, and the team will decide what goals will be addressed in music therapy and how the services will be delivered (direct service or consult service) by a qualified music therapist. More in-depth information about music therapy as a related service can be found in Chapter 6.

Least Restrictive Environment

Schools must provide appropriate education for students with disabilities in the least restrictive environment (LRE). This principle is frequently practiced in terms of mainstreaming, integration, or inclusion, although this terminology is not in IDEA. IDEA adopted the LRE principle to provide equal opportunities for students with disabilities to achieve independence, productivity, and inclusion in mainstream activities and the general curriculum. The LRE principle gives students with disabilities increased opportunities to interact and develop relationships with students who do not have disabilities. These relationships are important for all students to help them learn about diversity and respect for others. In addition, segregation goes against the constitutional foundation of equal treatment and equal rights for all individuals, along with the federal laws that prohibit discrimination based on disability (Section 504 and Americans with Disability Act).

This rule mandates that a school must educate a student with disabilities with students who do not have disabilities, to the maximum extent possible, for the students to benefit from education. If a student cannot benefit from being educated in a general education or inclusive setting, then that student may be placed in a more restrictive, less typical environment. This placement in a more restrictive, less typical environment may be made only after the school has utilized supplementary aids and support services in the general education setting. Special education services may be provided across a continuum of services from least restrictive to more restrictive. For example, the least restrictive environment would be the typical general education setting, and moving to more restrictive environments would be a resource room, special education classroom, special education school, home, or institution such as a hospital or treatment setting. Placement decisions are always made by the IEP team to determine the setting where the student will benefit from education in terms of academic, functional, and social development.

Schools must also provide opportunities for students with disabilities to participate in nonacademic instruction, general education activities, and extracurricular activities. This might include recess, meals, transportation, clubs, recreational activities, performance groups, and athletics. In short, schools must include students with disabilities in all academic, recreational, and other extracurricular activities to the maximum extent possible to provide equal opportunities to all students. When IDEA was reauthorized in 1997, Congress made it clear that special education is a service for children with disabilities, not a place where they are sent to be educated.

The key to determining the LRE for a student is to address how the placement benefits the student. According to a 1994 court case, several factors must be considered to determine the LRE for a student to receive an appropriate education:

- What are the educational benefits to the student in an integrated setting compared to a segregated setting? Will the student have increased benefits in one setting over the other?
- What are the nonacademic or social benefits for the student in an integrated setting, with peers who do not have disabilities? Will the integrated setting provide positive social experiences for the student to improve his or her ability to function in society?
- What effect does including the student with disabilities have on the other students and teachers in the general education setting? Is there a negative impact on the education of the other students? Is there a safety factor involved?
- What are the financial implications of providing services to the student in an inclusive setting? Do the costs of educating the student outweigh the benefits and limit funds for the education of the other students in the school?

Many factors must be considered when deciding LRE placement issues. The individual educational and social needs of the student must be considered, along with the impact and needs of the other students in the class (Bartlett et al., 2007; Turnbull et al., 2010).

Parental and Student Participation

This principle of IDEA gives parents and students rights to participate in the development, implementation, and decision-making process regarding special education services. Parental and student participation can enhance the educational benefits for the student and increase the effectiveness of the student's education. Parents are frequently involved in the evaluation process to determine eligibility for services and the necessary special education and related services. They are also a part of the IEP team and should be involved in the process of developing the initial IEP, evaluating progress and updating the student's IEP. Parents have many rights related to participation in their child's education.

Procedural Due Process

Schools are mandated by law to carry out the principles of IDEA. When parents or students think that schools are not following through with these principles or they want to challenge a decision of the school, they are allowed to do this through due process. Due process is a set of procedural guidelines or safeguards to protect students with disabilities and their parents from discriminatory, biased, or unfair practices that deny their rights under IDEA.

When parents disagree with a decision or practice of the school, they are encouraged to go through a mediation process to try to work out the problem. If a case cannot be resolved through mediation, or if the parents refuse to participate in mediation, the case then goes to a due process hearing. This due process hearing is similar to a trial, conducted before a due process hearing officer. Similar to a trial, there are usually lawyers to present the case, witnesses to shed light on the case, and the due process officer to make a judgment on the case. The side that does not win the case may appeal to a higher court, all the way up to the Supreme Court. Due process hearings can be time-intensive, expensive, and difficult for all parties involved (Rawson, 2000).

Additional Information about Laws Affecting Education

Comparison of IDEA and Section 504

The rights of students are protected under both IDEA and Section 504. There are many similarities and differences between these two laws, and these can cause confusion in regard to the purpose and effects of the laws. IDEA is a federally funded entitlement program that requires the provision of special education and related services to eligible students. Section 504 is a civil rights law that prohibits discrimination based on disability in any program that receives federal funding. Some of the primary factors for IDEA and Section 504 can be found in the comparison chart in Table 2.2.

Table 2.2 Components of IDEA and Section 504: A Comparison Chart

	IDEA: Special Education Law/Entitlement	Section 504: Civil Rights Law/Antidiscrimination
Purpose	To provide procedural safeguards and prescriptive mandates, and to ensure FAPE in LRE	To prevent discrimination against persons with disabilities
Eligibility	Lists specific disabling conditions to be eligible for services; evaluation for specific disability	Has broad-based definition for eligibility; evaluated for functional disability; more students eligible under 504 than IDEA
FAPE	Requires FAPE; specific written IEP for each child; requires a program designed for educational benefit for the student (benefit standard)	Requires FAPE; written accommodation plan—however, there are no specified procedures for the content of plan; required to provide services that are comparable to students without disabilities (comparability standard)
Funding	Funding provided by states for eligible students	No funding provided; financial sanctions to groups who receive federal funding and discriminate due to disability
Evaluations	Requires specific, comprehensive evaluation by multidisciplinary team; all areas related to disability assessed; re-evaluations required at least every 3 years	Less specific than IDEA; information is gathered and evaluated by people who know the student; re-evaluations required periodically
Placement	Placement decisions made by people who know the student and the service options, using a variety of documented information; placement to the maximum extent with students who are not disabled (LRE)	Same as IDEA
Responsible Federal, State, and Local Agencies/Programs	U.S. Office of Special Education Programs (OSEP); State Education Agency (SEA); Special Education	U.S. Office of Civil Rights (OCR); Local Education Agency (LEA); Regular Education

(Huefner, 2000; Hulett, 2009; Turnbull & Turnbull, 2000)

Americans with Disabilities Act (ADA) (1990)

In 1990, Congress passed the most sweeping antidiscrimination disability legislation to date, the Americans with Disabilities Act (ADA). While Section 504 applies only to recipients of federal funding, the ADA extends civil rights and nondiscrimination protection to most public and private programs, services, and agencies. ADA was created to eliminate barriers, physical barriers as well as the barriers of discrimination, for people with disabilities. ADA affects almost all sectors of society, to ensure access, full participation, equal opportunity, independent living, and job opportunities for people with disabilities (Turnbull & Turnbull, 2000).

ADA extends benefits to people with disabilities, based on the functional definition of disability in Section 504. According to this definition, a person has a disability if he or she is significantly limited in at least one of life's major functions, such as mobility, communication, learning, social skills, emotional well-being, employment, etc. The ADA prohibits discrimination based on disability related to employment; public services access, such as libraries and recreation facilities; use of public accommodations, such as restaurants, retail stores, and theaters; access to public and private transportation services; and telecommunications services. Since it is the role of special education to prepare students for successful employment and functioning in society upon completion of school, schools must teach students the skills necessary for employment, utilizing community and public services, transportation, and communication options. These important areas for learning are now accessible to students with disabilities due to the passage of the ADA.

Elementary and Secondary Education Act (ESEA) (commonly referred to as No Child Left Behind Act, NCLB) (2001)

In January of 2001, Congress passed P.L. 107-110, the latest version of the Elementary and Secondary Education Act, also known as No Child Left Behind Act (NCLB). This law represents an attempt at educational reform for all K–12 schools in the U.S. The ESEA focuses on several areas of educational improvement, including (a) increased accountability; (b) more choices for parents and students; (c) greater flexibility for states, school districts, and schools; and (d) a stronger emphasis on reading, especially for young children in primary grades (U.S. Department of Education, 2003).

Increased accountability: States are responsible for having strong academic standards and implementing statewide accountability systems for all schools and all students in the state. Assessment results must be listed to identify achievement by poverty, race, ethnicity, disability, and limited English proficiency. Schools that do not meet their achievement goals are subject to improvement measures to help them increase the success of their students. Schools that meet their goals and increase achievement of typically low performing groups are eligible for State Academic Achievement Awards.

More choices for parents and students: Students who attend schools that fail to meet state standards of achievement have the opportunity to attend a better performing school in the district. Funds may also be used to provide supplemental educational services for low-income students who are not achieving.

Greater flexibility for states, school districts, and schools: States and school districts in every state have more to say regarding how they spend federal education funding they receive each year. More decisions can be made at the local level to determine the best use of federal funds to support student achievement.

Stronger emphasis on reading: A strong focus of this Act is to ensure that all children can read by the end of the third grade. The Reading First initiative provides state grants to support screening and assessment to identify students at risk of reading failure and programs for professional development in reading instruction. Funding is also provided to support early language and literacy skills for preschool-aged children, especially those children from low-income families. In addition, schools that use scientifically based techniques to teach students to read are eligible for additional federal funds.

Entitlement and Antidiscrimination Laws

The federal government responded to disability discrimination through two types of laws—*entitlement laws* and *antidiscrimination laws.* Working together, these laws have different but complementary functions to provide a better environment for people with disabilities to live, learn, and work.

An *entitlement law* provides benefits to a person if that person meets specific standards of eligibility. These benefits help persons with disabilities respond better to the challenges they face due to their disability by diminishing the effect of the disability and augmenting existing capacities or developing new capacities for functioning. When an entitlement program is developed and delivered effectively, individuals with a disability are more likely to be able to accommodate to the demands imposed on them in a world that is primarily nondisabled. These accommodations are meant to help individuals adapt and function optimally when faced with disability-related difficulties in areas such as learning, communicating, mobility, etc. IDEA is an example of an entitlement program, where services are provided to children who meet eligibility requirements, and interventions are developed to diminish the effect of the disability on learning and functioning. Entitlement programs are one way to improve opportunities for an individual's functioning, but they are not enough to provide for the needs of individuals with disabilities.

Antidiscrimination laws prohibit discrimination against a person solely on the basis of a disability. Current antidiscrimination disability laws, specifically Section 504 and the Americans with Disabilities Act, are based on the legal precedents that prohibit discrimination on the basis of such differences as race or gender. Section 504 and the ADA prohibit discrimination and require access based on reasonable accommodations. Through improved access and appropriate accommodations, a person with a disability has increased opportunities to function in society.

Entitlement laws and antidiscrimination laws provide the basis for the principle of dual accommodations for individuals with disabilities. With entitlement laws, individuals are provided services to help them accommodate to their environment, and with antidiscrimination laws, the environment must accommodate to the individual with disabilities (Hulett, 2009; Turnbull & Turnbull, 2000). With these two-part accommodations in place, students with disabilities have the legal support necessary for appropriate educational services in an accessible environment.

Summary

There are many social, legal, and legislative events throughout our history that served as catalysts for educational reform, especially related to the education of students with disabilities. Through each decade in U.S. history, significant issues in special education prompted legal and legislative actions that led to current practice (see Table 2.3). Educational services for students with disabilities have moved from an exclusionary model to a model built on inclusion. Based on the current law, IDEA 2004, all students have the right to a free and appropriate public education in the least restrictive environment.

Events that Led to Current Educational Practices

Table 2.3 Significant Issues and Developments in Special Education, 1800s–2000s

Date	Issues in Special Education	Legal/Legislative Actions
1800s	• Segregated students with special needs, if educated at all	
Early 1900s	• Beginning to recognize worth and dignity of students • Students with disabilities educated in asylums or government institutions • Many had no educational opportunities	
1930s–1940s	• Decline in special education services due to the great depression • Low success rate/ineffective curricula • Poorly trained teachers • Sweeping segregation from general education classroom • Primarily custodial care	• *1930 White House Conference on Child Health and Protection*—1st time special education received national recognition as a justifiable component of education
1940s–1950s	• Parents started getting involved, renewal of interest in special education • Curriculum expanded, with emphasis on social participation and vocational skills • Basic rights being considered: due process, equal protection, protection from cruel and unusual punishment/treatment	• *Brown v. Board of Education* (1954): 1st landmark case that affected special education; civil rights case; separate is not equal, related to the education of white and black children; separate education did not provide equal education

Date	Issues in Special Education	Legal/Legislative Actions
1960s	• Increase in funding opportunities; increase in training institutions • Most students with severe disabilities continued to be institutionalized	• *Elementary and Secondary Education Act of 1965 (ESEA)* • *Elementary and Secondary Education Amendments of 1968*—authorized support of regional centers for education of handicapped children • *Handicapped Children's Early Education Assistance Act (1968)*—authorized pre-school and early education programs for handicapped children
1970s	• 8 million children with disabilities in the U.S.; half were not being educated appropriately • Movement to deinstitutionalize people with disabilities • Increased integration into communities • Practice of mainstreaming began • Problems: funding, identification of eligible students, competition for funds, little cooperation between special ed and general ed	• *PARC v. Commonwealth* (1971) and *Mills v. Board of Education* (1972): both of these cases established the constitutional basis for providing education for students with disabilities; denial of education and due process violates the 14th Amendment to the Constitution; framework from the Mills decision was foundation for P.L. 94-142 (now *IDEA*) • *Rehabilitation Act, Section 504* (1973): Programs that received federal funds could not discriminate on the basis of a disability • *P.L. 94-142, Education for All Handicapped Children Act (EAHCA)* (1975): Support for special education in order to provide FAPE; individualization, LRE, and due process must be provided; later became known as *IDEA* (Rothstein, 2000)
1980s	• Increased focus on special education reform • Regular Education Initiative	• Amendments to *EAHCA*: expanded services to ages 3–5 with incentives for birth–2 early intervention programs

Date	Issues in Special Education	Legal/Legislative Actions
1990s	• Movement from mainstreaming to full inclusion models	• Amendments to *EAHCA*, now renamed *IDEA*, 1990: changes in terminology (disabilities rather than handicaps); transition services and assistive technology listed as related services • *Americans with Disabilities Act (ADA)*, 1990: major civil rights legislation prohibiting discrimination on the basis of disability • IDEA reauthorized in 1997 (Rothstein, 2000)
2000s	• Continued movement toward education of students with disabilities with same-aged peers without disabilities • Early intervention services • Increased focus on accountability for the achievement of all children, especially related to ability to read	• Reauthorized *Elementary and Secondary Education Act (ESEA) (No Child Left Behind Act)* (2001) • *IDEA* amended in 2004 *(Individuals with Disabilities Education Improvement Act 2004)*
2010s	• Schools continue to struggle to meet the standards of ESEA regarding students with disabilities • States are allowed to exempt only 2% of student population from standard assessment procedures • Some districts eliminating programs such as music, art, and physical education to focus on "core academic subjects"; these may be the program areas where some students with disabilities excel	• *ESEA* up for reauthorization

KEY POINTS FROM THE CHAPTER

Eligibility for special education and related services:
   ♦   IDEA focuses on the educational needs of students ages 3 through 21. Students who have a disability that adversely affects their ability to learn may be eligible for special education and related services. IDEA uses a categorical approach to define eligibility for special services. Services also available for children with disabilities or at risk of developing disabilities, ages birth through 2.

Six principles of IDEA:

♦ Zero reject, free and appropriate public education (FAPE) must be provided for all children with disabilities.

♦ Nondiscriminatory evaluations must be used to determine eligibility and need for services.

♦ Services must be individualized to meet the needs of the student (Individualized Education Program, IEP).

♦ Educational services must be provided in the least restrictive environment (LRE).

♦ Parents have the right to be included and involved in the development of their child's educational program.

♦ Procedural protections must ensure that the requirements of the law are met (due process).

Entitlement and antidiscrimination laws:

♦ Entitlement laws provide benefits to a person if that person meets specific standards of eligibility. IDEA is an example of an entitlement law.

♦ Antidiscrimination laws prohibit discrimination against a person solely on the basis of a disability. The Americans with Disabilities Act is an example of an antidiscrimination law.

REFERENCES

Adamek, M. (2002). In the beginning: A review of early special education services and legislative/regulatory activity affecting the teaching and placement of special learners. In B. Wilson (Ed.), *Models of music therapy interventions in school settings* (2nd ed.). Silver Spring, MD: American Music Therapy Association.

Bartlett, L., Etscheidt, S., & Weisenstein, G. (2007). *Special education law and practice in public schools* (2nd ed.). Upper Saddle River, NJ: Pearson.

Boyle, J. R., & Weishaar, M. (2001). *Special education law with cases.* Needham Heights, MA: Allyn & Bacon.

Guernsey, T., & Klare, K. (2001). *Special education law* (2nd ed.). Durham, NC: Carolina Academic Press.

Hallahan, D., Kauffman, J., & Pullen, P. (2009). *Exceptional learners: An introduction to special education* (11th ed.). Boston: Pearson.

Huefner, D. S. (2000). *Getting comfortable with special education law.* Norwood, MA: Christopher-Gordon.

Hulett, K. (2009). *Legal aspects of special education.* Upper Saddle River, NJ: Pearson.

Jellison, J. (2000). A content analysis of music research with disabled children and youth (1975–1999): Applications in special education. In *Effectiveness of music therapy procedures: Documentations of research and clinical practice* (pp. 199–264). Silver Spring, MD: American Music Therapy Association.

Rawson, M. J. (2000). *A manual of special education law for educators and parents.* Naples, FL: Morgen.

Rothstein, L. F. (2000). *Special education law* (3rd ed.). New York: Longman.

Solomon, A. (1980). Music in special education before 1930: Hearing and speech development. *Journal of Research in Music Education, 28,* 236–242.

Stainback, W., Stainback, S., & Bunch, G. (1989). Introduction and historical background. In S. Stainback, W. Stainback, & M. Forest (Eds.), *Educating all students in the mainstream of regular education* (pp. 3–14). Baltimore: Paul H. Brookes.

Turnbull, H. R., & Turnbull, A. P. (2000). *Free appropriate public education: The law and children with disabilities* (6th ed.). Denver, CO: Love.

Turnbull, A., Turnbull, R., & Wehmeyer, M. (2010). *Exceptional lives: Special education in today's schools* (6th ed.). Upper Saddle River, NJ: Merrill.

U.S. Department of Education. (2003). *The No Child Left Behind Act of 2001.* Executive summary. Retrieved from http://www2.ed.gov/nclb/overview/intro/execsumm.html

Villa, R. A., Thousand, J. S., Meyers, H., & Nevin, A. I. (1996). Teacher and administrator perceptions of heterogeneous education. *Exceptional Children, 63,* 29–45.

Weiner, R. (1985). *P.L. 94-142: Impact on the schools.* Arlington, VA: Capitol.

Will, M. (1986). Educating children with learning problems. A shared responsibility. *Exceptional Children, 52,* 411–415.

Winzer, M. (1993). *The history of special education: From isolation to integration.* Washington, DC: Gallaudet University Press.

Winzer, M. (2007). Confronting difference: An excursion through the history of special education. In L. Florian (Ed.), *The Sage handbook of special education* (pp. 21–33). Thousand Oaks, CA: Sage.

Yell, M. L., & Drasgow, E. (2005). The Individuals with Disabilities Education Act (IDEA). *Encyclopedia of behavior modification and cognitive behavior therapy.* Retrieved March 24, 2010, from http://www.sage-ereference.com/cbt/Article_n3077.html

Chapter 3

Inclusion Principles and Practices

CHAPTER OVERVIEW

IDEA and other entitlement and antidiscrimination laws provide a legal framework for equal access and inclusive education for students with disabilities. There is an expectation of shared responsibility for including all students in the full range of possible educational opportunities in today's schools. Although inclusive practices are sometimes difficult to implement, inclusion is an important aspect of education in the U.S. As teachers, administrators, parents, and students grapple with the ever-changing needs of students with disabilities, inclusive practices continue to be expanded and implemented more effectively nationwide.

This chapter includes information on the following topics:
- ♦ Philosophical foundations of inclusion
- ♦ Benefits and outcomes of inclusion
- ♦ Barriers to successful inclusion and strategies to overcome them
- ♦ A continuum of service

Philosophical Foundations of Inclusion

Current educational efforts have evolved from focusing solely on the individual's deficits and deficits in the environment, to focusing on the whole student, the environment in which the student lives and learns, and the interactions between the individual and the environment. There are many basic ideas that provide the foundation for the inclusion movement. Underlying principles of inclusive education are based on issues of social justice, equity, tolerance, pluralism, and individual rights (Ayers, Quinn, & Stovall, 2009; Thomas & Loxley, 2007). Strategies based on these foundation principles continue to develop to strengthen the educational system for students with disabilities. Below are some of the basic philosophical ideas upon which inclusion is based (Kochhar, West, & Taymans, 2000):

1. The *human potential movement* is based on the belief that all people have the desire to develop in positive ways. This philosophy promotes a society that provides basic rights and equal opportunities for all individuals, including educational and social service opportunities. These educational opportunities and support services must be appropriate to the individual's developmental level and needs, and extra supports may be required to compensate for a person's disabilities.

2. The *general system theory* is based on the premise that educators must examine the student as a whole person and collaborate with others to provide an integrated approach to the individual's education. Individuals are viewed as more than the sum of their parts so that all aspects of a student, the student's environment, and the interaction between the two must be addressed. Using this approach, the teacher will look at the needs of the student and the impact of the environment on the student's behavior and learning.

3. The *principle of normalization* reflects the belief that individuals with disabilities should have experiences as close as possible to normal. This idea provided a foundation for the civil rights movement for people with disabilities, and it has many implications for the classroom and school setting. With normalized experiences, the student has the opportunities for increased community integration, social integration with peers, and improved quality of life.

4. The *self-determination movement* promotes students' and families' empowerment and decision making regarding services impacting the future. Characteristics and skills such as assertiveness, creativity, problem solving, flexibility, self-esteem, and decision making are developed throughout early educational years to promote self-determination as an adult.

Benefits and Outcomes of Inclusion

While there are many challenges to successful inclusion, the benefits of inclusion for students, teachers, families, schools, and communities can surpass the difficulties. Below is a brief list of some of the many possible benefits of inclusion that may be outcomes of successful inclusive practices.

Benefits to *students with disabilities* included in the general education classroom (Kochhar et al., 2000; Loreman, Deppeler, & Harvey, 2005):

*   Develops higher expectations and more appropriate social role models
*   Offers a wider circle of friends and support
*   Creates opportunities to promote self-determination and self-advocacy by working with peers
*   Improves quality of life by experiencing a broader array of meaningful experiences

Benefits for *peers without disabilities:*
- Increases acceptance of students who are different from themselves
- Promotes better understanding of individual's strengths and weaknesses
- Provides opportunities to function as a positive role model, mentor, or peer tutor
- Provides leadership opportunities

Benefits to *teachers and schools:*
- Provides for atmosphere of acceptance, diversity, and understanding of individual differences
- Provides teachers with opportunities to individualize to the needs of students
- Improves instructional strategies when teachers individualize or alter instructional methods

Barriers to Successful Inclusion and Strategies to Overcome Them

Much progress has been made in the past three decades to improve the quality of education for students with disabilities. Schools have had to undergo complex changes in order to implement the special education laws regarding access and structure of educational services. Although services have dramatically improved, there remain several barriers to successful inclusion that can be summarized in three main areas: organization, attitude, and knowledge (Jha, 2007; Kochhar & West, 1996; Loreman et al., 2005). Barriers to educational access may be physical in nature, or they may be unseen elements that impede successful inclusion. It is important for teachers to recognize and understand these possible barriers and to identify possible solutions within their school or classroom.

Organizational Barriers

Organizational barriers relate to the ways schools and classrooms are structured, how goals for students with disabilities are defined, how instruction is delivered, and how classrooms are managed.

Music educators typically teach dozens, if not hundreds, of students each day. Some of the major concerns voiced by music educators relate to lack of time to gather information and plan for students with disabilities, lack of support from administrators, and difficulty with classroom management (Darrow, 1999). In addition, some music educators are given teaching assignments for which they may not be trained or qualified, such as teaching students with severe disabilities in self-contained classrooms. These organizational barriers, if not addressed and resolved, may play a role in creating negative attitudes toward working with students who have disabilities.

Another organizational barrier is related to how the actual music classroom or rehearsal space is set up each day. Music rooms tend to be filled with instruments, chairs, risers, music stands, props, AV equipment, computers, and other assorted items. If not organized in a thoughtful manner, these objects create structural barriers for students who have physical disabilities, visual disabilities, or attention or behavior problems.

Strategies to overcome this barrier:
- Discuss concerns with administrators and offer solutions to solve the problems, rather than complaining. Always keep the needs of the students in the forefront and explain why the current situation is detrimental to the education of the students, if that is the case.
- Choose one or two students to focus on at a time, rather than all of the students who have disabilities. For these one or two students, gather basic information regarding strengths, needs, IEP goals, and effective intervention strategies. It is likely that once this information is understood and utilized, the information will generalize to fit the educational needs of other students.
- Educate administrators in the distinct differences between music education and music therapy. In some situations, music therapists who have extensive training and experience working with students with special needs may serve students with severe disabilities more effectively than music educators. Music therapists also can work as consultants to classroom teachers and music educators to help develop effective music-based interventions that are appropriate for the age and functioning level of the student.
- Set up the music room or rehearsal space in a way that provides an adequate structure for the needs of the students who are in the classes. For a child in a wheelchair, be sure there is plenty of room for him or her to enter, move about, and exit the class with the same ease as the students who are independently mobile. For a student who is blind or has a visual disability, set up the room in a consistent way each day so the student can learn the map of the room. If changes are made, give the student verbal directions so he or she can learn the new set-up and adapt his or her map of the room. For a student with attention or behavior problems, make sure that distracting or tempting instruments are not easily accessible or within easy reach or view.

Attitudinal Barriers

Attitudinal barriers relate to the beliefs and attitudes that teachers may have about educational services for students with disabilities, including how students are accommodated in the general education setting, interaction with parents and guardians, and students' participation in school-wide and community activities. The attitudes of students who do not have disabilities toward students who have disabilities may be a reflection of those modeled by the teacher.

Negative attitudes may stem from lack of information, misinformation, previous experiences, or difficult situations that remain unresolved or unsuccessful. Teachers may have misconceptions about working with students who have disabilities, or have fears that they will not be effective teachers in an inclusive setting. Teachers may also be concerned with how inclusion will affect the classroom climate and the education of students who do not have disabilities. Inclusion requires new ways of thinking about teaching, new approaches to communication and collaboration, and new attitudes about sound educational practices.

Positive attitudes may be developed and enhanced in many different ways. Teachers are encouraged to discover students' strengths and design instructional methods and adaptations that build on those strengths. In addition, developing a relationship with individual students helps teachers humanize the experience and learn about the student, beyond the disability. Peers may need structure and direction from the teacher to enhance socialization, interaction, and respect for each other (Humpal, 1991; Jellison, Brooks, & Huck, 1984).

Strategies to overcome this barrier:
- Find out information about the strengths and accomplishments of a few of the students who have disabilities in the music class. What can these students do to contribute to the positive climate of the classroom or the music environment?
- Talk to other teachers or professionals about ways to solve difficult problems related to students with disabilities in the classroom. Collaborative efforts among teachers can provide support to teachers who are struggling with difficult students or difficult situations.
- Talk to students about the many ways that people can contribute to the class so students can see that all students have positive attributes that can enhance the classroom environment.
- Students might be afraid of students who have severe disabilities. They may need information and structured activities to get to know the students as individuals rather than just as a disability.
- Positive attitudes, language, and respect by the teacher provide an appropriate model for students to develop positive attitudes about students with disabilities in the class.

Knowledge Barriers

Knowledge barriers relate to the range of knowledge and skills that teachers need to provide effective services to students, such as adapting the curriculum and instructional methods, providing necessary classroom structure and management, and developing appropriate goals and interventions based on the age and functioning levels of the students.

Music educators must have adequate knowledge and information in order to educate and include students with disabilities in their classrooms. Some of this information may come from collaborating with the regular education and/or special education teachers, as well as other specialists who work with the students. Collaboration is key to successful inclusion. Through collaboration, the music educator can find out specific information about the students, including strengths and weaknesses, goals, and effective instructional methods used by other teachers. Music educators may develop their expectations for a student's participation in music based on information provided by the team.

Strategies to overcome this barrier:
- Educate yourself about the general characteristics of specific disabilities (e.g., if there are several students with autism, learn about typical behaviors and characteristics of children with autism).
- Talk with the team members (classroom teachers, specialists such as art and physical education teachers, and therapists such as the speech and language pathologist or occupational therapist) to determine the student's abilities, needs, and effective intervention strategies. Find out the student's IEP goals that could be addressed in music.
- Design intervention strategies and classroom accommodations to support the student's learning in music class. Use music that is age appropriate and music activities with which the student can be successful. Ask the question, "Would I use this music with same-aged students who did not have disabilities?" If the answer is no, find music that is better suited to the age of the student.

Eliminating the barriers related to organization, attitudes, and knowledge sets the stage for more effective inclusion practices. It takes continuous efforts by all professionals to make sure that integration and acceptance are infused in all aspects of the educational system, starting at the classroom level.

A Continuum of Services

The terms *mainstreaming* and *inclusion* may have many different functional definitions in different school districts or states. *Mainstreaming* was originally used in the 1970s after the passage of P.L. 94-142 to define the practice of placing students part-time in the general classroom setting. This term is still used today in some districts and suggests that the student is not a member of the general classroom but a visitor for a short time, and is the responsibility of the special education teacher. Currently, *inclusion* is the preferred terminology and approach. *Inclusion* refers to the practice in which students with disabilities are primarily educated in the general education class, under the responsibility of the general education teacher, with supplementary supports and services either within the classroom or, when justified, in another setting outside of the classroom. Since both terms are used to describe levels of educational services within the general education setting, music educators should become familiar with the specific uses and definitions of these terms in their school district.

The continuum of services has been an essential feature for providing appropriate educational services to students with disabilities. The continuum provides options for learning in typical and inclusive general education classrooms all the way to most restrictive and separate educational settings. Currently, the trend is to limit the need for more restrictive settings by creating partnerships between special educators and general educators. With these partnerships to accommodate the students' needs, more students can find success in a typical and inclusive classroom, thus decreasing the need for more restrictive educational settings. Two major issues that are central to the current inclusion debate are related to eliminating the need for a continuum of placements and increasing the amount of time students spend in the regular, inclusive classroom (Turnbull, Turnbull, & Wehmeyer, 2010).

Education for students with disabilities should be focused on providing appropriate education supports for each student, not on the place of educational services. However, many variations exist in approach and location of services, and music professionals (therapists and educators) must work within each system and be familiar with the potential approaches. Educational services for students with disabilities can be provided in a number of different ways and in a variety of settings. IDEA mandates that the student be educated in the least restrictive environment (LRE), which means that the student must be educated in a setting that is as close as possible to the general education program while still meeting the unique needs of the individual student. A continuum of services provides a structure for considering the most appropriate LRE for each student.

There is no one universal model of the continuum of services; however, the basic approach is similar state to state. Each state has different ways to articulate and demonstrate inclusive education for students with disabilities. In order for inclusion to be successful, schools must not only provide the physical access to integrate students with disabilities, but they must also accept and support students' individual differences that become an integral part of the schools' programs and activities. Below is a list of several models along the continuum of services that can be implemented to provide instruction in the least restrictive environment, with implications for the music educator (Dover, 1994; Mastropieri & Scruggs, 2000). School districts across the country have varied educational philosophies and approaches, so not all of these models will be utilized in every district. Music educators must adapt instruction for the entire continuum of skills presented in every class, from gifted students to those students with severe disabilities. For all of these models, the music educator may need to consult with the classroom teacher, special educator, music therapist, or other professionals to develop appropriate instructional adaptations to provide the most effective educational experience for students who have disabilities.

Inclusion model: The student is placed in the general education classroom most, if not all, of the time. The classroom teacher collaborates with special education experts as partners in teaching, along with adaptation ideas and support.

- Student attends music classes with classmates. The music educator may need to consult with the classroom teacher, special educator, music therapist, or other professionals to develop appropriate instructional adaptations.

Social mainstreaming model: The student with severe disabilities is included during regular education classroom instruction, with the goal of providing social interaction with same-aged peers (without disabilities), rather than mastering educational concepts. The student is not expected to complete the same assignments as the rest of the class.

- Student attends music classes with same-aged peers. The music educator should create age-appropriate adaptations to include the student and to provide socialization experiences with nondisabled peers.

Resource room, pull-out model: The student is educated primarily in the general education inclusive classroom. Special education professionals provide individualized services for the student outside of the regular classroom, pulling the student out of the class for individual or small group instruction. Instructional needs, social support, and specific interventions such as speech, physical, or music therapy may be delivered in a pull-out model. These therapies may also be delivered in the regular classroom.

- Student typically attends music class with students in his or her regular classroom.

Mainstreaming model: The student participates in selected general education classes with same-aged peers. Typically the student is expected to maintain appropriate performance levels and behavior. Some students participate with same-aged peers only in specialist classes such as art, music, and physical education. In this case, instructional adaptations may need to be made to support the student's abilities.

- Student attends music with same-aged peers from the regular classroom where he or she is mainstreamed throughout the day. Expectations are the same in music as they are in the other mainstreamed classes. Music educators should find out what is expected of the student and follow through with those expectations. Music educators can work with classroom teachers to make sure that the student arrives and departs with the other students, making the situation as normalized as possible.

Self-contained model: The student is educated in a segregated special education classroom for the all or most of the day. The self-contained classroom is usually focused on the needs of a small number of students who have similar severe disabilities and low functioning levels. This model typically has several paraprofessionals to support the extensive needs of the students.

- Students may have a music class in their self-contained classroom taught by a music educator or music therapist. The focus of the adapted music class is music learning, through age- and functioning-appropriate music experiences.

The models listed above may still not provide an appropriate LRE for a student and other options may be necessary. In addition to the models listed above, students with severe disabilities may be educated in the following settings:

Separate school: Students may be educated in separate schools for students with specific disabilities. Certain schools are set up to educate students with a variety of disabilities, while other schools may specialize in the needs of students with a specific disability, such as students with behavior disorders or learning disabilities.

Residential facility: A small percentage of students are educated at residential facilities. These may be long-term or short-term placements, depending on the individual student's needs. Examples of these placements include programs for juvenile offenders, rehabilitation facilities for children with brain injury, and state facilities for people with severe cognitive and/or physical limitations.

Homebound or hospital placement: Due to a physical or emotional illness or disability, a student may need to have educational services provided at home or in/ out patient hospital settings.

- Music therapy might be offered in any of these segregated settings as an integral therapeutic approach to assist in the development of social/emotional skills, communication skills, academic/cognitive skills, or physical skills. Music therapists may also provide music experiences to promote music learning, since these students would not have access to the general music, vocal, or instrumental opportunities of the regular education setting.

Summary

Entitlement and antidiscrimination laws provide a legal framework for equal educational access for students with disabilities. Although inclusive practices can sometimes be difficult to implement, inclusion is a major feature of education in the U.S. IDEA mandates that students are to be educated in the least restrictive environment (LRE). General educators and special educators develop partnerships to provide the most appropriate individualized education for students in the most normalized and inclusive environment possible. Schools across the country offer different options to provide varying levels of support for the students in the least restrictive, most normalized environment. The team works together to determine the least restrictive environment needed by the student in order for that student to make educational progress. Models range from a full inclusion model (least restrictive) to separate schools and residential facilities (most restrictive).

KEY POINTS FROM THE CHAPTER

Philosophical foundations of inclusion:

These principles provide a foundation for the development of inclusion strategies in schools:

♦ The *human potential movement* is based on the belief that all people have the desire to develop in positive ways.

♦ The *general system theory* is based on the premise that educators must examine the student as a whole person and collaborate with others to provide an integrated approach to the student's education.

♦ The *principle of normalization* reflects the belief that individuals with disabilities should have experiences as close as possible to normal.

♦ The *self-determination movement* promotes students' and families' empowerment and decision making regarding services impacting the future.

Benefits and outcomes of inclusion:

♦ Benefits for students with disabilities include higher expectations, more appropriate role models, wider circle of friends and support, and a broader array of meaningful experiences.

♦ Benefits for students without disabilities include increased acceptance of others, opportunities to function as positive role model or peer tutor, and opportunities for leadership.

♦ Benefits to teachers and schools include creating an atmosphere of acceptance of diversity, and opportunities to individualize instruction and alter instructional methods to better serve all students.

Barriers to inclusion:

Several barriers negatively affect the successful inclusion of students in the general education setting:

♦ Organizational barriers

♦ Attitudinal barriers

♦ Knowledge barriers

Continuum of services:

Educational services for students with disabilities can be provided in a number of different types of settings, depending on the needs of the student and the approach of the school district. The names and structure of these models may vary from state to state.

Music educators must adapt instruction for the varied abilities of students in the class. Music therapists can assist music educators to develop appropriate instructional adaptations for students with severe disabilities. Music therapists may also work directly with students who have severe disabilities.

REFERENCES

Ayers, W., Quinn, T., & Stovall, D. (2009). *Handbook of social justice in education.* New York: Routledge.

Darrow, A. A. (1999). Music educators' perceptions regarding the inclusion of students with severe disabilities in music classrooms. *Journal of Music Therapy, 36,* 254–273.

Dover, W. (1994). *The inclusion facilitator.* Manhattan, KS: Master Teacher.

Humpal, M. (1991). The effects of an integrated early childhood music program on social interaction among children with handicaps and their typical peers. *Journal of Music Therapy, 38,* 161–177.

Jellison, J., Brooks, B., & Huck, A. (1984). Structuring small groups and music reinforcement to facilitate positive interactions and acceptance of severely handicapped students in the regular music classroom. *Journal of Research in Music Education, 32,* 243–264.

Jha, M. M. (2007). Barriers to student access and success. In G. K. Verma, C. R. Bagley, & M. M. Jha (Eds.), *International perspectives on educational diversity and inclusion* (pp. 33–43). New York: Routledge.

Kochhar, C., & West, L. (1996). *Handbook for successful inclusion.* Rockville, MD: Aspen.

Kochhar, C., West, L., & Taymans, J. (2000). *Successful inclusion. Practical strategies for a shared responsibility.* Upper Saddle River, NJ: Prentice-Hall.

Loreman, T., Deppeler, J., & Harvey, D. (2005) *Inclusive education: A practical guide to supporting diversity in the classroom.* New York: Routledge Falmer.

Mastropieri, M., & Scruggs, T. (2000). *The inclusive classroom: Strategies for effective instruction.* Upper Saddle River, NJ: Prentice-Hall.

Thomas, G., & Loxley, A. (2007). *Deconstructing special education and constructing inclusion.* Berkshire, England: Open University Press.

Turnbull, A., Turnbull, R., & Wehmeyer, M. (2010). *Exceptional lives: Special education in today's schools* (6th ed.). Upper Saddle River, NJ: Merrill.

Chapter 4

Teaching Strategies for Successful Inclusion

CHAPTER OVERVIEW

Music educators and music therapists who work in schools utilize a variety of strategies to support the educational needs of students with disabilities. In order to develop effective strategies, music professionals need to collaborate with other professionals in the school to gather information about students' abilities and special needs, and to share students' responses to music and their progress in music class. This chapter focuses on information to assist in collaborative efforts to promote students' success in the music setting.

This chapter includes information on the following topics:
♦ Collaboration
♦ Universal Design for Learning (UDL)
♦ Adaptations in the classroom: Accommodations and modifications

---

Collaboration

Students with disabilities have the legal right to a free and appropriate public education. In order for this to occur, teachers, specialists, administrators, community agencies, and parents must collaborate to develop effective partnerships. Successful collaboration begins with the development of good working relationships among all of the people involved in the individual student's education. Collaboration can occur formally though the IEP process or other formal team meetings, through co-teaching or directly serving a student with another professional, or informally through email and impromptu conversations or other times when a formal meeting is not possible.

Collaboration is an ongoing process among educational professionals and parents that is essential for the effective education of the students.

Collaboration involves cooperation, meaningful communication, problem solving, idea sharing, information sharing, and designing and facilitating useful strategies for students. Music educators and music therapists working in schools may develop collaborative partnerships with special education teachers, general education teachers, paraprofessionals, parents, and other team members (speech-language pathologist, occupational therapist, physical therapist, etc.). Darrow (1999) found that the majority of music educators interviewed identified collaboration or consultation as a critical issue related to successfully including students with severe disabilities in the music class. Some of the other critical issues mentioned by music educators included (a) obtaining information about students, disabilities, and IEP goals; (b) adapting curriculum materials, instruments, and music; (c) placement of students in the music classroom; (d) socialization between students with disabilities and students without disabilities in the music class; and (e) time for making adaptations, gathering information, and collaborating for successful inclusion practices.

It is typical for students with disabilities to be included in elementary music classes in districts where music is offered at that level. Students with disabilities are also included at the middle school/junior high and high school levels in vocal and instrumental performance classes and non-performance classes, such as music appreciation. Many schools include students with a range of disabling conditions in music class, even if the students have severe disabilities and are primarily educated in a self-contained special education classroom for the majority of the day. Special skills in collaboration, adaptations, and designing effective instructional strategies are necessary for successful inclusion in the music setting. Since music educators teach students with a wide range of abilities, they must be prepared to create instructional approaches that address the abilities and needs of the students in the school. More information on implanting Universal Design for Learning (UDL) and adapting instruction can be found later in this chapter.

Sharing Goals and Information

Collaboration means that teachers are working cooperatively with one another so that the students receive the best possible education throughout their school day. While the general education teacher or special education teacher might have primary responsibility for a student, all professionals work together to assist the student in the accomplishment of his or her IEP goals.

One of the first steps in working effectively with students who have special needs in music class or music therapy sessions is to find out some basic information about the students. Communication with the classroom teacher is essential to gain insight into the best ways to work with a particular student. Most music educators are unable to attend students' IEP meetings or even take the time to read each student's IEP. However, it is important to know basic information about students' goals and objectives, strengths and weaknesses, along with useful instructional approaches in order to develop appropriate instruction for students with special needs.

Music professionals can obtain specific information about a student quickly and efficiently by developing some sort of information-sharing tool that highlights specific information about a student. While most music educators' primary educational focus is to teach music skills, many would agree that developing appropriate classroom behaviors, cooperation, independence, and respect are essential non-music skills that can also be addressed through music experiences. Music teachers can develop strategies for including students in meaningful ways when they know and understand the students' IEP goals. In addition to knowing the IEP goals, teachers can learn about students' strengths and abilities in order to build on these positive attributes.

Teachers need basic information about students in order to design the best possible instructional interventions. Important information includes: (a) student's strength or special skills; (b) student's disability characteristics, limitations, or weaknesses; (c) IEP objectives that can be addressed in the music class; and (d) useful strategies for working with the student (Adamek, 2001; Ebeling, Deschenes, & Sprague, 1994; Fitzgerald, 2006; Lapka, 2006). Simple forms asking for this information can be created and then distributed to classroom teachers, special education teachers, administrators, specialists, parents, and, in some cases, the student. Music educators and music therapists can be proactive in obtaining pertinent information about a student before or soon after they begin working with the student. This simple and clear approach for information gathering provides a means for consistent teaching strategies and expectations among all of the student's teachers. Teachers who have appropriate information can also evaluate the student based on the individual's goals, objectives, and abilities. Music professionals can develop collaborative partnerships with other professionals by asking for information about the student and by sharing information about the student's experiences in music. These partnerships provide consistent support for the student throughout the school day and even from year to year. See Figure 4.1 for an example of a type of form that teachers can use to share information about students. Teachers are encouraged to develop similar forms to obtain important information that will increase students' successes in music.

Teachers who understand the process of collaboration, who can effectively communicate with team members, and who have information about students' strengths and IEP goals are ready to design effective interventions and develop adaptations to promote students' learning and success. Music educators and music therapists can be creative in applying adaptation techniques to music materials that are used in the classroom. Adaptations are developed and utilized to help students meet their educational objectives throughout their school day, including during music-based classes.

Figure 4.1 Student Information — "At a Glance" Sample Form

Student: Allen Southward
Teacher/Grade: Mr. Swanson, 6th grade inclusive class

Strengths/Special Skills	Disability/Limitations/Weaknesses
• Active participant in class • Very energetic • Responds to music, motivated by music • Has shown some leadership skills	• Low frustration tolerance • Difficulty getting along with other students at times • Hyperactive with limited focus of attention, easily distracted • Reads below grade level • Easily agitated in loud environments
IEP Objectives	*Useful Strategies*
• Follow teacher's one- and two-step directions • Focus on task for at least 10 minutes • Complete tasks when directed • Ask for help when needed or assistance when frustrated	• Peer buddy to assist with difficult tasks • Break down directions into one or two clear steps • Use positive reinforcement for completing work or getting along with peers (likes to earn tokens, social reinforcers) • Allow a brief time away with aide or peer buddy during loud activities

---

Working with Other Teachers and Paraprofessionals

Music educators and music therapists in the schools usually work with many, if not all, of the classroom teachers and special education teachers in their building. Good interpersonal skills and effective communication are essential characteristics for the successful music professional. Throughout each day, music specialists interact with many teachers who have different personalities and varied teaching approaches. One of the greatest challenges when working in a school is to have open and direct two-way communication between the teachers and the music specialist. Barriers to effective communication include lack of time to share about the students, attitudes held by certain professionals, or difficulties with interpersonal skills. A positive attitude towards the process and good interpersonal skills can lead to improved communication and better collaborative partnerships (McCord & Watts, 2006).

Several common elements are important for effective communication: active listening, depersonalizing situations, brainstorming possible solutions, summarizing goals and solutions, and follow-up to monitor students' progress (Gordon, 1987).

Active listening involves demonstrating to the speaker that you are listening, you have a serious interest in the topic, and you understand the content of the information being discussed. Verbal comments and nonverbal cues can indicate active listening. Comments such as "I understand" or "Yes, I agree" or restating or summarizing the main points of the discussion all demonstrate active listening. Nonverbal behaviors such as direct eye contact, leaning in towards the speaker, and nodding all indicate that you are intently listening and engaged in the discussion.

Depersonalizing the situation helps put the focus on the solution to a problem or the shared goals, rather than on who is to blame for a particular situation or lack of progress. If a teacher perceives that his or her character or skills are under attack, then ongoing communication and problem solving will likely be at-risk. It is important to avoid negative comments and focus on the needs and progress of the student.

Brainstorming possible solutions with other teachers or team members will help everyone identify several likely outcomes or approaches for a particular problem. When brainstorming, the group creates a list of possible solutions, without making value judgments, and then prioritizes the solutions based on what might be best in the situation at hand. Team members who are included in the problem-solving process are more likely to be invested in working together on solutions.

Summarizing goals and solutions prior to the end of a meeting helps to ensure that everyone is working toward the same outcomes. Summarizing provides an opportunity for clarification of any ideas and helps to prevent misunderstanding among the team members. After summarizing what is agreed upon, everyone involved should be aware of his or her role and responsibility in working with the students.

Follow-up to monitor students' progress ensures that the agreed-upon plan is being implemented and the student's progress is being evaluated. Often students behave differently in different situations or classes. Team members can use this information to help the student be more successful in areas where they are not achieving. Music specialists have important information to share with other team members since students might be more successful in music class or have different behaviors in music than in other classes. The music specialist can share this information with the team and offer ideas for incorporating music interventions or adaptations from music into other classes.

Effective communication with team members takes additional effort, but it is essential for understanding the education plan and progress for students with disabilities in one's class. In addition to working closely with and communicating with teachers and other professionals, music specialists also work closely with paraprofessionals. Paraprofessionals, sometimes called teachers' aides, frequently attend music classes to provide additional support to a student with special needs. While having an extra adult in the classroom can sound like a dream come true, this situation is not always without difficulties. Proactive discussions with the paraprofessional can help avert problems and create a positive classroom climate for everyone involved. Beninghof (1996) suggested that teachers discuss the following topics with paraprofesionals:

- Your teaching philosophy
- Classroom rules and discipline
- Objectives for the class and for the assigned student
- Your view of the role of the teacher and paraprofessional

- The paraprofessional's view of his or her role in the classroom
- Plan for continued communication throughout the year
- Needs of the student and how they can be met in the class
- A system to signal when things are not going well and discussion is not possible

In addition to this initial discussion, the music specialist should try to talk with the paraprofessional frequently about how things seem to be going in the class. This is also a good time to reinforce the paraprofessional and thank him or her for assisting in the class.

Sometimes paraprofessionals accompany a student to music classes to deal with health or safety needs in cases where a child is medically fragile and needs additional support to ensure basic safety. In other cases, a paraprofessional will accompany a child to music classes due to the student's severe cognitive, physical, or behavioral disabilities. In any of these situations, the music specialist can communicate with the supervising teacher and the paraprofessional to make sure that everyone understands the role and responsibilities of paraprofessionals when they attend music class. This communication is essential in designing and implementing the most advantageous learning environment for the student with special needs as well as the other students in the class. Open and direct communication about the paraprofessionals' responsibilities will help maximize their role in the music class and ensure a more normalized environment for the students.

Remember that the paraprofessional who is working one-on-one with a student knows that student very well, probably a lot better than specialists who see the student one or two times per week, at best. He or she can be a good source of information to help specialists understand some of the student's strengths, abilities, and challenges. In addition, the paraprofessional probably has a good understanding of effective adaptations or techniques for working with the student.

Sometimes a paraprofessional will sit in the back of music class and simply watch the student in case the student needs additional support (redirection, health issues, behavioral interventions, etc.) While this passive approach might be appropriate in some situations, a creative music specialist will work with the paraprofessional to get him or her involved in the class or rehearsal. Frequently the paraprofessional is interested in getting involved but does not know exactly what to do, so waits for directions from the music specialist. It is the job of the specialist to respectfully direct the paraprofessional to whatever active engagement is expected or appropriate for the class.

Here are some tips for maximizing the effects of the paraprofessional in music class (Hughes, Rice, DeBedout, & Hightower, 2002). Music specialists can ask paraprofessionals to:

- actively participate in the music activities, providing a good model for the students;
- move around the room in order to assist more students, rather than hover over the student with special needs. This creates a more normalized environment for the targeted student and gives additional support to the other students;
- redirect inappropriate behavior in a way that is respectful to the student. Rather than talking from across the room, ask the paraprofessional to redirect the student in close proximity;
- share with the music specialist any problems that the student might be having prior to the start of class;
- show the peers how to interact or support the student, and then let them step in to help as a peer buddy;
- ask questions when they are confused about what to do;
- make suggestions for accommodations or adaptations that they think would be useful;
- share information with the classroom teacher about the student's progress/ behavior in music.

The music specialist can also ask the paraprofessional to avoid the following behaviors:

- Sitting in the back and reading a book or newspaper
- Appearing bored or sleeping
- Using degrading or disrespectful language with the students
- Discussing a student in front of the other students
- Disciplining in a way that is in conflict with the music teacher's approach
- Leaving class for a break rather than staying to support the student

Communicating directly with the supervising teacher and the paraprofessional will help avert any misunderstanding related to the role of the paraprofessional in music. Paraprofessionals can be an enormous help in assisting the student, the music specialist, and the other students, when everyone understands the roles and expectations. Mutual respect is imperative to create and maintain this important collaborative partnership. This respect is demonstrated by open and direct communication, clear expectations, and acknowledgment for the assistance offered in class (Harding, 2009).

Universal Design for Learning (UDL)

In today's schools the student population is diverse, made up of students with disabilities, students who have motivation issues, students whose first language is not English, as well as students with typical learning needs. Instructional approaches can no longer be "one size fits all" but must address the individual differences of today's students. When the U.S. Congress reauthorized IDEA in 2004, they called for a whole-school approach for effective instruction and learning. The concept of Universal Design for Learning (UDL) embodies this directive.

Successful inclusive education requires that teachers provide accessible learning opportunities for students with and without disabilities. Educational reformers promote the idea of Universal Design for Learning (UDL) for all instruction, not just instruction for students with disabilities. UDL is the flexible design of instruction, instructional materials, and evaluation of student learning that can be used with all students, without the need for specialized design or adaptation. Rather than designing instruction for the average or typical student, a teacher using UDL principles will design instruction for students with a broad range of abilities, disabilities, reading levels, native languages, learning styles, motivations, and other characteristics. UDL promotes learning for all by providing supports for learning that enable students to gain knowledge and skills while reducing barriers to learning. Instruction can incorporate inclusive attributes that accommodate learner differences without excluding students or compromising academic standards. UDL is a strategic approach to instruction, focusing on the process of learning for all students (Bowe, 2000; Burgstahler, 2007a, 2007b; McCord & Watts, 2006; Rose & Meyer, 2006). Another term for this same concept is *Universal Design for Instruction,* or UDI. These terms are used interchangeably in the special education literature.

UDL refers to the development, adaptation, and implementation of instructional materials and strategies for access by all students. UDL calls for multiple means of *representation,* or a variety of ways that students can acquire information; *multiple means of action and expression,* by providing a variety of ways that students can demonstrate understanding; and multiple means of *engagement,* to motivate, capture, and sustain students' attention (see Figure 4.2). This means that general education instruction and materials become accessible for students with disabilities, and through this process, materials become more accessible to all students in the class. UDL benefits not only students with disabilities but also students without disabilities who may benefit from alternative instructional materials and approaches (CAST, 2010).

When utilizing the principles of UDL, a teacher must consider three different elements. The first is related to how the teacher presents the materials to the students. There may be multiple means of presentation of materials, including the use of technology to make the materials more readily understood and accessible. The second consideration is related to how the student responds to the materials and demonstrates knowledge and understanding. The third consideration is how to engage the student in the learning process by determining what interests and motivates the students.

Burgstahler (2007a, 2007b) categorized guidelines and performance indicators to consider when planning instruction. Teachers can consider developing instruction with the following guidelines in mind:

1. Class climate – demonstrate high value for all students; avoid stereotyping; be approachable and available; address individual needs inclusively rather than segregating or drawing attention to an individual's need for special accommodations
2. Interaction – encourage cooperative learning with varying leadership roles; make sure communication is accessible to all group members
3. Physical environments and products – make sure equipment is available and accessible to all students; organize a physical environment that is safe for all students
4. Delivery methods – utilize flexible, accessible instructional methods that motivate and engage all learners
5. Information resources and technology – ensure that course materials are accessible to all students; utilize flexible technology to assist in delivery of information
6. Feedback – provide feedback on a regular basis to all students
7. Assessment – assess student progress regularly and in a variety of ways
8. Accommodation – plan for specific accommodation needs for students whose needs are not met by UDL, specifically for students with severe disabilities

UDL enhances learning for all students, including students with disabilities, students who are English Language Learners, students who may learn differently, and students who are motivated to learn in different ways. Many music educators and music therapists already utilize Universal Design strategies by implementing visual, auditory, and kinesthetic experiences into instruction. Many highly effective teachers use these strategies on a daily basis to promote students' learning. UDL is a way to consider the needs of all students when designing curriculum, instructional strategies, and evaluation.

Figure 4.2 Universal Design for Learning Guidelines Version 1.0 (CAST, 2008)

Provide Multiple Means of Representation
Provide options for perception
Customize the display of information
Provide alternative s for auditory information
Provide alternatives for visual information
Provide options for language and symbols
Define vocabulary and symbols
Clarify syntax and structure
Decode text and mathematical notation
Promote cross-linguistic understanding
Illustrate concepts non-linguistically
Provide options for comprehension

Provide Multiple Means of Representation
Provide or activate background knowledge
Highlight critical features, big ideas, and relationships
Guide information processing
Support memory and transfer

Provide Multiple Means for Action and Expression
Provide options for physical actions
Provide varied ways to respond
Provide varied ways to interact with materials
Integrate assistive technologies
Provide options for expressive skills and fluency
Allow choices of media for communication
Provide appropriate tools for composition and problem solving
Provide ways to scaffold practice and performance
Provide options for executive functions
Guide effective goal setting
Support planning and strategy development
Facilitate managing information and resources
Enhance capacity for monitoring progress

Provide Multiple Means of Engagement
Provide options for recruiting interest
Increase individual choice and autonomy
Enhance relevance, value, and authenticity
Reduce threats and distractions
Provide options for sustaining effort and persistence
Heighten salience of goals and objectives
Vary levels of challenge and support
Foster collaboration and communication
Increase master-oriented feedback
Provide options for self-regulation
Guide personal goal-setting and expectations
Scaffold coping skills and strategies
Develop self-assessment and reflection

Teachers must be flexible in thinking about and implementing UDL in their classes. UDL promotes the need for multiple approaches to instruction and learning.

Unlike some other subjects, music provides opportunities for many different types of alternative means of presenting and responding to materials. In addition, music educators can find meaningful motivators through the music to actively engage students in the learning process. More information about creating alternative teaching approaches utilizing UDL concepts can be found throughout this chapter.

Adaptations in the Classroom: Accommodations and Modifications

Whenever possible, music educators and music therapists should employ principles of UDL in the classroom. However, there may be times when a particular student is unable to benefit from instruction and needs additional support. Some students with disabilities need some sort of specific adaptation in their educational program in order to be successful in a general or special education setting. Adaptations are any adjustment in the environment, instruction, or materials for learning that enhances the student's performance and allows for at least partial participation. Adaptations should be made for individual students based on their specific learning needs and should be based on their abilities as well as their limitations.

Although IDEA does not specify what accommodations and modifications must be made, there is a general agreement as to the definition of these terms. An accommodation is used when the teacher believes that the student can achieve the same level of participation or accomplishment as the rest of the class, but just needs some additional support. An accommodation allows a student to complete the same assignment or activity as the other students in the class, but the student is offered a change in such things as formatting, setting, amount of time needed, or type of response that is required. When making an accommodation, a teacher might give the student extra time to learn a skill, extra peer support during class, or additional instruction after class in order for the student to participate and achieve at the same level as the other students in the class. An accommodation does not change the nature of what the assignment or test measures or the final skill that the student develops. Either the approach to instruction can be changed, or the way in which the student demonstrates understanding can be changed. The teacher makes changes in instructional approaches so that the student with disabilities can perform the same tasks as the other class members.

> Example 1: *Kendra has a visual disability. She loves to sing and participates in the high school choir. In order for her to complete the worksheet in choir, her teacher enhances the font to 36 point. Kendra is able to complete the same worksheet as the other students in the class, only with a slightly different format.*

> Example 2: *The 7th grade music class is learning three chord songs on guitar. Due to her learning disability, Johanna needs extra time to learn and practice the songs. Ms. Kessel, the music teacher, lets her*

practice guitar at lunch in order to give her more time to learn the material.

Example 3: Davis's 4th grade music class is learning an Orff arrangement for the song "Shoo Fly." Davis has a cognitive impairment and she has difficulty reading the patterns to play the xylophone part. The music teacher pairs Davis up with a peer buddy to model the pattern, and gives them extra practice time in the back of the room while the rest of the class learns the vocal part. With this extra support and extra practice time, Davis is able to play the xylophone part successfully with the rest of the class.

Other students with severe disabilities might not be capable or expected to achieve at the same level or learn all of the same information as the rest of the students. If this is the case, the teacher might develop a modification to help the student participate and learn at the highest possible level for his or her individual abilities. A modification is used when the student is not able to complete the same assignment or participate in the same way as the rest of the class due to the severity of his or her disabilities. A modification changes the standard of participation or the extent of what an assignment or test measures. Modifications are changes to what the student is expected to learn. A student needing modifications might be asked to complete a part of an assignment rather than the entire assignment or participate partially in a music activity. In this situation, the teacher will help the student compensate for his or her limitations by assigning an alternative activity that is within the abilities of the child. This might involve creating a simple rhythm for a child who cannot manage a complex rhythm, creating a percussion part if the child is unable to play a recorder with the class, or offering a child who is nonverbal an accompaniment part to play rather than singing.

The goal is to have the student participate in the educational experiences at the highest level possible for the individual student. Teachers need to be aware of the student's strengths and abilities, what the student can do—not just what he or she cannot do, and build on these abilities when creating educational modifications.

Example 1: Johnny reads at a level that is 3 years behind his classmates. He is unable to read and understand all of the test questions about music concepts, so his teacher circles 3 of the questions for Johnny to answer. The rest of the class will answer all 30 questions.

Example 2: Due to impulsive behavior and short attention span, Sally is unable to remain in the music class for the entire 45 minutes, but she can usually fully participate with her peers for about 20 minutes. She comes to music class with the rest of the 6th grade but leaves for another activity after 20 minutes, during which time she successfully participates with the rest of the students.

Example 3: *Donald has severe physical disabilities due to cerebral palsy. He has limited range of motion in his arms and has extreme difficulty controlling his upper body movements. Donald participates in the 7th grade band as a member of the percussion section. Since Donald is unable to play the instruments requiring a precise rhythmic beat, the teacher adds a percussion part to the band arrangement and has Donald play the wind chime at the beginning and end of the piece as introduction and coda. This part adds to the musicality of the performance and includes Donald in a way that highlights what he can do while compensating for his disability.*

There are many ways to make adaptations to enhance the learning abilities of students with disabilities. Adaptations may involve changes in the way the teacher delivers instruction, alternative means for student responses, variations in the environment, or curricular changes to meet the student's needs (de l'Etoile, 2005; Ebeling et al., 1994; Hammel, 2004; Kochhar & West, 1996; Mitchell, 2008). General adaptations can be utilized in a variety of ways in the music education class and music therapy session. Several types of adaptations are presented here as a foundation for music educators and music therapists to create individualized, appropriate, and effective accommodations and modifications for their students. Remember that IDEA mandates individualized education for students with disabilities. Some students may need very few of these adaptations, while others might require a variety of accommodations or modifications in order to benefit from their education. Notice how the principles of Universal Design for Learning are apparent in many of the sections below. In some instances, utilizing the UDL principles will alleviate the need for further adaptations, but other times might necessitate a specific adaptation for an individual student.

Adapting Instructional Strategies and Curriculum

Participation: Vary the level of participation that is expected of the student. Partial participation occurs when the teacher adapts the level of participation or extent to which a student is involved in the activity. Most students with special needs attend music classes with their same aged peers; however, students with severe disabilities might not be able to participate fully in all of the activities of the music classroom because of their level of functioning. The teacher can create opportunities for partial participation that build on the students' abilities in order to provide the best possible learning experience. Partial participation might involve having a student who has severe physical disabilities only play in the rhythm section of a song arrangement rather than participate in the singing and movement sections. A student with autism might have difficulty with overstimulation in music class when many loud instruments are being played. He could leave class when the noise level increases, or he could listen to music with headphones during times of overstimulation.

Example: *Jenny is a student with severe behavior disorders. In addition, she has been diagnosed with ADHD and has difficulty attending during the entire 30-minute 5th grade general music class. She is able to focus on the task and participate for up to 15 minutes of the class if she is actively involved in music making with her peers. In order to build on Jenny's strengths and minimize her areas of deficit, the music educator begins class with active music making, which helps Jenny focus and successfully participate immediately. When Jenny begins to lose focus, she becomes verbally and physically aggressive to the students and teacher. Since the team is aware that Jenny has difficulty attending for the entire music class time, they decided to schedule her for her 1:1 resource room time after the first 15 minutes of music class. With this schedule, Jenny is able to participate successfully at her level of ability with her peers. Before she reaches the point of aggression and frustration, she is involved in a different setting. Jenny's time and involvement in music class (partial participation) can be increased as she builds the social and emotional skills to handle more time in one setting.*

Input: *Adapt the way that instruction is delivered to the students.* Teachers can vary the ways that material is presented to the students by using visual aids, hands-on learning, active participation, and cooperative group exercises. By using a multimodal approach to instruction, teachers are able to build on the strengths of the students and compensate for areas of deficit. Music learning fits in naturally to a multimodal approach to instruction. Music activities can utilize auditory, visual, tactile, and kinesthetic modalities. Children can learn music through singing, moving, playing instruments, reading, creating, and listening. Teachers can use all of these approaches to instruct the students and enhance their understanding of the material.

Some students have disabilities that make it necessary for the teacher to vary the ways that material is presented. For instance, a student who is deaf might need visual cues, such as directions written on the board or a chart with the words and melody of the song. That same student would need the teacher to deliver instruction facing the class (as opposed to talking when writing on the board), so the student could use residual hearing or speech reading to enhance learning.

Example: *Ms. Pratt teaches vocal music in an inclusive middle school. There are several students with visual disabilities in the classes since her school has specialized services for students who are blind and visually disabled. Ms. Pratt makes a point to always describe what she is doing to assist the students who are unable to see her. For instance, rather than saying, "Do this" or "Follow my hand with your voice," she might say "Clap the beat with me" or "Make your voice sound like a siren—start low and move higher." By describing her intentions more clearly, the students who cannot see her can participate at the same level as the students who do not have visual difficulties.*

Output: *Adapt how the students can respond to instruction.* A student might be able to answer a question verbally, or through movement, rather than in writing. Some students use assistive communication devices or communication books to respond to questions rather than using verbal or written responses. Similar to the adaptation of varying the input by the teacher, adapting the way a student can respond also fits in naturally in a music setting. Rather than write a response to rhythmic notation, a student could demonstrate understanding by moving to the rhythm patterns. A student with no speech could respond to whether a melody goes up or down by playing a glissando on a xylophone rather than giving a verbal response or singing.

> Example: *Kyle is unable to speak due to severe physical disabilities; however, he has appropriate cognitive development for his age. Kyle uses a computerized touch talking assistive communication device to communicate with others. The speech and language pathologist (SLP) at the school preprogrammed several typical music words such as "melody," "rhythm," "quarter note," "half note," "beat" into his communication device and taught Kyle how to use them in music class. Now when the music teacher asks the students to identify a rhythm or a music term, Kyle is able to respond to the question by using his touch talker. The music teacher must work with the SLP to identify appropriate words for preprogramming, and then the music teacher must phrase questions that can be answered using those terms.*

Difficulty: *Adapt the skill level, the type of problem, or the rules on how a student may approach a task.* Most music classrooms are made up of students with a variety of skill levels related to music. Music tasks can be made less difficult for some students by giving alternative but complementary tasks, such as having some students play only on the strong beat or steady beat, while other students are playing a more complex rhythm pattern. Difficulty can also be adapted by having some students play an instrument that has an easy part (egg shakers) along with students who are playing a more difficult melody line on recorders.

> Example: *The 10th grade "Music from Around the World" class is learning African percussion techniques for ensemble playing. Kya is a student with intellectual and some physical disabilities. Although Kya cannot play complex rhythms, she can keep a steady beat throughout an entire song. Since the song has many levels of rhythmic complexity, Kya can contribute to the ensemble by playing the djembe drum on a steady beat, while other students play the more complex rhythms. Kya is still an important part of the ensemble, but is participating at a difficulty level where she can be successful.*

Time: *Adapt the amount of time allotted for completing a task, taking a test, or learning a new skill.* Some students with disabilities will need additional time to be able to complete the same task as their peers. The music teacher can work with the general education or special education teacher to arrange for extra time for learning a skill or completing the task. Students might take time during a free hour, study hall, or lunch to work on the music skill. Teachers might structure additional time in the classroom for individual students or for all of the students to master a new skill.

> Example: *Thornton has a learning disability and struggles with learning new songs on his trumpet in beginning band. Although he enjoys learning the trumpet, he becomes frustrated when the band director introduces a new note or skill before he masters the previous skill. His band director lets Thornton practice his trumpet in the practice room during his free time as long as he has finished his other work. He is able to master the skills presented in class before he is challenged by new skills. Thornton feels better about his abilities in band and gets less frustrated because he is experiencing more success.*

Size: *Adapt the number of items or amount of material that a student is expected to learn or complete.* Some students might not be able to answer all of the questions on the weekly music worksheet, but they can answer a few of them. In an active music-making situation, some students with disabilities might be able to learn one or two of the rhythm parts but not all of the rhythm parts for a particular song.

> Example: *Lavonne has Down Syndrome. She loves to participate in music making, especially instrument playing. When it comes time to do a music worksheet or take a written test, she is unable to complete the work that all of the other students are able to complete. The music teacher circles the first two questions on the test or worksheet, which she makes very simple, and tells Lavonne that she is expected to answer those two questions while the rest of the class completes the entire assignment. Rather than announce this adaptation to the entire class, the teacher talks to Lavonne individually so that she is not singled out or set apart from the other students.*

Alternate goals: *While using the same materials for all students, adapt the outcome expectations or goals.* Students with severe disabilities might be included in a music class primarily for the purposes of socialization and interaction with typically developing peers. Although they can participate in music at some level, their goals would be related more toward socialization than music learning. Students might be several grade levels behind their peers in music class and not have the level of skill to achieve the same goals as the rest of the class, even though they can participate in some or all of the activities.

> Example: *The 6th grade students are learning a multi-layered Orff piece to enhance their study of the blues. Sherika has severe intellectual and*

physical disabilities and functions at a level many years younger than her peers. She is unable to understand much of the material in class, but enjoys being with her same aged peers. While the other students are expected to be able to play a blues piece and then improvise a brief section, Sherika is expected only to move her arm to play the shaker when prompted. The goal for Sherika is related to socialization and responding to cues, while the goal for the other students is to learn about the blues.

Substitute curriculum: *Provide different curriculum or instructional materials to meet the individual student's goals.* Some students are not appropriate for full inclusion music class because of the severity of their disability. Students with disruptive behaviors who endanger other students or negatively impact the learning of others might be better served in an individual or small group adapted music instruction or music therapy setting.

Example: *Luke is a 6th grade student with autism. He is nonverbal and has difficulty communicating his wants and needs to others. He can be extremely disruptive in classes and has been violent with peers for no apparent reason. Luke spends most of his day in a self-contained classroom with the additional support of a one-to-one assistant. He is not appropriate for the inclusive music class at this time due to his aggressive behavior. However, Luke seems to respond positively to some music, some of the time. The school hired a music therapist to work with Luke to reduce agitation and to find nonverbal means of expression. Even though all of the other students in the 6th grade attend either inclusive music or adapted music classes, Luke has different needs and so has a different type of music experience.*

Altering the Environment

Managing the physical space: *Adapt the classroom arrangement to best suit the needs of the students.* All students need some level of structure in their environment in order to succeed in school. Some students need a high level of structure in their environment to help them stay focused on the primary learning tasks. Music classrooms are typically filled with interesting visual and tactile stimuli such as pictures, song charts, instruments, scarves, etc. At the elementary level, it is usually necessary for the music educator to set up the room for the entire day, with a variety of props and instruments that will be used by some classes but not others. In order to manage the environment, the teacher should be aware of the distractions in the room and create an environment that will help the students focus on the music activities rather than the external stimuli. For instance, the Orff xylophones can be lined up in the back of the room, ready to play at the end of class. The students enter the classroom and sit in front, away from the instruments until it is time to play them.

At all levels, managing the physical space can also mean that the seating arrangements for students are managed to provide optimal placement in the room. For example, students who need good role models or peer support can be placed near an appropriate peer, students who are disruptive can be seated in an optimal position such as close to the teacher, or students who need extra room can be seated away from distractions or equipment. Students with physical disabilities and visual disabilities have specific needs for a safe environment. If a student who uses a wheelchair is coming to class, the teacher should arrange the classroom in such a way that the student can enter and maneuver around in the class in the most normalized way, eliminating the need to rearrange once the child enters the classroom. Additionally, a student who uses a wheelchair should be seated among peers when possible, not always at the end of the row for convenience. A student with a visual disability will usually have better mobility when the classroom structure is constant. That way the student can learn the pattern of the room and be more independent moving safely from one place to the next.

> Example: *Ian is a 2nd grade student who has disruptive behaviors and difficulty paying attention in class. The class typically sits on the floor in music, and when he is seated at the end of the row, he rolls around the floor rather than pay attention and participate in the music activities. The teacher makes a point of seating Ian between students who are able to pay attention and who are willing to encourage Ian when necessary. With that sort of appropriate placement, he is able to focus on the class for a longer period of time and usually participates in the entire music class with proper classroom behaviors.*

Adaptive instruments: *Provide instruments that students can play successfully.* Students with physical disabilities might have problems playing all of the classroom music instruments or band instruments due to limitations of strength, range of motion, fine and gross motor skills, or mobility. General music teachers can help students choose instruments from the regular classroom inventory that a child with physical disabilities will be able to play, such as a light-weight African basket shaker (for students with strength, range of motion, and grasp problems), a large drum played with a large mallet or a hand drum (for students with accuracy problems related to range of motion), or a chime tree on a stand (for students with limited movement or accuracy). These are the same instruments that the rest of the class is playing and this creates a more normalized environment for students with special needs. They are not singled out by playing something different, but are included as part of the music-making experience with their peers.

Sometimes it is not possible for a student to use the regular classroom instruments, so adaptive instruments might need to be created or purchased. Several manufacturers have developed adaptive instruments to help students overcome some of the barriers to playing classroom instruments. These adaptive instruments can provide a vehicle for full participation in music-making activities for some students.

Most of the adaptive instruments on the market are rhythm-based instruments such as adapted mallets (light-weight, short stick, and transverse), drum holders that attach a paddle drum to a wheelchair, instrument holders that attach to a wheelchair tray or table, Velcro shaker eggs, and large picks with wooden handles for strumming. There is even an adapted recorder that can be permanently individualized for the specific physical needs of a student related to finger dexterity or finger functioning problems. While these adaptive instruments can be very useful in some situations, they are not the "normalized" or same instruments that the rest of the class is using.

Adaptive instruments can also be developed by creative teachers to help students fully participate in classroom activities. For example, mallet handles can be built up with foam rubber or tubing to help a student grasp the mallet, or a large pick for guitar or autoharp can be cut from a stiff plastic sheet. Always check with the occupational therapist to make sure that the adaptation is not contra-indicated for the student's specific needs. When creating your own adaptive instruments, keep in mind the principle of normalization. If you are asking a student with disabilities to strum the autoharp with a kitchen utensil such as a rubber spatula while all of the other students are using "real" instruments, you are inadvertently singling that student out as different from the rest of the class. It is best to use instruments that are as close to normal as possible to create a more natural environment for all of the students. Of course, if you are making a kitchen band and all of the students are playing on kitchen utensils, you are no longer singling out the student with disabilities but are including him or her in the same experiences as the rest of the class.

> Example: *Due to a birth defect, Julia's fingers are not all properly developed and some of the fingers on her right hand are very short. Her class is beginning to learn the recorder and Julia is unable to reach all of the finger holes on her recorder. The teacher orders a special recorder for Julia to compensate for her physical problems. The adapted recorder is made with one joint for each finger hole, and the joints can be rotated to the side or front of the recorder depending on the finger length, dexterity, and strength of the student. Once the placement of the finger holes is correct, the music teacher glues the joints in place and Julia has a custom fitted recorder that she can play along with the rest of the class.*

Band instruments are more difficult to adapt than elementary classroom instruments. Instrument selection may be the key to success for some students. Band directors need to consider the student's physical abilities related to strength, control, and fine motor skills when assisting with instrument selection. Some instruments may be more suitable than others for students with physical disabilities, depending on the individual student's abilities and interests. Instruments may also be adapted to provide support if a student is not strong enough to hold the instrument for a long period of time, or the way an instrument is played may also be adapted. See Chapter 15 for more information about including students with disabilities in beginning band.

Example 1: *Johan has difficulty moving and controlling his left arm due to cerebral palsy, and is willing to work very hard to be part of the group. Due to his left arm/hand motor problems, it is unlikely that he would be successful on the flute, clarinet, or saxophone. However, he might be able to play a brass instrument such as trumpet or baritone, or percussion. By choosing an instrument that fits his physical abilities, Johan will be able to join the band with the other students in his grade.*

Example 2: *Krista suffered a head injury and suffered paralysis on her right side. She uses a wheelchair although his right arm is fully functioning. He wants to be in the band but can move from her chair to a chair or higher stool in band. She plays keyboard percussion in the orchestra, playing all of her music with her left hand. She has become proficient with using several mallets at one time. Rather than standing to play, she sits on a stool modified with additional support so she does not fall over. Krista is a strong musician and makes excellent contributions to the percussion section.*

Increasing Student Support

Level of support: Increase amount of support from others. Some students need additional assistance from another person in order to accomplish a task or even pay attention in class. Additional support might be from a peer buddy or from another adult (teacher's aide, classroom teacher, therapist working in the classroom, etc.). In order to maintain as normalized an environment as possible for the student, it is usually best to have peers provide the necessary additional support. Peer tutoring can provide the benefits of increased learning for both parties, increased self-esteem for all involved, and increased flexibility for the teacher. In order for peer tutoring to be effective, it must be structured and implemented judiciously. Teachers should carefully consider how to select, train, and monitor peer tutors (see Figure 4.3) (Beninghof, 1996; Vaughn, Wanzek, & Denton, 2007). Responsibilities of a peer buddy or tutor can range from sitting next to a student in class and acting as a role model, to helping the student utilize materials. More in-depth peer tutor relationships might involve working with a peer outside of class to remediate music skills for an upcoming performance. In any event, effective support through the use of peers needs to be guided by the music specialist so that a positive outcome is likely for all of the students involved. If appropriate peer support is not available, then an adult might have to be utilized to give additional support to the student.

Figure 4.3 Techniques for Selecting, Training and Monitoring Peer Tutor Relationships (Beninghof, 1996)

Selecting peer tutors:
   •   Is the student willing and interested in becoming a peer tutor?
   •   Does the student have the necessary skills to help/teach other students?
   •   Is this student a good role model who follows directions well?
   •   Does this seem to be a good match of personalities between students?
   •   Does the student have time (if needed) outside of the classroom to work with peers?

Training peer tutors—topics to discuss prior to peer tutoring sessions:
   •   How to give simple directions and reinforce correct responses/behaviors
   •   How to interest and motivate the student and keep the student's attention throughout the lesson or practice session
   •   How to redirect behaviors or correct incorrect responses
   •   How to adapt instruction to the specific needs of the student

Monitoring and evaluating peer tutors:
   •   Teach peer tutor simple data-taking methods to document progress
   •   Observe peer tutoring and give feedback to both parties
   •   Interview both parties to see how they feel about the relationship
   •   Make adjustments based on observations and feedback from students

Careful arrangement of students can also provide additional support to a student by giving the student ready access to the teacher and providing the teacher ready access to the student. A student who is impulsive or inattentive might function better in class when seated in close proximity to the teacher. The teacher can then provide unobtrusive support in terms of reinforcement (eye contact, tokens), reminders ("look at me," "pay attention"), and assistance in completing tasks (proper placement of instrument or finding correct page in the book). Additional support for students can range from a limited, infrequent amount of extra assistance to continuous and extensive extra help.

> Example: *Victor has multiple physical disabilities. He frequently needs assistance with placement of instruments and material and with movement around the room. Each day Victor chooses a peer buddy to help him when he needs assistance in music class. Since Victor likes to be as independent as possible and do things on his own, the peer buddy helps him only when he asks for help.*

Additional Strategies/Teacher Behaviors to Promote Students' Success

There are many different strategies and behaviors that teachers implement to help students learn better in the classroom. These strategies are all elements of effective teaching, rather than simply different ways to work with students who have special needs. All students need variety, individualized attention, positive relationships, and high expectations. Here are some ideas to keep in mind when planning and teaching students in full-inclusion music classes or self-contained music in special education classes (Adamek, 2001; Ebeling et al., 1994; Gordon, 1987). You might notice similarities between the principles and guidelines of Universal Design for Learning and these ideas for effective teaching.

1. *Structure lessons to include a blend of auditory, visual, and experiential/hands-on activities.* Vary the ways that you introduce information, and vary the ways that students respond to information.

2. *Have high expectations for students.* Understand the current level of functioning for students with disabilities, then plan for their next level of achievement. Do not underestimate what students can do just because they are not at the same level of functioning as their peers.

3. *Use age-appropriate activities* that meet the current functioning level of the students. Adolescents who have the cognitive functioning level of a 5-year-old should not be singing preschool songs. An effective music educator and music therapist will be creative in making music choices that are age appropriate but still within the functioning level of the individual students.

4. *Be flexible.* Planning is important, but if the student is unable to function at that level, you will need to vary the lesson plan or approach.

5. *Develop relationships with students* through active interactions. Some students might be difficult to get to know due to socialization, communication, cognitive, or physical disabilities. Each student is an individual, with abilities and limitations. As you get to know the students, you will have a much easier time adapting activities and creating interventions that are appropriate for their age and ability level.

6. *Provide consistency* along with a structured and predictable approach. Be clear with directions and rules, making sure that there is follow-through for consequences in a consistent manner. Students feel secure and function better when they know what to expect and what is expected of them.

7. *Maintain a positive attitude* about working with students with special needs. Willingness to work with these students along with increasing knowledge and understanding of the individual students, general disability characteristics, and effective approaches all demonstrate a positive attitude toward working with all students along the continuum.

8. *Be willing to work collaboratively* with special education teachers, regular education teachers, music educators, music therapists, parents, and other specialists on the team; this is critically important for the students' success.

9. *Provide frequent feedback* to students to let them know how they are doing. Positive reinforcement can be used to let the student know that he or she is doing the right thing, which will increase the likelihood of the student continuing that behavior.

10. *Patience, humor, and warmth* are personal characteristics that can help in relationship-building as well as getting through a difficult day.

Summary

All students with disabilities have the legal right to a free and appropriate public education. Since music professionals work with students with disabilities in the music education or music therapy setting, they need to be prepared to develop and adapt instructional practices to allow the student to participate at the highest possible level. Collaboration with other professionals in the school is an essential practice to develop effective strategies for successful participation in the music setting. Teachers can to share information about the student, goals and objectives, and strategies that they have used that are effective in increasing the student's level of functioning.

Music educators and music therapists who work in schools interact with many teachers and paraprofessionals each day. Effective communication is important when working with a large number of other professionals. Such elements as active listening, depersonalizing situations, identifying and sharing goals and solutions, and monitoring students' progress are essential for effective communication and collaboration in schools.

Universal Design for Learning takes into account the needs of a broad spectrum of student abilities, disabilities, cultural differences, language differences, and learning styles. UDL is a flexible approach to curriculum, instructional design, and evaluation that eliminates the need for many accommodations. However, some students with severe disabilities continue to need individualized, specific adaptations of instruction. There are numerous strategies for adapting for an individual's needs. A music educator or music therapist can adapt instructional strategies and curriculum, adapt the way that instruction is delivered, and adapt how the students respond to instruction. In addition, other factors such as level of difficulty, amount of time allotted, goals, and the environment can also be adapted to provide the best opportunities for student learning and success.

KEY POINTS FROM THE CHAPTER

Gathering information and collaboration:
♦ Music professionals who work with students with disabilities can collaborate with other school personnel to ensure an appropriate educational experience for the students. Collaboration involves effective communication, sharing of information, cooperation, and problem-solving skills. By working together with the rest of the team, music educators and music therapists can develop strategies to promote students' success in music.
♦ Teachers need basic information about students in order to work with them effectively. Important information includes: (a) student's strength or special skills; (b) student's disability characteristics, limitations, or weaknesses; (c) IEP goals that can be addressed in the music class; and (d) useful strategies for working with the student (Adamek, 2001).

♦ It is important to gather information about students in a concise and efficient manner. A tool such as an IEP summary can structure the acquisition of pertinent information to assist in program planning for students with disabilities.

♦ Respectful communication is necessary when working with other teachers and paraprofessionals in the school. When a paraprofessional attends music class with a student, the music educator or music therapist has the responsibility to work with the paraprofessional to maximize his or her efforts on behalf of the students.

Universal Design for Learning (UDL):

♦ UDL is a flexible approach to developing instruction to accommodate the needs of all learners in the class.

♦ UDL refers to the development, adaptation, and implementation of instructional materials and strategies for access by all students. This means that general education materials are made accessible for students with disabilities, and through this process, materials become more accessible to all students in the class.

♦ Rather than plan for the typical or average students, teachers design instruction to be accessible to students of varying abilities, disabilities, cultural differences, learning differences, language abilities, and other characteristics.

♦ UDL benefits all students by enhancing learning opportunities, motivation, and engagement. Teachers utilize a variety of strategic instructional approaches to promote learning.

♦ Some students with severe disabilities will also need specific adaptations to benefit from instruction.

♦ *Universal Design for Instruction* (UDI) is another term for the same concept. These terms are used interchangeably in the special education literature.

Adapting instruction to meet the needs of students:

♦ An **accommodation** is used when the teacher believes that the student can achieve the same level of participation or accomplishment as the rest of the class but needs some additional support. An accommodation allows a student to complete the same assignment or activity as the other students in the class, but the student is offered a change in such things as formatting, setting, amount of time needed, or type of response.

♦ A **modification** is used when the student is not able to complete the same assignment or participate in the same way as the rest of the class due to the nature of his or her disabilities. A modification changes the standard of participation or the extent of what an assignment or test measures.

♦ Adapting for students' needs could involve methods for adapting instructional strategies and curriculum, altering the environment, or increasing student support.

♦ Additional interventions to promote students' learning might include using a variety of visual, auditory, and kinesthetic experiences in class, having high expectations for students, and being flexible when the situation warrants.

REFERENCES

Adamek, M. (2001). Meeting special needs in music class. *Music Educators Journal, 87*(4), 23–26.

Beninghof, A. M. (1996). *Ideas for inclusion: The classroom teacher's guide to integrating students with severe disabilities.* Longmont, CO: Sopris West.

Bowe, F. (2000). *Universal Design in education: Teaching nontraditional students.* Santa Barbara, CA: Praeger.

Burgstahler, S. (2007a). *Equal access: Universal Design of Instruction.* Seattle: DO-IT, University of Washington. Retrieved March 15, 2010, from http://www.washington.edu/doit/Brochures/Academics/equal_access_udi.html

Burgstahler, S. (2007b). *Universal Designing of Instruction (UDI): Definition, principles guidelines, and examples.* Seattle: DO-IT, University of Washington. Retrieved March 15, 2010, from http://www.washington.edu/doit//Brochures/Academics/instruction.html

CAST. (2008). *Universal Design for Learning guidelines version 1.0.* Wakefield, MA: Rose. Retrieved March 29, 2010, from http://www.udlcenter.org/aboutudl/udlguidelines/downloads

CAST. (2010). *What is Universal Design for Learning?* Wakefield, MA: Rose. Retrieved May 29, 2010, from http://www.cast.org/research/udl/index/html

Darrow, A. A. (1999). Music educators' perceptions regarding the inclusion of students with severe disabilities in music classrooms. *Journal of Music Therapy, 36,* 254–273.

de l'Etoile, S. (2005). Teaching music to special learners: Children with disruptive behavior disorders. *Music Educators Journal, 91*(5), 37–43.

Ebeling, D., Deschenes, C., & Sprague, J. (1994). *Adapting curriculum and instruction in inclusive classrooms: A teacher's desk reference.* Bloomington, IN: Center for School and Community Integration – Institute for the Study of Developmental Disabilities.

Fitzgerald, M. (2006). "I send my best Matthew to school every day": Music educators collaborating with parents. *Music Educators Journal, 92*(4), 40–45.

Gordon, T. (1987). T.E.T.: *Teacher effectiveness training.* New York: David McKay.

Harding, S. (2009). Successful inclusion models for students with disabilities require strong leadership: Autism and behavioral disorders create many challenges for the learning environment. *The International Journal of Learning, 16*(3), 91–103.

Hammel, A. (2004). Inclusion strategies that work. *Music Educators Journal, 90*(5), 33–37.

Hughes, J., Rice, B., DeBedout, J., & Hightower, L. (2002). Music therapy for learners in comprehensive public school systems: Three district-wide models. In B. Wilson (Ed.), *Models of music therapy interventions in school settings* (2nd ed.). Silver Spring, MD: American Music Therapy Association.

Kochhar, C. A., & West, L. L. (1996). *Handbook for successful inclusion.* Gaithersburg, MD: Aspen.

Lapka, C. (2006). Students with disabilities in high school band: "We can do it!" *Music Educators Journal, 92*(4), 54–59.

McCord, K., & Watts, E. (2006). Collaboration and access for our children: Music educators and special educators together. *Music Educators Journal, 92*(4), 26–33.

Mitchell, D. (2008). *What really works in special and inclusive education.* New York: Routledge.

Rose, D. H., & Meyer, A. (2006). *A practical reader in Universal Design for Learning.* Cambridge, MA: Harvard Education Press.

Vaughn, S., Wanzek, J., & Denton, C. (2007). Teaching elementary students who experience difficulties in learning. In L. Florian (Ed.), *The Sage handbook of special education* (pp. 360–377). Thousand Oaks, CA: Sage.

Chapter 5

Management Techniques to Promote Motivation, Responsibility, and Learning

---

CHAPTER OVERVIEW

Behavior problems in the music class can turn an otherwise perfect lesson into a disaster. No matter how good a teacher is at creating and facilitating lesson plans to teach music skills, behavior problems can eliminate any sense of successfully teaching the students. Classroom management should be seen as a total process that affects all aspects of the classroom climate, not only as a way to deal with students' behavior problems. Music educators and music therapists need to utilize practices that promote an optimal learning environment for all students.

This chapter includes information on the following topics:
♦ Factors contributing to behavior problems
♦ Creating a positive classroom environment to enhance learning and prevent problem behaviors
♦ Interventions to deal with problem behaviors

Factors Contributing to Behavior Problems

Most beginning music professionals are well equipped to teach music, but few are prepared to deal with the array of behavior problems that frequently occur in the music class. Motivating students to want to learn and managing behaviors so that all students can learn are skills that take understanding and practice. Many music student teachers do their training in well-established programs with procedures already in place to minimize behavior problems. In this type of situation, student teachers have few opportunities to practice the skills necessary for behavior management. The real awareness usually comes when they begin working independently at their first jobs and suddenly realize how difficult it can be to motivate some students to want to follow directions and learn. Students with difficult behavior can challenge even seasoned professionals. Music professionals can strengthen behavior management skills and improve teaching effectiveness by reviewing behavior management techniques, practicing new interventions, and obtaining feedback from a fellow teacher.

Teachers can use selected techniques to create a positive behavioral environment in which the students can learn. The teacher needs an array of behavior management techniques to redirect or decrease negative behaviors when students do not follow the classroom rules and exhibit problem behaviors in the music class. The best approach is to prevent problem behaviors, but not all problem behaviors can be prevented. A clear and direct behavior management system with consistent follow-through and consequences is needed to ensure a classroom environment suitable for learning.

> Scenario: *Julia was an exceptional undergraduate music education major while in college. She was a superior flutist, playing in all of the premier school ensembles, had high academic achievement, and had good leadership skills. When it was time for Julia to student teach, she was placed with a successful veteran teacher in a K–6 general music setting. Although the transition from student to teacher was difficult at first, Julia quickly learned the classroom procedures set in place by her cooperating teacher, and the students responded well to their new student teacher. Julia experienced minimal behavior problems and thoroughly enjoyed the role of elementary music teacher.*

> *The next fall when Julia was hired as a general music teacher in a different school district, the situation was much different. Now she was the teacher responsible for setting the classroom climate, including supporting positive behaviors, preventing behavior problems, and effectively dealing with problem behaviors in class. Julia had not had to practice these techniques in her student teaching because the cooperating teacher had everything in place. Julia did not even realize all of the variables in her student teaching classroom that were structured to encourage positive behavior. She just thought that all students would respond to her in the same respectful and "eager to learn" manner as those students in her pre-professional training. She was wrong. Julia had to start from the beginning to set a positive climate for successful behaviors in her music classroom. In addition to reviewing materials from her undergraduate curriculum on behavior management, she sought out the help of an experienced teacher at her new school to serve as her mentor. Julia realized that she needed to develop management skills to prevent behavior problems and to*

learn to deal with behavior problems effectively in order to be an effective teacher.

Teachers and students can contribute to behavior problems in the classroom. Based on research literature and classroom experiences, Kauffman, Pullen, and Akers (1986) suggested the following teacher characteristics that can negatively affect classroom behavior and student learning:

- Inconsistency in management techniques
- Reinforcement of the wrong behavior
- Formation of inappropriate expectations for children
- Nonfunctional or irrelevant instruction
- Insensitivity to children's legitimate individuality
- Demonstration or encouragement of undesirable models
- Irritability and overreliance on punishment
- Unwillingness to try new strategies or to seek suggestions from other professionals (p. 2)

Students with negative behaviors usually have limited academic success. In addition, students with problem behaviors can cause stress for the teacher as well as for other students in the classroom. The following are some of the most common student characteristics that contribute to behavioral and academic problems (Kauffman et al., 1986):

- Overdependence on the teacher
- Difficulty concentrating and paying attention
- Becoming upset under pressure to achieve
- Sloppiness and impulsivity in responding
- Teasing, annoying, or interfering with other children
- Negativism about work, self, teacher, or peers
- Poor personal hygiene
- Extreme social withdrawal or refusal to respond
- Self-stimulation or self-injury
- Physical or verbal aggression toward teacher or peers (p. 2)

These characteristics can cause negative reactions from both teachers and students' peers, which can be detrimental to a positive learning environment. Teachers need to have the skills to create a positive classroom climate in order to prevent problem behaviors. In addition, they must have the skills to deal with problem behaviors effectively.

Creating a Positive Classroom Environment to Prevent Behavior Problems

There are many ways to set the stage for positive behaviors in the music classroom. Appropriate curriculum, pacing, the teacher's attitude, interactions with students, and arrangement of the physical environment can all contribute to students' positive behaviors in class. Although these factors may not eliminate all problem behaviors, teachers should consider what variables might encourage positive behavior for all students. Students' learning and engagement in music experiences will be enhanced in a classroom environment with few or no behavior problems. Various ways to promote positive behaviors in students are listed below, along with descriptions and suggested ideas for implementation (Brophy, 1987; Colvin, 2002; Evertson & Poole, 2008; Kauffman et al., 1986; Pankake, 2006; Wilson & Bruce, 1996; Wood, 1998).

Positive Teacher Attitude with High Expectations for Students' Learning

The teacher's attitude can influence students' behaviors in positive and negative ways. Teachers who have a positive self-concept, a high level of self-confidence, and are satisfied with their positions can contribute to students' feeling secure in the class. They can begin to identify ways in which their own behaviors and attitudes influence the behaviors and attitudes of their students. Teachers might reflect on the following questions when evaluating their attitudes and expectations (Wood, 1998):

- Do I convey confidence in my voice, behaviors, and preparation?
- Do I have a positive self-concept and believe that I can do a good job teaching?
- Do I have a good attitude about teaching music at this level?
- What is my attitude about teaching children? What is my attitude about teaching children with disabilities?
- Do I have high expectations for all children?
- Do I have realistic expectations for myself and for my students?
- Can I admit when I make a mistake?
- Do I have an appropriate sense of humor in the classroom?
- Can I laugh at myself and still maintain self-respect?
- Do I listen attentively to students, parents, and other professionals in the school?
- Do I show respect to students?

Students learn appropriate behavior through appropriate models. Teachers can model the appropriate behaviors and attitudes and set the tone for positive or negative student behaviors

Clear Expectations, Known by All Students

Students must know the rules if they are expected to follow the rules of the classroom or the school (Wilson & Bruce, 1996). Music educators should develop specific expectations for student behavior and participation in their classes, and then make sure all the students understand these expectations. Many teachers develop classroom rules that are sometimes developed in conjunction with the students. Rules should be brief, clear, and stated in a positive manner. The classroom rules can be as broad as "respect yourself and others," "listen," "participate in all music activities," and "follow directions." Or, when necessary, rules can address very specific behaviors such as "keep hands to self," "listen when others are talking," "be gentle with instruments," and "stay in your assigned area."

Here are some guidelines for setting classroom rules:
- Involve students in formulating the rules, when possible and appropriate.
- Keep the list of rules short, with only a few rules.
- State rules in a positive manner ("listen" rather than "don't talk when someone else is talking").
- Remind students of the rules often, not just when someone is breaking the rules. With young children, you can practice following the rules such as "Who can show me 'hands to self'?" Also practice consequences such as removal of instruments or removal from the activity. ("What happens if you are playing when it is not your turn? Right—you lose the instrument until the end of the song.")
- Notice students who are following the rules and set them up as good examples. Use positive reinforcement for students who are following the rules. ("Jane is listening." "Jonah is in his place." "Erica has her hands to herself.")
- If needed, have additional rules for different activities: rules for instrument playing ("place instruments on the floor unless it is your turn to play"); or rules for movement ("during movement activities, keep enough space between students so you do not bump").
- Create only rules that can be enforced.
- Follow through on consequences, making sure students understand the connection between not following the rules and having a consequence.

Literature on effective teaching has focused on managing the classroom environment through developing and maintaining rules and procedures (Englert, 1984; Marzano, 2003). Teachers are encouraged to present rules and consequences at the beginning of the year, model examples of appropriate and inappropriate behaviors, have the students practice the behaviors, give specific feedback and positive reinforcement to students, review and monitor rules throughout the year, and follow through with consequences immediately and consistently. Students can have responsibility for managing their own behavior by participating in developing the rules and monitoring their behaviors through self-evaluation procedures.

In addition to having clear rules for the class, teachers are encouraged to have reasonable expectations for students. Expectations related to behavior can be addressed in the rules for the class. Teachers might also have expectations related to students' participation, effort, and achievement. Students can get frustrated, act out, or stop trying when expectations are too high. When expectations are too low, students can get bored, act out, and not follow through with assignments or activities. In either case, students might become resentful and develop a pattern of nonparticipatory or negative behaviors. In order to set reasonable expectations, teachers need to understand what typically developing students should be able to do, as well as know the abilities and needs of students in class who are not typically developing or have some type of special needs. Teachers are likely to be successful setting appropriate expectations for students when they understand typical development, have information about the functioning levels of students with disabilities in the class, and are flexible in their teaching.

Appropriate and Motivating Curriculum

Students need to have the appropriate level of challenge and difficulty in order to be motivated to learn. Students may become bored if the music experiences are too easy, and they may become frustrated if the tasks are too difficult and unattainable. In addition to finding the appropriate level of difficulty for students, teachers should prepare lessons that have meaningful learning objectives. Students need to be aware that the material they are learning is both important and valuable in its own right, or that it is a meaningful part of a bigger, more complex task for which they are preparing. For example, students may be more motivated to practice rhythm patterns when they realize that the patterns are recurring in the upcoming music arrangement that the entire group will put together.

Students are poised to pay attention and actively participate as directed when they are motivated to learn and are engaged in the music experiences. On the other hand, if students are bored with the content, frustrated by the level of expectations, or otherwise not engaged, they are more likely to exhibit behavior problems. Music educators need to be able to increase or decrease the difficulty of the activity to meet the functioning level of the students. Flexibility on the part of the teacher is a must. Fortunately, many music activities can be made more challenging or simpler by varying the complexity of the music itself. For example, Orff Schulwerk activities usually are layered arrangements with a variety of parts. Some of the parts may be more difficult or complex musically than others, and other parts may be quite simple to play. Students can participate at many different levels of difficulty while still participating in a music-making experience together.

Pacing

Similar to having an appropriate and motivating curriculum, the pacing of the class is an important variable to keep students engaged, on-task, and following directions. Pacing that is too slow can cause boredom and the possibilities for behavior problems increase. Pacing that is too fast may frustrate students and they may not stay engaged in the activity due to their lack of ability to keep up or understand the concepts.

Do some students need extra time on a concept or skill while others have mastered the skill? How can the music teacher keep the lesson moving forward when some students still need practice? Students might work in cooperative learning groups, with the students who have achieved mastery integrated into all of the groups, possibly even functioning as leaders or peer tutors for the students who need additional help. This way, the students who need more time are able to review and practice the materials, while the students who have attained the skill level can now function in a different role as teacher/mentor.

Giving Clear Directions

Students need to understand the expectations, rules, and procedures in the classroom. Teachers have the responsibility to make sure that the directions they give to students are clear, unambiguous, and easily understood. Students can follow directions only if they understand them. Also, it is important to make sure that students have an opportunity to ask questions in case they do not understand a direction. If one student does not understand a direction, it is likely that other students also might not understand. Clear and specific directions are essential.

Structure in Teaching

Teachers typically have a clear idea of the intended student outcomes or goals. In order to reach those goals, the students learn through a series of logical steps, which build on their previous knowledge and abilities in order to develop new knowledge and skills. A well-structured music class could have a set structure in place where there is a clear beginning (warm-up time), middle (learning new information), and end (practicing or generalizing the information). A well-structured and focused approach is in contrast to a class where the teacher presents information or several activities that are unrelated and random in nature.

Structure in the Environment

Most music classrooms are full of instruments for classroom or performance use, equipment, props, and other interesting yet distracting materials. In addition, the music educator frequently works with a variety of age groups, so there might be materials in the room that are used only for a specific age or purpose. Students who have difficulty managing their own behaviors in class can become disruptive when they are in an environment with so many distractions close at hand. Music educators can eliminate some behavior problems by making sure the room is organized in a way that is less distracting.

- Do all of the instruments need to be out for every class, or is there an out-of-the-way place where those xylophones can be stored during classes when they are not being used?
- Do students need to be seated away from instruments until it is time for them to play?
- What about proximity to the teacher? Is there easy access to all of the students in case someone needs a small reminder to stay on task or to keep hands to self?
- Does a large open room, which is great for movement, create difficult transitions for students entering and leaving music class?
- Do the boys in chorus always need to be placed in the back, or can they be seated in the middle section with some students closer to the conductor? Or can the male and female voices be alternated to break up groups that might become distracting?
- Can the room be sectioned off into various areas for instruction, instrument playing, or movement?
- Does a particular student need to be seated closer to the teacher, or farther away from the teacher? Would that student be more successful sitting next to a different peer as a model?

These questions might stimulate some thoughts on better room structure and placement. Environmental factors can influence students' behaviors and support students' attention and learning.

Positive Teacher Responses

Teachers who create clear expectations and give specific directions are well on their way to setting the stage for positive behaviors, since everyone knows what they are supposed to do. That is only part of the challenge, however. In addition to setting up expectations, teachers need to let the students know when they are doing the right thing, meeting the expectations, and following the directions. A high level of positive teacher responses serves to reinforce students who are doing what is expected and alerts other students to what is expected of them. Teachers are quick to redirect students who are not doing the right thing in class, but they are less likely to make a positive comment when a student is following through correctly. A high percentage of positive teacher responses may promote appropriate behavior due to the reinforcing value of the comments and the modeling and vicarious learning effects of the appropriate behavior. Just as students can learn what not to do when someone suffers a consequence in class, they can learn what they should be doing when someone is reinforced for appropriate behaviors.

Often, children with behavior problems get attention in the form of reprimands or criticism when they misbehave in class, and then they are ignored when they are behaving appropriately. For some children, getting any attention (even negative attention such as criticism or reprimands) is better than getting no attention at all. It is especially important for students who have recurring behavior problems in music to receive positive attention from teachers. Teachers need to watch for any appropriate behavior and reinforce it with a positive comment or other positive reinforcement, even though it might be difficult at times. It is easy to identify times when some students are misbehaving and to redirect or reprimand them, but it is much more difficult (yet extremely important) to "catch them being good" and reinforce that appropriate behavior. Positive reinforcement functions to increase the likelihood that the preceding behavior will strengthen or occur again. The student is more likely to exhibit that appropriate behavior again if he or she receives some sort of positive reinforcement.

Follow Through

Teachers can set the stage for an environment conducive for learning by setting up clear expectations; understandable and positive classroom rules; logical, fair consequences; positive teacher responses; and classroom structure. The teacher should always follow through with predetermined consequences when efforts to prevent behavior problems fail and a student displays inappropriate behavior in music class. Students know when they can get away with not following directions or otherwise breaking the classroom rules, and they will continue to do so if they do not have to experience any consequences for their behaviors. Teachers who follow through with consequences in a fair and unemotional way are likely to have fewer behavior problems in their classrooms. Consequences should be fair, enforceable, and developmentally appropriate for the age and functioning level of the student.

Reflecting on Personal Teacher Characteristics

Teacher characteristics that can negatively affect classroom behavior and student learning were listed at the beginning of this chapter (Kauffman et al., 1986; Marzano, 2003). Teachers are encouraged to use this list and the questions below to reflect on their own teaching behaviors that positively or negatively affect students' learning.

1. Inconsistency in management techniques: *"Do I respond in a consistent manner to students' behaviors?"*

Students need to know the consequences for appropriate and inappropriate behavior in class. Teachers need to have clear expectations for students' behaviors, give clear directions, have specific consequences for behavior, and follow through consistently with rewards for positive behavior and consequences for negative behavior.

2. Reinforcement of the wrong behavior: *"Do I reinforce or reward the correct behavior, or do I continue to reinforce the behavior that is inappropriate?"*

Frequently teachers give too much attention to students who are exhibiting inappropriate behaviors. This attention can function to reinforce that behavior and increase the likelihood that the behavior will reoccur. Rather than cajoling, criticizing, or otherwise reinforcing inappropriate behavior, teachers should follow through consistently with any consequences for negative behavior and be generous with reinforcement for appropriate behaviors. Teachers must emember to "catch the students being good" and reinforce the behaviors they want to see again with praise, a pat on the shoulder, a nonverbal sign, or some other event that is reinforcing to the student.

3. Inappropriate expectations for children: *"Do I have reasonable expectations for the students in my class? Are these expectations in line with the abilities of the students, and am I able to vary my expectations based on the abilities of individual students?"*

Students need to be challenged and they need to feel a sense of accomplishment. In today's classroom, teachers can have the difficult job of varying expectations for individual students in the class due to the student's disability or other special needs. When students are not challenged due to low expectations, they can become bored and exhibit negative behaviors. Similarly, when expectations are too high and students are unable to be successful, they may become frustrated and give up academically or behaviorally. Students need a balance between challenge and success in order to maintain interest and positive behaviors in the class.

4. Nonfunctional or irrelevant curriculum: *"Is the music curriculum relevant and functional for the lives of the students? Have I chosen the most important information and material to teach?"*

Sometimes students are unable to see the value in what they are learning in music class. They may not understand how what they are learning in music is meaningful in their lives, and so they may not take learning seriously. Behavior problems may arise when this happens. Teachers might need to help students understand the value of what they are learning by pointing out how it fits into their lives and the lives of others. Many types of music can be used to teach concepts, and most students enjoy some type of music. Students respond best when the curriculum is interesting, meaningful, and in some way relevant to their lives.

5. Insensitivity to children's individuality: *"Am I sensitive to the needs of individual students? Do I respect the need for students to explore their individuality?"*

An inclusive classroom consists of students with varied individual needs and abilities. Although it may be difficult for music educators to know all of the individual needs of the many students in their classes, it can be important to have some information about students who have challenging behaviors in order to make music class a good experience for all of the students. Music class can be an exciting place for students to explore their creativity and individuality through music making alone and with others. Teachers who allow creative exploration may be encouraging students' individuality rather than stifling their curiosity or originality.

6. Presenting or encouraging desirable models: *"Are there many desirable models for the students to emulate throughout the class?"*

We all want students to be respectful of others and follow the rules and expectations for the class. Children tend to imitate others around them, both adults and peers, so they need to have good models to imitate. Teachers can model respect for students in order to teach respect of others. Even during a difficult day, teachers should model in their own behavior the type of behavior they are looking for in their students. Teachers can reinforce the desirable behavior of students in the class by calling attention to specific students who demonstrate appropriate behaviors. Strong peer role models can be developed and maintained through this approach (e.g., "Molly has her instrument on the floor and her hands in her lap; so do Joe and Libby").

7. Irritability or frequent use of punishment: *"Am I frequently crabby and short-tempered with the students? Do I use punishment to control the students rather than manage their behaviors through positive reinforcement and role models?"*

Teachers who are irritable and short-tempered can set a negative tone in the class. In this environment, students may respond with defiance and general lack of motivation. In addition, teachers may contribute to a negative classroom climate when they are quick to punish students for negative behavior and are reticent to offer students approval for positive behaviors. Behavior management is not simply responding to students' inappropriate behaviors, but it also sets the stage for students to have positive behaviors. Redirection or giving consequences for inappropriate behavior is only one part of behavior management.

8. Unwillingness to seek advice or try new strategies from other professionals: *"Do I seek out help from other teachers or district professionals? Do I try new strategies to improve students' success in music?"*

Teachers are more likely to succeed when they collaborate with others. By collaborating, teachers can learn from each other and build on the skills and successes of other teachers in similar situations. Teachers who try to handle everything on their own are typically fearful of feedback from their peers or are afraid of being seen as not qualified to manage the class. Collaboration could be simply sharing about students and strategies during lunch break, having a weekly meeting to discuss specific students' needs, or asking a veteran teacher to observe and provide consultation to help deal with a difficult class.

Tolerating Selected Behaviors

Teachers should consider the students' abilities, level of functioning, and developmental stages before immediately instituting interventions to modify behaviors. Long and Newman (1980) suggested three situations where teachers may need to tolerate certain behaviors rather than giving consequences, including (a) when a student is learning a new skill (learner's leeway), (b) when a student exhibits behaviors that are due to a disability, and (c) when a student exhibits behaviors that are typical of a developmental stage.

Learner's leeway: Students who are learning a new skill cannot be expected to master that skill right away. They need to practice the skill, make mistakes, get feedback, and continue to practice until they achieve mastery. This is true for learning music skills as well as learning social skills and appropriate behavioral skills. All students need time and practice to learn a new skill, and some students with disabilities need additional time to learn and practice new skills. Teachers who give some leeway and tolerate certain behaviors can support the students as they make small gains over time. This approach may serve to decrease the students' frustration level and increase motivation. Some students need repeated feedback, modeling, and directives from the teacher in order to understand and master some skills. For instance, when a student is given a reminder from the teacher to stay in a particular place, other students usually learn from this example and are reminded to stay in their space. A child with a cognitive disability may not pick up cues through incidental learning and may need several specific reminders in order to learn this classroom rule (Wood, 1998).

Behaviors due to a disability: Throughout this book we stress the importance of gathering information about students in the class who have disabilities so that the teacher can accommodate the needs of the students when necessary. Behaviors such as impulsivity from a student who has ADHD may be symptomatic of the disability and might need to be tolerated while the student is becoming regulated on medication or learning new coping skills in class. Tolerating behaviors does not mean that these behaviors go unnoticed, overlooked, or without redirection. Music professionals should seek out assistance from the classroom teacher to determine procedures for consistent interventions to support the student in learning and practicing new behaviors.

Behaviors that indicate developmental stages: Certain behaviors are typical of a specific age or developmental level. For instance, preschool and early elementary aged children tend to be fidgety and impulsive at times, whereas children in the upper elementary grades are expected to focus for longer periods of time and display patience and self-control in class. A young child would not be reprimanded or suffer consequences for that impulsivity that is developmentally expected, while an older child might. Behaviors that are tolerated in young children may not be tolerated in older children due to different expectations based on developmental levels. Developmental progress for some students with disabilities might be slower than for students without disabilities. Teachers might need to tolerate some behaviors of students whose skills are at a different developmental level than the rest of the class, while providing redirection and support (Long & Newman, 1980; Wood, 1998).

Interventions to Deal with Problem Behaviors

The first part of this chapter describes several ways for teachers to set the tone for positive behaviors in the music class and possibly prevent problem behaviors from occurring. However, not all problem behaviors can be eliminated through proactive behavior management techniques. Teachers also must be aware of and be comfortable using a variety of interventions to decrease or eliminate problem behaviors in the classroom. Behavior problems in the classroom disrupt students' ability to learn and teachers' ability to provide effective instruction. Teachers can create an environment conducive to active participation and learning through effective behavior management interventions. *Surface behavior techniques* and *positive reinforcement* are two approaches that can be used easily and effectively in the music class.

Surface Behavior Techniques

Some students have behavior problems that warrant long-term behavior management interventions, while other students may exhibit less serious behavior problems that do not require such extensive interventions. Surface behaviors are problem behaviors in class that require some attention but do not require a total behavior management program to decrease or eliminate the behavior (Long & Newman, 1980; Walker, Shea, & Bauer, 2007). Surface behaviors are those minor infractions that teachers deal with frequently throughout their day. These techniques are considered to be stopgap measures to redirect or diffuse a minor behavioral problem during class and are not meant to replace a well-designed behavior management system. Teachers may use many different techniques to deal with these behaviors in order to maintain the best possible environment for learning for all students. When using surface management techniques, teachers need to match the proper technique with the behavior, implementing the intervention immediately when the behavior occurs.

Planned ignoring: This technique is also called extinction, and although it is a simple technique, it is one that requires patience on the part of the teacher. When a student engages in an inappropriate behavior, the teacher ignores that behavior and immediately reinforces the student when he or she exhibits the appropriate behavior. For instance, a student may impulsively call out the answer rather than raising his hand in class. Instead of scolding or reprimanding the student, the teacher ignores him. The first time he raises his hand without calling out, the teacher calls on him for his answer and reinforces him for his appropriate behavior. With planned ignoring, the inappropriate target behavior usually increases before it decreases. This is due to the fact that the student is used to getting some attention, any attention at all, for that behavior. If he does not get the expected response from the teacher, he is likely to continue to try, even harder, to get the expected attention. This is where patience comes in. The teacher must realize that this increase will happen and that a decrease will then usually occur after the student is not reinforced over time for the inappropriate behavior. It is very important for the teacher to remember to consistently reinforce the appropriate behavior as soon as it occurs to let the student know what is expected. This technique is useful for decreasing behaviors that may be annoying and inappropriate but are not typically harmful to anyone.

Signal interference: Teachers use a vast array of nonverbal signals to convey disapproval or the need for redirection. Nonverbal techniques such as eye contact, hand gestures, finger snapping, or clearing the throat can provide enough of a cue to alert a student to get back on task or to otherwise meet the set behavioral expectations. The signal (e.g., finger snapping or "the look") functions to interrupt the behavior and immediately notify the student that he or she needs to stop the behavior and resume more acceptable actions. These signals are best used at the onset of a behavior infraction rather than waiting until the behavior has been ongoing and is escalating.

Proximity control: Just being near a student who is beginning to have problem behaviors can be effective in eliminating the problem. A teacher can move about the room in a seemingly random fashion, yet situate himself or herself close to a student who needs additional support and guidance. This might be all a student needs to get back on track academically or behaviorally.

These first three techniques—*planned ignoring, signal interference,* and *proximity control*—have the added advantage of not embarrassing a student or even actually identifying students who are having the problems. Students' behavior can escalate in an effort to save face with their peers when they are singled out or embarrassed in class.

Defusing tension through humor: Well-placed humor can reduce an anxiety-producing situation to a comical interlude. The alternative to humor might be scolding the students, giving a consequence, or making a comment that, in some way, belittles someone else. For example, let's say that the music teacher plays an accompaniment on the piano and makes a few mistakes, causing the choir to stop and restart the piece several times. One student makes a rude comment about the teacher's piano skills, to which she replies, "Maybe I should try taking my mittens off and play with all ten fingers!" The other students laugh and they continue their rehearsal. In this instance, the teacher could have scolded the student for being rude or sent him or her out of the room as a consequence for the comment. Such actions would have disrupted the rehearsal even more and the student would have received more attention for the negative comment. As it was, they were able to move on and finish the rehearsal without the tension that follows negative interactions.

Support for routine: Classroom structure helps promote a secure and predictable environment. Some students need more structure than others to feel secure and relaxed in a classroom. Certain elements in a class can cue students to what is going to happen. For example, early elementary students may know that class is beginning when the music teacher sings a greeting song, or high school choir students know that class is beginning when they hear the warm-ups cued on the piano. A predictable, structured environment is especially important for some students who have disabilities, in particular students with autism and students with behavior disorders. Most music classrooms have a predictable class structure, due to the large number of classes that a teacher has in one day or to make the most efficient use of rehearsal time. A predictable structure allows students to come into class with some idea of what is expected of them, what they will be doing in class, and how they will be evaluated for their progress.

Interest boosting: For this technique, the teacher needs to know some of the interests of the students in the class. When a specific student is off-task or on the verge of problem behavior, the teacher goes over to the student, mentions something that the student is interested in, and engages him or her in a brief conversation. This is difficult to do when the teacher is working with the entire class, but it can be useful when students are working in cooperative groups or individually during music. Discussion could easily revolve around musical interests, such as favorite types of music, favorite song on the radio, the instrument or music they are playing in band, or other recreational music interests. This brief encounter lets students know that the teacher is paying attention to them and is able to acknowledge some of their interests. This attention functions to redirect a student from off-task behavior and to reconnect the student to the teacher who has expectations of positive behavior.

Removing distracting objects: Students can become distracted by an array of interesting objects that they might bring into the music classroom. Teachers are rarely able to compete for the student's attention when toys, electronic equipment, or other interesting objects are available. Usually a comment to put the item away during class will eliminate the problem; however, sometimes the teacher might need to confiscate the object until the end of class. Some students with disabilities, in particular, some students with autism, might need a transition object to help them feel secure and to reduce anxiety as they move from their regular classroom to the music classroom. This might be a small toy, a nerf ball, or some other object from their classroom or home. Music teachers should discuss with the classroom teacher what is allowed in the regular classroom and the function of the object for the student. Every effort should be made to be consistent in the music class to help the student make a secure transition. Students are usually able to fade out using these transition objects as they become more comfortable in the music class. The fading process could go like this: (a) the student brings the object to class and holds it in her hand during class; (b) as the student becomes more comfortable in music class, she is asked to place the object on the teacher's desk in plain sight during music with the reassurance that it will be returned to her at the end of class; (c) as the student becomes even more comfortable and has fewer problems transitioning to music class, she is asked to give the object to the classroom teacher when entering the music class; and (d) finally, the student is able to leave the transition object in her classroom when she comes to music. Students who do not need these objects will usually understand that it is important for their peer to have it in class, even though they are not allowed to bring in toys or other objects.

Antiseptic bouncing: When a child's behavior has reached the point where nonverbal or verbal cues do not suffice, the teacher might ask a child to leave the area or the room for a brief time in order to gain self-control. This is a nonpunitive type of approach to give the student an opportunity to get away from the situation, calm down, and refocus. There is no intention to punish the child, but simply to help the student get over such feelings as anger or disappointment, or to help him or her to overcome giggling or hiccups. For instance, a teacher might ask a student who is giggling uncontrollably to take a short break and maybe go get a drink of water. When the student returns, the giggling will be under control and the student can resume active participation in the class. This technique can be very useful with students who have a low frustration tolerance, or when the teacher can tell a student's behaviors are escalating out of control. Some students with behavior problems may be asked to indicate when they need to leave in order to gain control. A teacher's aide or a trusted student might accompany the student in order to diffuse the situation and give the student time to self-regulate. Antiseptic bouncing can be difficult to facilitate if there is no safe, nonpunitive place to send the student, or if there is not appropriate support to assist a student when needed.

Additional Procedures for Changing Students' Behaviors in Music

When students have extreme behaviors or they do not respond to surface management techniques, teachers need to utilize other procedures to change students' behaviors in music class. Teachers may need to utilize more complex behavior management procedures to support behavioral changes for students who are frequently or consistently disruptive in class. This brief overview outlines additional ways to modify students' behavior in music class (Long & Newman, 1980; Wood, 1998).

One way to attempt to modify behavior is to use a functional analysis of behavior. The functional analysis is used to determine specific environmental variables that are affecting behavior, and to find ways to predict and control behavior through manipulating these variables. According to Deno (1980), the functional analysis of behavior consists of the following elements:

- the target behavior;
- the events that precede the target behavior (antecedents);
- the events that follow the target behavior (consequences);
- the contingency relations among those three elements.

Heavy emphasis is usually placed on the fact that behavior can be strengthened by changing the events that follow a behavior, and making sure that change is contingent upon the occurrence of the target behavior. However, it is just as important to be aware of how the antecedent events, or events that precede the behavior, affect the students' behavior. According to Deno (1980):

> *The first term of the contingency (preceding, antecedent or discriminative stimulus events) is as much a part of the analysis as the second and third terms. Rarely are we concerned with strengthening*

*or weakening behavior without regard for the occasion upon which
that behavior occurs (the preceding events). In fact, we cannot judge
behavior as appropriate or inappropriate in a social system unless we
know the situation (the preceding events) in which the behavior has
occurred. (p. 244)*

The events prior to the target behavior and immediately following the target
behavior are important events to observe and manipulate. In terms of preceding
events, teachers should consider what directions have been given, what expectations
have been communicated, what the other students are doing at the time, what
distractions are occurring in the room, etc. These might be factors that can be varied
to modify the target behavior in the future. The events that follow a behavior are also
powerful factors in affecting that behavior in the future. When a positive behavior
occurs and that behavior is reinforced immediately and consistently, it is likely that
the behavior will be maintained or increased in the future. Students' behavior can
be reinforced many different ways, both verbally and nonverbally, and through extra
privileges and honors. The important factor to remember is that the reinforcement
must be motivating for the student and something that the student likes or values.

Steps to modify behaviors:

1. The first step is to *identify the target behavior,* which is the behavior that
needs to be changed. Clear, specific, and observable behaviors should be identified
in order to be able to focus on exactly what is the problem behavior. For instance,
rather than saying that Stephanie disrupts the class, the teacher might say that
Stephanie gets out of her seat, talks out, and hits peers seated by her.

2. The next step in the behavior change process is to *record the frequency of
occurrence* of the target behavior. Choose one of the target behaviors and attempt
to note each time that behavior occurs in class. The teacher needs to know the
starting point of the behavior in order to determine if the behavioral interventions
are effective. This can be difficult to do while teaching an entire class, but it is
worthwhile to document the success or failure of interventions. A simple slash on a
piece of paper each time the behavior is observed may be sufficient to get an idea
of the baseline number of occurrences.

3. Another step is to *change some conditions,* either the antecedents (what
usually happens prior to the behavior occurring) or the consequences (what happens
after the behavior occurs). Teachers can change preceding events such as the
instructions; type of materials the student is using; the environment, such as placing
the child next to the teacher or a good model; or the number of examples the student
is expected to complete. Changing the consequences immediately following the
behavior usually produces the most positive changes. Positive reinforcement is a highly
effective means to increase target behaviors, such as staying in one's seat, raising a
hand to talk, following directions, etc. Positive reinforcement functions to increase
or maintain a behavior. Teachers must use an appropriate reinforcer, one that is truly

reinforcing and motivating for the student, and reinforce the student immediately after the student exhibits the target behavior. Reinforcers might be social (praise, pat on the back), tangible (star on paper, prize), or activity-related (extra music time, free time). The following guidelines are important to consider when implementing a behavior change program using positive reinforcement (Wood, 1998):

- Select reinforcements that are appropriate for the student.
- Reinforce only those behaviors that need to be changed or modified.
- Reinforce the target behavior immediately.
- Reinforce the target behavior each time it occurs, initially.
- After the target behavior is established, reinforce intermittently.
- Use a social reinforcer along with tangible or activity reinforcers.
- Fade out the tangible or activity reinforcement and maintain the social reinforcement.

Reinforcement must be immediate, continuous, and consistent during the period of time when the appropriate behavior is being established.

Praise is frequently used as a positive reinforcement to improve students' behavior. Praise is a teacher's detailed or intense response to a student's behavior, meant to express approval or to commend the student for a particular response or behavior (Brophy, 1981). In order to be effective, praise should have the qualities of **contingency**, **specificity**, and **sincerity/variety/credibility** (O'Leary & O'Leary, 1977).

- *Contingency.* The teacher's praise must be contingent on the exhibition of the target behavior. For example, if the teacher is attempting to increase a student's time working on assignments, praise should be given when the student has been working on assignments for a predetermined amount of time.
- *Specificity.* The teacher's praise should state specifically what behaviors are being reinforced. For instance, "Donovan, you have been working on your assignments for 10 minutes; good for you."
- *Sincerity/variety/credibility.* Praise from the teacher should sound sincere and should be varied to address the individual differences and preferences of students and situations. Using the same phrase such as "good job" over and over has no variety, may not sound sincere, and does not specifically state what the student is doing that is so good.

4. After a period of time where reinforcement has been applied, teachers should *evaluate the effectiveness* of the interventions by noting if the target behavior has changed according to plan. If not, the plan should be reevaluated and changes made to elicit a more positive response from the student.

Token economy and *contingency contracting* are two additional procedures used to modify students' behavior in school. In the *token economy* system, the desired changes in behavior are specified, effective reinforcers are identified and made potentially available, a token such as a chip or a star is earned by the student when the specified behavior occurs, and, finally, the student is given opportunities to exchange the token for a selected reinforcer. Many classrooms already have token economy systems in place. The music educator can collaborate with the classroom teacher to participate in the token system that will provide consistent behavioral expectations and reinforcement between the classroom and the music class. *Contingency contracting* is a procedure developed between a student and the teacher that focuses on changing (increasing or decreasing) the target behavior, whether it is academic achievement or appropriate behavior in class. The student and teacher work together to set up the contract, including setting up target behaviors, and identifying reinforcement and criteria for success. Classroom teachers may want to use additional music time, individual music lessons, or other music-related reinforcement to motivate students to complete academic work. Collaboration between the classroom teacher and music teacher is essential for the success of this type of contingency contract with music as reinforcement.

Music educators may have difficulty implementing behavior plans for all of the students who have problem behaviors, since they teach so many students each week. This can be an overwhelming process when classes are back-to-back all day, when the teacher is moving from school to school, or when he or she is working with hundreds of students each week. However, teachers can work to modify behaviors in class as they occur and improve the learning environment in the class by using the principles of reinforcement to increase positive behavior. In addition, collaboration with the classroom teacher is highly recommended when certain classes consistently exhibit difficult behaviors in music, or when individual students consistently have behavior problems in music. The classroom teacher may have a behavior management plan in place that can also be used in music. By collaborating with the classroom teacher, the music specialist can gain insight and information about specific students who have behavior plans already in place. Many times the music educator can piggyback on the classroom behavior plan that is already established and functioning. The students benefit from this consistency, and they learn that the same behaviors are expected in the music class as are expected in the regular classroom. Music educators and music therapists who work in smaller settings such as self-contained classrooms may be able to implement their own behavior plans or collaborate with the classroom teacher again to utilize the same or similar plans.

Summary

Effective classroom management is a total process that significantly affects learning environment. The first step in the behavior management process is to create a positive environment to prevent some behavior problems. Positive teacher attitude, clear expectations, and motivating classroom activities are a few elements that contribute to a positive classroom environment. There will be times when preventative measures are not enough and additional techniques need to be implemented to manage students' behaviors. Music educators and music therapists might need only to apply surface management techniques or they might need to attempt to modify more difficult behaviors through a structured behavior management plan. Effective behavior management procedures in the music setting can be developed, implemented, and enhanced through collaboration with classroom teachers, special educators, and classroom aides.

KEY POINTS FROM THE CHAPTER

♦ Teachers can contribute to motivation and behavior problems in the class by having inconsistent management techniques, reinforcing the wrong behaviors, having inappropriate expectations for students, and being unwilling to try new strategies, among other characteristics.

♦ Student characteristics that contribute to behavior or academic problems include difficulty concentrating or paying attention; impulsivity; negative attitude towards self, peers, and/or teacher; and verbal or physical aggression, among other characteristics.

♦ Teachers can create a positive environment to help prevent behavior problems through such features as positive teacher attitude and high expectations, clear expectations, structure, motivating curriculum, and follow through on consequences.

♦ Surface management techniques can be used to deal with minor infractions of the rules before they become difficult behavior issues.

♦ A functional analysis can be used to determine specific environmental variables that are affecting a student's behavior and to find ways to predict and control behavior through manipulating these variables. A functional analysis of behavior consists of identifying of the target behavior to be changed, determining the events that precede the behavior (antecedents), and determining consequences (events that will follow the behavior).

♦ Positive reinforcement can increase the likelihood of a behavior occurring again. There are several important steps for using positive reinforcement to change behavior.

♦ Token economy and contingency contracting are additional behavior management procedures that are frequently used to modify students' behavior in school.

REFERENCES

Brophy, J. (1981). Teacher praise: A functional analysis. *Review of Educational Research, 51,* 5–32.
Brophy, J. (1987). Synthesis of research on strategies for motivating students to learn. *Educational Leadership, 45*(2), 40–48.
Colvin, G. (2002). Designing classroom organization and structure. In K. Lane, F. Gresham, & T. O'Shaughnessy (Eds.), *Interventions for children with or at risk for emotional and behavioral disorders.* Boston: Allyn & Bacon.

Deno, S. L. (1980). Contingency management in (special) education: Confusions and clarifications. In N. J. Long, W. Morse, & R. Newman (Eds.), *Conflict in the classroom: The education of emotionally disturbed children* (4th ed.). Belmont, CA: Wadsworth.

Englert, C. (1984). Measuring teacher effectiveness from the teacher's point of view. *Focus on Exceptional Children, 17,* 1–16.

Evertson, C., & Poole, I. (2008). Proactive classroom management. *21st century education: A reference handbook.* Retrieved March 24, 2010, from http://www.sage-ereference.com/education/Article_n14.html

Kauffman, J. M., Pullen, P. L., & Akers, E. (1986). Classroom management: Teacher-child-peer relationships. *Focus on Exceptional Children, 19*(1), 1–10.

Long, N. J., & Newman, R. (1980). Managing surface behaviors of children in schools. In N. J. Long, W. Morse, & R. Newman (Eds.), *Conflict in the classroom: The education of emotionally disturbed children* (4th ed.). Belmont, CA: Wadsworth.

Marzano, R. J. (2003). *Classroom management that works: Research-based strategies for teachers.* Alexandria, VA: Association for Supervision and Curriculum Development.

O'Leary, K., & O'Leary, S. (Eds.). (1977). *Classroom management: The successful use of behavior modification* (2nd ed.). New York: Pergamon.

Pankake, A. (2006). Classroom management. *Encyclopedia of Educational Leadership and Administration.* Retrieved March 24, 2010, from http://www.sage-ereference.com/edleadership/Article_n91.html

Walker, J., Shea, T., & Bauer, A. (2007). *Behavior management: A practical approach for educators* (9th ed.). Upper Saddle River, NJ: Prentice-Hall.

Wilson, E., & Bruce, C. (1996). *Classroom management to encourage motivation and responsibility.* Arlington, VA: Educational Research Service.

Wood, J. W. (1998). *Adapting instruction to accommodate students in inclusive settings* (3rd ed.). Upper Saddle River, NJ: Prentice-Hall.

Chapter 6

Music Education and Music Therapy Service Delivery Options

CHAPTER OVERVIEW

Music education is offered in most school districts in the U.S., providing opportunities for students to participate in general music, instrumental music, and choral music classes and performances. Through all of these types of music experiences, music educators and music therapists working in schools may engage in a variety of different roles in the education of students who have disabilities.

This chapter includes information on the following topics:
- Current practice in schools
- Music education and music therapy: Collaborative possibilities
- Mainstreaming and inclusion
- Roles of music educators and music therapists in special education: An overview
- Music therapy as a related service
- Music therapy in a district-wide special education setting
- Music therapist as a consultant to music education, general education, and special education teachers

Current Practice in Schools

The principles of IDEA provide an important framework for the education of students with disabilities. Of those six principles (zero reject, nondiscriminatory evaluation, appropriate education, least restrictive environment, parent and student participation, and procedural due process), music educators and music therapists will be primarily involved with practices related to the least restrictive environment, individualized education, and nondiscriminatory evaluation. These three principles as they relate to music education and music therapy services in schools are addressed in this chapter. Music professionals should understand the six principles of IDEA that were discussed in detail in Chapter 2.

Least Restrictive Environment

One of the six principles of IDEA is that of *least restrictive environment* (LRE). This principle requires that schools educate students with disabilities together with students without disabilities to the maximum extent appropriate (Turnbull, Turnbull, & Wehmeyer, 2010). The 1997 Amendments to IDEA strengthened the idea further stating that, whenever possible, students should be educated in the general classroom setting. Many court cases have interpreted the LRE principle and have concluded that students have a right to participate in academic, extracurricular, and other programs in general education, to the maximum extent possible for the individual and the setting (Bartlett, Etscheidt, & Weisenstein, 2007; Richards & Martin, 2006; Turnbull & Turnbull, 1998). In addition, schools must consider the *educational benefits* of an integrated setting compared to a segregated setting, the nonacademic or *social benefits* for the student with disabilities interacting with students without disabilities, the *effect of the student* with disabilities on the general classroom milieu, and the costs necessary to sustain a student in an integrated environment. It is the responsibility of the school personnel to determine the benefits of the educational environment and make adjustments if the student is not benefiting. This means that if a student is educated in an inclusive classroom and is making meaningful progress on educational goals, then this inclusive environment is benefiting the student and the placement is appropriate. However, if the student is not making meaningful progress on educational goals in that environment with the addition of appropriate supports, then the inclusive setting is not benefiting the student and inclusion is not appropriate and not required. The least restrictive environment will be different for different students, depending on the individual needs of each student. In all cases, LRE refers to the educational setting where the student is able to demonstrate progress on IEP goals in the most normalized setting as possible (i.e., with students who do not have disabilities). For most students, the LRE is the general education classroom with additional support from special education personnel, but for other students the LRE is a self-contained classroom with minimal or no inclusion in the general education milieu.

Music Education and Music Therapy: Collaborative Possibilities

Music education and music therapy are distinct disciplines and professions, yet there is great potential for collaboration between the two. Music educators focus primarily on music-related goals such as learning to sing, perform, compose, and analyze music. The Music Educators National Conference (1994) developed

National Standards for Music Education (see Figure 6.1) to focus instruction and achievement in music learning.

Figure 6.1 National Standards for Music Education (1994)

1. Students will be able to sing, alone and with others, a varied repertoire of music.
2. Students will be able to perform on instruments, alone and with others, a varied repertoire of music.
3. Students will be able to improvise melodies, variations, and accompaniments.
4. Students will be able to compose and arrange music within specified guidelines.
5. Students will be able to read and notate music.
6. Students will be able to listen to, analyze, and describe music.
7. Students will be able to evaluate music and music performance.
8. Students will be able to understand relationships between music, the other arts, and disciplines outside the arts.
9. Students will be able to understand music in relation to history and culture.

Music therapy is the use of music to achieve non-music goals and can address students' development in cognitive, behavioral, physical, emotional, social, and communication domains. For some students, participation in music therapy can stimulate their focus of attention and can serve as a motivation for students to participate more fully in their education. While music therapists use the same media as music educators, namely music, music therapists use the music for a different purpose. For instance, a student with a behavior disorder might be involved in a percussion group during a music therapy session. In order to be successful, the student must listen to directions, imitate others, take turns, and control impulses. Opportunities for these target behaviors are structured into the session by the music therapist, who knows what non-music goal areas the student is working on in class. The percussion group sets the stage for practice of these targeted non-music behaviors, while the student participates in the music-making experience. Even though the student engages in music learning, the learning of specific percussion skills is not the primary instructional focus of the group. The same student might also participate in a percussion group during general music class or band, where the focus is primarily on learning the percussion pattern, fitting parts together to make an ensemble sound, playing the music in a style authentic to the African culture, or simply keeping a steady beat. In this music education setting, the primary instructional focus is on developing music skills and learning about music.

Mainstreaming and Inclusion

Practices related to educating students with disabilities have had a great impact on the jobs of music educators over the past 30 years. The role of the music educator continues to evolve, beginning with the practice of *mainstreaming* in the mid-1970s and continuing with IDEA's directives to educate students with disabilities in general education classes as much as possible. Soon after the passage of the law in 1975 that mandated a free and appropriate public education for all students (FAPE), the term *mainstreaming* was used to describe the practice of including students with disabilities in general education classes for a portion of the day. For the majority of the day, these students were usually educated in a separate, self-contained special education classroom for students with disabilities. Students would join their peers without disabilities for part of the day, either in class for an academic subject or in a more social time, such as lunch or recess. In many instances, one of the student's first mainstreaming experiences included joining the music, art, and/or physical education class. Music is still a popular choice for a student's initial placement in general education classes.

The current practice of *inclusion* refers to educating students with disabilities in the same classroom as their nondisabled peers. Additional supports for the student are provided within the regular classroom, rather than removing the student to a separate setting for special education services. In a full inclusion model, students with mild to severe disabilities are educated in the regular education classroom with their peers for the entire day. Special education personnel work closely with the general education teachers to provide appropriate educational interventions for the students within the typical educational environment.

Due to these dramatic educational changes in how students are placed in schools and who is responsible for educating students with disabilities, music therapists and music educators have an even greater need and opportunity for collaboration. Students with disabilities have participated in the general music class for over 30 years, and this practice is now commonplace in the United States. As previously mentioned, music class is frequently one of the first inclusive experiences for a student who is primarily educated in a self-contained classroom (Jellison & Gainer, 1995). General music classes consist of students who demonstrate a continuum of skills and abilities, from students who are gifted to students who have severe disabilities, with many students having different abilities in between. The music educator can assist the IEP team or special education team in deciding if the music class is an appropriate placement based on the educational benefits and/or the social benefits that a student is receiving in that setting (Patterson, 2003). Rather than consenting to the practice of placing all students with disabilities into the general education music class with their same-aged peers, the music educator can suggest the most educationally beneficial placement for the child. Placement suggestions can be made based on:

- the characteristics of the student, including the student's abilities;

- the primary focus of the music class (a class that focuses on music making rather than music theory might be more appropriate for a student with severe intellectual disabilities);
- the general education options that are available for that student in the school (is the student placed in the music class because it is the only option, or is there a more appropriate general education class for this student?);
- opportunities for partial participation (if the student is unable to successfully participate in the entire class every time, is there a possibility for the student to join the class for a portion of the class time and then move to another setting?).

When making placement decisions for students, the team needs to understand what is required for successful participation in the music class. Many people do not understand the wide array of skills that are utilized in music classes, and sometimes they need to be educated by the music professionals to help them understand that all music classes are not alike. The music educator is in a position to make positive contributions to the decision-making process regarding placement in music classes. In order to be proactive in this process, music educators are encouraged to develop course descriptions for their classes, especially those at the junior and senior high school levels (Hughes, Rice, DeBedout, & Hightower, 2002). These course descriptions might include prerequisite courses or skills needed; class size; skills required for successful participation (such as good listening skills, self-discipline, ability to read, etc.); required homework or performances; and amount and type of assistance needed. The team can then use this information to carefully place a student into a music class that is the most appropriate setting for the student's abilities. This proactive approach can facilitate communication between the music educator and the classroom teacher or special education team and will ultimately benefit all the students in the class.

Collaboration is one of the keys to developing effective music education plans and expectations for students with disabilities and for successfully including all of the students in some capacity. Music educators can seek out support and instruction from music therapists, special education teachers, and general education teachers to create the best possible learning environment for all students. Collaboration with other professionals, including music therapists, can strengthen teaching skills and provide a basis for possible improved outcomes for the students. Music professionals can become isolated from other teachers because of busy schedules, back-to-back classes, and the large number of students in music classes. All of these factors make it difficult to find time to interact with other teachers in the school. Even though it takes time to seek out other professionals to share ideas, discuss students' progress, and even commiserate over difficult students' behaviors, the benefits are usually well worth the time spent. The increased teaching effectiveness, improved feelings of success with students, and overall improved job satisfaction will more than compensate for the extra time and effort it takes to collaborate with other professionals (McCord & Watts, 2006).

Music classes can provide positive group experiences where the strengths of each individual student are recognized and built upon. Music educators are faced with the challenge each day to provide experiences that are musically, educationally, and socially beneficial to all of the students in their classes.

Roles of Music Educators and Music Therapists in Special Education: An Overview

While both music educators and music therapists engage students in music-making experiences, the goals for each discipline are different. Specific job descriptions and roles for music educators and music therapists in schools vary across the U.S. Job descriptions vary from state to state and even within states, depending on the autonomy of the districts and the schools within the districts.

Here are a few examples of the variety of roles for music educators and music therapists in the schools:

- In addition to teaching students in standard inclusive music classes (general music, band, chorus, orchestra, etc.), some music educators also teach "adapted music" classes or "special music education" classes with students who have severe disabilities. These students are typically educated in self-contained classrooms and are not usually included in the general education music class due to the severe nature of their disabilities or the lack of appropriate inclusive music classes. For example, a high school may have several performing groups for students, including chorus, band, and orchestra. Students with severe disabilities who may not have the prerequisite skills for a performance group but may enjoy music participation are educated in a special "adapted music" class taught by the music educator. Students learn about music by engaging in music-making activities such as singing, instrument playing, and movement experiences at their level of ability. Performance is not a focus of this class; however, the students may perform for their peers in a reverse mainstreaming type of situation. Elementary and junior high schools may also have students who would benefit from an adapted music class. *Primary instructional focus: Providing opportunities for students to participate in music experiences with others and to learn basic music skills at a developmentally appropriate level of difficulty.*

- In another district, a music therapist who is trained to work with students with disabilities facilitates this type of "adapted music" class or "special music education" class, while the music educators teach the regular education inclusive classes. This could be the same situation as listed above, but the school uses a music therapist to deliver the instruction due to the therapist's extensive education and experience with children who have disabilities. Adapted music classes can be created at all age levels, from very young children through young adults. *Primary instructional focus: Providing opportunities for students to participate in music experiences with others and to learn basic music skills at a developmentally appropriate level of difficulty. Therapist also structures music experiences to address students' IEP goals.*

- The music therapist might serve as a consultant to the music educator to help with various adaptations necessary for improved student achievement in an inclusive music education setting or adapted music setting. *Primary instructional focus: Providing opportunities for students to participate in music experiences with others and to learn basic music skills in an inclusive classroom setting. The music therapist assists the music educator to develop Universal Design for Learning strategies and to adapt instruction to meet the abilities and educational needs of students with disabilities.*

- The music therapist provides district-wide music therapy services for students in special education, including small group music therapy sessions focusing on the students' IEP goals, and one-to-one sessions for students who qualify for music therapy as a related service. In this situation, the music therapist usually travels to several schools to provide services to students with disabilities. The music therapy sessions focus on students' general IEP goals, such as increased attention to task, improved socialization, or improved academic skills. For some students, this could be in addition to their inclusive music education class, or it could take the place of the inclusive experience. *Primary instructional focus: Using music for development in non-music functional areas necessary for educational progress, such as increased communication skills, improved academics, or improved behavior.*

- The music therapist might travel throughout the entire district and provide music therapy only as a related service to those students who qualify for such services. Music therapy as a related service is discussed later in this chapter. In order for the school to provide music therapy as a related service, the music therapist assesses a student for eligibility to determine if music therapy is necessary for the student to benefit from special education. If music therapy as a related service is recommended, the team will decide if the service will be provided, and, if so, in what type of setting (direct services one-to-one or group, or consultative services). The music therapy services in this instance are focused only on the student's specific IEP goals that can be addressed in music therapy. *Primary instructional focus: Using music to assist individual students' progress on IEP goals.*

- Some music therapists are dual-certified in music education and music therapy. These teacher/therapists often provide the range of services throughout a school or district from regular education music to music therapy services for groups and individual students. *Primary instructional focus: Both music learning and using music for non-music development related to IEP goals.*

Any of these roles might be combined for both the music educator and music therapist, depending on the music professional's certification, licensure, training, and experience.

Music Education in an Inclusive Setting

Inclusive education is the norm in schools across the country. All music educators can expect to work with students who have disabilities in the regular music class setting, including general music, band, choir, orchestra, and other music programs. The typical music education class is made up of students across a wide continuum of abilities, and this can create an additional challenge for the music educator. One way to accommodate the needs of all students is to utilize the principles of Universal Design for Learning (UDL) when developing teaching materials and strategies. UDL calls for flexibility in teaching to enhance learning for students with different learning styles, skills, and deficits. More information on the principles of UDL can be found in Chapter 4.

In addition to utilizing the principles of UDL, music educators may also need to adapt instruction to accommodate the specific learning abilities of the students in the class. The nature of the adaptation will vary depending on the student's abilities and the type and severity of the student's disability. Students who have behavior problems might need some sort of behavior management system implemented in the class, while students who have intellectual disabilities might need simplified instructions. Each student will need different types of accommodations, because each student has different needs and abilities. In order to work effectively with all students, music professionals must be informed about the needs of the students and be willing and able to adapt the music instruction so that all of the students in the class can participate and achieve at their highest possible level.

Music educators and music therapists who work in an inclusive music classroom should (a) know the impact of the student's disability on his or her ability to participate and learn in the class, (b) implement instructional accommodations that will assist the student in achieving the highest level possible in class, and (c) create opportunities for positive interactions between students with disabilities and students without disabilities (Adamek & Darrow, 2008). Chapter 4 in this book contains ideas for gathering information about students and outlines many examples of specific types of adaptations that are appropriate for use in the inclusive music class.

Collaborative teaching can be challenging and requires changes to roles and responsibilities of those professionals involved (Thousand, Nevin, & Villa, 2007). Music therapists might be called in to team-teach or consult with the music educator to assist in development of appropriate instructional interventions, or to take primary responsibility working with students in special education. Typically, music educators are the primary teachers in the inclusive music classroom, unless the co-teaching or consulting music therapist is dual-certified in music education and music therapy. Collaborative co-teaching and consulting efforts are most likely to occur when music therapists are already working in the school or the district. However, it is possible for a school to hire a music therapist on a consultation basis to assist the music education staff with specific difficult situations. Students and teachers alike can benefit when professionals work together to create effective educational opportunities that are accessible for all students.

Cooperative Learning in the Inclusive Music Classroom

Some students might be placed in music class for the social benefits obtained by interacting in a normalized setting with peers who do not have disabilities. Social integration among students is a concern for music educators (Darrow, 1999), and positive interaction requires some direct intervention on the part of the teacher or therapist. Cooperative learning is one approach that can be used to facilitate instruction and increase interactions among students in the class. In a cooperative learning activity, small groups of students work together to maximize their own and each other's learning (Johnson, Johnson, & Holubec, 1991). Cooperative learning strategies can help move a student from isolation to interaction by engaging students with varied abilities in shared learning experiences. Classmates can get to know each other's strengths, in addition to weaknesses, as they work together to achieve a group goal. Extensive research has been focused on the effects of cooperative learning strategies on the interactions of students in inclusive classrooms. Research outcomes have been positive, noting higher levels of social and verbal interaction among students when cooperative learning strategies are used, compared to competitive or individual approaches (Putnam, 1993). Researchers have found that students with disabilities and students without disabilities have increased positive interactions in music class when cooperative learning strategies are used. However, the interaction does not occur automatically and usually must be structured and directed by the teacher. Positive social interactions can occur in music when the teacher sets up a positive teaching environment, opportunities for cooperative work, and reinforcement for appropriate social interactions (Humpal, 1991; Jellison, Brooks, & Huck, 1984; Kostka, 1993, Mitchell, 2008).

Cooperative lessons in an integrated music class must be carefully planned, with consideration for the abilities and limitations of students with special needs. Based on ideas from previous research, Nevin (1993) expanded on eight strategies for structuring and facilitating cooperative lessons:

1. Select instructional objectives and materials that are somewhat connected to the student's IEP objectives and related to the student's ability level.
2. Assign groups to ensure proper size, heterogeneity, and diversity of students within each group.
3. Arrange the environment to ensure that the students are working face-to-face and the teacher can move between groups freely.

4. Design the intervention so that students focus on the goal, have opportunities for interdependence, and can be rewarded for working together to achieve the goal.
5. Give specific criteria for success, including what constitutes a successful outcome (task) and what constitutes successful interactions (interpersonal/ social) among group members.
6. Observe group members working together on the task.
7. Get involved with the group when necessary to assist with task performance or cooperative skills.
8. Give feedback to the students to evaluate their work on the group task and their ability to work as a cooperative group.

Music activities can naturally be structured as cooperative learning experiences for the students, and these experiences can create an environment for positive social interactions. Cooperative learning activities increase interactions among all students because students are required to work together to complete tasks. Music professionals need to consider how they can structure direct, meaningful, and consistent opportunities for interaction between students with and without disabilities (Nevin, 1993).

> Example: *Sara, Judy, and David are students with autism who are primarily educated in a self-contained special education classroom. All three students are included in the 5th grade music class with their same-aged peers two times each week. The music teacher understands the importance of setting up the environment to integrate the students from the special education class with the other students. She creates cooperative learning groups to practice improvising a call and response rhythm activity, which will then be shared with the entire class. Sara, Judy, and David are each assigned to different groups so that the students can all get to know each other. The students sit in small circles to work on their improvisations together, while the teacher moves from group to group listening to their work. Groups that work together, share instruments, create an improvisation to present, and include all of the students in the group earn extra free time to experiment with instruments at the end of class. By using this approach, the teacher is providing a structure for music learning and for appropriate interactions among all of the students in the class.*

Music Education/Adapted Music in a Self-Contained Special Education Setting

For some students with severe disabilities, the inclusive general education classroom is not an appropriate placement, and the self-contained special education classroom becomes the least restrictive environment. These students might not attend an inclusive music class but would likely have music instruction in a smaller, self-contained adapted music classroom that is designed to meet the needs of the students with a specific or severe disability. The primary instructional focus of the adapted music class is to give the students opportunities to experience music (through singing, moving, playing, listening, and creating) and to enhance music learning at an appropriate developmental level and age level for the students.

In some districts, the music educator teaches adapted music classes with students who have severe disabilities. In other districts, music therapists are hired to teach adapted music with students who have severe disabilities. Currently, more and more music educators are being assigned the role of teaching adapted music classes, so it is more important than ever for music educators to be aware of the needs of students with severe disabilities. Music therapists might serve as consultants to these music educators to help them develop music curriculum and teaching strategies for adapted music classes.

> Example: *The four students in Ms. Elkhart's primary autism classroom are unable to participate in the inclusive general music class due to difficulties with severe behavior problems and impulse control. Three of the boys are nonverbal and are unable to sing. In this smaller environment, the students learn some of the same music activities as their same-aged peers, but the music educator/therapist uses more visuals; breaks down the activity into very small, achievable steps; and focuses on movement and rhythm instead of singing. In addition, she sees the class two times per week for 20 minutes each session, rather than 40 minutes one time per week, as in the general music classroom. The students are able to stay on task with appropriate behaviors for the shorter class period, making the adapted music class a successful educational experience for them. The focus of this class is still on music learning and active participation in music experiences, in preparation for future inclusive music experiences with same-aged peers. The teacher adapts the instruction to meet the behavioral, learning, and social needs of this small group of students. The teacher also makes sure that the materials used are age appropriate, making adaptations to complexity and instructional delivery when needed to compensate for the students' cognitive and learning styles.*

Teaching music in a self-contained classroom gives teachers the advantage of working with students with similar abilities and disabilities, focusing instruction to address the specific needs of the students, and teaching fewer students so that more attention and support can be offered to the students. A major disadvantage of the self-contained music classroom is that the students do not have opportunities to interact with peers who are not disabled. Experts disagree on the merits of the inclusive classroom versus the self-contained classroom (Adamek & Darrow, 2008).

Some experts promote the value of the inclusive setting for improved academic and social benefits, while other experts suggest that students with some types of disabilities can be better served in the smaller self-contained classroom with more individualized instruction (Darrow & Schunk, 2002). To compensate for this lack of peer interaction in a self-contained classroom, it is possible to provide social interaction and positive role models through a practice called reverse mainstreaming. In reverse mainstreaming, students from the general education class join students in the self-contained music class and actively participate with the students who have disabilities. This approach can be used to increase interactions between students with and without disabilities and to provide positive role models for students who have behavior problems or difficult classroom behaviors. Reverse mainstreaming can also be a good transition step as the student moves from the self-contained music class to the inclusive music class.

> Example: *Three students from Ms. Barnes' 2nd grade class join the weekly adapted music class in Ms. Stokley's room, which is a special education class for six 1st and 2nd grade students with severe cognitive and behavior problems. The students from the general education class are excellent role models for taking turns, passing instruments, playing the instruments correctly, and raising their hands. Ms. Stokely's students enjoy having these new peer buddies come to music each week, and they all enjoy the extra time provided for socializing together after music.*

In some instances, a student has music in a self-contained setting initially and is later moved to the inclusive music class as the student's behaviors or skills improve. The music educator or therapist who works with the student in the self-contained music class needs to communicate with the general education music teacher to determine the skills necessary for the student to succeed in the larger inclusive music setting. This communication is extremely important as the student is prepared to move to the less restricted environment of the inclusive music class. During a transition from a self-contained music class to an inclusive class, it is helpful to provide the student with both smaller, self-contained classes along with inclusive class experiences. The student can build some appropriate skills (music skills and behavioral skills) in the self-contained class and later practice those skills in the larger inclusive class.

> Example: *Tony has severe behavior problems and is educated primarily in a self-contained class with four other students with similar disabilities. Due to his behavioral problems, Tony has not been able to successfully participate in the 5th grade general music class. At the beginning of the school year, Tony attended adapted music class with the rest of the students in his special education classroom; however, his behaviors are improving and his teachers want him to begin participation in the inclusive general education classes. To prepare*

Tony for successful participation in the 5th grade music class, his music therapist (or possibly music educator) is teaching him some of the concepts and materials from the 5th grade curriculum, along with focusing on improved classroom behaviors and impulse control. Tony will have music skills and knowledge similar to the rest of the class when he attends the general education music class, which will improve his chances for appropriate behavior and success in the new environment.

Using Age-Appropriate Materials

Students with severe disabilities typically function developmentally far below the level of their same-aged peers. When working with students with severe disabilities, teachers may find it challenging to find materials that are appropriate to both the functioning level and the age level of the students. Music professionals should always use age-appropriate activities when planning music curriculum or interventions for students who have severe developmental delays, and they should use materials that are similar to those for same-aged peers (Adamek, 2001; Adamek & Darrow, 2008; Nevin, 1993). This can be a difficult task at first, but through creative lesson planning, music lessons that are functionally appropriate and age appropriate can be developed and facilitated. For instance, a 13-year-old student with intellectual disabilities might be functioning at the level of a 5-year-old. The adapted music teacher needs to develop music experiences that are within the functioning level of the student and also use music that is age appropriate and engaging for the student. Rather than using a preschool song to reinforce steady beat, the music teacher could use a recording of an African percussion group and have the student play a steady beat to the recording. This activity would reinforce the developmentally appropriate music skill of maintaining a steady beat while using music that is similar to that used with other students of the same age.

The use of age-appropriate music activities and materials allows students to function in a more normalized environment, an environment that is closer to that of students their same age who do not have disabilities. Many songs in our culture can be categorized as songs for preschool children or songs for young children. Just by hearing the melody of "Ring Around the Rosie," one immediately thinks of young children. If a music educator or music therapist changes the words to the song but uses that same melody, the song still has the connotation of an early childhood song and is not age appropriate for anyone older than early childhood. Music that does not evoke this type of association can be more age appropriate for older students with severe disabilities. World music, folk music, traditional music, and classical music are a few examples of music that can span the age ranges. This music can then provide an age-appropriate music foundation for the development of functionally appropriate music activities.

Some music educators have expressed concerns that they do not feel prepared to work with students who have severe disabilities due to limited training and experience (Darrow, 1999; Gfeller, Darrow, & Hedden, 1990; Gilbert & Asmus, 1981; Wilson & McCrary, 1996). These teachers might need additional training or consultation with a music therapist or other special education professional in order to increase their skills and work successfully in a self-contained or inclusive classroom with students who have disabilities.

Music Therapy as a Related Service

A student is eligible for special education services if he or she has a disability, and because of that disability, needs specially designed instruction in order to progress educationally (Turnbull et al., 2010). According to IDEA, this special education must consist of instruction specifically designed to meet the individual needs of a student with a disability.

Individualized Education

Each student who qualifies for special education is entitled to *individualized education* as an element of the required free and appropriate public education (FAPE). Although the definition of appropriate education has been interpreted in different ways, an appropriate education consists of instruction specifically designed for the student at no cost to the parents or guardians. This education may be delivered in the general education classroom, the special education classroom, or in a variety of settings including home, hospital, or institution, depending on the needs of the student.

Individualization is the key to providing appropriate education for a student in special education. When the team of school personnel and parents determines that a student is eligible for special education, the next step is to determine the necessary specific special education services and **related services** for the student. Related services are those services that are related to special education, but are not a typical part of the education setting. Related services are those services that are necessary to help the student

1. advance appropriately toward attaining the annual goals,
2. be involved and progress in the general education and to participate in extracurricular activities and other nonacademic activities, and
3. be educated and participate with other children with disabilities and nondisabled children in those extracurricular and nonacademic activities. (Turnbull & Turnbull, 1998, p. 151)

The law defines *related services* as

> *transportation, and such developmental, corrective, and other supportive services (including speech-language pathology and*

audiology services, interpreting services, psychological services, physical and occupational therapy, recreation, including therapeutic recreation, social work services, school nurse services designed to enable a child with a disability to receive a free appropriate public education as described in the individualized education program of the child, counseling services, including rehabilitation counseling, orientation and mobility services, and medical services, except that such medical services shall be for diagnostic and evaluation purposes only) as may be required to assist a child with a disability to benefit from special education, and includes the early identification and assessment of disabling conditions in children. (IDEA, 2004)

The listing of related services in IDEA is not meant to be an exhaustive list. IDEA lists some typical related services that could be required for a student to achieve educational benefits, but not all possible related services. Music therapy can be considered a related service (Bartlett et al., 2007). Although music therapy is not specifically mentioned in the listing of related services, the original notes that accompanied the law did cite music therapy as a possible related service (Wilson, 2002). These notes were removed when editorial revisions were made to IDEA 1997, apparently to streamline the document. Because the law does not currently list music therapy as a related service, some school districts interpret this to mean that music therapy does not qualify as a related service. This misinterpretation is clarified in a publication released in June 2010 by the U.S. Department of Education, which discusses IDEA 2004 and the provisions related to IEPs, evaluations and reevaluations. This document states:

The Department's long-standing interpretation is that the list of related services in the IDEA and the Part B regulations is not exhaustive and may include other developmental, corrective, or supportive services (such as artistic and cultural programs, art, music, and dance therapy), if they are required to assist a child with a disability to benefit from special education in order for the child to receive FAPE. (U.S. Department of Education, 2010)

The document goes on to say:

If a child's IEP Team determines that an artistic or cultural service such as music therapy is an appropriate related service for the child with a disability, that related service must be included in the child's IEP under the statement of special education, related services, and supplementary aids and services to be provided to the child or on behalf of the child. 34 CFR §300.320(a)(4). These services are to enable the child to advance appropriately toward attaining the annual goals, to be involved and make progress in the general education curriculum, and to participate in extracurricular and other nonacademic activities, and

*to be educated and participate with other children with and without
disabilities in those activities. 34 CFR §300.320(a)(4)(i)-(iii). If the
child's IEP specifies that an artistic or cultural service such as music
therapy is a related service for the child, that related service must be
provided at public expense and at no cost to the parents. 34 CFR
§§300.101 and 300.17. (U.S. Department of Education, 2010).*

Based on this interpretation of the law, it is clear that music therapy should be
considered as a viable related service for individual students.

IDEA mandates one of two types of individualized plans, namely the Individualized
Education Program (IEP) for students ages 3 through 21, and the Individual Family
Service Plan (IFSP) for students ages birth through 2. Related services, such as music
therapy, are added to the individualized plan when the team determines that the
particular related service is necessary for the student to benefit from special education.
This means that if a student is not making progress on IEP goals, or is making very
little progress, specific related services must be provided for the student. However,
it is important to keep in mind that "appropriate education" does not mean the "best
possible" education. If a student is making progress on IEP goals, one can conclude
the student is benefiting from an appropriate education. While it might be true that
the student could benefit even more from additional related services such as music
therapy or speech therapy, the school is not required to provide those services if
the student is currently progressing.

Team members must determine the specific related services that are required
for the student to receive benefit from special education. In order for music therapy
to be included on a student's IEP as a related service, a music therapy eligibility
assessment must be completed and must demonstrate that the student needs music
therapy in order to make progress on IEP goals. Based on the outcome of the
music therapy eligibility assessment, the IEP team will decide if music therapy will
be provided as a related service for the student, and, if so, how the services will
be delivered. Music therapy as a related service may be delivered to the student in
various ways including: (a) *direct service to the student,* usually in a one-on-one
setting but sometimes in a group setting; (b) *consult to the student,* working with
a student in a classroom setting and working with teachers to implement music
strategies targeting IEP goals; or (c) *a combination of direct service and consult
services* (Brunk & Coleman, 2002).

Eligibility Assessment for Music Therapy as a Related Service

Nondiscriminatory Evaluation

Another one of the six IDEA principles is the need for *nondiscriminatory
evaluation* (fair and unbiased evaluation) of students. The purpose of the
nondiscriminatory evaluation is first to determine if a student has a disability, and,
second, to decide the nature of appropriate and necessary special education and

related services. IDEA has guidelines for nondiscriminatory evaluations (see Figure 6.2) that are important for music therapists to be aware of when conducting music therapy assessments (Overton, 2003).

Music therapy as a related service can be included on a student's IEP after the team has decided that the student needs music therapy to benefit from his or her special education. In order to make that determination, a music therapist must complete a thorough assessment of the student to ascertain if music therapy services will likely promote significant progress on the student's IEP goals.

Figure 6.2 IDEA Guidelines for Nondiscriminatory Evaluation for Services

---

- Nondiscriminatory evaluation occurs before the beginning of services.
- Parents must be notified and provide written consent before a student is evaluated or reevaluated.
- Students must be reevaluated every three years or more frequently, if requested by parents or teacher, or if the situation warrants reevaluation.
- Qualified professionals must complete the evaluation process related to the specific area of expertise (i.e., only a qualified music therapist must complete a music therapy assessment).
- If parents disagree with the outcome of the school's evaluation, the parents have a right to an evaluation by an outside, independent evaluator.
- Parents are entitled to a written justification from the school if their request for an evaluation is refused.

Types of Assessment in Music Therapy

Music therapists in schools work with a diverse population of students with special needs. Students' skills, abilities, and needs related to cognitive, communication, physical, social, and emotional domains could be extremely varied depending on the individual's type of disability, the severity of the disability, and the number of disabilities. Some students have strong cognitive skills but severe deficits in physical or social skills. Other students may have strong physical skills but lack a useful communication system. Any number of possibilities may exist. The music therapy assessment will focus on skills in any of these domains related to the student's educational needs that could be enhanced through music interventions.

Music therapy assessments are conducted with individuals for a variety of reasons. Some assessments evaluate a child's development in motor, affective, social, cognitive, and communication domains through participation in music activities (Boxill, 1985). Other assessments use music tasks to determine a child's cognitive level of functioning (Rider, 1981) or use music interventions to evaluate a child's skills and adaptive abilities (Grant, 1995). Some music therapy assessment procedures integrate standardized assessment information from other disciplines for a particular purpose, such as evaluating language development (Gfeller & Baumann, 1988). Typically, these types of music therapy assessments are used to determine the student's current level of functioning in order to develop an appropriate music therapy treatment approach for general music therapy services. When music therapy is being considered as a related service, a more specific music therapy eligibility assessment based on the student's IEP goals will be developed and facilitated by a qualified music therapist.

The decision to offer music therapy services in educational settings is made one of two ways. First, music therapy can be listed on the IEP as a related service, determined by the IEP team to be a necessary service. For this to happen, a music therapy eligibility assessment must be completed to determine whether the student requires music therapy services in order to make progress on IEP goals and objectives. An eligibility assessment must be completed by a qualified music therapist and presented to the IEP team for discussion and a decision whether to provide the student with music therapy services. In this scenario, each student who is referred for a music therapy assessment is assessed individually. The purpose of this type of music therapy assessment is to demonstrate to the team how well a student performs on IEP goals with the assist of music interventions compared to the student's performance on IEP goals without music interventions. Based on the outcome of the assessment, the IEP team will decide whether music therapy should be provided as a related service. If the IEP team agrees that music interventions appear to be necessary for the student to progress on IEP goals and objectives, music therapy should be added to the student's IEP as a related service.

In a different scenario, a school district could decide to provide music therapy services to students with disabilities to enhance their development and support their educational progress. This is sometimes referred to as a district-wide model, where the music therapist works with several students throughout the district on general educational goals and objectives. Frequently students in entire special education classrooms or special education programs receive music therapy services throughout the school year. In this situation, a music therapist is not required to complete eligibility assessments on the students. Eligibility to receive music therapy services is determined by the district or school administrators and is not listed on the students' IEPs as a related service. The music therapist will assess the students' current levels of functioning in order to develop appropriate interventions and document changes, but will not utilize an eligibility assessment to determine need for services.

Special Education Music Therapy Assessment Process (SEMTAP)

The first step in determining eligibility for music therapy as a related service is the referral. Any member of the IEP team may request that a music therapist complete an assessment process to determine if music therapy services should be provided as a related service. While many students might benefit from music therapy services, not all students are eligible for music therapy as a related service. Students who are making progress on their IEP goals and objectives would not be referred for a music therapy assessment. However, a student who is not making progress on goals and objectives could be a candidate for a music therapy assessment. If the student seems to be highly interested in music, motivated by and attentive to sound and music, or interested in rhythm and/or songs, a music therapy assessment might be appropriate. Brunk and Coleman (2000) have identified several questions that might help determine if a music therapy assessment is appropriate for a student (see Figure 6.3).

Figure 6.3 Questions One Might Ask to Help Determine if a Music Therapy Assessment is Appropriate (Brunk & Coleman, 2000)

- Is the student motivated to begin or complete tasks through the use of music?
- Is music a favored activity or subject? Does the student focus attention on music-type tasks longer than non-music tasks?
- Would an additional means of communication benefit the student?
- Does the student initiate activities using music or musical instruments at school or at home?
- Does the student retain information presented in a song better than information presented without the use of a song?

When music therapy is being considered as a related service for a student, the IEP team will decide if a music therapy assessment is appropriate for the student, and, if so, a qualified music therapist will complete an individual assessment. The purpose of this assessment is to determine if the student performs significantly better on IEP goals and objectives when responses to music therapy strategies are compared to responses to non-music based strategies. Brunk and Coleman (2002) developed an individualized music therapy assessment process that helps music therapists determine if music therapy is necessary for the student to make progress on educational goals and objectives. This assessment process is called the Special Education Music Therapy Assessment Process (SEMTAP) and is designed to provide specific information to the IEP team. The music therapist using the SEMTAP compares a student's performance related to IEP goals and objectives with and without the use of music therapy interventions, makes a recommendation for services, and justifies the recommendation with documentation of quantitative and qualitative information. Music therapy will be added to the IEP as a related service if, based on the outcome of the assessment, the team decides that music therapy is a necessary service for the student to benefit from special education.

When utilizing an assessment process such as the SEMTAP, the music therapist will evaluate the student's responses to tasks related to the IEP goals and objectives both with and without music interventions. Since the assessment process is based on each student's IEP, the music therapist must develop specific music therapy interventions to address the student's objectives. For instance, David is a student with cognitive deficits who has an IEP objective to count to 10 with a 1 to 1 correspondence, which means the student can count 1 to 10 items correctly (e.g., there are three drums and the student can count the drums, "1, 2, 3"; or the student can play the drum five times and count or respond to the numbers "1, 2, 3, 4, 5"). The music therapist will create a music activity to work on this counting skill, and then compare David's response on the music-based counting activity to a non-music-based counting activity. Since not all students have the same IEP goals and objectives, the music therapist must create appropriate music interventions for each student based on the individual's IEP.

Brunk and Coleman (2002) describe the steps contained in the SEMTAP, which include:

1.   The formal request for assessment
2.   The music therapy assessment process
   a.   review of documentation
   b.   interviews
   c.   observation in a non-musical setting
   d.   preparation of the assessment
   e.   administration of the assessment
   f.   preparation of the assessment report and documentation
3.   Presentation of the report and recommendations (p. 73)

Music Therapy Assessment Process

Any member of the IEP team, including parents, can make **a formal request for a music therapy assessment** either during the annual IEP meeting or at a specially called IEP meeting to address the needs of the student. This is a request only for a music therapy assessment, not for music therapy services. The school district will provide music therapy as a related service only after a music therapy assessment has been completed and the IEP team decides that music therapy is necessary for the student to benefit from special education. If a parent makes a formal request for a music therapy assessment and the school denies this request, the parents have the right to receive a written, detailed justification for the denial. If the request for a music therapy assessment is granted, there are several steps involved in the assessment process. These steps will be briefly outlined here, but for a more detailed explanation of the assessment process, see Brunk and Coleman (2002) and Bradfield, Carlenius, Gold, and White (2007).

The music therapy **assessment process** is a multi-step approach that involves gathering information from many areas related to the individual student, developing and facilitating a music therapy assessment, documenting responses, and developing an assessment report to present to the IEP team.

Gather Information: This assessment process involves a focus on the student's IEP goals and objectives, so the first step is to gather information about the student. The music therapist should review the student's IEP and any other records to determine the student's current level of functioning and IEP goals and objectives. It is important to follow the confidentiality procedures for the school and receive permission to review confidential files. After reviewing the IEP, the music therapist should interview members of the IEP team to determine the areas of the IEP where the student is not making progress. Information can come from parents, classroom, and special education teachers, speech therapists, and any other professionals who work with the student. The music therapist can also find out why a music therapy assessment was requested and what particular behaviors of the student seem to be influenced by music. Based on the information gathered from the reports and interviews, the music therapist should choose a limited number of objectives that could be addressed in music therapy, making sure the objectives are observable and measurable. Usually four to six objectives can be addressed in a one- or two-session assessment period. The music therapist should choose objectives carefully so the objectives are ones that can be readily addressed via music therapy interventions (i.e., objectives related to academic skills, movement, imitation, following directions, focusing attention to task, communication skills, sharing, making choices, etc.).

Now that the targeted IEP objectives are chosen, the music therapist should schedule a time with the teacher to observe the student working on those objectives in a non-music setting such as the classroom or resource room. Observations should be thoroughly documented via explicit notes, audio recording, or video recording to ensure adequate information for comparison of response.

Develop, Facilitate, and Document Assessment Procedure: The music therapist creates a music therapy session plan to address the specific IEP objectives that can be completed within one or two individual music therapy sessions. If an objective is related to interacting with peers in a group, one session might be in a small group setting in order to focus on that objective. Music-based interventions must be directly related to the specific IEP objectives and give the student an opportunity to respond in a way that is observable and can be documented. After all of the information is gathered (through reading files, interviewing, and conducting assessment), the therapist writes a report that documents all of the steps involved in the assessment process. The report should contain information such as the purposes of the assessment, documentation of the student's responses to IEP objectives in both settings, and recommendations for music therapy services (Brunk & Coleman, 2002).

Presentation of Assessment Outcome and Recommendations for Services: Upon completion of the music therapy assessment, the IEP team will hold a meeting to learn about and discuss the assessment results. The music therapist who completed the assessment should be present at the meeting to explain in detail the responses of the student in the various settings and to justify the recommendations on the assessment report. If the music therapist determines that the student received a considerable assist or motivation from music therapy interventions, a recommendation for music therapy services might be made to the IEP team. The music therapist must be able to justify the recommendation with documented information about the assessment process and the student's responses.

If music therapy as a related service is recommended, the music therapy service could be in the form of direct service, consultation service, or a combination of both direct and consultation services. If music therapy does not appear to make a difference in student responses, and the student does not seem to benefit from music-based interventions, music therapy as a related service will not be recommended. See Figure 6.4 for more information regarding the assessment outcomes and recommendations.

Figure 6.4 Potential Recommendations Following a Music Therapy Assessment

---

Direct music therapy service
- Assessment findings: Music therapy provides a considerable assist for the student to make progress on IEP goals.
- Music therapist provides music therapy services directly with the student, usually in a pull-out, one-to-one setting.
- Goals are taken directly from the IEP; schedule and number of sessions are determined by the team.

Consult to student service
- Assessment findings: Music therapy assists student when involved in classroom activities (such as working with peers, sharing, completing tasks).
- Music therapist provides services to the student within the classroom or in other therapy settings (speech therapy, occupational therapy) and offers suggestions to teachers on how to implement music-based interventions throughout the school day.
- Goals are taken directly from the IEP; schedule and number of times the music therapist works with the student and teacher are determined by the team.

Combination of direct service and consult to student service
- Assessment findings: Music therapy assists the student on IEP goals individually and when involved in classroom activities.
- Music therapist provides both individual 1-to-1 music therapy with the student as well as works with the student in the classroom and with the teachers.
- Goals are taken directly from the IEP; schedule and number of times the music therapist works with the student and teacher are determined by the team.

No music therapy services
- Assessment findings: When comparing responses to music-based and non-music-based interventions, there was not a difference between the student's responses. Music therapy did not significantly assist the student to make progress on IEP objectives.

Additional Suggestions: The music therapist may also offer additional suggestions for including music in the student's life in the home, community, or extracurricular school music experiences. These suggestions could be made regardless of the outcome of the music therapy assessment and related services recommendations. The music therapist might recommend private music therapy sessions, adapted music lessons, participation in an inclusive community choir or in a community choir for persons with disabilities, participation in a community-based percussion group, or other music experiences that could benefit the student in some way. The school district would not be required to pay for these services; however, the school staff might assist the parents in getting the student involved in various additional music activities. When music therapy is listed on the student's IEP as a related service, the music therapist works on goals taken directly from the student's IEP. New goals can be added to the IEP if the team determines that is appropriate and necessary for the education of the student. If the student's parents choose to engage the student in additional music therapy outside of the school setting (a service for which the school would not be required to pay), the music therapist in that setting could work with the student on additional goals that are not on the IEP in a non-school setting.

> Example of music therapy as a direct service: *Upon completion of a music therapy eligibility assessment and recommendations from the music therapist, the IEP team agreed that music therapy as a related service should be provided for Dane, a student with autism. The team decided that the music therapist should provide direct service, one-to-one with Dane, two times per week for 30 minutes each session. The music therapist develops session plans based on Dane's IEP goals, including increasing communication skills and improving classroom behaviors. Dane engages in music therapy activities with the therapist in order to acquire and develop skills in these specific areas.*

> Example of music therapy as a consult to student: *Upon completion of a music therapy eligibility assessment and recommendations from the music therapist, the IEP team decided that Shawna should have music therapy as a related service, provided as a consult to the student. Shawna has severe behavior problems and needs additional practice on appropriate social interaction and cooperation with peers. The music therapist works with the classroom teacher to develop music-based activities based on Shawna's IEP goals. These activities are created to help Shawna practice appropriate social behaviors in class. The music therapist is scheduled to co-teach a small group of students (including Shawna) with the classroom teacher two times per month. In addition, the music therapist creates music-based activities to promote appropriate social interaction that the classroom teacher can facilitate throughout the week.*

Example of combined direct service and consult service: *Based on the outcome of the music therapy eligibility assessment, the IEP team determined that Jessie should receive music therapy as a related service. Due to Jessie's positive response to music therapy and her minimal response to other forms of instruction, the team recommended weekly one-to-one direct service sessions with the music therapist. In addition, the music therapist was scheduled to meet monthly with the classroom teacher to provide consult services. These consult services were deemed necessary to support the student in class during non-music therapy times. The music therapist facilitated one-to-one sessions based on Jessie's IEP goals and worked with the teacher each month to help her utilize music activities to enhance Jessie's response to instruction.*

Music educators who work with students in an inclusive setting are in a unique position to observe individual students' responses to music. When a student seems to be highly motivated by music or demonstrates significant assistance in learning from a music stimuli, the music educator can recommend to the IEP team that music therapy as a related service be considered for the student. In some situations, the music educator might have to educate the IEP team about the benefits of music therapy in an educational setting and the differences between music education and music therapy. This valuable information can help expand the educational options for students who have unmet educational needs (Patterson, 2003).

The music therapist needs to be aware of the fact that the school district or even some IEP team members might oppose the addition of music therapy as a related service for students in special education. One must remember that if a related service is found to be necessary for a student to make progress on IEP goals, the school is legally bound to provide (and pay for) those specific related services. Most schools are reticent to pay for any extra services for a student, not because they do not care about what is best for each student, but because educational budgets are usually tight and funds are limited. With a thorough and well-documented assessment, the music therapist has to be able to justify a recommendation for music therapy as a related service. Many times the music therapist must educate members of the team to inform them of the benefits of music therapy services in an education setting. In a district or school where music therapy is not currently being provided as a related service, the music therapist can use the assessment report as an educational tool to inform team members and school officials of the valid role of music therapy in special education (Brunk & Coleman, 2002).

Music Therapy in District-Wide Special Education Setting

Music therapy is provided in many school districts as a comprehensive special service available to students who are served in special education. A district-wide music therapy program stems from the school's mission to provide services that facilitate educational progress for students who have disabilities. In this type of model, students from early childhood through high school can benefit from music therapy services to enhance academic, social, communication, physical, and behavioral development. Funding for these services is usually from a combination of federal, state, and local funds distributed for special education services.

Music therapists in district-wide programs usually provide services to a large number of students in several schools throughout the district. These services are not generally mandated on students' IEPs unless the music therapy is also provided as a related service. In this model, the music therapist develops goals and objectives for groups of students based on their pre-existing IEP goals, and then uses the music therapy interventions to help all of the students progress on educational goals. Typical goal areas might be to improve language development for students with communication deficits, to increase academic skills and readiness for at-risk preschool students, or to improve behavior for students with challenging classroom behaviors. It is likely that the music therapist will collaborate on goals and objectives with music educators, general education teachers, special education teachers, speech and language pathologists, and occupational and physical therapists to provide the most appropriate educational interventions for the students.

Although a music therapy eligibility assessment is not required for services in a district-wide program model, assessments are still an important part of the educational process. The purpose of music therapy assessments in a district-wide model is to determine students' current level of functioning related to educational needs and to use that information for planning and implementing services and for evaluating and documenting students' progress. Students' progress can be documented informally through reports to the IEP team and through general progress reports to teachers and parents. Formal progress reports are usually completed at variable intervals, from quarterly to yearly, depending on the district guidelines for student evaluations.

The role of the music therapist in a district-wide model may be all-inclusive. The music therapist could teach or co-teach in a music education inclusive classroom, teach adapted music or facilitate music therapy sessions in a self-contained classroom, work with individual students who have music therapy as a related service on their IEP, consult with teachers about including music into the curriculum, and work on inclusive community events involving music participation and performance (Hughes et al., 2002). These specific responsibilities might change from year to year depending on the variable needs of the students in the district and the type of programs that are offered in the school and community. School administrators and team members will usually work with the music therapist to establish the job responsibilities and expectations for the music therapist in a district-wide program.

> Example: *Joan is a music therapist in a school district in central Minnesota. Throughout the week, she travels to 8 different schools to provide music therapy services across the continuum of special*

*education programs in the district. On Monday and Tuesday, she works
with students with severe disabilities, teaching music skills and working
on non-music functional skills such as improved behavior and attention
to task. On Wednesday, she works with students who are included in
the regular music class to remediate their music and behavior skills
in order to be successful in the class. On Thursday and Friday, she
works one-to-one with students who have music therapy on the IEP
as a related service, completes eligibility assessments for students who
have been referred for a music therapy assessment, and consults with
district teachers to help them utilize music in the classroom.*

Music Therapist as a Consultant to Music Education, General Education, and Special Education Teachers

Music therapists have special training related to the needs of students with
disabilities in school music settings. They have knowledge and experience in making
accommodations to help students succeed in the music class, including adapting
instructional methods and managing difficult student behaviors. Frequently, music
therapists act as **consultants to music educators** who are looking for effective ways
to include a student in the general music class, band, choir, or any other music
experience (Patterson, 2003). As a consultant, the music therapist works with
the teachers to develop strategies for (a) adapting music materials, curriculum,
or equipment to meet the specific needs of a student; (b) behavior management
and improved participation of students with difficult behaviors; (c) improved social
integration among students with disabilities and students without disabilities; and
(d) collaboration with other teachers to improve flow of communication related to
students with disabilities.

The music therapist will first meet with the teacher to gather information about
the student and to learn about what instructional approaches have already been used
with the student. Then, if possible, the therapist will observe the student in the music
setting and develop alternative instructional or behavioral interventions. Since there
are many ways to make instructional adaptations, the music therapist should offer a
variety of practical ideas that could be implemented by the music educator to help
the student achieve success in the music class.

In addition to serving as a general consultant to music educators, the music
therapist can serve as an **inclusion facilitator for music education programs**
(Darrow, 1999). A music therapist in this role might have some of the following
responsibilities:

1. Schedule consultation appointments with teachers to discuss placement
    issues
2. Disseminate selected pertinent IEP information to music educators

3. Provide in-service training for music educators and paraprofessional staff concerning:
   a. Making adaptations in the music classroom (instructional strategies and materials)
   b. Problem solving for difficult situations
   c. Classroom management procedures
   d. Appropriate and useful music materials for instruction
4. Provide assistance to music educators in the classroom

Successful inclusion in the music classroom does not just happen; it needs to be facilitated by trained, effective, and dedicated professionals. Music therapists can provide an important service to support and train music educators in their role to teach students having a wide range of disabilities. The role of the music educator continues to evolve as more students with disabilities are educated in the general education classroom. Through collaborative efforts between music educators and music therapists, students with disabilities can experience success in the many facets of music education.

Example: *Andy works as a music therapist in a school district in Louisiana. In addition to his work directly with students, he is frequently called upon to serve as a consultant to music educators who need assistance with students who have disabilities. About once a month, the band or choir director asks Andy to observe a rehearsal and recommend adaptations or ideas for partial participation that would be appropriate for a student. In preparation for the spring choral concert, the choir director asked for help including a student with autism (J.) who loves music but does not sing. This student was very rhythmical and could play a solid steady beat. Andy suggested that the student be given a percussion part to play during certain sections of one piece on the program. The director found a peer buddy to help J. with his part during rehearsals. J. performed his part with the song on the spring concert, and sat quietly listening during the other songs.*

Andy is frequently asked to assist the general music teacher who teaches students with severe disabilities. He observes the students in music class and makes suggestions for implementing UDL principles and for adapting the curriculum, activities, or materials to support the students' learning.

Music therapists can also serve as **consultants to general education and special education classroom teachers** who are interested in incorporating instructional interventions that include music. Therapists can provide (a) music resources such as songs and recordings to teach and reinforce academic skills, (b) ideas for using music activities to build social or cooperative skills, (c) music activities to serve as reinforcement for student learning, and (d) other music related ideas to enhance students' success in the classroom.

Just as the job descriptions for music educators and music therapists vary from state to state, educational policies and rules for certification of professionals also vary. Some states or school districts require that music therapists have a valid state teaching license along with music therapy credentials to work in the schools. Other states or school districts require only that music therapists have an approved credential of the profession, which is either the MT-BC (Music Therapist-Board Certified), the RMT (Registered Music Therapist), or the CMT (Certified Music Therapist). Smith and Hairston (1999) found that of those school music therapists who responded to their survey, approximately 40% were required to have a valid state teaching license for employment. Requirements for specific professional credentials may also depend on the role of the music therapist in the school. If a music therapist is teaching full inclusion music education classes, then it is likely that he or she would be required to have a teaching license in addition to certification in music therapy. However, a music therapist who is primarily servicing students who have music therapy listed as a related service on the IEP would not necessarily need teacher licensure. School administrators need to understand the differences between music education and music therapy in order to determine the appropriate professional designation (teaching license and/or music therapy credential) for employment.

Experienced music professionals may have a wide range of beliefs about the most appropriate and effective music education practices for students with special needs in schools. The following issues and ideas are important to remember when working with all students in today's schools:

1. The fundamental importance of understanding child development in context, as a basis for understanding the identification of special education needs
2. The value of knowing that you do not know everything, and believing that change is possible
3. The need to communicate understanding and resolve differences between the people who have useful knowledge
4. The need to recognize the school as a site for the development of teaching expertise and the creation of knowledge. (Kershner, 2007, pp. 494–496)

Over 30 years ago, Alley (1977) stated that if music therapy is to be considered and accepted as an educational discipline, then music therapy services must be "(1) unique enough to be viewed as complementary to, but not overlapping with, standard educational disciplines; (2) specific to educational objectives communicated in educational jargon; (3) accountable for pupil progress; and (4) competitive for available funding resources" (p. 50). These factors remain important today when providing music therapy in the schools, and, in particular, music therapy as a related service. A thorough music therapy assessment, completed by a qualified music therapist, is one way to demonstrate the value of music therapy as an educational discipline for students with disabilities.

Summary

IDEA requires that students are educated in the most normalized and least restrictive environment (LRE). Students with disabilities should be educated together with students who do not have disabilities, to the maximum extent appropriate for the students. In order to determine the most appropriate educational setting for students, school personnel need to consider the educational benefits and social benefits for the student with disabilities, the effect of the placement on the classroom milieu, and the costs involved. An appropriate educational environment is one in which the student with disabilities is able to make meaningful progress on IEP goals. This means that the LRE may vary from one student to the next, depending on the individual needs of each student.

The U.S. Supreme Court interpreted IDEA as giving students the right to an *appropriate* education, but *not necessarily the best* education possible. This interpretation of the law, sometimes referred to as the benefit standard, means that a student is not receiving an appropriate education if he or she is regressing or making only minimal progress. The students must benefit from their special education, as demonstrated by making progress on IEP goals. The amendments to IDEA emphasize the importance of students' progress toward annual goals and ongoing reporting to parents about the students' progress (Turnbull et al., 2010). Even though the music therapist might think that the student could make even better progress on IEP objectives with music therapy, if the student is making educational progress without music therapy (i.e., the student is benefiting from special education), then music therapy as a related service would not be recommended.

IDEA provides the framework from which services to students with disabilities are delivered. Depending on the needs and abilities of the students, music experiences in school can range from an inclusive music education setting to self-contained music education or music therapy, to one-on-one music therapy as a related service. Collaboration is one key factor that contributes to effective teaching and learning. Music educators and music therapists have many different opportunities to work together to enhance the education of all students in the music setting.

KEY POINTS FROM THE CHAPTER

Roles of music educators and music therapists in schools:
♦ Music education and music therapy are distinct disciplines and professions, yet there is potential for collaboration between music educators and music therapists working in schools.

♦ Music educators may teach students with disabilities in the inclusive music classroom (or performance group) or in a self-contained adapted music class.

♦ Music therapists may co-teach with a music educator in a music class, work with students with disabilities in a self-contained classroom, facilitate group music therapy in a district-wide programmatic model, or provide music therapy as a related service for students who need music therapy to progress on their educational goals.

♦ Music therapists may also serve as consultants to music educators to help them successfully include students with disabilities into the music class. Music therapists may also consult with other teachers to help them use music in the class to enhance learning or improve behaviors.

♦ In order for a student to have music therapy as a related service listed on the IEP, a qualified music therapist must facilitate an eligibility assessment and present the recommendations to the IEP team for a decision for services.

Eligibility assessments for music therapy as a related service:
♦ A music therapy eligibility assessment may be requested to determine if a student needs music therapy to benefit from special education.

♦ A qualified professional (music therapist) must complete this assessment.

♦ The Special Education Music Therapy Assessment Process (SEMTAP) is one assessment that can be used to determine if a student should be eligible for music therapy as a related service.

♦ A student may receive music therapy as a related service in a direct service or consultative model, or a combination of the two.

Ideas to enhance instruction in a self-contained or inclusive setting:
♦ Structured cooperative learning experiences in the music class can be used to facilitate instruction and increase interactions among students in the class.

♦ Students with severe disabilities typically function below the developmental level of their peers. Music educators and therapists should strive to use materials that are appropriate to the age and functioning level of the students.

♦ Music therapists can facilitate inclusion for music education programs by assisting with appropriate placement decisions, adapting instructional strategies and materials, and providing assistance to music educators when needed.

REFERENCES

Adamek, M. (2001). Meeting special needs in music class. *Music Educators Journal, 87*(4), 23–26.

Adamek, M., & Darrow, A. A. (2008). Music therapy in special education. In W. Davis, K. Gfeller, & M. Thaut (Eds.), *An introduction to music therapy theory and practice* (3rd ed., pp. 405–426). Silver Spring, MD: American Music Therapy Association.

Alley, J. M. (1977). Education for the severely handicapped: The role of music therapy. *Journal of Music Therapy, 14*, 50–59.

Bartlett, L. Etscheidt, S., & Weisenstein, G. (2007). *Special education law and practice in public schools* (2nd ed.). Upper Saddle River, NJ: Pearson.

Boxill, E. H. (1985). *Music therapy for the developmentally disabled.* Rockville, MD: Aspen Press.

Bradfield, C., Carlenius, J., Gold, C., & White, M. (2007). *MT-SEAS: Music Therapy Special Education Assessment Scale manual.* Grapevine, TX: Prelude Music.

Brunk, B., & Coleman, K. (2000). Development of a special education music therapy assessment process. *Music Therapy Perspectives, 18*, 59–68.

Brunk, B., & Coleman, K. (2002). A special education music therapy assessment process. In B. Wilson (Ed.), *Models of music therapy interventions in school settings* (2nd ed., pp. 69–82). Silver Spring, MD: American Music Therapy Association.

Darrow, A. A. (1999). Music educators' perceptions regarding the inclusion of students with severe disabilities in music classrooms. *Journal of Music Therapy, 36*, 254–273.

Darrow, A. A., & Schunk, H. (2002). Music therapy for learners who are deaf/hard-of-hearing. In B. Wilson (Ed.), *Models of music therapy interventions in school settings* (2nd ed., pp. 291–318). Silver Spring, MD: American Music Therapy Association.

Gfeller, K., & Baumann, A. A. (1988). Assessment procedures for music therapy with hearing impaired children: Language development. *Journal of Music Therapy, 25*, 192–205.

Gfeller, K., Darrow, A. A., & Hedden, S. (1990). The perceived effectiveness of mainstreaming in Iowa and Kansas schools. *Journal of Research in Music Education, 38*, 90–101.

Gilbert, J., & Asmus, E. P. (1981). Mainstreaming: Music educators' participation and professional needs. *Journal of Research in Music Education, 29*, 283–289.

Grant, R. E. (1995). Music therapy assessment for developmentally disabled clients. In T. Wigram, B. Saperston, & R. West (Eds.), *The art and science of music therapy: A handbook.* Switzerland: Harwood Academic.

Hughes, J., Rice, B., DeBedout, J., & Hightower, L. (2002). Music therapy for learners in comprehensive public school systems: Three district-wide models. In B. Wilson (Ed.), *Models of music therapy interventions in school settings* (2nd ed., pp. 319–368). Silver Spring, MD: American Music Therapy Association.

Humpal, M. (1991). The effects of an integrated early childhood music program on social interaction among children with handicaps and their typical peers. *Journal of Music Therapy, 28*, 161–177.

Individuals with Disabilities Education Improvement Act of 2004, 20 U.S.C. § 1400 *et seq.* (1990). (Session law # P.L. 101-476).

Jellison, J., Brooks, B., & Huck, A. (1984). Structuring small groups and music reinforcement to facilitate positive interactions and acceptance of severely handicapped students in the regular music classroom. *Journal of Research in Music Education, 32*, 228–247.

Jellison, J., & Gainer, E. (1995). Into the mainstream: A case study of a child's participation in music education and music therapy. *Journal of Music Therapy, 32*, 228–247.

Johnson, D. W., Johnson, R. T., & Holubec, E. J. (1991). *Cooperation in the classroom.* Edina, MN: Interaction Book Company.

Kershner, R. (2007). What do teachers need to know about meeting special educational needs? In L. Florian (Ed.), *The Sage handbook of special education* (pp. 486–498). Thousand Oaks, CA: Sage.

Kostka, M. (1993). A comparison of selected behaviors of a student with autism in special education and regular music class. *Music Therapy Perspectives, 11*, 57–60.

McCord, K., & Watts, E. (2006). Collaboration and access for our children: Music educators and special educators together. *Music Educators Journal, 92*(4), 26–33.

Mitchell, D. (2008). *What really works in special and inclusive education.* New York: Routledge.

Music Educators National Conference. (1994). *National standards for music education.* Reston, VA: Author.

Nevin, A. (1993). Curricular and instructional adaptations for including students with disabilities in cooperative groups. In J. Putnam (Ed.), *Cooperative learning and strategies for inclusion.* Baltimore: Paul H. Brooks.

Overton, T. (2003). *Assessing learners with special needs: An applied approach* (4th ed.). Columbus, OH: Merrill Prentice Hall.

Patterson, A. (2003). Music teachers and music therapists: Helping children together. *Music Educators Journal, 89*(4), 35–38.

Putnam, J. (1993). The process of cooperative learning. In J. Putnam (Ed.), *Cooperative learning and strategies for inclusion.* Baltimore: Paul H. Brooks.

Richards, D., & Martin, J. (2006). *2006 IDEA final Part B regulations: What you need to know.* Danvers, MA: LRP Publications.

Rider, M. (1981). The assessment of cognitive functioning level through musical perception. *Journal of Music Therapy, 18,* 110–119.

Smith, D. S., & Hairston, M. J. (1999). Music therapy in school settings: Current practice. *Journal of Music Therapy, 36,* 274–292.

Thousand, J., Nevin, A., & Villa, R. (2007). Collaborative teaching: Critique of the scientific evidence. In L. Florian (Ed.), *The Sage handbook of special education* (pp. 417–428). Thousand Oaks, CA: Sage.

Turnbull, R., & Turnbull, A. (1998). *Free appropriate public education: The law and children with disabilities* (5th ed.). Denver, CO: Love.

Turnbull, A., Turnbull, R., & Wehmeyer, M. (2010). *Exceptional lives: Special education in today's schools* (6th ed.). Upper Saddle River, NJ: Merrill.

U.S. Department of Education. (2010). *Questions and Answers on Individualized Education Programs (IEPs), Evaluations, and Reevaluations.* Retrieved August 9, 2010, from http://idea.ed.gov/explore/home

Wilson, B. (2002). Changing times: The evolution of special education. In B. Wilson (Ed.), *Models of music therapy interventions in school settings* (2nd ed., pp. 25–40). Silver Spring, MD: American Music Therapy Association.

Wilson, B., & McCrary, J. (1996). The effect of instruction on music educators' attitudes toward students with disabilities. *Journal of Research in Music Education, 44,* 26–33.

Part II

Students with Specific Disabilities:
Characteristics, Music Education, and
Music Therapy Services

Chapter 7

Students with Behavior Disorders

CHAPTER OVERVIEW

Most teachers will report that managing students with behavior disorders is the greatest barrier to effective classroom instruction. Students with behavior disorders are generally unhappy individuals, and they are often successful at making everyone around them unhappy as well. They are generally disliked by their peers, their teachers, their siblings, and often even their parents. In addition to their challenging behaviors, these students are frequently diagnosed with accompanying disorders—such as learning disabilities, attention deficit and hyperactivity disorders, depression, and suicidal tendencies (Stahl & Clarizio, 1999). Even though music is a highly desirable activity for most students, music educators have indicated that students with behavior disorders are the most difficult to mainstream in the music classroom (Darrow, 1999). Unfortunately, students with behavior disorders are often seen simply as troubled students vying for attention, and not as students with a disability who are deserving of the same educational provisions as students with physical, cognitive, or sensory disabilities.

There is no doubt that students with behavior disorders present significant challenges to their teachers and peers. They typically exhibit unacceptable patterns of behavior, are nonconforming to the norms of the classroom, and often make the learning environment unproductive for other students. To make the problem worse, teachers often have misguided expectations of students with behavior disorders. Students who are blind are not expected to see when they enter the classroom, and students who are deaf are not expected to hear when they enter the classroom. However, teachers often expect students with a behavior disorder to suppress their disability and "behave" when they enter the classroom. These students, like most students with disabilities, require instructional interventions to manage their disability and to assist them in becoming educated and sociable adults.

This chapter includes information on the following topics:
+ Definition and classification of behavior disorders
+ Causes of behavior disorders
+ Effects of behavior disorders
+ Identification and assessment of behavior disorders
+ Intervention approaches for students with behavior disorders and ADHD
+ Music education for students with behavior disorders and ADHD
+ Music therapy for students with behavior disorders and ADHD

Definition and Classification of Behavior Disorders

Estimates of the prevalence of behavior disorders range from 8% to as high as 20%, with boys outnumbering girls 5 to 1 (U.S. Department of Education, 2009). The definition of these disorders, like many disability definitions, has been the source of debate and controversy. A standardized definition of behavior disorders is difficult for a number of reasons. First, and most importantly, behavior is a social construct, and there is no clear consensus on what constitutes good or bad behavior. What is considered acceptable behavior is quite different, in certain situations, for different authority figures or across various cultural or ethnic groups. There are, however, three criteria that must be met in order for a student's behavior to be considered disordered (Heward, 2008):

1.   *Chronicity:* The behavior must be exhibited over a period of time.
2.   *Severity:* The behavior must be extreme and outside the bounds of typical behavior.
3.   *Pervasiveness:* The behavior must be present across school settings and adversely affect school performance.

The terms *emotional disturbances* and *behavioral disorders* are often used interchangeably to refer to students whose behaviors depart significantly from the norm. Though IDEA still uses the term *emotional disturbance,* some special educators prefer the term *behavioral disorders* (Turnbull, Turnbull, & Wehmeyer, 2010). The term emotional disturbance has been criticized by many professionals in the field of special education because of its negative connotation, and because teachers often view students with the label as less susceptible to change than students who are considered behavior disordered (Kauffman & Landrum, 2009). Students classified under either label exhibit significant behavioral excesses or deficits.

Behaviors are classified for the purposes of communication among professionals, assessment and placement purposes, or planning educational interventions. Children exhibiting one type of behavior will frequently engage in other similar behaviors. Behaviors that are related in some way are grouped together and may be identified as symptomatic of a disorder type (Hunt & Marshall, 2005). Several authors in the field of special education have described various classifications of behavior disorders (Hall & Hall, 2003; Hallahan, Kauffman, & Pullen 2009; Hardman, Drew, & Egan, 2008; Wicks-Nelson & Israel, 2005). These classifications are summarized below.

- *Conduct disorder*—is overtly aggressive (both physically and verbally), disruptive, negative, and irresponsible.
- *Oppositionally defiant*—argues with authority figures, loses temper frequently, exhibits defiant behaviors associated with anger and resentment.
- *Anxiety-withdrawal*—is self-conscious, overly shy or anxious, easily embarrassed, hypersensitive, generally fearful, depressed or sad.
- *Attention problems-immaturity*—has short attention span and poor concentration; is passive, sluggish, easily distracted, and often daydreams; may play with younger children or objects that are developmentally inappropriate.
- *Socialized aggression*—engages in delinquent subculture behaviors such as stealing and truancy from school, damages school property, engages in fights with other students, uses drugs or alcohol, and generally associates with others who exhibit similar related behaviors.
- *Psychotic behavior*—expresses implausible ideas, engages in repetitive speech, exhibits highly unusual or bizarre behavior.
- *Motor excesses*—is restless, tense, unable to sit still, overly active (verbally or physically).

Another frequently used system of broad classification is categorization of behaviors as *externalizing* or *internalizing* (Hallahan et al., 2009; Hardman et al., 2008; Heward, 2008; Hunt & Marshall, 2005; Turnbull et al., 2010). Externalizing behaviors are typified as overt, antisocial, disruptive, aggressive, acting out, usually directed toward others, and noncompliant. Examples are:

- shows aggression toward objects or persons
- argues excessively
- forces the submission of others through physical and/or verbal means
- is noncompliant with reasonable request
- exhibits persistent patterns of stealing, lying, and/or cheating
- frequently exhibits lack of self-control and acting-out behaviors
- throws tantrums
- hits, spits, scratches, bites
- throws objects

- sets fires
- harms animals

Internalizing behaviors are typified as withdrawing from others; excessive fantasizing or crying; feigning illness; conveying frequent feelings of sadness, fear, or depression. Examples are:
- plays alone
- suddenly or frequently cries
- complains of severe headaches or other somatic problems (stomach aches, nausea, dizziness, vomiting) as a result of fear or anxiety
- shows decreased interest in activities that were previously of interest
- rarely speaks
- has problems with sleeping or sleeping too much, daydreaming
- shows little affect or sad affect, depression
- expresses feelings of worthlessness
- is excessively teased, neglected, and/or avoided by peers
- has severely restricted activity levels
- shows signs of physical, emotional, and/or sexual abuse
- exhibits other specific behaviors, such as withdrawal, avoidance of social interactions, and/or lack of personal care to an extent which prevents the development or maintenance of satisfactory interpersonal relationships

Internalizing behaviors are not identified as frequently because they are not as disruptive in the classroom as externalizing behaviors; however, they should be considered as serious and detrimental to the child's well-being personally and educationally.

Hyperactivity and Attention Deficit Disorders

Although Attention Deficit Hyperactivity Disorder (ADHD) is not technically a behavior disorder, it is included in this chapter because the symptoms that characterize the disability are similar to those of some behavior disorders. ADHD is not considered a separate disability under IDEA, but is included under *Other Health Impairments*. Behaviors exhibited by students with ADHD are often disruptive, and, as a result, are susceptible to interventions used with students who have behavior disorders. Some research has indicated that nearly half of all students with ADHD also have a behavior disorder (Stahl & Clarizio, 1999). There is also considerable overlap with learning disabilities (Hardman et al., 2008).

ADHD has been called ADD (Attention Deficit Disorder); however, ADHD is the updated clinical term as it most accurately describes all aspects of the condition, both inattention and hyperactivity. ADHD is characterized by: difficulty in maintaining attention, limited ability to concentrate, impulsive behaviors, and hyperactivity. In addition to these symptoms, a child with ADHD may have trouble sitting still, finishing tasks, or following directions. According to the *Diagnostic & Statistical Manual for Mental Disorders (DSM-IV-TR)* (American Psychiatric Association, 2000), for someone to be diagnosed with ADHD, behaviors must have lasted for at least 6 months and be severe enough to disrupt school and other aspects of the individual's life. The *DSM-IV-TR* identifies three subtypes of ADHD:

1. ADHD, Predominantly Inattentive Type: Inattention but not hyperactivity-impulsivity behaviors.
2. ADHD, Predominantly Hyperactive-Impulsive Type: Hyperactivity-impulsivity but not inattention behaviors.
3. ADHD, Combined Type: Both inattention and hyperactivity-impulsivity behaviors.

Specific behaviors distinguish the two main types of ADHA. Examples of hyperactivity-impulsivity symptoms of ADHD include:

- Fidgeting
- Squirming
- Getting up often when seated
- Running or climbing at inappropriate times
- Having trouble playing quietly
- Talking excessively or out of turn
- Interrupting

Examples of inattention symptoms of ADHD include:
- Not paying attention to detail
- Making careless mistakes
- Failing to pay attention and keep on task
- Not listening
- Being unable to follow or understand instructions
- Avoiding tasks that involve effort
- Being distracted or forgetful
- Losing things that are needed to complete tasks

Symptoms of either type can be a serious challenge to academic instruction, social relationships, and classroom management. The Centers for Disease Control and Prevention (CDC) publication *Vital and Health Statistics* (2007) states there are 4.5 million children ages 3 to 17 (7% of this age group) with ADHD, with boys outnumbering girls about 5 to 1.

The cause of ADHD is generally considered to be biologically based, neurological (congenital or trauma-based), or inherited. The fact that ADHD tends to run in families suggests that children may show tendencies to develop ADHD from their parents. ADHD is also considered to have a neurological component since some experts believe an imbalance of brain chemicals that transmit nerve impulses may be a factor in the development of ADHD symptoms. Because it is considered a biological disorder, pharmaceutical interventions are often used. Common medications are Adderall, Dexedrine, and Ritalin. Cognitive-behavioral techniques have also been shown to be effective (Turnbull et al., 2010) and are often preferred by parents due to the side effects of some stimulant drugs.

Causes of Behavior Disorders

Various factors influence the way we perceive one's behaviors. These factors are related to home and school environments, ethnic and cultural norms, the social and economic climate of the community, the responses of peers and authority figures, as well as the biological and social-emotional characteristics of the individual exhibiting the behavior (Hardman et al., 2008; Kauffman & Landrum, 2009). Other factors include:

- our values or beliefs regarding behavior,
- our tolerance for certain behaviors,
- our perceptions of what is considered normal behavior,
- the context in which a behavior occurs, and
- the frequency with which a behavior occurs. (Heward, 2008)

Although various factors have been identified that may influence behaviors, there are two generally accepted broad categories of factors related to causation: biological and environmental. Under the biological category, problem behaviors are related to factors such as intellectual disabilities, autism, childhood schizophrenia, attention deficit hyperactivity disorder, or Tourette's disorder. Under the environmental categories, problem behaviors are often related to family, school, and cultural factors. There is, however, no consensus on the etiology of behavior disorders. Turnbull et al. (2010) make two very important points about determining the cause of behavior disorders: (a) it is likely that a range of factors contributes interactively to behavior disorders, and (b) determining the cause is useful only to the extent that it leads to the development of effective interventions and preventions.

Effects of Behavior Disorders

A behavior disorder is a social disability and, as such, affects students in any area that requires interpersonal interactions. Nearly all academic and social activities require interpersonal interactions; therefore, a behavior disorder can affect every area of a student's development: intellectual, educational, and social. Without effective intervention, students with behavior disorders are at risk for dropping out of school and for finding employment. Students with behavior disorders have the highest dropout rate (about 50%) of all students receiving special education services, and they engage in drug use at significantly higher rates than students without behavior disorders (Cullinan, 2007).

- Students with behavior disorders were once thought to be above average in intelligence; however, more recent research indicates that they are generally in the normal to slightly below normal range (Hardman et al., 2008).
- Though generally having normal intelligence, students with behavior disorders rarely do well in school. The disruptive and defiant behaviors that characterize the disability interfere with learning and academic achievement (Bauer & Shea, 1999). Conversely, students who experience difficulties in learning often develop behavior problems.
- Students exhibiting either externalizing or internalizing behaviors have difficulty making and maintaining friendships. Without friends and with few opportunities for social interaction, their social and emotional development is adversely affected (Cartledge & Milburn, 1995).
- In addition to their peers, students with behavior disorders also have difficulty in relating to their parents, teachers, and other adults (Gresham & MacMillan, 1997).

Identification and Assessment of Behavior Disorders

Direct observation is the most widely used method of obtaining information regarding a student's problem behavior. Once a target behavior—one that is both observable and measurable—has been identified, observers watch and record the problem behavior across settings. The most common problem behaviors are aggressive acts such as hitting or throwing objects, and acts of defiance, particularly in response to authority figures. These behaviors and others are measured on several dimensions: rate, intensity, duration, and age appropriateness.

- Rate refers to how often a behavior occurs in a given time period.
- Intensity refers to the strength or magnitude of the behavior.
- Duration refers to the length of time a behavior lasts.
- Age appropriateness refers to how fitting the behavior is to the student's chronological age. (Hunt & Marshall, 2005, p. 242)

Measurements based on these dimensions are used to determine whether a behavior is considered to be outside the bounds of normal behavior.

Behavior measurements, as well as scales and checklists, are used to obtain information from parents, teachers, and others about the symptoms and functioning of students in various settings. Noting and recording symptoms is necessary to appropriately assess behavior disorders and to monitor treatment. Generally, symptoms must be present in more than one setting for a student to be diagnosed as having a behavior disorder. There are several behavioral rating scales that are used frequently in schools: Conners' Behavior-Rating Scale, Peterson-Quay Behavior-Rating Scale, Behavior Dimensions Rating Scale, and the Social Behavior Scales, which has assessments for school as well as home and community (Hall & Bramlett, 2002; Lund & Merrell, 2001; Merrell, 1993). A list of other behavioral assessments with descriptions can be found online at PsychTests.com (http://www.psychtests.com/).

Another frequently used source for diagnosing behavior disorders is the *Diagnostic and Statistical Manual of Mental Disorders of the American Psychiatric Association* (4th ed., 2000), commonly known as the *DSM-IV-TR*. The *DSM-IV-TR* is a manual that groups behaviors into diagnostic categories, and lists specific behaviors and other criteria that must be present for a diagnosis. Observations of the child in various settings are made and then compared to the categories and descriptions in the *DSM-IV-TR*. A physician must be involved in the assessment if medication is to be prescribed for reducing symptoms such as tics or hyperactivity.

Although observations, scales, checklists, and diagnoses all help to identify students with behavior disorders, they provide little information about structuring instructional objectives, or the type of intervention that might be helpful. Consequently, the 1997 IDEA amendments require that a functional behavioral assessment (FBA) be administered to students who have been identified as having a behavior disorder (IDEA Amendments, 1997). The purpose of a functional behavioral assessment is to determine the uses and function of the problem behaviors, and to identify positive strategies and substitute behaviors that can serve the same function as the problem behaviors. By identifying significant, pupil-specific social, affective, cognitive, and/or environmental factors associated with the occurrence of problem behaviors, or the non-occurrence of desired behaviors, behavioral interventions can better address the causes of student misbehaviors.

Brady and Halle (1997) identify three components of a functional behavior assessment:

1. Interviews with the student, parents, teachers, and classmates about the occurrence of the behavior and surrounding circumstances;
2. Observations of the student when the behavior occurs, noting antecedents and consequences to the behavior, as well as what occurs during the behavior;
3. Manipulation of specific variables (called analog probe) such as setting, activity, or participants to gain a better understanding of when and why the behavior occurs.

The first two components are generally considered functional assessments, and the third is considered functional analysis. Of the two assessments, the more reliable method is to directly observe students' behaviors in their natural environment and analyze the behaviors' antecedents (environmental events that immediately precede the problem behaviors) and consequences (environmental events that immediately follow the problem behaviors).

Three important outcomes are achieved through a functional assessment (Hardman et al., 2008):

1. A concrete definition of the problem behavior
2. One or more predictions regarding when, where, and under what conditions the problem behavior will occur
3. Identification of the function the problem behavior serves, such as to get attention, to avoid work, or to control others

Information gathered from a functional behavioral assessment is used to determine what initiates, sustains, or ends a behavior; and with that information, a behavior intervention plan (BIP) is developed. This plan should include positive behavioral support strategies designed to teach appropriate replacement behaviors (Hallahan et al., 2009). The Positive Behavioral Support (PBS) approach is discussed in the following section.

Intervention Approaches for Students with Behavior Disorders and ADHD

Most schools have established programs for dealing with problem behaviors. Many of these school programs are based on or utilize the principles of two approaches that are used widely in schools today: Applied Behavioral Analysis (ABA) and Positive Behavioral Support (PBS). The term *approach* is important, as ABA and PBS are not specific interventions, but intervention approaches. That is, they do not identify specific techniques to be used, but rather important strategies that are a part of the approach. Cognitive Behavior Modification, a blend of behavior modification and cognitive therapy, is used less often and primarily with students who exhibit internalizing behaviors.

Applied Behavioral Analysis (ABA) is a process of systematically applying the methods of science (description, quantification, and analysis) to improve behaviors of social significance and to demonstrate that the interventions employed are responsible for the improvement in behavior (Baer, Wolf, & Risley, 1987; Madsen & Madsen, 2000; Sulzer-Azaroff & Mayer, 1991). Behaviors are identified that need to be extinguished, as well as those that are to be taught and reinforced. ABA focuses on clearly defining the problem behavior within the context of the environment, reliably measuring and objectively evaluating the target behavior, arranging the environment and providing consequences for decreasing undesirable behaviors, and teaching desirable behaviors through reinforcement-based opportunities for response (Hunt & Marshall, 2005).

Empiricism is the basis of ABA—meaning that knowledge is guided not by speculation, personal opinion, or the logic of common sense, but rather by objective observation based on thorough description and precise quantification of the behavior under study. Problem behaviors are defined objectively. Imprecise terms such as *anger, aggression,* or *disruptive* are redefined in terms of behaviors that are observable and measurable, so their frequency, duration, or other measurable properties can be recorded (Sulzer-Azaroff & Mayer, 1991). For example, a child's disruptive behavior might be defined as "yelling out, leaving seat, or hitting other students." The goal of "developing classroom discipline" might be defined as "requesting permission to leave seat, raising hand before speaking, completing work assignments in allotted time."

The use of single-case experimental design to evaluate the effectiveness of individualized interventions is an essential component of programs based upon ABA methodologies (Kazdin, 1982). This is a process that includes the following components:

- Selection of interfering behavior or behavioral skill deficit
- Identification of goals and objectives
- Establishment of a method of measuring target behaviors
- Evaluation of the current levels of performance (baseline)
- Design and implementation of the interventions that teach new skills and/or reduce interfering behaviors
- Continuous measurement of target behaviors to determine the effectiveness of the intervention
- Ongoing evaluation of the effectiveness of the intervention, with modifications made as necessary to maintain and/or increase both the effectiveness and the efficiency of the intervention (Alberto & Troutman, 1999; Cooper, Heron, & Heward, 1987; Sulzer-Azaroff & Mayer, 1991)

Behavioral-based approaches have been found to be effective with a broad range of problem behaviors in music education and music therapy (Standley, 1996).

Positive Behavioral Support (PBS) refers to a range of preventive and positive interventions designed to create a supportive and successful environment for students who exhibit social or academic problems. PBS is a comprehensive research-based approach intended to address all aspects of a student's problem behavior. PBS involves a proactive, collaborative, assessment-based process to develop effective, positive individualized interventions for individuals with challenging behavior. Along with reducing problem behaviors, the approach is structured to address quality of life issues and plans for the student's future. It is an approach that merges values regarding the rights of people with disabilities with practical application of how learning and behavior change occur. The principal goal of PBS is to improve the daily life of students and their support providers in home, school, and community settings (Hallahan et al., 2009; Turnbull et al., 2010). PBS is supported by recent mandates, including the 1997 amendments to the Individuals with Disabilities Education Act, which call for the use of functional behavioral assessment and positive supports and strategies (IDEA, 2004).

Positive Behavioral Support (PBS) has three primary features: (a) functional (behavioral) assessment, (b) comprehensive intervention, and (c) lifestyle enhancement (Kauffman & Landrum, 2009). As discussed earlier in the chapter, functional assessment is a process for identifying the events that prompt and maintain problem behavior. This process involves information gathering through record reviews, interviews, and observations and the development of summary statements that describe the behavioral patterns identified and their functions.

A comprehensive plan is developed that includes multiple proactive strategies. These strategies are structured to (a) change the environment so that triggering events are removed, (b) teach new skills that can replace problem behaviors, (c) eliminate or minimize natural rewards for problem behavior, and (d) maximize rewards for new replacement behaviors. The key principle of PBS is the comprehensive approach to improving multiple areas of students' lives: personal relationships, social and academic activities, and health (Turnbull et al., 2010).

PBS outcomes include lifestyle enhancements such as building and maintaining meaningful relationships, expressing personal preferences and making choices (self-determination), and participating in community activities. Such lifestyle enhancements are facilitated by establishing a positive long-range vision with the student and his or her family, and then, through effective collaborations, assembling natural supports to realize the vision (Kauffman & Landrum, 2009).

Cognitive Behavior Modification (CBM) is a therapeutic approach used to treat a range of neuroses and anxiety disorders. In cognitive behavior modification, a student who is exhibiting internalizing behaviors (crying, excessive sleeping, social withdrawal, etc.), as a result of anxiety or depression, is trained to recognize destructive or harmful thought patterns or behaviors and to replace them with helpful or constructive thoughts and behaviors (Corey, 2009). By making thought patterns conscious, students are able to recognize when they are about to perform undesirable behaviors, such as crying or complaining, or when they are engaged in negative thoughts that are not supported by logic or reality. The CBM approach then calls for a student to halt the behavior or thought and consciously replace it with a desired thought or behavior. CBM effectiveness is dependent upon a student's ability to self-regulate (de l'Etoile, 2005). This type of intervention is not administered in the classroom, but rather individually in the sessions with the school counselor or psychologist.

Students who exhibit internalizing behaviors require a different approach than students exhibiting externalizing behaviors. Internalizing behaviors are often covert and do not generally disrupt instruction in the classroom. Students who are anxious or depressed, however, often experience difficulties in their school work and in their social lives. They are frequently bullied and ostracized by their peers. The debilitating effects of anxiety and depression can lead to physical ailments and to dropping out of school. Teachers need to be as attentive to students exhibiting internalizing behaviors as they are to those exhibiting the more disruptive types of externalizing behaviors. Both types of behaviors are detrimental to students' academic success and to their personal well-being.

Teaching students with behavior disorders requires the use of multiple strategies that are matched to the needs of the student. Unfortunately, there is not one universal strategy that works for all students. Any useful strategy, such as contingency contracting, class-wide or cross-age peer tutoring, or self-monitoring, can be incorporated within the comprehensive PBS and ABA approaches described above.

Music Education for Students with Behavior Disorders and ADHD

As music educators, we are fortunate that music is a highly desirable activity for most students. Students with behavior disorders often find the music room the one classroom where they are motivated to conform and to succeed. Structuring for their success, as well as the success of all students, requires careful planning. Students with behavior disorders learn music as other students do, through singing, playing instruments, moving, listening, reading, and creating. Their disability does not require adapted instruments or music. However, adapting the environment, instruction, expectations, and attitudes can be useful in teaching music to students with challenging behaviors.

Students generally engage in disruptive behaviors when they are not actively engaged, or when the environment prompts these behaviors (de l'Etoile, 2005). Students with problem behaviors generally perform better when they are (a) in close proximity to the teacher, (b) sitting beside model students, and (c) actively engaged in a desirable activity. Moving a student to the front of the room or wisely placing him or her next to appropriate peers is not difficult; however, planning learning activities that are motivating is difficult unless the teacher is knowledgeable about a wide range of curricular options.

Instructional accommodations are often used for students with behavior disorders. As explained in Chapter 4, an accommodation is used when the teacher believes the student can achieve the same level of participation as his or her classmates, but needs additional support. An instructional accommodation allows a student to engage in the same musical activity as other students in the class, but some change is made in setting, presentation of the information, or the type of accepted response. Some suggestions for instructional accommodations are:

- Give clear, uncomplicated directions. Students often misbehave when they are confused about what they are supposed to do.
- Use the student's name and look at him or her. Students are more likely to misbehave when they think they are anonymous.
- Define expectations for classroom behavior and be consistent in administering consequences for misbehavior. Students often misbehave because they do not know what behavior is expected.
- Make a desirable activity (e.g., using the Karaoke machine) contingent upon a less desirable activity (e.g., completing sight-singing exercises). Many teachers use reinforcement menus (lists of desired activities such as listening to CDs, playing music Bingo).

- Think "do" when you think "don't." Asking students to *do* something is a more positive approach than telling them *don't do* something—"Watch me" instead of "Don't bury your head in the music."
- Think "approval" when you think "disapproval." Reinforcing students who **are** doing what you want them to do creates a more positive learning environment than admonishing students who **aren't** doing what you want them to do.
- Set the occasion for problem students to be reinforced. It is difficult to "catch the student being good" if they aren't being good. Ask them to help move risers, put instruments away—any activity that will allow you to reinforce good behavior and allow them to feel good about themselves.

Teaching Discipline (Madsen & Madsen, 2000) includes helpful information related to the suggestions listed above, as well as other suggestions for managing students' behavior:

- Avoid labeling students, such as "troublemakers" or "bad students." Students often live up to their label.
- Reserve emotions—choose your battles. Students with behavior disorders are difficult; it is their disability. Decide which problem behaviors interfere the most with learning, and prioritize which behaviors will receive your time and attention.
- Use peers as solutions. Solicit classmates to engage in peer tutoring or as a part of the management strategy. Students with behavior problems often respond more readily to the approval and disapproval of their peers than of their teachers.
- Analyze problem situations as to antecedents and consequences. Problem behaviors rarely occur in isolation. There are events that trigger the behavior and consequences that either reinforce or extinguish the behavior.

As stated in the introduction to this chapter, teachers often expect students with a behavior disorder to suppress their disability and "behave" when they enter the music classroom. Our expectations of students, as well as their instruction, often have to be adapted. Like all new behaviors, appropriate behaviors have to be shaped—shaped through successive approximations to the desired behavior. Shaping desired behaviors takes time. Students rarely instantly transform from being a problem student to a model student. In the initial stages of shaping a problem student's behavior, accept and reinforce behaviors that come close to the appropriate behavior.

Finally, we often have to adapt our attitudes about teaching students with behavior disorders. Most teachers have negative attitudes about teaching problem students (Darrow, 1999). Madsen and Madsen (2000) discuss the strategy of "act yourself into a new way of thinking." There is research to support the notion that engaging in positive behaviors can result in more positive thoughts (Strack, Martin, & Stepper, 1988). Developing a positive attitude about students with behavior disorders can do much to reduce the stress of teaching these students. There are many other constructive outcomes that result from teaching students who have behavior disorders:

- They require us to practice patience.
- They motivate us to plan more effectively.
- They keep us on task in the classroom.
- They prompt us to be more organized.

If students with behavior problems can affect us in these ways, how can teaching them be negative?

Music Therapy for Students with Behavior Disorders and ADHD

Music is a highly desirable activity for even the most challenging student. As a result of its desirability, the contingent use of music can be easily incorporated into a behavioral management program to reinforce appropriate behaviors. In addition, selected musical behaviors that are incompatible with inappropriate or negative behaviors can be taught. Music can also be used to induce mood change and relaxation in students who are anxious or stressed. These techniques have been used successfully with children and adolescents in residential treatment centers, juvenile detention centers, and public schools (Epstein, Pratto, & Skipper, 1990; Rio & Tenney, 2002; Saperston, 1989; Silverman, 2003; Wilson, 1975).

Music as a Competing Behavior

There are many musical behaviors that are incompatible with undesirable behaviors. For example, a student cannot play a guitar while striking another student, or play the piano while walking around the room. A student cannot sing while swearing or yelling in classroom. Musical behaviors should be selected that compete with the problem behaviors a student exhibits. Most students would choose to play the drums rather than throw paper airplanes or any number of other inappropriate behaviors.

Using Music as a Contingency

Much of the early music therapy research related to children and adolescents with behavioral or emotional problems was carried out in residential treatment facilities or hospitals (Mitchell, 1966; Wasserman, 1972). Since the mid 1970s, most children and adolescents with behavior disorders have attended public schools, although some students with severe emotional disorders are still enrolled in special outpatient or residential programs where they receive music therapy services. The use of contingent music has been used for many years by music therapists to effectively modify challenging behaviors. Music has been used contingently to modify inappropriate bus behaviors (McCarty, McElfresh, Rice, & Wilson, 1978), verbal behaviors to parents (Madsen & Madsen, 1968), and disruptive classroom behaviors

(Montello & Coons, 1998; West et al., 1995). Computer and electronic music is especially effective in managing the behaviors of adolescents (Krout, 1988). Such music, along with popular teen music, is particularly attractive to adolescents and, consequently, can be used in relatively simple ways to encourage prosocial behaviors. Savan (1999) found that even the use of classical background music resulted in the reduction of students' aggressive behaviors. Periods of preferred listening are often an effective reward for students with behavior disorders to initiate or maintain appropriate classroom behaviors such as:

- staying in their seats,
- completing work assignments,
- being punctual,
- raising their hands to speak, or
- participating in class activities.

Music Learning to Modify Inappropriate Behavior

Learning music, such as a new instrument, requires many behavioral prerequisites—sitting still, holding an instrument, manipulating the instrument, and reading music. The process of music learning increases the likelihood that students with behavior disorders will engage in these adaptive behaviors, and that the musical product itself will motivate continued engagement (Gardstrom, 1987; Kivland, 1986). For students with behavior disorders, the positive sense of self that comes from learning a musical skill does much to enhance their confidence and, consequently, their willingness to socialize appropriately with others. While learning music, students can participate in various musical organizations that allow for rewarding social contacts with their peers. An additional benefit of participation in musical organizations is that they often require regular school attendance as well as satisfactory grades and conduct reports. The development of performance skills can do much to enhance a student's sense of self. Participation in various musical activities aids in the development of adolescent independence and of a healthy self-concept.

Using Music to Modulate Mood

Depression is a frequent secondary condition of students with behavior disorders (Heward, 2008). According to researchers, one of the benefits of music for individuals with depression is its ability to induce or to alter mood states (Keneally, 1998; Mornhinweg, 1992; Silverman, 2003). Music has also been found to alter the behaviors and cognitive thought processes of depressed individuals (Williams & Dorow, 1985). Although music can be used to modify a student's affect or to elicit socially appropriate behaviors, it may also encourage inappropriate behaviors in certain situations (Durand & Mapstone, 1998). Furthermore, students with varying diagnoses such as ADD and ADHD have been shown to react differently to background music; some students may find that background music focuses their attention, while others are distracted by it (Pratt, Abel, & Skidmore, 1995). Musical preferences of the students must be considered as well as the sedative or stimulative characteristics of the music itself. Listening to preferred music, regardless of style (heavy metal, rap) has been shown to induce positive changes in mood. Thus, adolescents who prefer heavy metal music may experience an increase in positive affect upon listening to their preferred kind of music. Although heavy metal music and rap are often blamed for encouraging aggressive and violent behaviors in teenagers, some researchers do not support this premise (Took & Weiss, 1994), although others (Dimsdale & Friedman, 1998) suggest that adolescents who experience strong negative emotions to music are at an increased risk of participating in risk-taking behaviors. Research shows that, contrary to popular belief, adolescent listeners do not pay close attention to lyrics and are therefore not significantly influenced by them (Wanamaker & Reznikoff, 1989).

Using Music to Modulate Physical and Cognitive Activity

Sedative or stimulative music can be used effectively to modulate students' physical activity (Harris, Bradley, & Titus, 1992; Skaggs, 1997). Students will often remain in their seats in order to listen to their preferred music. Music that sedates hyperactive or inappropriate behavior may be a quick, efficient, and noninvasive way to manage difficult behavior (Saperston, 1989). Although stimulative music such as rap and heavy metal may stimulate muscle activity, preferences for these kinds of music do not predict behavior problems (Epstein et al., 1990).

Children with ADHD require interventions to modify not only their physical behaviors, but also their cognitive behaviors, such as attending and focusing on a task. A recent study found that music combined with neurofeedback significantly improved the executive function and attention scores of children with ADHD (Miller, 2007). Executive functions require the completion of tasks and attention to detail. While not a practical classroom intervention, music combined with neurofeedback holds promise for students with ADHD, a growing population of students who experience problems in learning and in managing their behaviors.

Using Lyric Analysis in Counseling Students with Behavior Disorders

Students with behavior disorders often choose inappropriate ways to express their emotions. Music therapy can provide these students with an alternative means of communication, and an opportunity to express their emotions through song writing or lyric analysis. Adolescents' preferred music can be used as a structure and impetus for discussing issues such as substance abuse, suicide, and coping with stress (Mark, 1987; Pelletier, 2004; Trzcinski, 1992). Lyric analysis relies on the text component of music. The music therapist or the student can select songs to use as the impetus for discussion. The music therapist can also write a song for a student to convey an emotion or message. Trained music therapists also have a variety of songwriting techniques that allow students to successfully write their own song. The content of the song may describe relevant issues the student is dealing with in his or her life. It may also be a way to explore what is missing in a student's life, such as a parent, friends, or love.

Music therapy can also facilitate the development of prosocial skills and the suppression of negative behaviors (Rickson & Watkins, 2003). In order to be successful, however, the music therapist must adapt the broad range of treatment techniques to the individualized needs of the student. As students practice and gradually acquire new relational and behavioral skills, the music therapist must facilitate the transfer of these skills outside the music therapy context and into the students' home and school environments. Layman, Hussey, and Laing (2002) have devised a music therapy assessment for students with emotional disorders that is useful for evaluating music therapy interventions.

The advantage of using music with students who have behavior disorders is that music is inherently nonthreatening and an inviting medium. Music offers the reluctant student a safe environment in which to explore emotions (Duerksen & Darrow, 1991). Music is extremely adaptable in ways such as style, age appropriateness, and sophistication, and, as a result, is capable of targeting problem behaviors across a wide age range of students. Nearly all students respond to music. Their response to music assists in establishing a strong foundation for engaging in therapeutic work. Students' natural interest in music is enhanced by the fact that they are occupied in activities associated more with play or fun than work or therapy (Hussey & Layman, 2003).

Summary

Teachers and therapists who work successfully with students who have behavior disorders are generally exceptional individuals. Heward (2008) refers to two important affective characteristics professionals must have in order to be successful with students who have behavior disorders: maintaining differential acceptance of the student, and having an empathic relationship with the student. Differential acceptance refers to the ability to not respond in kind to a student who exhibits extreme behaviors—to accept the student, but not the behaviors. Having an empathic relationship refers to the ability to understand the nonverbal cues that indicate a student's emotional needs. Patience is, of course, another important personal quality that is useful when working with students whose behaviors are demanding. Despite the challenges involved, having students with behavior disorders in the music classroom or clinic can be one of the most gratifying experiences music educators or music therapists can have in their professional lives. It is like making an "A" in the most demanding class you have ever taken. Helping students with behavior disorders to become productive and accepted by their peers contributes not only to the life of the student, but also to the lives of those around them.

KEY POINTS FROM THE CHAPTER

Definition and classification of behavior disorders:

♦ An emotional or behavioral disorder is a chronic condition that is characterized by behavioral or emotional responses that differ from age, cultural, or ethnic norms to such a degree that educational performance, including both academic and social skills, is adversely affected.

♦ Although estimates of the prevalence of behavior disorders range from 8% to as high as 20%, approximately 8.6% of the school-aged population with disabilities is generally considered to have behavior disorders, with boys outnumbering girls 5 to 1.

♦ Three criteria must be met in order for a student's behavior to be considered disordered: chronicity, severity, and pervasiveness.

♦ Several authors in the field of special education have described the following classifications of behavior disorders: conduct disorder, oppositionally defiant, anxiety-withdrawal, attention problems-immaturity, socialized aggression, psychotic behavior, and motor excesses.

♦ Behaviors are also sometimes classified as externalizing and internalizing.

Causes of behavior disorders:

♦ There is no consensus on the cause of behavior disorders, although it is widely believed that a range of factors, both biological and environmental, contribute to the existence of behavior disorders.

Effects of behavior disorders:

♦ A behavior disorder can affect every area of a student's development: intellectual, educational, and social.

♦ Though generally having normal intelligence, students with behavior disorders rarely do well in school.

♦ Students with behavior disorders have the highest dropout rate (about 50%) of all students receiving special education services, and engage in drug use at significantly higher rates than students without behavior disorders.

♦ Students with behavior disorders often have difficulty relating to their parents, teachers, and other adults.

♦ The most common problem behaviors associated with behavior disorders are aggressive acts such as hitting or throwing objects, and acts of defiance, particularly in response to authority figures.

Identification and assessment of behaviors disorders:

♦ Direct observation is the most widely used method of obtaining information regarding a student's problem behavior. Behaviors are measured on several dimensions: rate, intensity, duration, and age appropriateness.

♦ Several behavioral rating scales are frequently used in schools, along with the *DSM-IV-TR.*

♦ A functional behavioral assessment (FBA) is used to determine the uses and function of problem behaviors, and to identify positive strategies and substitute behaviors that can serve the same function as the problem behaviors. This information is used to create a behavior intervention plan (BIP.)

Attention deficit and hyperactivity disorders:

♦ ADHD is characterized by difficulty in maintaining attention, limited ability to concentrate, impulsive behaviors, and hyperactivity.

♦ It is estimated that 3–5% of school-aged children may have ADHD, with boys outnumbering girls about 5 to 1.

♦ Because the cause of ADHD is generally considered to be biological, pharmaceutical interventions are often used to treat ADHD, although cognitive-behavioral techniques have also been shown to be effective.

Interventions for students with behavior disorders and ADHD:

♦ Applied Behavior Analysis (ABA), Positive Behavioral Support (PBS), and Cognitive Behavior Modification (CBM) are approaches that are commonly used to deal with problem behaviors. The first two approaches are used with students exhibiting externalizing behaviors, and the third with students exhibiting internalizing behaviors.

Music education for students with behavior disorders and ADHD:

♦ Music educators should adapt the environment, instruction, expectations, and attitudes when teaching students with behavior disorders and ADHD.

♦ Teachers should recognize the constructive outcomes that arise from teaching students with behavior disorders.

Music therapy for students with behavior disorders and ADHD:

♦ Music can be used as a contingency for appropriate behavior.

♦ Participation in music activities often requires behaviors that are incompatible with inappropriate behaviors.

♦ Music can be used to aid relaxation and improve the mood of students who are anxious, stressed, or depressed.

♦ Sedative or stimulative music can be used to elicit a desired physical response in students with behavior disorders.

♦ Lyric analysis and songwriting can help students with behavior disorders and ADHD to express and understand their emotions, and it can provide a starting point for discussion of important issues.

REFERENCES

Alberto, P. A., & Troutman, A. C. (1999). *Applied behavior analysis* (5th ed.). Columbus, OH: Merrill.

American Psychiatric Association (APA). (2000). *Diagnostic and statistical manual of mental disorders* (4th ed.). Washington, DC: Author.

Baer, D., Wolf, M., & Risley, R. (1987). Some still-current dimensions of applied behavior analysis. *Journal of Applied Behavior Analysis, 20,* 313–327.

Bauer, A. M., & Shea, T. M. (1999). *Learner with emotional and behavioral disorders: An introduction.* Upper Saddle River, NJ: Prentice-Hall.

Brady, N. C., & Halle, J. W. (1997). Functional analysis of communicative behaviors. *Focus on Autism and Other Developmental Disabilities, 12,* 95–104.

Cartledge, G., & Milburn, J. F. (1995). *Teaching social skills to children and youth: Innovative approaches* (3rd ed.). Boston: Allyn & Bacon.

Centers for Disease Control. (2007, September). *Vital and Health Statistics* (Series 10, No. 234). Washington, DC: U.S. Department of Health and Human Services.

Cooper, J. O., Heron, T. E., & Heward, W. L. (1987). *Applied behavior analysis.* Columbus, OH: Merrill.

Corey, G. (2009). *Theory and practice of counseling and psychotherapy.* Belmont, CA: Thomson Brooks/Cole.

Cullinan, D. (2007). *Students with emotional and behavioral disorders: An introduction for teachers and other helping professionals* (2nd ed.). Upper Saddle River, NJ: Pearson/Merrill Prentice Hall.

Darrow, A. A. (1999). Music educators' perceptions regarding the inclusion of students with severe disabilities in music classrooms. *Journal of Music Therapy, 36,* 254–273.

de l'Etoile, S. K. (2005). Teaching music to special learners: Children with disruptive behavior disorders. *Music Educators Journal, 91*(5), 37–43.

Dimsdale, J., & Friedman, L. (1998). Adolescent emotional response to music and its relationship to risk-taking behaviors. *Journal of Adolescent Health, 23*(1), 1–2.

Duerksen, G. L., & Darrow, A. A. (1991). Music class for the at-risk: A music therapist's perspective. *Music Educators Journal, 78*(3), 46–49.

Durand, V. M., & Mapstone, E. (1998). Influence of "mood-inducing" music on challenging behavior. *American Journal on Mental Retardation, 102,* 367–378.

Epstein, J. S., Pratto, D. J., & Skipper, J. K., Jr. (1990). Teenagers, behavioral problems, and preferences for heavy metal and rap music: A case study of a southern middle school. *Deviant Behavior, 11,* 381–394.

Gardstrom, S. C. (1987). Positive peer culture: A working definition for the music therapist. *Music Therapy Perspectives, 4,* 19–23.

Gresham, F. M., & MacMillan, D. L. (1997). Social competence and affective characteristics of students with mild disabilities. *Review of Educational Research, 67,* 377–415.

Hall, J. D., & Bramlett, R. K. (2002). Screening young children's social behaviors: An examination of decision reliability with alternative measures. *Special Services in the Schools, 18*(1–2), 83–91.

Hall, P. S., & Hall, N. D. (2003). *Educating oppositional and defiant children.* Alexandria, VA: Association of Supervision and Curriculum Development.

Hallahan, D. P., Kauffman, J. M., & Pullen, P. C. (2009). *Exceptional learners: An introduction to special education* (11th ed.). Boston: Allyn & Bacon.

Hardman, M. L, Drew, C. L, & Egan, M. W. (2008). *Human exceptionality: School, community, and family* (9th ed.). Boston: Houghton Mifflin.

Harris, C. S., Bradley, R. J., & Titus, S. K. (1992). A comparison of the effects of hard rock and easy listening on the frequency of observed inappropriate behaviors: Control of environmental antecedents in a large public area. *Journal of Music Therapy, 29,* 6–17.

Heward, W. L. (2008). *Exceptional children: An introduction to special education* (9th ed.). Upper Saddle River, NJ: Merrill/Prentice Hall.

Hunt, N., & Marshall, K. (2005). *Exceptional children and youth: An introduction to special education.* Boston: Houghton Mifflin.

Hussey, D. L., & Layman, D. (2003). Music therapy with emotionally disturbed children. *Psychiatric Times, 20.* Retrieved February 16, 2005, from http://www.psychiatrictimes.com/p030637.html

Individuals with Disabilities Education Act Amendments of 1997 (P.L. 105-17). (1997). 20 U.S.C. Chapter 33.

Individuals with Disabilities Education Improvement Act of 2004, 20 U.S.C. § 1400 *et seq.* (1990). (Session law # P.L. 101-476).

Kauffman, J. M., & Landrum, T. J. (2009). *Characteristics of emotional and behavioral disorders of children and youth* (9th ed.). Upper Saddle River, NJ: Merrill Prentice-Hall.

Kazdin, A. E. (1982). *Single case research designs: Methods for clinical and applied settings.* New York: Oxford University Press.

Keneally, P. (1998). Validation of a music mood induction procedure: Some preliminary findings. *Cognition and Emotion, 2*, 11-18.

Kivland, M. J. (1986). The use of music to increase self-esteem in a conduct disordered adolescent. *Journal of Music Therapy, 23*, 25-29.

Krout, R. E. (1988). Using computer and electronic music resources in clinical music therapy with behaviorally disordered students, 12 to 18 years old. *Music Therapy Perspectives, 5*, 114-118.

Layman, D. L., Hussey, D. L., & Laing, S. J. (2002). Music therapy assessment for severely emotionally disturbed children: A pilot study. *Journal of Music Therapy, 39*, 164-187.

Lund, J., & Merrell, K. W. (2001). Social and antisocial behavior of children with learning and behavior disorders: Construct validity of the Home and Community Social Behavior Scales. *Journal of Psychoeducational Assessment, 19*, 112-122.

Madsen, C. H., & Madsen, C. K. (2000). *Teaching discipline: A positive approach for educational development* (4th ed.). Raleigh, NC: Contemporary.

Madsen, C. K., & Madsen, C. H., Jr. (1968). Music as a behavior modification technique with a juvenile delinquent. *Journal of Music Therapy, 5*, 72-76.

Mark, A. (1987). Adolescents discuss themselves and drugs through music. *Journal of Substance Abuse Treatment, 3*, 243-249.

McCarty, B. C., McElfresh, C. T., Rice, S. V., & Wilson, S. J. (1978). The effect of contingent background music on inappropriate bus behavior. *Journal of Music Therapy, 15*, 150-156.

Merrell, K. W. (1993). Using behavior rating scales to assess social skills and antisocial behavior in school settings: Development of the School Social Behavior Scales. *School Psychology Review, 22*, 115-133.

Miller, E. B. (2007). *Getting from psy-phy (psychophysiology) to medical policy via music and neurofeedback for ADHD children.* Unpublished dissertation, Bryn Mawr College, Graduate College of Social Work and Social Research, Bryn Mawr, PA.

Mitchell, G. C. (1966). Bedtime music for psychotic children. *Nursing Mirror, 122*, 452.

Montello, L., & Coons, E. E. (1998). Effects of active versus passive group music therapy on preadolescents with emotional, learning, and behavioral disorders. *Journal of Music Therapy, 35*, 49-67.

Mornhinweg, G. C. (1992). Effects of music preference and selection on stress reducing. *Journal of Holistic Nursing, 10*, 101-109.

Pelletier, C. L. (2004). The effect of music on decreasing arousal due to stress: A meta-analysis. *Journal of Music Therapy, 41*, 192-214.

Pratt, R. R., Abel, H. H., & Skidmore, J. (1995). The effects of neurofeedback training with background music on EEG patterns of ADD and ADHD children. *International Journal of Arts Medicine, 4*, 24-31.

Rickson, D. J., & Watkins, W. G. (2003). Music therapy to promote prosocial behaviors in aggressive adolescent boys: A pilot study. *Journal of Music Therapy, 40*, 283–301.

Rio, R. E., & Tenney, K. S. (2002). Music therapy for juvenile offenders in residential treatment. *Music Therapy Perspectives, 20*, 89–97.

Saperston, B. M. (1989). Music-based individualized relaxation training (MBIRT): A stress-reduction approach for the behaviorally disturbed mentally retarded. *Music Therapy Perspectives, 6*, 26–33.

Savan, A. (1999). The effect of background music on learning. *Psychology of Music, 27*, 138–146.

Silverman, M. J. (2003). The influence of music on the symptoms of psychosis: A meta-analysis. *Journal of Music Therapy, 40*, 27–40.

Skaggs, R. (1997). Music-centered creative arts in a sex offender treatment program for male juveniles. *Music Therapy Perspectives, 15*, 73–78.

Stahl, N. D., & Clarizio, H. F. (1999). Conduct disorder and comorbidity. *Psychology in the Schools, 36*, 41–50.

Standley, J. M. (1996). A meta-analysis on the effects of music as reinforcement for education/therapy objectives. *Journal of Research in Music Education, 44*, 105–133.

Strack, F., Martin, L. L., & Stepper, S. (1988). Inhibiting and facilitating conditions of the human smile: A nonobstrusive test of the facial feedback hypothesis. *Journal of Personality and Social Psychology, 54*, 768–777.

Sulzer-Azaroff, B., & Mayer, R. (1991). *Behavior analysis for lasting change*. Fort Worth, TX: Holt, Reinhart & Winston.

Took, K. J., & Weiss, D. S. (1994). The relationship between heavy metal and rap music and adolescent turmoil: Real or artifact? *Adolescence, 29*, 613–621.

Trzcinski, J. (1992). Heavy metal kids: Are they dancing with the devil? *Child and Youth Care Forum, 21*(1), 7–22.

Turnbull, A., Turnbull, R., & Wehmeyer, M. (2010). *Exceptional lives: Special education in today's schools* (6th ed.). Upper Saddle River, NJ: Merrill.

U.S. Department of Education, National Center for Education Statistics (2009). *Digest of Education Statistics, 2008* (NCES 2009-020) (Chapter 2).

Wanamaker, C. E., & Reznikoff, M. (1989). Effects of aggressive and nonaggressive rock songs on projective and structured tests. *The Journal of Psychology, 123*, 561–570.

Wasserman, N. M. (1972). Music therapy for emotionally disturbed in a private hospital. *Journal of Music Therapy, 9*, 99–104.

West, R. P., Young, K. R., Callahan, K., Fister, S., Kemp, K., Freston, J., & Lovitt, T. C. (1995). The musical clocklight: Encouraging positive classroom behavior. *Teaching Exceptional Children, 27*(2), 46–51.

Wicks-Nelson, R., & Israel, A. C. (2005). *Behavior disorders of childhood* (6th ed.). Upper Saddle River, NJ: Prentice Hall.

Williams, G., & Dorow, L. G. (1985). Changes in complaints and noncomplaints of a chronically depressed psychiatric patient as a function of an interrupted music/verbal feedback package. *Journal of Music Therapy, 20*, 143–155.

Wilson, C. V. (1975). The use of rock music as a reward in behavior therapy with children. *Journal of Music Therapy, 13*, 39–48.

Chapter 8

Students with Cognitive Disabilities: Mental Retardation, Learning Disabilities, and Traumatic Brain Injury

CHAPTER OVERVIEW

Students with cognitive disabilities comprise the largest number of students served under IDEA. Cognitive disabilities may be seen in children having learning disabilities, mental retardation, and traumatic brain injuries, among others. In 2007, over 2.5 million students with learning disabilities received special education services. This is 44% of the total population of students with disabilities served that year, making learning disabilities the most prevalent disability category for students served under IDEA. During that same school year, close to 500,000 students with mental retardation were served under IDEA. This is approximately 8% of the total population of students with disabilities served that year, making mental retardation the fourth most prevalent disability category for students, behind students with learning disabilities (44%), students with speech and language disorders (19%), and students with other health impairments (11%). The number of students with traumatic brain injuries is much smaller, with approximately 24,000 students, or less than 1% of the special education population having this diagnosis (Data Accountability Center, 2007). The disability category "developmental delay" indicates that a young child, ages 3 through 9, may have delays in cognitive, adaptive, social, language, and/or physical motor domains. Based on this information, it is highly likely that music educators and music therapists in schools today will have daily contact with several students who have cognitive disabilities.

This chapter includes information on the following topics:
- Mental retardation/intellectual disabilities
- Learning disabilities
- Traumatic brain injuries
- Music education for students with cognitive disabilities
- Music therapy services for students with cognitive disabilities

Mental Retardation

Terminology – Mental Retardation and Intellectual Disability

Mental retardation is listed as one of the 13 IDEA disability categories for special education service. This terminology is also used in other government documents and policies to delineate specific services, rights, and responsibilities for individuals. Historically, terms such as *feebleminded, idiot, moron, mentally deficient,* and others, were used as a name for the disability of limited intellectual functioning. Today these terms are clearly seen as demoralizing and pejorative and would not be used in any professional venue. The term *intellectual disability* is increasingly being used in the U.S. to replace the term *mental retardation.* This change reflects current professional practice that focuses on functional behaviors and individualized supports in a social and ecological framework (Schalock, Luckasson, & Shogren, 2007). Many people find the new terminology better to promote dignity and respect rather than a sense of devaluation of the individual person. Professionals might use these two terms interchangeably, since the definition and criteria remain the same. In this book we will use the terminology *mental retardation* primarily when referring to the IDEA category and diagnosis, but will use the preferred terminology *intellectual disability* in most other instances.

Definition and Characteristics of Mental Retardation

Mental retardation is functionally defined as fundamental limitations in learning and performing important skills of daily living. Mental retardation is not a medical condition or a mental disorder. According to the American Association on Intellectual and Developmental Disabilities (AAIDD, 2010), mental retardation is "a state of functioning that begins in childhood and is characterized by limitations in both intellectual functioning and adaptive skills." In order for a person to function at his or her highest possible level, the structure and expectations of the environment must correspond with the individual's capabilities. There are several different definitions for mental retardation as well as several ways to categorize levels of functioning. The AAIDD definition states that mental retardation is a disability characterized by limitations in intellectual functioning and adaptive behavior. These limitations are evident in conceptual, social, and practical adaptive skills.

Mental retardation is characterized by sub-average intellectual functioning, as documented by an IQ score of below approximately 70. However, limitations in intellectual functioning alone do not constitute mental retardation. Concurrent with the limited IQ, a person must have adaptive behavior limitations in at least two different areas. Adaptive behaviors are skills that are important to function safely and effectively in everyday life. Limitations in adaptive behaviors can negatively affect a person's ability to respond appropriately to his or her environment or to a particular situation. Adaptive behavior areas are central to successful functioning and include such broad areas as communication, self-care, home living, social skills, community use, self-direction, health and safety, functional academics, and work. These adaptive skills can be categorized as *conceptual skills* (receptive and expressive language, reading and writing, money concepts, self-directions), *social skills* (interpersonal, responsibility, self-esteem, gullibility, naiveté, following rules and laws), and *practical skills* (eating, dressing, toileting, mobility, using the telephone, managing money, using transportation). Limitations in adaptive behavior and intellectual ability must be evident before the age of 18 (American Association on Mental Retardation, 2002; Harris, 2006; Odom, Horner, Snell, & Blacher, 2007).

Over 25 years ago, the American Association on Mental Retardation (AAMR) (now the American Association on Intellectual and Developmental Disabilities, AAIDD) classification system categorized people with mental retardation into four categories based on IQ ranges (Grossman, 1983) (see Table 8.1).

Table 8.1 Previous AAMR Classification System

IQ Range	1983 AAMR Classification	Previously Used Educational Classification
50–55 to 70	Mild mental retardation	Educable mental retardation
35–40 to 50–55	Moderate mental retardation	Trainable mental retardation
20–25 to 35–40	Severe mental retardation	Severely/multiply handicapped
Below 20 or 25	Profound mental retardation	Severely/multiply handicapped

At that time in our history, students with mild mental retardation were thought to be "educable" and able to achieve academically at about the third or fourth grade level. Students with moderate mental retardation were thought to be "trainable" and able to learn basic self-help skills and basic social skills but would not be able to learn to read. Although the terms *educable* and *trainable* may still be used by some, these terms are outdated and limiting by creating low expectations on the part of teachers and parents. As the field of education moved away from a medical model to a more holistic model, the current definition is based on the belief that students with mental retardation have the potential to learn and develop skills when appropriate supports and services are provided.

Since special education is a system of supports based on the student's abilities and limitations, a student's functioning and need for supports must be assessed related to intellectual functioning and adaptive skills, psychological and emotional considerations, physical health and etiology considerations, and environmental considerations of family and community. Students' needs and supports are identified in nine potential support areas: human development, teaching and education, home living, community living, employment, health and safety, behavioral, social, and protection and advocacy (AAMR, 2002). An environment is created to provide the services and structure necessary to allow a person with mental retardation the highest quality of life and independence. The level of support needed by individuals will vary in duration and across life stages and situations. Services need to be designed to provide the appropriate level of support to meet the individual's specific needs. These supports range from intermittent support to pervasive support (AAMR, 2002) (see Table 8.2).

Table 8.2 Intensity of Supports Needed by Individuals

Intermittent	Episodic in nature; support provided on an as-needed basis
Limited	Time limited, such as during a transition period when person needs additional assistance
Extensive	Regular involvement, consistently, in at least some environments; ongoing, not time-limited
Pervasive	High intensity supports in all environments; could be necessary for sustaining life (e.g., feeding, breathing support)

School districts in different states use a variety of terminology to identify and classify students' levels of functioning. Some use older terminology such as EMR (educable mentally retarded) or TMR (trainable mentally retarded), mild/moderate/severe or profound mental retardation. Other districts use a broader terminology such as *cognitively impaired* (CI) or *developmentally disabled* (DD), or they will use the current preferred terminology, *student with an intellectual disability*.

Causes of Mental Retardation

The cause of mental retardation/intellectual disability is known for only about 40-50% of all cases. Known causes can be linked to a number of different risk factors that can be categorized by biomedical factors, social factors, behavioral factors, and educational factors (see Table 8.3). Mental retardation may develop during prenatal (before birth), perinatal (during the birth process) and postnatal (after birth) periods (Turnbull, Turnbull, & Wehmeyer, 2010). Many known causes of mental retardation can be linked to inadequate and adverse social and economic conditions. While poverty itself does not cause mental retardation, factors related to poverty such as malnutrition, poor health care, undesirable living conditions, and lack of educational resources and stimulation have been linked to the development of cognitive disabilities in children (AAMR, 2002).

Table 8.3 Etiology of Mental Retardation

Etiology of Mental Retardation/Intellectual Disability	Specific Examples
Biomedical Factors	Factors related to biological processes such as nutrition and genetic or chromosomal abnormalities • Various syndromes such as Down Syndrome, Fragile X Syndrome, Phenylketonuria (PKU), Rett Syndrome, Williams Syndrome, Prader-Willi Syndrome • Prenatal exposure to drugs or alcohol, rubella, syphilis • Infections such as meningitis, encephalitis, or brain malformation • Anoxia (lack of oxygen to the brain) any time pre/peri/post birth • Seizure disorder • Head injury from fall, accident, abuse, or other trauma • Presence of and ingestion of lead paint
Social Factors	Factors related to family and social interaction, including appropriate stimulation and responsiveness from adults • Poverty • Poor nutrition during prenatal development • Domestic violence • Lack of access to prenatal/postnatal care • Lack of adequate stimulation or care giving
Behavioral Factors	Factors related to dangerous or injurious activities or maternal substance abuse • Parental drug use, smoking, alcohol use • Parental abandonment • Child abuse and neglect • Domestic violence • Social deprivation
Educational Factors	Factors related to the availability of educational supports to promote intellectual development and development of adaptive skills • Parents without supports for limited cognitive abilities • Impaired parenting • Inadequate early intervention programs • Inadequate educational services and family supports

Developmental Characteristics of Students with Intellectual Disabilities

Mental retardation/intellectual disability is considered to be a developmental disability, occurring during the time when a child is developing cognitive, communication, social/emotional, and physical/motor skills. Most experts agree that children with intellectual disabilities develop skills in the same way that children without disabilities develop skills, only they develop these skills at a slower rate. The student's level of achievement is usually limited by the severity of the intellectual disability. Students with the least severe disabilities will develop the highest levels of skills in all areas. While all students do not develop in exactly the same way, children with intellectual disabilities share some common characteristics in their development of skills needed for success in school and in daily life.

Cognitive Skill Areas

Students with intellectual disabilities have limitations in cognitive skills that impair their learning processes. Limitations of *attention, memory, generalization,* and *motivation* are typical problem areas for these students. These students may have difficulty attending to tasks, and they may have trouble distinguishing what to attend to when there are competing stimuli in the room. They may also have difficulty with sustained attention over a longer period of time. A student with intellectual disabilities may need additional cues from the teacher to "look" or "listen" when his or her attention is wandering, or if the teacher sees that the student is not attending to the primary feature of the class. Proximity and other nonverbal cues may also help the student focus on the appropriate task.

In addition to focus-of-attention problems, students are likely to have problems with memory, particularly short-term memory. Students may have difficulty remembering multiple-step directions and will need to have simple one- or two-step directions in order to follow through with tasks. They may need additional review time when learning new skills in music class, including words to songs, rhythms, or music concepts. Music can be used as a mnemonic device to assist in recall of information. Words to familiar songs can be changed to cue a student to complete the steps to a task, such as steps to getting dressed or steps to playing a game. This is an easy thing to do with young children, since many familiar children's songs are repetitious, easy to recall, and can be reworked into a song to cue memory. However, the music professional should remember the importance of using age-appropriate music with students so as not to stigmatize or socially separate students by using songs with older children that are part of the music repertoire for much younger children.

Generalization of skills is also an area of difficulty for students with intellectual disabilities. Students may have difficulty transferring skills or behaviors from their home classroom to the music classroom, or from one music activity to another music activity. They may have difficulty understanding the expectations from one environment to the next when each environment is different. So when it is time for music, the student is now facing the expectations of another teacher, in a different environment, and, possibly, in a class with a different group of students (if joining an inclusive or mainstreamed music class). This area alone highlights the importance of collaboration between the music professionals and the classroom teachers, working together to create similar expectations across environments to support transfer of skills and behaviors.

Motivation is not usually a problem in a music classroom. Most students are eager to participate in well-structured, interesting music experiences. However, for students who have experienced many failures in school, motivation can be a problem. Researchers have addressed the issues of learned-helplessness, where individuals who experience repeated failures set low expectations for themselves and look to others for cues for solving problems (Seligman, 1975). Students with intellectual disabilities may have experienced failures in unsupportive environments, and they may look to others to make choices for them or to solve problems. Recent approaches to teaching these students focus on helping the students to develop self-determination and decrease their outer-directedness or reliance on others to solve problems or achieve successes (Wehmeyer, 1999).

Because of these deficits in attention, generalization, memory, and motivation, students with mental retardation may have difficulty learning basic academic skills. Their skills in reading, writing, and math are typically well below those of same-aged peers without disabilities. These students learn information at a slower rate, and they need concrete examples, repetition, and many opportunities for practice and success. In some instances, teaching songs, instrumental parts, or other music activities by rote may be more accessible for the students than teaching through reading. Music teachers can easily use auditory, visual, and kinesthetic approaches to present and reinforce information to support students' learning.

Language skills and social skills are also affected due to cognitive limitations and developmental delays. Students with intellectual disabilities will most likely have language and communication skills more congruent with their functioning level than with their chronological age. Similarly, students with intellectual disabilities may have delayed social skills that correspond more to their level of cognitive functioning than their chronological age.

Adaptive Skill Areas

As previously mentioned, a person with the diagnosis of mental retardation has significantly below-average intelligence and deficits in at least two adaptive skill areas. These are skills or behaviors that are necessary to function in a person's environment. Appropriate adaptive skills or behaviors change over time according to a person's age and environmental expectations (Turnbull, Turnbull, & Wehmeyer, 2010). Listed below are 10 adaptive skills and behaviors with examples of how these might impact the student in school (see Table 8.4). Not all individuals with intellectual disabilities have deficits in all of these areas, so it is important not to generalize this information to all students with this disability. In addition, the amount of delay or deficit depends on the severity of the disorder; for instance, a student with mild intellectual disabilities will most likely have much better communication skills than a student who has more severe intellectual disabilities.

Table 8.4 Summary of Adaptive Skills and Behaviors

Adaptive Skills and Behaviors	Examples Related to School Functioning
Conceptual Area	
Communication	• Delayed or limited ability to express self (expressive language) or understand others (receptive language). • May use adaptive communication system, functional signs, or gestures to communicate.
Functional academics	• Functional skills that have direct application to one's life, such as using math to assist in shopping, reading labels to enhance nutrition. • Functional academics should be directly related to skills needed to function in society at some level.
Self-direction	• Making choices for oneself, decision-making. • Students may rely on others to make decisions due to lack of confidence or understanding. Self-determination approach provides support and choices so students can have opportunities to have choices and make decisions.
Health and safety	• Skills related to staying safe and healthy, such as proper nutrition, safety, sexuality, first aid, and prevention of illness or accidents.
Social Area	
Social	• May have difficulty with appropriate interactions with others, including peers in school. Language deficits and cognitive limitations may also affect social skills. • Self-care issues related to hygiene may also impact social interactions.
Leisure	• Developing a variety of leisure activities, based on preferences, age appropriateness, and cultural norms.
Practical Area	
Self-care	• Hygiene, toileting, dressing, eating, etc. • Students with severe disabilities will probably need assistance throughout the school day, and may have an aide or assistant to help them with these tasks.
Home living	• Tasks related to functioning in a home, such as cooking, shopping, washing clothes, budgeting, etc. • Students will likely participate in authentic experiences such as creating a shopping list and purchasing food to work on functional math skills.
Community use	• Ability to use community resources effectively.
Work	• Developing work skills for employment. • Behavior, social interactions, and specific work skills may all be involved in training.

Communication/Social/Self-direction

Three adaptive skill areas of particular interest for music educators and music therapists are *communication, social,* and *self-direction*. Strengths and deficits in these areas may dramatically affect a student's academic and social success in music settings.Children with intellectual disabilities follow typical patterns of development for language skills, but due to their cognitive limitations, their language develops at a much slower rate than their typically developing peers. Most children with intellectual disabilities exhibit language deficits in quantity of speech and content and structure of language. Students with severe cognitive impairments may have little or no language due to neurological damage in the language centers of the brain. In addition, physical/motor problems such as those associated with cerebral palsy or even Down Syndrome can affect a student's communication abilities. These students may use augmentative or adaptive communication systems to assist with communication at an appropriate level of understanding.

Language and communication deficits negatively affect a student's ability to interact with others. Limitations in social skills may be due to the student's language deficits, attention problems, frustration tolerance, and difficulty understanding abstract ideas (Jones, 1996). In addition, since students with intellectual disabilities develop at a slower pace than their nondisabled peers, their social skills will likely not be congruent with other children their age, and they could be isolated or rejected by peers because of their limited skills. All students need good role models, successful social experiences, and quality interactions with others to build good relationships and self-esteem. The music classroom provides excellent opportunities for structuring social interaction between children with and without disabilities through music activities. Appropriate social interactions may need to be modeled and reinforced in order for students to develop meaningful relationships with peers (Jellison, Brooks, & Huck, 1984).

Self-direction, which is also known as self-determination, a principle guided by the value and respect of an individual's right to autonomy and independence, refers to such concepts as making choices, decision making, self-regulation, and self-management (Wehmeyer, 2001). Elements of self-determined behavior are expected for students without disabilities in music class, and so should also be expected for students who have disabilities. Choice-making, decision-making, and problem-solving skills are all necessary and important skills used in music class regularly. Students are also expected to set goals and follow through with a plan, problem solve, and, at times, self-instruct to learn new skills. Additionally, in music class students are able to demonstrate leadership skills, increase self-awareness, and observe and evaluate one's abilities. These are all skills related to self-direction or self-determination that students with intellectual disabilities can also work on with their peers during music. Remembering the student's cognitive, language, and social skills limitations, the teacher may need to provide additional support or structure to assist the student in the development of these important skills.

Music educators and music therapists need to understand students' abilities and limitations in the adaptive skill areas of communication, social skills, and self-direction. Music therapists might address students' limitations in functional academics, self-care, health and safety, leisure, community use, and work skills as a focus of music therapy interventions. Of course, all students do not have limitations in all of these adaptive skill areas, nor do all students have the same level of abilities in these areas. Music professionals gain understanding and direction for their work with students with intellectual disabilities by reviewing students' IEPs and collaborating with other teachers. Adaptations in the music classroom should be based on the students' strengths as well as their limitations in all of these areas.

Students with intellectual disabilities may also have problems with behavior that need to be addressed in the music classroom. Behavior problems may stem from a student's inability to understand directions, expectations, or consequences. They may also be due to low frustration tolerance, repeated failures, and lack of self-esteem. These students may have difficulty making the connections between their behaviors and the consequences of their behaviors, and they will need individualized behavioral interventions to help develop appropriate behaviors in school. Behavior management techniques discussed in Chapter 5 can be useful for developing a behavior management plan in music to prevent as well as remediate problem behaviors. Teachers need to remember to make concrete rules and expectations along with clear consequences to support the student's behavioral growth.

In addition to the cognitive limitations and deficits in adaptive skills previously discussed, children with intellectual disabilities may also have physical disabilities ranging from mild to severe. Children who have extensive neurological damage causing severe cognitive limitations are likely to have additional physical disabilities. It is not unusual for a child with severe intellectual disabilities to also have cerebral palsy, which is a disorder of movement that can significantly affect a person's mobility, language, and self-care. Students with intellectual and physical disabilities are considered to have multiple disabilities, and classroom interventions should be adapted based on the student's cognitive as well as physical limitations. Information about children with physical disabilities can be found in Chapter 13.

Learning Disabilities

Definition and Characteristics of Learning Disabilities

Learning disabilities are neurologically based processing problems. They can negatively impact an individual's ability to learn basic skills such as reading, writing, or math, and they can also interfere with higher-order skills such as problem solving, time management, and abstract thinking. The definition of *learning disabilities* has been debated since the term was first used in 1963. Students who qualify for special education services due to a learning disability must demonstrate a severe discrepancy between their potential and their achievement, as measured by intelligence tests and achievement tests. For example, a student may score high on a verbal intelligence test but have very low reading abilities. This would be a discrepancy. The learning disability cannot be from other factors such as mental retardation, hearing impairment, or emotional disturbance, or from extrinsic factors such as limited opportunities or cultural differences (Turnbull et al., 2010).

IDEA lists "specific learning disability" as one of the 13 categories of disability in the law. The term *specific learning disabilities* describes a heterogeneous group of disabilities that may be related to reading, writing, math, or memory skills. A student may have trouble with listening, thinking, and understanding or using spoken or written language. As with the other disability categories, a student with a learning disability may have mild to severe forms of the disability, and he or she may have only one specific learning disability or a combination of specific learning disabilities. *Learning disabilities* is an umbrella term that may describe one or more specific disabilities such as:

- Dyslexia – a language and reading disability
- Dyscalculia – difficulty with math concepts and processes
- Dysgraphia – a writing disorder that results in illegible handwriting
- Dyspraxia – a sensory integration disorder that causes motor coordination problems
- Central auditory processing disorder – difficulty with mental processing and remembering language-related tasks
- Nonverbal learning disorders – difficulty understanding nonverbal cues such as body language
- Visual perceptual/visual motor deficit – letter reversal, difficulty copying accurately, loses place frequently
- Language disorder (aphasia/dysphasia) – difficulty understanding spoken language, poor reading comprehension

(Learning Disabilities Association of America, 2010)

Types of learning disabilities can be identified by the particular processing area that is affected. Problems can be related to accessing information (input—auditory or visual perception difficulty), making sense of information (integration—problems with sequencing, abstraction, and organization of information), storing and later retrieving information (memory—problems with working memory, short-term memory, or long-term memory), and responding with information through words, writing, or gestures (output—language disability or motor disability). Students with learning disabilities may have a variety of additional presenting problems that limit their academic and social success in school, including social withdrawal, inattention, hyperactivity, and low frustration tolerance (Forness, 1996).

Learning disabilities are caused by a central nervous system dysfunction; however, the cause of this dysfunction is still not known. There is evidence of a strong connection between family history and learning disabilities in children. Additionally, environmental factors, such as exposure to chemicals, during critical periods of brain development may cause neurological dysfunction. Alcohol and drugs that are ingested by the mother during the development of the fetus have been linked to the development of learning disabilities as well as other disabling conditions in the developing child (Turnbull et al., 2010).

Students with learning disabilities may or may not have problems in the music classroom. Each child is different in abilities and needs. Students' level of difficulty or success will depend on their problem area (e.g., reading, math, etc.) and how much that area is used within the music classroom. Many students may even excel in music since the information typically is presented through auditory, visual, and kinesthetic means. They may be able to compensate for their area of deficit if the teacher uses a multimodal approach to instruction. Some social and emotional problems, such as low frustration tolerance, difficulty with peers, and lack of attention or hyperactivity, may cause problems for the student and will need to be addressed through collaboration with the classroom teacher and development of appropriate instructional accommodations. Instructional strategies and accommodations for students with behavior problems can be found in Chapter 7.

Traumatic Brain Injury

Definition and Characteristics of Traumatic Brain Injury

Accidents are the leading cause of all traumatic brain injuries (TBI), accounting for over half of all traumatic brain injuries each year. These injuries result from motor vehicle accidents, bicycle accidents, and pedestrian-motor vehicle accidents. Head injuries from falls are the next leading cause of TBI, followed by brain injuries caused by violent incidents such as child abuse, shaken-baby syndrome, or other assaults (Turnbull et al., 2010).

Traumatic brain injuries can cause mild to severe disabilities in children across all domains of functioning. These brain injuries may affect cognitive abilities related to focus of attention, concentration, ability to learn, memory, problem solving, perception, and abstract reasoning. The student may have difficulty with social skills, such as relating to others and being socially appropriate with others. The student may develop a low frustration tolerance and have erratic behavior or low motivation, and he or she may seem to have a different personality than before the accident. Language and motor skills may also be negatively affected depending on where in the brain the injury occurred. Rehabilitation services will help the student regain some skills that were lost due to a brain injury, but many deficits in functioning may be ongoing. Cognitive retraining may be used to help the student improve cognitive, communication, social, and behavioral skills.

Music educators and music therapists should find out the nature and scope of the student's abilities and needs. Even though a student may appear to have recovered physically from an accident, he or she still may have many deficits needing adaptations and rehabilitation for a long time post accident. Since these students may have needs across all domains (cognitive, communication, social, emotional, physical), teachers may use adaptations and instructional interventions from the various specific disability chapters in this book. For instance, a child with a traumatic brain injury might have difficulty with memory skills as well as low frustration tolerance and social difficulties with peers. A music educator or music therapist needs to consider the student's cognitive deficits as well as the social/emotional deficits when planning instructional accommodations.

Music Education for Students with Cognitive Disabilities

Educational Approaches/Strategies for Effective Teaching

Universal Design for Learning strategies can be very useful to address learning needs of students with cognitive disabilities, especially those with mild cognitive disabilities. Students who have more severe disabilities may need additional adaptations in order to access learning in the music classroom. Due to the variability of needs of the students with cognitive disabilities, no one set of strategies or adaptations would be useful or practical with all students. As previously stated, adaptations should be made based on the abilities and the limitations of the individual student. Teachers can use these general strategies for adaptations combined with strategies based on individual student needs to promote success in the music classroom.

Students with cognitive disabilities have varying abilities and limitations, with the severity of the disability ranging from mild to severe. The majority of students with intellectual disabilities have mild to moderate disabilities, and teachers can usually develop reasonable UDL strategies and other adaptations for these students in music class. However, music educators may have more difficulty developing instructional adaptations for students who have severe intellectual disabilities. Music educators typically have fewer problems making appropriate adaptations for students with learning disabilities since music learning usually takes place in a multimodal environment, and some students with learning disabilities may not need specific accommodations in music class. Accommodations for students who have a traumatic brain injury may be related to cognitive skills, social/emotional skills, language skills, or communication skills, depending on the areas of deficit caused by the injury. Again, some students who suffer a traumatic brain injury will need few, if any, instructional accommodations due to the mild nature of the resulting disability, while other students will need extensive additional support in the classroom.

Because a music educator may have 20–30 students in a class, it can be difficult to know how to include a student with severe disabilities in meaningful ways. Students may have little or no language, minimal response to others or their environment, and physical disabilities prohibiting independent mobility or movement. What can a teacher do to include this student with the rest of the students in the class? The first step is to find out why music class was chosen as a class for inclusion. The following statements are all reasons why a student with severe disabilities may be part of the music classroom:

- The student is a member of that class full-time so, of course, he or she would come to music with the rest of the students.
- The student has social goals on the IEP that can be addressed in music and other specialist classes such as art and physical education.
- The student responds positively to music (smiles, lifts head, makes sounds) when music is in the environment or when someone is singing directly to him or her.
- All students with severe disabilities in the school are integrated into the music class.

These are all standard reasons why a student is in music class. The next question to ask is, "What expectations do the teachers and parents have for this student's participation in music?" Some students with severe multiple disabilities will be unable to participate meaningfully in a class, especially if it is an upper-level class, which makes the discrepancy even greater. Music educators can discuss expectations with the classroom teacher or team to gain insight into what others see as meaningful inclusion for the student. By doing this, the music educator is working collaboratively for the good of the student and not in an isolated manner. Everyone might have different opinions on what is meaningful involvement in integrated classes, so it is important to discuss this issue when there are students who function at extremely low levels compared to the other students in the class. The music educator might seek out assistance from a music therapist to determine effective adaptation strategies, or he or she could encourage the school to look into music therapy for these students in addition to or in place of full inclusion music education classes.

Several strategies for adapting instruction for students with disabilities are described in Chapter 4. Many of these strategies are appropriate for use with students who have intellectual disabilities, learning disabilities, and traumatic brain injuries to support their learning and increase social success and positive behavior in music class. Listed below are examples of how some of these strategies might be implemented in the music setting. This is not an exhaustive listing, but it presents various ideas for making adaptations that are appropriate for students with cognitive disabilities. Teachers are encouraged to use these ideas as a catalyst to develop their own unique interventions. These adaptations can be used in an inclusive music class, a self-contained music class, or music therapy setting.

- *Participation—Vary the level of participation that is expected of the student.*
  - » Students with severe cognitive disabilities may not be able to participate in every element of every music activity. Teachers can make decisions about partial participation for the student to determine the highest level of participation that the student can handle with as much independence

as possible. This may mean that a student participates in some but not all of the activities in the music session. For instance, a student with severe disabilities may not be able to play recorder along with the other students in the class, but might be able to accompany the class as part of a rhythm section while the recorders are playing.

- *Input—Adapt the way that instruction is delivered to the students.*
  - » Information presented should be concrete and simple rather than abstract and complex. Keep in mind that since students with intellectual disabilities, learning disabilities, and traumatic brain injuries may have problems with attention and memory, they need one- and two-step directions, repetition, and cues to focus on the teacher or main event in class.
  - » Using varied modalities will assist the student in understanding the information presented. Information presented via visual, auditory, and kinesthetic modalities will give the student many opportunities to process the information. Other students might understand the concepts better by using these modalities to reinforce and practice skills.
- *Output—Adapt how the students can respond to instruction.*
  - » Students with cognitive limitations might need to have fewer, simpler questions to respond to on a test in music.
  - » Give students the option to respond verbally or through movement to evaluate understanding, rather than insisting on reading test questions and writing responses.
  - » Understand the use of augmentative and alternative communication methods and enhance students' system with music terminology or other responses that will be used in the music class. This can be especially important for students with severe cognitive and language disabilities.
- *Difficulty—Adapt the skill level, the type of problem, or the rules on how a student may approach a task.*
  - » Simplify music to meet the cognitive functioning level for the student. Use color coding or write out letter names of notes if the class is learning keyboard or recorder.
  - » Adapt a music arrangement to the level where the student can be challenged but successful. That might mean changing rhythm patterns from complex to simple or giving additional structure or cues for a music improvisation on Orff instruments.
  - » Make sure that the student has success in music to increase motivation and self-esteem.
- *Time—Adapt the amount of time allotted for completing a task, taking a test, or learning a new skill.*
  - » Students may need additional time to complete tasks, since they are developmentally behind their peers who do not have cognitive disabilities. Students with mild intellectual disabilities are likely to be able

to accomplish many of the same tasks as the rest of the class, but they might need additional time or support in order to do so.

- *Alternate goals—While using the same materials for all students, adapt the outcome expectations or goals.*
  - » While students with mild cognitive disabilities might be able to complete the same tasks and assignments as the rest of the class, students with severe cognitive disabilities are unlikely to be able to do the same. Expectations for these students may need to be adjusted based on their level of functioning. Sometimes students are included in music class primarily for the social aspects of interacting with peers, without the expectation of learning music concepts or literacy.
- *Managing the physical space—Adapt the classroom arrangement to best suit the needs of the students.*
  - » If a student has difficulty with focus of attention, be sure to place that child in close proximity to the teacher or another support person to assist with focus and redirection.
  - » Move interesting or enticing instruments so they are not within easy reach if the student is likely to be distracted by the instrument.
  - » Some students with cognitive disabilities also have problems with behavior. Make sure that the room will accommodate the student's behavior needs, such as clear structure so the student knows where to be at any time or a time-out space if necessary (or a place to go to settle down). Some students need clear physical boundaries, while others need some space to move around when agitated.
- *Adaptive instruments—Provide instruments that students can play successfully.*
  - » Students with mild cognitive disabilities will probably not need any instrument adaptations. However, students with severe disabilities are likely to have physical limitations necessitating use of adaptive instruments. Whenever possible, use instruments that are typically used in the class and choose from these instruments ones that the student will be able to play. If that is not possible, use adaptive instruments to allow students to participate at the highest level in the most normalized way.
- *Level of support—Increase amount of support from others.*
  - » Peer buddies or adult aides may be needed to assist the student in music class, but the student should be supported by these helpers rather than people who do the task for the students.
  - » In keeping with the idea of self-direction or self-determination, teachers can offer students the opportunities to make choices, make decisions, and take risks in music class. Students may appear to be helpless or might wait for others to complete tasks for them. Peers and teachers need to remember that students may need additional time, additional support,

or other adaptations to complete a task, but there are many things that the student should be able to do rather than having everything done for him or her.

Music Therapy Services for Students with Cognitive Disabilities
Music Therapy as a Related Service and District-wide Service

Students with cognitive disabilities may be eligible for music therapy services as a related service (see Chapter 6 for information about Music Therapy as a Related Service). A variety of goals from the student's IEP might be considered for music therapy, including those goals related to academic skills (using music interventions to teach/reinforce academic concepts), social/emotional skills (using music interventions to teach/reinforce social skills and emotional expression), physical skills (using music interventions to develop gross and fine motor skills), communication skills (using music interventions to practice language and communication skills), and leisure skills (using music interventions to develop new leisure skills such as learning an instrument or participating in a choral group).

Also discussed in Chapter 6, music therapy can be a provided service to many students in a school district to enhance their educational services and increase their educational successes. In this type of district-wide model, the music therapist usually works with small groups of students who have similar goals. Students with mild to moderate cognitive disabilities will most likely be educated in inclusive settings, while students with severe cognitive disabilities may be educated in self-contained classrooms for all or a portion of the day. Students may receive additional support within the classroom or they may receive additional one-to-one services outside of the classroom. Since students with mild disabilities are typically educated in an inclusive setting, the music therapist might be called on to assist the music educator in finding ways to adapt instruction for the student in the inclusive music class. Music therapists are more likely to work in small groups with students who have more severe disabilities and are primarily educated in self-contained classrooms. In some schools, these students do not participate in inclusive music education classes, so music therapy might take the place of that type of music experience.

Music therapy has been shown to be an effective approach for improving the functioning of individuals with cognitive disabilities. Music therapy activities can be designed to meet the needs of individuals and groups with various needs and functioning levels (Boxill, 2007; Braithwaite & Sigafoos, 1998; Claeys, Miller, Dalloud-Rampersad, & Kollan, 1989; Furman & Furman, 1996; Hairston, 1990; Perry, 2003; Robb, 1996; Wagner, 2000; Wylie, 1996). Examples of goal areas (domains) and how music therapy could be implemented to address related goals are listed in Table 8.5.

Table 8.5 Sample Music Therapy Goal Areas for Students with Cognitive Disabilities

Domain	Skills Addressed	Music Interventions
Cognitive	Pre-academics and academics, following directions, attention to task	Music activities focusing on academic concepts such as colors, numbers, letters, reading, memory
Social/Emotional	Sharing, taking turns, interacting with peers, leadership, self-expression	Group music-making activities such as playing instruments and movement to music; sharing instruments; leading group
	Self-determination, self-direction	Making choices for self through music activities; setting goals and determining/following through with steps to reach goals; sharing about self
Communication	Receptive and expressive communication, auditory awareness and discrimination	Singing and songwriting; listening to various instruments to identify by timbre or location
Physical Motor	Sensory integration	Vibrotactile stimulation through percussion instruments; acceptance of sensory input from others; awareness and response to sensory input; increased interaction with others through sensory activities
	Coordination and motor planning	Participation in movement to music activities; playing percussion instruments to a steady beat; use of rhythm to organize movements
Leisure	Develop skills for productive leisure activities	Learn instrument for individual or group leisure activity; group singing as preparation for participation in a community choral group; music activities in the community—planning, attending, and follow-through with community-based activity

Music Therapy to Improve Cognitive Skills

Students with cognitive deficits may have difficulty with skills that are necessary for the learning process, including focus of attention, appropriate attention span, and the ability to follow directions. Students with intellectual disabilities or other cognitive deficits have difficulty filtering out the extraneous stimuli and focusing their attention on the important features of the class. In order to be an effective learner, first a student must be able to focus on the important elements of the class or situation. The next step is to increase the student's attention span so that he or she is able to attend to an activity or event for longer periods of time, thus increasing opportunities to learn. Following directions can also be difficult for students with cognitive disabilities, due in part to problems with attention (not paying attention when the direction is given), problems with memory (unable to remember multiple-step directions), and problems understanding expectations.

Music therapy interventions can be developed to help the student improve skills in these pre-academic areas. For all of these skills, music and music activities provide an interesting and motivating means for the student to respond, learn, and practice new skills. There are many ways that music activities can be developed to improve a student's focus of attention, attention span, and ability to follow directions. Using age-appropriate music and interesting and engaging materials, the therapist can structure appropriate interventions based on the student's needs and interests. For instance, a group percussion activity can be very engaging and motivating for students who are interested in the instruments. The therapist can use the sounds of the instruments to gain attention, encourage focus of attention for longer periods of time through playing and passing instruments, and increase opportunities for active participation and engagement. Directions can be delivered nonverbally through sound cues ("stop when the music stops, play when the music plays") or verbally as simple one-step directions, then building to more complex directions. The therapist can use auditory cues, visual cues, and movement to focus and engage students and increase these skills that are necessary for learning.

Students with cognitive disabilities may have difficulty with academic subjects such as math and reading. These students typically learn at a slower rate and need additional adaptations, supports, and interventions to assist them in the process. Memory problems, difficulty understanding complex information, and focus-of-attention problems all contribute to a student's learning problems in school. Music therapy activities can be developed to teach and reinforce academic concepts such as shapes, colors, numbers, and concepts. Using music activities, students can develop skills related to object classification (identification of shapes and colors using instruments and songs about colors and shapes), spatial relationships (up/down, in/out, front/back), seriation (organizing by size or number), and temporal relationships (understanding relationships such as first, second, last) (Gfeller, 1990). Songs and chants can be used as mnemonics for memory skills/organizing information. For instance, the therapist can write a song to help students remember the steps necessary for completing a math problem or for getting ready to leave school and get on the bus (e.g., first we pack our bag, then we put on our coat, next we zip our coat and put on our gloves, then we line up and walk to the bus—remember to get on the right bus!).

Music Therapy to Improve Social, Communication, and Leisure Skills

Music therapy activities can help students with cognitive disabilities improve social and communication skills. Goal-directed music activities are developed to provide training and practice through increased interaction with peers, working together on a group music task, decision making, listening to others, group leadership, and other similar tasks. Music provides the motivation, interest, and structure for students to develop and improve their skills.

Music engagement can provide many hours of productive and enjoyable leisure activities for students with disabilities. Students with cognitive disabilities may need additional support to develop age-appropriate leisure skills. This may be especially important for students with severe disabilities who do not have the independence to explore leisure opportunities that improve their quality of life. Students may be interested in participating in adapted music lessons on guitar, keyboard, or percussion to learn basic music skills that they can practice and enjoy by themselves and with others. Some students might participate in a community choir program for individuals with disabilities or an integrated chorus for people of all functioning levels. These community music groups can provide normalized social experiences as well as satisfying musical experiences for the participants.

Summary

Students may have cognitive disabilities due to mental retardation, learning disabilities, or traumatic brain injuries, as well as other diagnoses. Cognitive deficits range from mild to severe, and these disabilities can also impact other areas such as language and social skills. Music educators and music therapists need to determine the student's level of functioning in all areas to develop appropriate adaptations for the music setting.

KEY POINTS FROM THE CHAPTER

Mental retardation
Prevalence and characteristics:
- ♦ Mental retardation is defined as fundamental limitations in learning and performing important skills of daily living. A person with mental retardation has sub-average intellectual functioning along with limitations in at least two different adaptive skill areas. These limitations must be evident before age 18.
- ♦ Mental retardation may be caused by genetic factors, environmental factors, or brain factors (such as lack of oxygen, head injury, infections, or prenatal exposure to drugs or alcohol).
- ♦ Students with mental retardation have difficulty in the areas of cognitive skills and adaptive skills.

♦ Students with severe mental retardation are more likely to have multiple disabilities such as cerebral palsy due to extensive damage to the brain.

♦ The term *mental retardation* is used in IDEA, but the preferred terminology is *intellectual disability*. Both terms refer to the same disability and can be used interchangeably.

Learning disabilities
Prevalence and characteristics:

♦ Learning disabilities are neurologically based processing problems that affect a student's ability to access information (input), make sense of information (integration), store and retrieve information (memory), and communicate information back to others (output).

♦ Approximately 44% of students who receive special education services are diagnosed learning disabled.

♦ Specific learning disabilities may be in reading, writing, math, or memory skills.

♦ Students with learning disabilities may also have other problems, such as attention problems, social problems, or low frustration tolerance.

Traumatic brain injuries
Prevalence and characteristics:

♦ Traumatic brain injuries can cause problems in all areas of functioning, including cognitive, social/emotional, physical/motor, and communication, depending on the nature, severity, and location of the injury.

♦ Less than 1% of students who receive special education services have traumatic brain injuries.

Educational considerations:

♦ Students with cognitive disabilities may need additional support in the music classroom in order to be successful.

♦ Music teachers should collaborate with the classroom teacher and the special education team to determine the goals for the student's participation in the general education music class. After the goals are clear, the teacher can structure learning interventions to promote the student's success at an appropriate and reasonable level.

♦ Students with severe disabilities may be appropriate for self-contained music education or music therapy sessions. These smaller groups allow the student to progress at a slower pace or to work on functional skills that are not a typical component of the music education curriculum.

REFERENCES

American Association on Intellectual and Developmental Disabilities (AAIDD). (2010). Retrieved March 30, 2010, from http://www.aamr.org

American Association on Mental Retardation (AAMR). (2002). *Mental retardation: Definition, classification and system of supports* (10th ed.). Washington, DC: Author.

Boxill, E. (2007). *Music therapy for developmental disabilities.* Austin, TX: ProEd.

Braithwaite, M., & Sigafoos, J. (1998). Effects of social versus musical antecedents on communication responsiveness in five children with developmental disabilities. *Journal of Music Therapy, 35,* 88–107.

Claeys, M. S., Miller, A. C., Dalloud-Rampersad, R., & Kollan, M. (1989). The role of music and music therapy in the rehabilitation of traumatically brain injured clients. *Music Therapy Perspectives, 6,* 71–78.

Data Accountability Center. (2007). *Individuals with Disabilities Education Act (IDEA) data: Part B data and notes.* Retrieved April 6, 2010, from https://www.ideadata.org/PartBData.asp

Forness, S. (1996). Social and emotional dimensions of learning disabilities. In B. J. Cratty & R. L. Goldman (Eds.), *Learning disabilities: Contemporary touchpoints.* Amsterdam: Harwood Academic.

Furman, C., & Furman, A. (1996). Uses of music therapy with people having mental retardation: An update of a previous analysis. In C. E. Furman (Ed.), *Effectiveness of music therapy procedures: Documentation of research and clinical practice* (2nd ed., pp. 279–296). Silver Spring, MD: National Association for Music Therapy.

Gfeller, K. (1990). A cognitive-linguistic approach to language development for the preschool child with hearing impairment: Implications for music therapy practice. *Music Therapy Perspectives, 8,* 47–51.

Grossman, H. J. (Ed.). (1983). *Classification in mental retardation.* Washington, DC: American Association on Mental Deficiency.

Hairston, M. (1990). Analyses of responses of mentally retarded autistic and mentally retarded nonautistic children to art therapy and music therapy. *Journal of Music Therapy, 27,* 137–150.

Harris, J. (2006). *Intellectual disability: Understanding its development, causes, classification, evaluation and treatment.* New York: Oxford University Press.

Jellison, J. A., Brooks, B. H., & Huck, A. M. (1984). Structuring small groups and music reinforcement to facilitate positive interactions and acceptance of severely handicapped students in regular music classrooms. *Journal of Research in Music Education, 32,* 243–264.

Jones, C. J. (1996). *An introduction to the nature and needs of students with mild disabilities.* Springfield, IL: Charles C. Thomas.

Learning Disabilities Association of America. (2010). Retrieved April 27, 2010, from http://www.ldanatl.org

Odom, S., Horner, R., Snell, M., & Blacher, J. (2007). The construct of developmental disabilities. In S. Odom, R. Horner, M. Snell, & J. Blacher (Eds.), *Handbook of developmental disabilities* (pp. 3–14). New York: Guilford Press.

Perry, M. M. (2003). Relating improvisational music therapy with severely and multiply disabled children to communication development. *Journal of Music Therapy, 40,* 227–246.

Robb, S. (1996). Techniques in song writing: Restoring emotional and physical well being in adolescents who have been traumatically injured. *Music Therapy Perspectives, 14,* 30–37.

Schalock, R. L, Luckasson, R. A., & Shogren, K. A. (2007). The renaming of mental retardation: Understanding the change to the term intellectual disability. *Intellectual and Developmental Disabilities, 45*(2), 116–124.

Seligman, M. E. P. (1975). *Helplessness: On depression, development, and death.* San Francisco: Freeman.

Turnbull, A., Turnbull, R., & Wehmeyer, M. (2010). *Exceptional lives: Special education in today's schools* (6th ed.). Upper Saddle River, NJ: Merrill.

Wagner, K. (2000). The effects of music therapy upon an adult male with autism and mental retardation: A four-year case study. *Music Therapy Perspectives, 18,* 131–140.

Wehmeyer, M. L. (1999). A functional model of self-determination: Describing development and implementing instruction. *Focus on Autism and Other Developmental Disabilities, 14,* 53–61.

Wehmeyer, M. L. (2001). Self-determination and mental retardation: Assembling the puzzle pieces. In H. N. Switzky (Ed.), *Personality and motivational differences in persons with mental retardation*. Mahwah, NJ: Lawrence Erlbaum Associates.

Wylie, M. E. (1996). A case study to promote hand use in children with Rett Syndrome. *Music Therapy Perspectives, 14*, 83–86.

Chapter 9

Students with Speech and Language Disorders

CHAPTER OVERVIEW

Close to 20% of students who receive special education services under IDEA have a communication disorder, either a disorder of speech or a disorder of language (Data Accountability Center, 2007). *Speech* is defined as the method of producing sounds for language, while language is the method for communicating thoughts and ideas. Disorders of speech include problems related to voice (strained, breathy), articulation (inaccurate articulation, making it difficult to understand), and fluency (stuttering) (Mastropieri & Scruggs, 2000). Language disorders are related to language use, language comprehension, and language expression. Students with speech and language disorders will most likely be educated in an inclusive classroom unless they also have other areas of severe disability. Music educators and music therapists may need to collaborate with a speech and language pathologist to determine the most effective approaches for working with individual students.

This chapter includes information on the following topics:
- ♦ Characteristics of students with speech and language disorders
- ♦ Music education for students with speech and language disorders
- ♦ Music therapy for students with speech and language disorders

---

Characteristics of Students with Speech and Language Disorders

In young children, differences in language ability can be attributed to a language delay or a language disorder. A child who has a *language delay* develops typical language competencies, but at a slower rate than would be expected for his or her chronological age and functioning level. The language delay might be related to a later-than-normal onset of language skills, a slower rate of language development, or variations in the sequence in which language skills are learned. A child with a *language disorder* has language skills and behaviors that are not typical of normally developing language skills (Paul, 2007; Vinson, 2007).

Language disorders can cause deficits in language related to:

- Content (Semantics)—Children with content deficits may have late onset of language, slow vocabulary development, difficulty with temporal or spatial concepts, and difficulty understanding synonyms and antonyms.
- Form (Phonology, Syntax, and Morphology)—Children with form deficits may have difficulty sequencing or organizing letter sounds to form words (problem with phonology); difficulty using the rules of grammar and language structure appropriately (problem with syntax); and difficulty with category words or words used to distinguish one item from another, or difficulty using parts of language to change verb tense or make plural (problem with morphology).
- Functional use (Pragmatics)—Children with functional use deficits have difficulty using language to communicate in different social contexts, such as using appropriate social greetings, giving feedback or initiating conversations, or requesting information. These children may have difficulty maintaining a conversation or focusing a conversation on a topic, and may converse with little regard for the listener.

Causes of Language Delays and Language Disorders

Language delays and language disorders can be the result of many different etiological factors. While it is not always essential for the music professional to know the specific cause of a student's language disorder, it is important to realize that language disorders are frequently characteristic of several disabling conditions. Language delays and language disorders may be the result of genetic or chromosomal disorders, motor or sensory deficits, prenatal exposure to alcohol or drugs, neglect or limited stimulation, developmental delay such as mental retardation or autism, or an accident or head trauma. Table 9.1 lists causes of several language delays and disorders (Vinson, 2007).

Table 9.1 Sample Causes of Language Delays and Disorders with Characteristics

Disorder/Diagnostic Label	Caused by	Language Characteristics
Down Syndrome/ Fragile X	Chromosomal abnormality	• Deficits from mild to severe • Delayed language • Linked to typical hearing loss (Down Syndrome) and cognitive functioning level • May be echolalic or perseverate on words (Fragile X)

Disorder/Diagnostic Label	Caused by	Language Characteristics
Cerebral Palsy	Motor deficits caused by damage to the brain	• Child's exploration limited due to physical limitations • Cognitive deficits are common • Language delayed • Articulation difficult due to motor problems
Hearing Impairment	Damage to inner ear (sensorineural hearing loss) or middle ear (conductive hearing loss)	• Language skills dependent on when hearing loss occurred—either prelingual, perilingual, or postlingual (see Chapter 12 on students who are deaf or hard of hearing) • Language delay likely due to limited language experiences • Difficulty with form, content, and use of language • May use American Sign Language (ASL) or some other form of sign language
Prenatal exposure to drugs or alcohol	Damage to the brain during formation	Language delays associated with cognitive deficits, limited environmental stimulation
Premature birth	Possible neurological deficits	Developmental delays in language and other domains
Failure to thrive	Neglect, malnutrition, limited stimulation	Developmental delays in language and other domains
Cytomegalovirus (CMV) infection	Viral disease that results in brain damage—contracted prenatal or postnatal	Delays due to cognitive disabilities, sensory deficits, and motor disabilities
Mental retardation	Damage to the brain—prenatal, perinatal, or postnatal	Language deficits range from mild to severe, depending on severity of the disorder
Autism	Neurological disorder—see Chapter 10 for indepth discussion of autism and autism spectrum disorder (ASD)	Language deficit is key feature of the diagnosis; may range from mild to severe; echolalia and other stereotypical speech patterns possible; deficits in expressive and receptive language skills
Traumatic Brain Injury	Acquired damage to the brain caused by an external force such as blow to the head in a car accident or fall	Aphasia, memory problems, information processing problems, reduced attending skills

Language disorders can be acquired, either before the child develops language (pre-lingual), during the period of language development (peri-lingual), or after the child has developed typical language skills (post-lingual). A virus such as meningitis, a convulsive disorder, or some type of head trauma may cause brain damage resulting in an acquired language disorder. Trauma from traumatic brain injuries (TBI) may be from head injuries from falls, car accidents, and physical abuse, or hypoxia from near drowning. Traumatic brain injuries can cause pervasive disorders for children in cognitive, social/emotional, physical, and communication areas. Aphasia is a severe acquired language disorder that may affect a child who has had a traumatic brain injury. Children with aphasia may have effortful or nonfluent speech, impaired repetition skills, difficulty with reading and writing, syntax problems, and comprehension problems. They also might have difficulty with speech production, with understanding figurative or abstract language, or with attention (Vinson, 2007). These students may have trouble understanding language or using language that they had little difficulty with prior to the injury. Language deficits such as aphasia can severely affect the student's ability to succeed academically and socially.

Some children have Specific Language Impairments (SLI) that cannot be attributed to sensory, motor, or cognitive deficits. These children may have language that is *different* from typically developing children, or language that is *delayed*. They may have difficulty expressing themselves or understanding language, and many children with SLI are thought to have central auditory processing problems. Central auditory processing problems limit abilities in auditory discrimination, auditory attention, and auditory memory, all of which are important to the understanding and use of language. Because of these language problems, students may have difficulty with academic and social success in school (Vinson, 2007).

In addition to having language deficits, students with identified language delays or language disorders may also experience problems with attention, comprehension, reading/writing, problem solving, motor functioning, and social skills. Depending on the severity of the disorder, music teachers and music therapists may need to make instructional adaptations in many areas to accommodate students in the music class and music therapy setting.

Music Education for Students with Speech and Language Disorders
Strategies for the Music Classroom

Students with mild speech and language disorders may not need additional accommodations in the music class, and it is unlikely that a student with only a mild language disorder would be recommended for music therapy. In fact, music educators may not even know which students have language delays or language disorders unless the disorders are moderate to severe and significantly impede the student's success in music class. Teachers of students with moderate or severe language disorders usually need to make some adaptations to instructional interventions to help the student succeed in music class. The first step is to obtain information from the classroom teacher and other professionals who work with the student to determine effective strategies for supporting the student's language needs. Students with multiple disabilities, in addition to a language disorder, may require several types of adaptations in order to successfully participate in the music classroom.

Several strategies for adapting instruction for students with disabilities are described in Chapter 4. Many of these strategies are appropriate for use with students who have speech and language disorders to support their learning in music class. Some examples of how some of these strategies might be implemented in the music setting are listed below. This is not an exhaustive listing, but it presents some ideas for making adaptations that could be appropriate, depending on the needs of the students. These adaptations can be used in an inclusive music class, a self-contained music class, or a music therapy setting.

- *Input—Adapt the way that instruction is delivered to the students.*
  - » Use visuals, movement/gestures, and other nonverbal formats for giving directions or sharing information and ideas.
  - » Speak slowly, when necessary, to help the student comprehend information; use repetition and allow time for processing when asking for a response. Create a relaxed environment so students do not feel pressured or anxious.
- *Output—Adapt how the students can respond to instruction.*
  - » Know if the student typically uses any type of alternative or augmentative communication device and allow the student to use that device to respond in class; make sure it is programmed with terminology to express thoughts and ideas in music class.
  - » Depending on the abilities of the student, encourage spontaneous language opportunities, along with opportunities to respond using full sentences rather than simply "yes" or "no" answers.
  - » The student may need to respond physically rather than verbally, such as through pointing to an instrument ("Which one is in the percussion family?"), pointing to make a choice ("Which instrument do you want to play, the djembe or the bongo?") or by dramatizing an answer ("Did the melody go up or down?").
- *Time—Adapt the amount of time allotted for completing a task, taking a test, or learning a new skill.*
  - » Give the student plenty of time to give a response in class if a verbal response is required. Students may have difficulty processing directions or requests from the teacher, or they may have difficulty finding words or making actual speech sounds. Refrain from jumping in too quickly (or letting other students jump in) to provide the correct answer.

»   Students may need extra time to respond using an alternative or augmentative communication device, as they need to find the right letter/word/picture to give a response.

• *Level of support—Increase amount of support from others.*
    »   Use peer buddies to assist the student when needed.
    »   Taper off support from others to increase students' independence when appropriate.
    »   Music activities can be highly motivating for students. Share music activities and songs with the speech and language therapist so the student can work on speech and language skills using the songs and other activities used in music. The student can build language skills as well as be more prepared to be successful in music class.

Music Therapy for Students with Speech and Language Disorders

Music therapy has been shown to be effective in improving language and communication skills with children and adults who have language disorders. Studies document the use of music therapy in assisting children with language delays and apraxia to develop language skills (Adamek, Gervin, & Shiraishi, 2000; Cohen, 1994; Krauss & Galloway, 1982; Seybold, 1971) as well as the use of music therapy in language rehabilitation of persons with brain injuries (Claeys, Miller, Dalloud-Rampersad, & Kollan, 1989; Cohen, 1988, 1992; Robb, 1996). Music therapy in early intervention and preschool classes may contribute to improved language development of young children with disabilities (Davis, 1990; Humpal, 1990).

Music Therapy as a Related Service and District-wide Service

Some students with language disorders may be eligible for music therapy as a related service. Goals for music therapy as a related service will be taken directly from a student's IEP (see Chapter 6 for more information about Music Therapy as a Related Service). Primarily, goals will be focused on improving communication skills, but may also focus on improving social, academic, physical, or leisure skills, depending on the needs of the students.

As discussed in Chapter 6, music therapy can also be an educational service to many students in a school district to enhance their educational program. Students with speech and language disorders are likely to be integrated into the regular education classroom and to be a part of the music education classroom. They may receive some additional special education services directly in the classroom or in a separate resource room for more intensive one-to-one or small group services. Students who have severe multiple disabilities may be educated in a self-contained classroom for part or all of the school day, and it may be at these times that a music therapist would provide services to a small group of students. Examples of goal areas for students with language disorders, along with ideas for goal-directed music therapy interventions, are listed below.

Music Therapy Goals and Intervention Strategies

Students with language disorders may be referred to music therapy if a parent or professional thinks that music therapy interventions might stimulate, reinforce, or develop a student's speech and language abilities. Music therapy goals for students with speech and language disorders will primarily focus on communication skills. Secondary areas of focus include improvement of social skills, academic skills, physical skills, and leisure skills. Music therapy can be a highly motivating and flexible approach for working on these various goals. A structured music therapy activity could involve the student in listening, singing, playing, moving, or responding in other ways, both verbally and nonverbally. A student can work on several skills through just one goal-directed music therapy activity. Communication skills, social skills, and academic skills might all be addressed in a music and movement activity where the students make choices, improvise ideas, follow directions, interact with a partner, and learn about AB form.

Music Therapy to Improve Receptive and Expressive Language Skills

Music therapists use the elements of music to create a rich language environment for students to practice and improve their speech and language skills. Music therapy interventions can be facilitated to encourage expressive language and increase receptive language skills. Auditory awareness and auditory discrimination, skills needed for language development, can be addressed through music activities focusing on being aware of sounds, locating sounds, tracking sounds, and identifying sounds.

Expressive language skills may be enhanced through a variety of verbal and nonverbal methods. Examples include singing simple and repetitive songs, sharing ideas about songs and music, making choices related to preferred songs or instruments, or participating in imitation and call-and-response rhythmic activities. Students can develop vocabulary by describing the music or the sounds they hear, writing and performing songs about their experiences, and learning new words from songs. Receptive language skills may also be improved through verbal and nonverbal music interventions. Students may be asked to follow the direction of a drum beat by moving to the beat as it speeds up and slows down, then stops. They may be directed to move their bodies the way the music sounds, for instance, using a glissando for smooth movements, using a large drum for heavy movements, and using finger cymbals for light movements. Students may also be directed to follow verbal directions as to how to play, move, or sing within the session. The possibilities for enriching language and communication skills through music are limited only by the imagination and creativity of the music therapist.

Music Therapy to Improve Social Skills

Language is a key factor for socialization with others, so it is likely that students with severe language delays or language disorders will also have social skill deficits. Music therapy interventions can be structured to give students opportunities to practice social skills. Through music making with others, students can work on taking turns, sharing, listening, self-expression, leadership, and other social skills needed for active involvement with others. Demonstration of these skills may be in a nonverbal form, such as during an instrument ensemble intervention, or they may be demonstrated in a verbal form through feedback during or after a music activity.

Music Therapy to Improve Cognitive Skills (focus of attention, memory, problem solving)

The development and enhancement of cognitive skills may also be the focus of music therapy. Students with language disorders may have difficulty with focus of attention, memory, or problem solving, especially those students who have a language disorder related to a head injury or brain damage. Music activities can be broken down into small steps, then increased in complexity to challenge a student's memory skills. Nonverbal forms of input, such as rhythms played on percussion instruments, can be used for an imitation and call-and-response activity to improve memory and focus of attention. Other nonverbal forms of interventions include movement to music, playing simple rhythmic parts in an ensemble, or developing an improvisation on an Orff instrument to go along with a song. Verbal music interventions to increase memory and focus of attention include learning words to a song, creating song lyrics and performing the song, discussing song lyrics, or giving directions for leading a song or an ensemble (deciding what comes first, who plays when, ending the song, etc.). Preferred music can provide a motivating foundation for keeping a student interested and involved, even when the task is challenging. Table 9.2 lists sample goals areas along with ideas for music therapy strategies.

Table 9.2 Summary of Goal Areas and Examples of Music Therapy Interventions

Goal Area	Sample Music Therapy Strategy
Expressive language skills	• Writing songs to express ideas • Making choices about songs, instruments, movement • Learning and practicing new words through simple, repetitive songs
Receptive language skills	• Responding to verbal cues in songs such as "move like a monkey" • Responding to nonverbal cues, such as cues given on instruments—to stop when the drum stops, move when the drum plays

Goal Area	Sample Music Therapy Strategy
Social skills	• Working together in group music making, such as tone chime ensemble or percussion ensemble • Playing then passing instruments; sharing • Leading group music making; making decisions about how to play a piece • Working on a performance using leadership skills, listening, responding, decision making
Cognitive skills	• Using simple, motivating activities to gain focus of attention • Increase length/complexity of the music activities to improve attention skills • Imitation of rhythms; call and response to increase memory skills

Summary

Communication disorders affect a large percentage of students with disabilities in schools today. While this chapter focused on students with language delays and specific language impairments, students with many other diagnoses may also have moderate or severe communication problems. Most music educators and music therapists will work with students with communication disorders in the various classroom settings. Students with severe communication deficits may require significant adaptations, but students with mild or moderate problems may simply require additional time or patience on the part of the teacher.

KEY POINTS FROM THE CHAPTER

Language delay and language disorders
Prevalence and characteristics:

♦ Language delays and language disorders may be caused by such disorders as cerebral palsy, mental retardation, autism, brain injury, hearing impairment, or other neurological impairment.

♦ Language disorders can be acquired before, during, or after the development of typical language skills.

♦ A child with a language delay develops typical language competencies but at a slower rate than would be expected, while a child with a language disorder displays language skills and behaviors that are not typical of normally developing language skills.

♦ Language disorders may be related to content (semantics); form (phonology, syntax, and morphology); or functional use (pragmatics).

Educational considerations:

♦ Students with mild speech and language disorders may not need additional accommodations in music class.

♦ Students with multiple disabilities, including a language disorder, may require several different types of instructional or curricular adaptations in order to successfully participate in the music classroom.

♦ Music therapy may be an appropriate intervention to improve a student's receptive and expressive language, improve social skills, and improve such cognitive skills as focus of attention, memory, and problem solving.

REFERENCES

Adamek, M., Gervin, A. & Shiraishi, I. (2000). Music therapy and speech rehabilitation with brain-injured patients: Research, intervention models and assessment. In *Effectiveness of music therapy procedures: Documentation of research and clinical practice* (3rd ed., pp. 113–134). Silver Spring, MD: American Music Therapy Association.

Claeys, M. S., Miller, A. C., Dalloud-Rampersad, R., & Kollan, M. (1989). The role of music and music therapy in the rehabilitation of traumatically brain injured clients. *Music Therapy Perspectives, 6*, 71–78.

Cohen, N. (1988). The use of superimposed rhythm to decrease the rate of speech in a brain damaged adolescent. *Journal of Music Therapy, 25*, 85–93.

Cohen, N. (1992). The effects of singing instruction on the speech production of neurologically impaired persons. *Journal of Music Therapy, 29*, 87–102.

Cohen, N. (1994). Speech and song: Implications for therapy. *Music Therapy Perspectives, 12*, 8–14.

Data Accountability Center. (2007). *Individuals with Disabilities Education Act (IDEA) data: Part B data and notes.* Retrieved April 6, 2010, from https://www.ideadata.org/PartBData.asp

Davis, R. K. (1990). A model for the integration of music therapy with preschool classrooms for children with physical disabilities or language delays. *Music Therapy Perspectives, 8*, 82–84.

Humpal, M. (1990). Early intervention: The implications for music therapy. *Music Therapy Perspectives, 8*, 30–35.

Krauss, T., & Galloway, H. (1982). Melodic intonation therapy with language-delayed, apraxic children. *Journal of Music Therapy, 19*, 102–113.

Mastropieri, M., & Scruggs, T. (2000). *The inclusive classroom: Strategies for effective instruction.* Upper Saddle River, NJ: Merrill/Prentice Hall.

Paul, R. (2007). *Language disorders from infancy through adolescence: Assessment and intervention* (3rd ed.). St. Louis, MO: Mosby Elsevier.

Robb, S. (1996). Techniques in song writing: Restoring emotional and physical well being in adolescents who have been traumatically injured. *Music Therapy Perspectives, 14*, 30–37.

Seybold, C. D. (1971). The value and use of music activities in the treatment of speech delayed children. *Journal of Music Therapy, 8*, 102–110.

Vinson, B. P. (2007). *Language disorders across the lifespan* (2nd ed.). Clifton Park, NY: Thomson.

Chapter 10

Students with Autism Spectrum Disorders (ASD)

CHAPTER OVERVIEW

According to data collected for the U.S. Department of Education, over 258,000 students with autism received services under IDEA in 2007 (Data Accountability Center, 2007). This is more than three times the number of students with autism served just 5 years earlier in 2002. Approximately 1 in 100 children are diagnosed with ASD, and this disorder is four times more prevalent in boys than in girls. The number of individuals diagnosed with autism is increasing rapidly by a rate of 10–17% each year (Autism Society of America, 2010). Although autism is considered a low incidence disorder, many music educators and music therapists work with students with autism each week in schools.

This chapter includes information on the following topics:
♦   Characteristics of students with autism spectrum disorders (ASD)
♦   Educational implications
♦   Music education for students with autism spectrum disorders
♦   Music therapy services for students with autism spectrum disorders

---

Characteristics of Autism Spectrum Disorders

Autism Spectrum Disorder (ASD) includes autism as well as other disorders that are like autism but do not meet all of the same diagnostic criteria for autism, including Rett's Disorder, Childhood Disintegrative Disorder, Asperger's Disorder, and Pervasive Developmental Disorder Not Otherwise Specified (PDD-NOS). These are all listed in the *Diagnostic and Statistical Manual of Mental Disorders (DSM-IV-TR)* (American Psychological Association, 2000) under Pervasive Developmental

Disorders. As a spectrum disorder, various possible disorders and characteristics exist, which have differing levels of developmental delay ranging from mild to severe. Students with ASD usually require similar types of educational interventions, adapted to their specific needs and abilities. Autism and ASD affect children of all social classes, financial levels, educational levels, cultures, and races throughout the world (Scott, Clark, & Brady, 2000; Turnbull, Turnbull, & Wehmeyer, 2010).

Children who are diagnosed with autism or other ASD have qualitative impairments in communication skills and social skills. These students may have difficulty with expressive and receptive language or interacting with others, and they usually are unable to understand that others' thoughts, feelings, and perspectives might be different from their own (Coleman, 2005; Mastropieri & Scruggs, 2000; Scott et al., 2000). Some students with autism are nonverbal, while others may be highly verbal but have difficulty with interpretation or meaning in language. In addition to communication and social problems, they have a limited range of interests and activities when compared to typically developing peers, and they may exhibit unusual stereotypic and self-stimulating behaviors. Many, but not all, children with autism also have intellectual disabilities; however, children with Asperger's syndrome do not have delays in intellectual functioning and can be very intelligent. Individuals with Asperger's syndrome have significant challenges and delays in social functioning but do not have significant delays in language skills.

The characteristics of autism may be present in a wide combination of behaviors and levels of severity, so a group of children all diagnosed with autism can have very different abilities, personalities, and skills. As a spectrum disorder, the range of abilities and degree of developmental delay manifest as individual differences unique to each child; however, all children with autism have some sort of difficulty with communication and social skills (see Table 10.1). Children with autism can learn and make developmental gains in many areas of functioning when provided with appropriate educational support and treatment.

Table 10.1 Continuum of Abilities and Limitations for Persons with Autism

Area of Functioning	Variability Levels
Measured Intelligence	Severely impaired------------------------------------- Gifted
Social Interaction	Aloof ----------------- Passive ----------------Active but odd
Communication	Nonverbal ---Verbal
Behaviors	Intense -- Mild
Sensory	Hyposensitive -------------------------------- Hypersensitive
Motor	Uncoordinated------------------------------- Coordinated

(Adamek, Thaut & Furman, 2008, p. 120)

Children who are typically developing have intact sensory systems that help them perceive the world around them. Their senses of vision, hearing, touch, taste, and smell work together to help them make sense of their environment and understand what they are experiencing. Some children with autism have sensory integration problems that can cause oversensitivity or undersensitivity to certain stimuli. For a child with sensory integration problems, the environment may be confusing, painful, or frightening because these systems are not working together to help him or her decode and understand the environment. For instance, children with autism might be particularly sensitive to high or loud sounds and, when presented with this type of sound, they will shriek, hold their ears, or be aggressive in some way. Teachers should be aware of a child's reactions to certain stimuli and adapt or avoid certain sounds or movements when appropriate. This is especially important in a music class, where sounds and movement are a primary focus of the class. Children with autism may have atypical, inappropriate, or unusual behaviors in class because they process and respond to information in different ways. Students may exhibit aggressive or self-injurious behaviors when they are unable to understand or unable to communicate their confusion, but not all children with autism exhibit these types of behaviors.

Children with autism or ASD may display some of the following characteristics. It is important to note that not all children with this diagnosis have all of these traits, and the severity of the disorder varies by individual.

- Difficulty with communication and expressing needs; may point, use gestures, or use other nonverbal forms of communication such as pictures or icons
- Repeating words or phrases, echolalic
- Unresponsive to verbal cues or directions; may appear to be deaf due to unresponsiveness
- Difficulty interacting with peers; minimal spontaneous socialization
- Oversensitivity or undersensitivity to stimuli or to pain
- Resistance to change; insistence on routine
- Minimal direct eye contact
- Odd or unusual play, particularly sustained play or attachment to objects

    (Autism Society of America, 2010; National Education Association, 2006)

Contrary to some beliefs, children with autism or ASD may make eye contact, develop good functional language and communication skills, socialize with peers, and show affection. Their skills in these areas might be different or less sophisticated than typically developing peers, but it is very likely that with appropriate educational and social interventions, children with autism and ASD may develop functional and appropriate skills in all of these areas.

Educational Implications

Communication Skills

One of the primary deficits for students with autism and other ASD is communication, so it is important to help the student develop effective communication skills. Students who have severe autism may have little or no receptive or expressive language, while students with mild forms of autism may have developed language skills that allow them to communicate with others. There are many alternative and augmentative communication (AAC) systems available to either enhance a student's verbal communication skills or become a student's primary means of communication. These alternative systems help a student express wants and needs, initiate and maintain conversations, and receive and understand information from others. A team of speech and language professionals assesses the students in all areas to match the students' needs and abilities to the best AAC system. AAC systems can be a simple system of pointing to pictures, words, or letter boards, or more sophisticated methods, such as use of sign language, voice output computers, or visual tracking devices (Mitchell, 2008; National Research Council, 2001; Scott et al., 2000; Turnbull et al., 2010). Communication systems can provide a means for students to communicate with others in a meaningful way and allow two-way, interactive communication between the student with autism and others.

The Picture Exchange Communication System (PECS) is a good example of an AAC system that is used in many classrooms. PECS is a behavioral system that teaches students to use pictures and symbols to initiate conversations, respond to others, and ask for wants and needs. Using PECS, a student learns the meaning of a set of pictures or symbols by exchanging those symbols for something he or she wants or needs. Using a sentence strip that says "I want _____," the student learns to fill in the blank with a picture (attached to the sentence strip with Velcro) that stands for whatever he or she wants, and then hands the sentence strip back to the teacher in exchange for the desired object (Bondy & Frost, 1994; Frost & Bondy, 1994; Kravits, Kamps, Kemmerer, & Potucek, 2002; Mitchell, 2008). For instance, in music class, when students are given an opportunity to choose an instrument to play, the student using PECS could fill in the blank with a picture of a drum to indicate that he or she wants to play the drum during instrument time. The student then gives the completed sentence strip to the teacher in exchange for the drum. This approach, like all AAC systems, takes consistent training and use to develop skills for effective communication. The student uses the AAC throughout the day at school, at home, and during recreational or free time activities to promote communication. Other AAC systems might simply be a picture/symbol book, board, or wallet that the student uses to point to what he or she wants or to respond to a question. Some students may use functional sign language to communicate with others. More sophisticated technology such as computers with voice output systems can also provide an effective means of communication for students with communication deficits. With this type of system, the student might have a keyboard or picture board that is programmed to "say" the word when it is spelled out or a picture is touched. A speech and language pathologist usually programs these with ideas from teachers and parents for appropriate words and functionality. The music educator and music therapist can offer useful ideas for words or phrases that will help the student communicate and participate at the highest possible level in the music setting (McCarthy, Geist, Zojwala, & Schock, 2008). Some possible responses added to a student's AAC system for use in music education or music therapy include:

- Yes or No
- Icon to represent music, or a picture of the music room
- Pictures or drawings of instruments used in music
- Pictures or drawings of props used in music
- Names of favorite songs sung in music
- Iconic representation of note values, such as whole note, half note, quarter note, eighth note
- Pictures related to the schedule or order of events in music, such as "hello song or opening song," "movement time," "play instruments," or "sing songs"
- Picture or name of peer buddy in music
- Picture or name of music teacher or music therapist
- Functional signs used for directions such as "stop," "play," "dance"

Use of Visuals and Structure to Enhance Receptive and Expressive Communication

Teachers may need to give additional thought to the organization and facilitation of instruction to promote the most successful outcomes. Organizing instruction includes such preparatory tasks as preparing visual structure for the student, developing a schedule for classroom activities, preparing adaptations of the lesson plan, and making sure the environment is conducive to the needs of the students. Music professionals can gain insight and ideas for structure from the classroom teachers and other professionals who work with the student each day. Whenever possible, similar adaptations and approaches should be utilized throughout the student's day to encourage generalization of skills and to support the student's understanding of the environment.

Visual cues are very important in the education of students with autism. Most of these students are more successful when presented with visual cues and instructions than when only verbal instructions are used. Visual cues can be used for giving directions, offering choices, teaching new skills, or providing structure for an activity. Through added visuals, it is possible to present the schedule for the class, teach and reinforce the classroom rules, and help the student focus and prioritize attention on the important material to be learned. In music class or music therapy sessions, visuals can be used in music class or music therapy sessions to support the student's learning and increase success in an inclusive setting. Visual cues may be icons, photos, or functional signs to convey information. Suggested uses for visuals include:

- describing classroom rules (listen, hands to self—by using drawings, pictures, or acting out the behavior);
- presenting the schedule for class activities—helps student understand order of events in a predictable manner;

- modeling movement that students can imitate;
- pairing pictures with songs to help students either to know what activity is next or to allow them to choose a preferred song (a sun for "Mr. Sun" or "You Are My Sunshine").

These visual enhancements do not need to be detailed or complex. Rather, they should be simple so that the student can make the connection between the visual and the task, object, or direction that is being communicated.

Thoughtful classroom structure and placement help the student organize and focus attention appropriately. Some students need to be close to others for structure and support, while other students may need more space due to tactile defensiveness or hyperactivity. Close proximity of the teacher or therapist to the students is important when working in a small group. This proximity allows the teacher or therapist to provide physical and gestural prompts when needed and gives the student a clear idea of where he or she should be looking for instruction.

Social Skills and Peer Interactions

Appropriate social skills are necessary for successful inclusion and normalization. Individuals with autism and ASD have core deficits in social interaction and social perception, which manifest in difficulty initiating interaction, difficulty maintaining social relationships, and difficulty understanding the perceptions of others (Prizant, Wetherby, Rubin, Laurent, & Rydell, 2006; Turnbull et al., 2010). Social skills are a major feature of a child's growth and development, and they play an important role in students' ability to function in integrated classroom or community settings. Students with autism may need direct training to improve social skills in a variety of settings. Students' social deficits can range from mild, such as difficulty making and maintaining eye contact, to more severe, such as inability to share experiences and interests with others. Some students with severe social deficits may seem oblivious to others and the environment, while other students with less severe deficits may interact spontaneously with others. Even students with higher functioning skills may have problems understanding the perspective of others, having difficulty understanding that the thoughts, beliefs, and intentions of others may be different than their own. Some children with autism stiffen and avoid physical contact, while others may be clingy and have inappropriate boundaries (always wanting to sit on the teacher's lap or right next to others in very close proximity). Social behaviors vary over time, and children with autism can develop more socially appropriate behaviors through social skills training. Since communication provides the foundation for developing and maintaining social relationships, students with autism need to develop functional communication along with social skills in order to enhance their abilities to interact with others, make friends, and be included in classroom and social activities.

A variety of techniques can be used to teach social skills. Teachers and therapists must keep in mind the age, language skills, developmental level, and interests of the student in order to develop effective approaches. Some current educational approaches used to teach social skills include:

- direct instruction—students taught to directly interact with peers with support from teacher prompts, modeling, or providing physical assistance during the interaction;
- social communication training—teaching students to ask questions and seek out information in a social setting;
- use of social stories—stories developed to teach social skill concepts and strategies; these stories can also be set to music to create social story songs;
- leisure related social skill development—teaching social interaction and rules of play through leisure skills; developing friendships through peer buddies;
- positive behavioral supports—tailoring the students' environments to their needs, interests and strengths.

(Kern, Wakeford, & Aldridge, 2007; Mitchell, 2008; Register & Humpal, 2007; Scott et al., 2000; Turnbull et al., 2010)

Example of a social story song about **waiting your turn** *in music (to the tune of ABC song):*

Wait your turn, wait today,
Then you'll have a chance to play.
First it's her, then it's him,
Round the circle back to you.
Wait your turn, wait today,
Then you'll have a chance to play.

It is always important to use instructional materials that are age appropriate for the students. Materials and activities that do not match the chronological age for the students involved can become stigmatizing and likely will not meet the standard for normalized experiences. With the goal of developing skills for maintaining meaningful social relationships, teachers and therapists must be creative in developing interventions that are age and developmentally appropriate for the students. Students need adults to provide instruction and numerous motivating opportunities for social interaction in order to develop long-term, meaningful social relationships with peers (Brown, Branston, Hamre-Nietupski, Pumpian, Certo, & Gruenewald, 1979; Jellison, Brooks, & Huck, 1984).

Managing Difficult Behaviors

Students with autism may have behaviors that are difficult to manage in an inclusive setting or in a self-contained classroom. Deficits in language and communication, social interaction, focus of attention, aggression, stereotypic or self-stimulating behaviors, oversensitivity to sensory input, and difficulty with generalization of skills are some characteristic features of autism that affect behavior (Coleman, 2005; National Research Council, 2001; Simpson & Miles, 1998). These behaviors can be among the most challenging and stressful factors for teachers as they strive to provide appropriate and effective educational experiences for the students. The child may exhibit problem behaviors due to inability to understand the expectations of the classroom or because of the inability to communicate wants and needs. Students may also be confused about the consequences of their behavior, especially in relation to the severe difficulty that these students may have in initiating and maintaining positive social relationships. Behaviors such as aggression towards others, self-injurious behaviors, noncompliance, and disruption of classroom routines may create difficult and frustrating situations for the teacher and other students in the class.

While no single intervention will deal effectively with all problem behaviors, most professionals recommend using a preventative approach to decrease problem behaviors and increase positive behaviors. A proactive approach, such as utilizing positive behavioral interventions and supports, can create an environment for students' success in the classroom. This approach, which builds on the strengths of the student, focuses on changes in the environment (class structure, amount of time in activities, appropriateness of setting), instructional changes (teaching skills to the student and those who work with the student to improve the student's academic, social, communication, and behavioral functioning), and behavioral consequences (to minimize impeding behaviors and increase positive behaviors) (National Education Association, 2006). Music educators and music therapists should utilize methods to promote positive behaviors, including:

- creating a sense of predictability and routine in the classroom—using a visual schedule, having a predictable room set up, using familiar materials *(for example: pictures that represent types of activities will help the student understand what is coming next. Small drawings to represent "opening song/ warm-up," "movement," "singing," "instrument playing," and "closing" will help the student understand the class schedule).*

- providing alternative or adapted goals, activities, and settings *(for example: give the student small, concrete tasks that can be completed before adding complexity; allow the student to complete work in a quiet setting, or do music tasks on the computer if he or she is getting overstimulated or distracted by the group).*

- using a functional approach to problem behaviors—identification of events that occur before the problem behavior and events that occur after the behavior and serve to reinforce the behavior *(for example: notice what happens to "set off" a student's outburst; Is the music very loud or is there a high amount of activity in the room? What happens after an outburst? Does the student get to leave the class or get to play anything he or she wants? Changing these factors may help improve the student's behavior).*

- providing positive reinforcement for appropriate behaviors *(for example: be sure to catch students doing what you want them to be doing, and reinforce them immediately, so they understand the expectations).*
- providing a means of communication for the student, and making sure that the communication system transfers to all school environments, including music *(for example: Does the student have a communication system that he or she uses in the classroom? If so, make sure there are music words included, and familiarize yourself with how the student can communicate and at what level. Is it a yes/no system or more complex?).*
- teaching peers how to interact in a positive way with the student *(for example: be sure peers know that this student has a disability that impacts language and behavior. If a student strikes out when someone touches him or her, be sure the peers know that the student needs additional space).*
- understanding the student's individual plan for creating positive behaviors and dealing with problem behaviors—this should be a part of the student's IEP *(for example: What does the classroom teacher do to manage behavior? Is there an approach that can also be used in music class? Does the teacher use tokens, a point system, or other behavior modification techniques that you can also use in music?).*
- implementing this individual plan in a consistent manner *(for example: use the same tokens, point system, rewards, and consequences each time so the student understands the system).*

Table 10.2 provides examples of the characteristic features of autism and how they might cause difficult behaviors in the music class or music therapy session.

Table 10.2 Examples of Autism Behaviors and Music Interventions

Characteristic Feature	Specific Difficulties	Possible Behavior	Interventions
Language and communication impairment	Student has difficulty understanding directions; student has difficulty expressing self and needs	Not following through with directions, may seem deaf due to lack of response to teacher; outburst such as screaming, hitting/biting self, hitting peer due to frustration of not getting needs met	Use visuals to give direction; get student's attention before giving directions; use alternative communication system making sure music terms are listed; learn basic signs/communication systems used by the student

Characteristic Feature	Specific Difficulties	Possible Behavior	Interventions
Social interaction difficulty	Student has difficulty reading social cues from others, may think that peers think/feel the same way he/she does; difficulty understanding the perspective of others	Difficulty interacting with others, sharing classroom materials, may want to always go first or sit in a specific chair and will push other student out of the chair; isolation from peers, minimal spontaneous interaction with peers	Use cooperative groups to encourage interaction; create clear rules/expectations for behavior and enforce them; reinforce positive interactions with verbal reinforcers; consequate negative behaviors such as pushing
Focus of attention problems	Student has difficulty processing information, focusing on the main feature of instruction (teacher?) and problems filtering out other distracters, such as auditory or visual distractions	Not following through with directions, tasks, or assignments; engaging in off-task or self-stimulating behaviors; inability to follow multi-step directions	Use visuals or signs to gain attention; place student where there are few distractions and close to teacher; use peer buddy to help with focus of attention
Aggressive, stereotypic or self-stimulating behaviors	Student gets frustrated—has difficulty communicating needs or understanding expectations; sensory integration problems so student provides own stimulation	Acting out towards others; rocking or hand flapping to provide sensory stimulation; "spacing out" by focusing visually on such things as flickering lights, fan blades, or shiny instruments; repeatedly playing an instrument close to ears	Assist with communication needs, making sure student has a way to communicate needs directly; choose instruments that do not reinforce self-stimulating behavior; make sure student has enough physical structure to create boundaries if needed; observe student's reaction to different sounds and avoid using sounds that elicit a negative response

Characteristic Feature	Specific Difficulties	Possible Behavior	Interventions
Oversensitivity to sensory input	Student has sensory integration and processing problems so he/she may not be able to handle tactile, visual, or auditory stimuli in the same way as other students. Some sensory stimulation, such as high-pitched instruments or tactile vibrations from a percussion instrument, could cause pain or uncomfortable sensations	Acting out or isolation; holding ears with hands; rejecting touch from others; refusal to play instruments that provide tactile stimulation; student may throw instrument, strike out, or scream if sensory input is too much	Observe student's reaction to different sounds, visual stimuli, or tactile stimulation and avoid using instruments that promote an undesirable reaction; use a peer buddy to work with student during times when sensory input might be problematic; allow the student time away from the class when sensory stimulation might be too much for him/her to handle
Difficulty generalizing behaviors	Student has difficulty applying skills learned in one situation to another situation	Difficulty with transition from classroom to music room; may act out physically, vocally, or refuse participation; difficulty transferring playing skills from one instrument to another without additional instruction	Work with classroom teacher to provide easier transition to music; some students need a transitional object to bring with them to new setting (such as a small toy or sensory object); use similar teaching methods as classroom teacher to promote generalization

Behavioral strategies are widely used to teach appropriate behaviors to students with autism. Using a behavioral approach, it is important to recognize antecedents (what happens before the target behavior) and consequences (what happens as a result of the behavior) in order to determine some possible causes and reinforcing events. The teacher/therapist can develop strategies and adaptations to promote students' appropriate behavior when they understand some of the potential causes of the inappropriate behavior. See Chapter 5 for in-depth information regarding managing students' behavior effectively and Chapter 7 for ideas related to working with children with behavior disorders.

Music Education for Students with Autism Spectrum Disorders

Some students with autism excel in music and may need few adaptations in order to be successful in an inclusive music classroom. Other students might need significant individualized adaptations due to severe social, communication, or behavioral difficulties. Each child with autism is different, so teachers and therapists must get to know the individual needs of the individual student.

Adaptations for the Music Classroom

In general, students with autism need a structured classroom that is predictable and consistent to help them learn. Information should be presented visually as well as verbally to support students' processing and understanding. Typically developing peers can provide models of appropriate behavior and age-appropriate social interaction for students with autism when engaged in structured experiences (Pierangelo & Giuliani, 2001; Turnbull et al., 2010). These general strategies, combined with strategies developed based on individual student needs, will promote success in the music classroom.

Educators and therapists should always consider using the principles of Universal Design for Learning (UDL) described in Chapter 4. Strategies such as using visuals, providing multiple means of instructional delivery, and proximity may all support the needs of students with autism without additional adaptations. However, some students will need additional adaptations due to their level of disability. Several strategies for adapting instruction for students with severe disabilities were described in Chapter 4. Many of these strategies are appropriate for use with students who have autism to support their learning and increase positive behavior in music class. Examples of how some of these strategies might be implemented in the music setting are listed below. These adaptations can be used in an inclusive music class, a self-contained music class, or a music therapy setting.

- *Participation—Vary the level of participation that is expected of the student.*
  - » For some students, partial participation might be most appropriate. For example, Johnny is a student with autism in the 5th grade. His class is learning a dance with Orff ensemble accompaniment for a familiar folk song. Johnny has great difficulty playing instruments as part of an ensemble, but he is able to do the movement part of the activity with assistance from a peer buddy. The music teacher decides to have Johnny focus only on the dance/movement aspect of the activity to build on his strengths, even though the other students rotate around the room playing instruments and dancing.
  - » Another student with autism might be able to successfully participate in the music class for only 20 minutes of the 40-minute period. After 20 minutes, the stimulation becomes too great and he becomes aggressive

to himself and others. Rather than making him stay in the class for the entire time, it might be more effective to have him participate for the first half of the class, then go to another setting for the remainder of the class (e.g., computer time back in his classroom with an aide or peer buddy). His time in music could be extended when he is better able to handle the stimulation in the class.

» Keep the student actively involved as much as possible, building on the student's abilities.

• *Input—Adapt the way that instruction is delivered to the students.*

» Using visuals to enhance directions, structure the class (i.e., schedule) and reinforce concepts that may be useful for students with auditory processing problems. Routines are very important. Be consistent whenever possible, and when a major shift in routine is imminent, work with the student (and teacher or aide) to prepare the student for the new schedule or routine.

» Break steps down into small steps or tasks.

» Use a direct approach to teach skills. Teach and model correct responses. If using a discovery approach or improvisation, give choices upon which the students can build.

» Discuss the student's communication system with the classroom teacher and speech and language pathologist and utilize a consistent approach in music.

» When giving the student choices, offer a limited number of choices initially, then increase number of options as the student becomes better at making decisions.

• *Output—Adapt how the students can respond to instruction.*

» Make sure that responses appropriate to music are a part of the student's alternative communication system, if used. Icons/words related to instruments, concepts (fast/slow), notation (half note, whole note) as well as yes/no responses can be a part of the student's communication system.

• *Alternate goals—While using the same materials for all students, adapt the outcome expectations or goals.*

» The goals related to music learning could be different for a student with autism, especially if the student has intellectual disabilities as well as autism.

• *Managing the physical space—Adapt the classroom arrangement to best suit the needs of the students.*

» Attempt to minimize distractions in the room, such as placing interesting-looking instruments out of sight or away from the students. Some students might be distracted by seeing their reflection in glass, or by looking at the hands on the clock.

» Structure the space depending on the needs of the student. Some students may need to be somewhat confined by sitting between other students to help them focus, while other students may need to have more space to accommodate excessive movement.

» Be aware of how the lighting or extraneous sounds are affecting the student. Some students have a high sensitivity to the flicker of lights or the sounds from electronic equipment. Other students have difficulty tuning out sounds from the playground or hallway and tuning in to the teacher.

- *Level of support—Increase amount of support from others.*
  » Ask peers to assist the student when the student needs additional help or support—be sure the peer buddy is aware of effective methods for working with the student to ensure the most success for both students.
  » Foster independence as much as possible, offering additional support when needed and tapering off support as student develops more skills.
  » Handle problem behaviors in a professional, non-emotional manner. Expect that students will have some inappropriate behavior that you will need to monitor and remediate. Have a plan that is consistent with the classroom behavior management plan to provide a stable learning environment for the student and generalization from one setting to another.

Music Education in Self-Contained Classroom – Adapted Music Education Class

Music educators might work with small groups of children with autism in an "adapted music class." Students with severe disabilities who may not be able to benefit from the inclusive music class can have an opportunity to have music education experiences through this type of class. This is not a music therapy session but a music education class with the focus on music learning. Music educators may not have had previous experience working with students with severe disabilities in a non-inclusive setting. They may find themselves floundering to create effective music education lessons for the students since the typical music education curriculum is not focused on the specific needs or abilities of students in this setting. Some of the suggestions for adaptations (above) may be helpful as music educators plan and facilitate these "adapted music classes." In addition, the following suggestions can help as one develops lesson plans.

- *Use age-appropriate music*—Consider the age of the student, not just the functioning level of the student. Always use age-appropriate music, or music that other students who are typically developing might enjoy. Avoid using songs for young children if the student is not of the intended age.
- *Use developmentally appropriate music*—Teachers may need to adapt music that is intended for higher functioning students to make it more accessible

to students with autism in the adapted music class. Songs and activities may need to be simplified, but teachers should try to maintain the integrity of the music.

- *Use age- and developmentally appropriate instruments*—Whenever possible, students should be given opportunities to make music with the same instruments that their same-aged peers are using in music class. This can help facilitate inclusion and generalization if the student is integrated into the inclusive music class in the future. Students should not be given instruments that are too young for their age. Teachers may need to make adjustments in how an instrument is used in order to adapt to the developmental needs of the student with autism.

- *Focus on experiencing and music learning*—Focus lessons on the development of music skills. Consider what music skills the students already have acquired, and build from there in a developmental manner. Can the students match pitch, keep a steady beat, play instruments correctly, make music with others, etc.? Think about the music skills one typically develops in school and use age- and developmentally appropriate materials to develop a curricular focus and lesson plans for the class.

  » Music educators can modify the early elementary music curriculum for young students with autism, since the music will be age appropriate. Music skills are addressed developmentally throughout the curriculum, so music educators can assess the development of music skills and build on what the students can do.

  » Music educators can be highly challenged when planning adaptive music classes for older students with severe disabilities. The music of the early elementary curriculum is no longer age appropriate, but the skill level of the students might still be very low. Again, thinking about building music skills developmentally, music educators can utilize age-appropriate music but continue to work on developing basic music skills, such as responding to sound, steady beat, matching pitch, and responding to music through movement.

Music Therapy Services for Students with Autism Spectrum Disorders
Music Therapy as a Related Service or District-wide Service

There are many students with autism who qualify for music therapy as a related service. Goals for music therapy as a related service are taken directly from a student's IEP (see Chapter 6 for more information about Music Therapy as a Related Service). A variety of goals might be considered for music therapy, including those goals related to academic skills (using music interventions to teach/reinforce academic concepts), social/emotional skills (using music interventions to teach/reinforce social skills and emotional expression), physical skills (using music interventions to develop gross and fine motor skills), communication skills (using music interventions to practice language and communication skills), and leisure skills (using music interventions to develop new leisure skills such as learning an instrument or participating in a choral group).

As discussed in Chapter 6, music therapy can also be a service to many students in a school district to enhance their educational services and increase their educational successes. In this type of district-wide model, the music therapist usually works with small groups of students who have similar goals and objectives. Music therapists can work with the entire class, or a group of students from the class, on some of the goals that they all share. Listed below are examples of goal areas and how music therapy could be implemented to address related goals.

Music Therapy Goals and Intervention Strategies

Music therapy has been found to be an effective approach for addressing language and communication skills, social skills, cognitive skills, and behavioral skills for children with autism (Allgood, 2005; Edgerton, 1994; Hairston, 1990; Kaplan & Steele, 2005; Kostka, 1993; Mahlberg, 1973; Nelson, Anderson, & Gonzales, 1984; Saperston, 1973; Staum & Flowers, 1984; Thaut, 1984; Walworth, 2007; Walworth, Register, & Engel, 2009). Music therapy goals for students with autism primarily focus on improving skills in the major areas of disability, namely communication, social interactions, and behavior. Secondary areas of focus include improvement of academic skills, physical skills, and leisure skills. Music therapy can be a highly motivating and flexible approach for working on these various goals. A structured music therapy activity could involve the student in listening, singing, playing, moving, or responding in other ways both verbally and nonverbally. A student can work on several skills through just one goal-directed music therapy intervention. For instance, an activity based around playing in a percussion ensemble could focus on communication (nonverbal communication and self-expression through drumming, making choices about what instrument to play); social skills (interacting appropriately with peers, taking turns playing, listening to others, taking leadership); and behavior (following directions, listening to the leader, following through with tasks).

Music Therapy to Improve Communication Skills

Children with autism have deficits in receptive and/or expressive communication skills. Some children with autism develop functional speech skills, while other children may have no speech skills and use nonverbal communication such as signs, gestures, computers, pictures, or icons to express their wants and needs. Music therapists use music in many ways to encourage communication and practice speech and language skills. The music therapist can use the elements of music (melody, rhythm, pitch, dynamics, form) to encourage expressive language and build receptive language skills. Auditory awareness and auditory discrimination are basic skills needed for language development that can be addressed through music therapy. Activities using the various elements of music can be developed for awareness of sounds, locating sounds, tracking sounds, and identification of sounds.

Music therapy sessions provide a rich opportunity for language experiences through age-appropriate and interesting music activities. Well-structured music activities can motivate a student to pay attention, actively participate, and respond both verbally and nonverbally. For instance, action songs, chants, and instrument playing can elicit vocal responses and physical responses to increase receptive communication skills. Rhythm can be used to accompany speech and encourage verbalizations and appropriate pacing. Call-and-response rhythm activities can be developed to increase imitation skills first on instruments, then in speech. Songs with repetition in the lyrics and melodies can help students remember information and important words. Students can understand the meaning of the song and specific information about target words by pairing songs with visuals and movement. For instance, language and concepts about weather, temperature, appropriate clothing, outdoor activities such as sledding or skating, and concepts such as up/down (snow is falling down) can be reinforced through a song about winter. Music can be a highly motivating tool to encourage imitative and spontaneous language in students with autism.

Music Therapy to Improve Social Skills

Children with autism have deficits in social skills and social interactions. This is a key factor for the diagnosis of autism or ASD. Teachers will find that students with ASD have a wide range of social skill abilities, and they may all be in one classroom. For students who have few social responses, music can be used as a mediating object to provide a mutual point of interaction between the child and the therapist. Structured use of an instrument with the therapist can support exploration and social contact. Social learning can also be developed through participation in active music making. Responding to others, taking turns, listening, sharing ideas, greeting others, and sharing equipment can all be practiced through music-making experiences. Students with autism can build social skills necessary for successful classroom and community participation beginning with just the therapist, if necessary, and then adding others to a small group. Students can learn skills for active group participation by engaging in singing, movement, and instrument activities that focus on interactions with others. Simple skills such as holding hands with a peer, listening to others, or starting and stopping with the group can be difficult but important skills for these students to develop. Students can learn and practice many social skills through motivating music activities.

Music Therapy to Improve Behavior

Behavioral difficulties are another key feature of autism spectrum disorders. Just as with all other characteristics of autism, behavioral skills vary from one student to the next, with some students having severe and disruptive behavior, while others might have unusual or stereotypical behaviors. Many times students' behavior problems are due to difficulty communicating or limited comprehension of the expectations and consequences of their behavior.

Music therapy can be structured to provide predictable experiences to practice appropriate behavior in a small group or in one-to-one sessions. Interventions taken step by step to improve skills and behavior can be layered with more complex music skills to challenge the students. For instance, a student in a small group percussion ensemble can learn basic steady beat patterns that can later be extended to include more complicated rhythms on a variety of instruments. Students who follow directions, meet expectations, and participate with others may be asked to perform for peers or parents. In this way, music can be used to improve self-esteem and leadership skills. Music can also be used as a reinforcement for appropriate behavior, offered as a reward for following through with expectations. Extra time playing instruments, listening to music, or making music with others may be highly reinforcing and motivating for some students.

Music Therapy to Improve Academic, Physical/Motor, and Leisure Skills

In addition to the main three areas of difficulty for students with autism (communication skills, social skills, and behavior), other areas of deficit such as academic skills, physical/motor skills, and leisure skills can be addressed through music therapy. Songs, chants, and rhythm activities can be used to reinforce math skills such as counting, one-to-one correspondence, and ordering. Songs with repetitive lyrics, rhythmic patterns, and added movements can give students many opportunities to count, add, subtract, and order in a fun and interesting way. Students can practice categorization by size, shape, color, and sound through simple music activities and musical instruments. Other concepts such as high and low, in and out, front and back, and slow and fast can be taught and practiced through music therapy interventions combining music and movement. Music therapists can incorporate movement along with songs and rhythm to give students different options for understanding and remembering the concepts, making the concepts come to life through music and movement. Music activities can also be developed to enhance focus of attention, memory skills, ordering of tasks, and task completion.

Some students with autism have physical/motor delay or disabilities. Music therapy interventions can focus on improving fine motor skills through instrument playing, such as piano/keyboard, guitar, or other small instruments requiring fine motor control. Gross motor skills can be enhanced through participation in movement to music activities and music making through playing instruments requiring large muscle use, such as hand drums or mallet instruments. In addition, eye-hand coordination can be improved through playing two-handed instruments or reaching to play a percussion instrument that is attached to a stand.

A student with communication, social, and behavior problems may have difficulty finding appropriate leisure activities. Music therapists can work with students to determine preferences of music and then teach the students how to engage in music making/listening experiences during leisure time. This could be as simple as learning how to use a radio or CD player, purchasing preferred music, and learning a few current dance steps. Music as a leisure skill could also involve teaching a student to play an instrument such as guitar, keyboard, or drums, or preparing the student for involvement in a community choir that is structured to support the needs of individuals with disabilities. Instruments and sheet music can be adapted through color-coding or adaptive playing techniques to make learning and playing instruments easier and more enjoyable. It is always important to find out what type of music the student prefers and what kind of music participation interests the student. Leisure music activities should be age appropriate, socially acceptable, interesting, and fun for the student. Whenever possible, leisure music activities should involve others to continue to improve social skills while sharing the joy of making music with others. Table 10.3 illustrates several goal areas with sample music therapy strategies (Kaplan & Steele, 2005; Walworth et al., 2009).

Table 10.3 Summary of Goal Areas and Examples of Music Therapy Interventions

Goal Area	Sample Music Therapy Strategy
Communication Skills	• Making choices through instrumental and vocal activities • Echoing verbalizations of therapist through songs • Following directions and being the leader (stop/go)
Social/Emotional Skills	• Practicing sharing/taking turns • Working together as a group to make music in an ensemble • Emotional expression/sharing of feelings through songs, instruments, and movement • Increasing self-esteem by learning new skills • Interacting with peers through music making
Behavior Skills	• Structuring music activities to practice following directions • Providing opportunities to be a leader in the group; opportunities to follow others' lead • Using preferred music to reinforce appropriate behavior
Academic Skills	• Counting songs/rhythm activities • Using movement to reinforce concepts such as in/out, high/low, in front/behind • Categorizing instruments; colors, size, shapes, sounds
Physical Skills	• Developing gross motor skills through movement to music • Developing fine motor skills through playing instrument • Providing gait training through rhythmic stimulation

Goal Area	Sample Music Therapy Strategy
Leisure Skills	• Developing playing skills on instruments such as guitar or piano for leisure time • Participating in a vocal music group in preparation for a community vocal group

KEY POINTS FROM THE CHAPTER

Autism and autism spectrum disorders
Prevalence and characteristics:

♦ Over 258,000 students with autism received services under IDEA in 2007.

♦ Approximately 1 in 100 individuals have autism or ASD.

♦ Autism Spectrum Disorder (ASD) includes autism as well as other disorders that are like autism but do not meet all of the same diagnostic criteria for autism. Children diagnosed with autism or ASD have qualitative impairments in communication and social skills, along with difficulty with language and communication.

♦ Asperger's Syndrome is an example of a disorder on the autism spectrum that shares some but not all of the characteristics of autism. Individuals with Asperger's Syndrome have challenges in social behavior but do not have the language deficits or intellectual deficits that are typical of a child with autism.

Educational considerations:

♦ Many students with autism or ASD use alternative communication systems to enhance verbal or nonverbal communication skills. This system may be as simple as pointing to pictures or letters, using sign language, or using computer devices.

♦ Most students with autism are more successful when visual cues and instruction are paired with verbal cues.

♦ Teachers can promote positive behaviors by creating a predictable environment, providing alternative goals and activities, providing positive reinforcement for appropriate behaviors, and using a functional approach to solving behavior problems.

♦ Music educators teaching in "adapted music classes" should consider age and developmentally appropriate music, songs, and instruments when planning lessons. Curricular focus can be on the development of basic music skills that are used in an inclusive music classroom.

♦   Music therapy has been shown to be effective to improve students'
    communication skills, social skills, and behavior, as well as improve academic,
    physical/motor, and leisure skills.

REFERENCES

Adamek, M., Thaut, M., & Furman, A. (2008). Individuals with autism and autism spectrum disorders (ASD). In W. B. Davis, K. E. Gfeller, & M. H. Thaut (Eds.), *An introduction to music therapy theory and practice* (3rd ed., pp. 117–142). Silver Spring, MD: American Music Therapy Association.

Allgood, N. (2005). Parents' perceptions of family-based group music therapy for children with Autism Spectrum Disorders. *Music Therapy Perspectives, 23,* 92–99.

American Psychological Association. (2000). *Diagnostic and statistical manual of mental disorders* (4th ed., text revision). Washington, DC: Author.

Autism Society of America. (2010). Retrieved from www.autism-society.org

Bondy, A., & Frost, L. (1994). The Picture Exchange Communication System. *Focus on Autistic Behavior, 9,* 1–19.

Brown, L., Branston, M. B., Hamre-Nietupski, S., Pumpian, I., Certo, N., & Gruenewald, L. (1979). A strategy for developing chronological, age appropriate and functional curricular content for severely handicapped adolescents and young adults. *Journal of Special Education, 13,* 81–90.

Coleman, M. (2005). *The neurology of autism.* New York: Oxford University Press.

Data Accountability Center. (2007). *Individuals with Disabilities Education Act (IDEA) data: Part B data and notes.* Retrieved April 6, 2010, from https://www.ideadata.org/PartBData.asp

Edgerton, C. (1994). The effect of improvisational music therapy on the communicative behaviors of autistic children. *Journal of Music Therapy, 31,* 31–62.

Frost, L., & Bondy, A. (1994). *PECS: The Picture Exchange Communication System training manual.* Cherry Hill, NJ: Pyramid Educational Consultants.

Hairston, M. (1990). Analysis of responses of mentally retarded autistic and mentally retarded nonautistic children to art therapy and music therapy. *Journal of Music Therapy, 27,* 137–150.

Jellison, J. A., Brooks, B. H., & Huck, A. M. (1984). Structuring small groups and music reinforcement to facilitate positive interactions and acceptance of severely handicapped students in regular music classrooms. *Journal of Research in Music Education, 32,* 243–264.

Kaplan, R., & Steele, A. L. (2005). An analysis of music therapy program goals and outcomes for clients with diagnoses on the autism spectrum. *Journal of Music Therapy, 42,* 2–19.

Kern, P., Wakeford, L., & Aldridge, D. (2007). Improving the performance of a young child with autism during self-care tasks using embedded song interventions: A case study. *Music Therapy Perspectives, 25,* 43–51.

Kostka, M. (1993). A comparison of selected behaviors of a student with autism in special education and regular music classes. *Music Therapy Perspectives, 11,* 57–60.

Kravits, T. R., Kamps, D. M., Kemmerer, K., & Potucek, J. (2002). Brief report: Increasing communication skills for an elementary-aged student with autism using the picture exchange communication system. *Journal of Autism and Developmental Disorders, 32,* 225–230.

Mahlberg, M. (1973). Music therapy in the treatment of an autistic child. *Journal of Music Therapy, 10,* 189–193.

Mastropieri, M., & Scruggs, T. (2000). *The inclusive classroom: Strategies for effective instruction.* Upper Saddle River, NJ: Merrill/Prentice Hall.

McCarthy, J., Geist, K., Zojwala, R., & Schock, M. (2008). A survey of music therapists' work with speech-language pathologists and experiences with augmentative and alternative communication. *Journal of Music Therapy, 45,* 405-426.

Mitchell, D. (2008). *What really works in special and inclusive education: Using evidence-based teaching strategies.* New York: Routledge.

National Education Association. (2006). *The puzzle of autism.* Washington, DC: Author.

National Research Council. (2001). *Educating children with autism.* Committee on Educational Interventions for Children with Autism. Division of Behavioral and Social Sciences and Education. Washington, DC: National Academy Press.

Nelson, D., Anderson, V., & Gonzales, A. (1984). Music activities as therapy for children with autism and other pervasive developmental disorders. *Journal of Music Therapy, 21,* 100–116.

Pierangelo, R., & Giuliani, G. A. (2001). *What every teacher should know about students with special needs: Promoting success in the classroom.* Champaign, IL: Research Press.

Prizant, B., Wetherby, E., Rubin, E., Laurent, A., & Rydell, P. (2006). *The SCERTS® Model: A comprehensive educational approach for children with autism spectrum disorders.* Baltimore: Paul H. Brookes.

Register, D., & Humpal, M. (2007). Using musical transitions in early childhood classrooms: Three case examples. *Music Therapy Perspectives, 25,* 5–31.

Saperston, B. (1973). The use of music in establishing communication with an autistic mentally retarded child. *Journal of Music Therapy, 10,* 184–188.

Scott, J., Clark, C., & Brady, M. (2000). *Students with autism: Characteristics and instruction programming.* San Diego, CA: Singular.

Simpson, R. L., & Miles, B. S. (1998). *Educating children and youth with autism.* Austin, TX: PRO-ED.

Staum, M., & Flowers, P. (1984). The use of simulated training and music lessons in teaching appropriate shopping skills to an autistic child. *Music Therapy Perspectives, 1,* 14–17.

Thaut, M. (1984). A music therapy treatment model for autistic children. *Music Therapy Perspectives, 1,* 7–13.

Turnbull, A., Turnbull, R., & Wehmeyer, M. (2010). *Exceptional lives: Special education in today's schools.* Upper Saddle River, NJ: Merrill.

Walworth, D. (2007). The use of music therapy within the SCERTS model for children with Autism Spectrum Disorder. *Journal of Music Therapy, 44,* 2–22.

Walworth, D., Register, D., & Engel, J. (2009). Using the SCERTS model assessment tool to identify music therapy goals for clients with Autism Spectrum Disorder. *Journal of Music Therapy, 46,* 204–216.

Chapter 11

Students with Vision Loss

CHAPTER OVERVIEW

Vision plays a critical role in a child's growth and development. Children typically learn much about the world around them by visual observation. Most students with limited vision have learned to use other senses to acquire much of the information that is transmitted in their environment; however, there is still information that is strictly visual and cannot be accessed in any other way. Teachers of children who have limited sight must provide their students with first-hand experiences and opportunities to learn by doing. All students who are blind or have low vision need adaptations to their environment as well as adapted materials and instructional strategies.

Many judgments made about individuals who are blind, as well as individuals with other disabilities, are made without adequately understanding the psychosocial aspects of the disability. Ray Charles, once commenting on the song "I Can See Clearly Now," described "seeing" a "bright sunshiny day" as a warm and happy day. A student of the author's who is blind once described going to "see" Christmas lights as great fun because she and her friends were huddled in the car laughing and singing Christmas carols. Another student who is blind was the only student in the class to correctly identify the teacher's daily cue that the lecture was about to begin—the transfer of his keys from his pocket to the table. From these individuals we learn that there is not just one way to experience the visual world—and who is to say that one way is better than another? Sounds, smells, and touch are probably not fully appreciated by individuals who rely on their sight.

This chapter includes information on the following topics:
- ◆ Definition of vision loss
- ◆ Levels of vision loss
- ◆ Types of vision loss
- ◆ Effects of vision loss
- ◆ Educational tools
- ◆ Assistive technology
- ◆ Adaptations to the music classroom
- ◆ Music education for students with vision loss
- ◆ Music therapy for students with vision loss

Definitions of Vision Loss

Visual acuity is determined by measuring the distance at which an individual can clearly identify objects—usually letters, numbers, or symbols on the familiar Snellen chart. Using such a measurement, persons who have 20/200 vision are considered *legally blind;* that is, standing at 20 feet, they can see what the typical person can see at 200 feet, although other individuals may be considered blind who have a *field of vision* that is extremely restricted. The normal eye is able to see objects within a range of approximately 180 degrees. A person may be also considered legally blind if he or she is able to see objects only within an area of 20 degrees or less from the normal 180-degree field. Such a person may be considered to have *tunnel vision.* Some people with limited fields of vision have good central vision, but their *peripheral vision* at the outer ranges of the visual field is poor or nonexistent. It is possible for some types of vision loss to have good peripheral vision and poor central vision. *Visual efficiency* and *functional vision* are terms denoting how well a person utilizes his or her residual sight. Visual efficiency includes specific skills such as paying attention to visual stimuli, adapting to varied visual stimuli in environments, controlling eye movements, and processing visual information (Barraga & Erin, 1992). Functional vision is residual vision sufficient for the execution of daily living tasks.

Levels of Vision Loss

The definition of visual disabilities in IDEA emphasizes the relationship between sight and how individuals experience and learn about the world around them—"an impairment in vision that, even with correction, adversely affects a child's educational performance." Students with visual disabilities represent a wide range of abilities—ranging from blindness to low vision to good residual vision. Educational classifications, such as low vision, functionally blind, and blind, describe students' ability to use their vision or tactile aids for learning.

Students with *low vision* can read print, although they may depend on optical aids, such as typical glasses, special magnifying glasses, or computers to enlarge the print. These students may or may not be legally blind, but they are able to use their vision for learning. Low vision is also sometimes referred to as *partial sight.*

Students who are *functionally blind* typically use Braille for reading and writing, although they may use their functional vision for mobility, cooking, dressing, and other daily life activities. These students use their vision to supplement their tactual and auditory senses for learning.

Students who are *blind* receive no useful input through their sense of vision. These students use their tactile and auditory senses for learning. Very few students are blind; in fact, nearly 80% of school-age students who receive services use their vision for learning. Although vision loss is a low incidence disability, services for students with vision loss are important and can be costly. The type of services needed will depend on the degree of loss and the age of onset.

Like hearing losses, visual losses can be *congenital* or *acquired*, and the *age of onset* has important implications for students' education. Children who have never experienced vision quite understandably have a different perception of the world around them than children who gradually lost their vision. Children who were blind at birth have learned through hearing, touch, tastes, and smells. Children who gradually lost their sight generally have a memory bank of visual experiences to draw upon, although inaccurate associations can be made when a child draws upon these visual memories. The author once commented to a classmate who was blind that she liked his red hair. He replied that he didn't like it—explaining that he didn't like it because "who wants hair the color of a fire engine?" Unfortunately, he did not remember the color of a new penny—the actual color of his hair.

Children who have lost their vision *adventitiously* (acquired their vision loss) will have to adjust to a world with limited or no visual information. The difficulty of such an adjustment, while profound, can be made considerably easier if they are given support from family, friends, and teachers. Many persons who have lost their sight report that the biggest difficulty is dealing with the attitudes and behaviors of those around them who assume that they are now helpless or somehow different.

Types of Vision Loss

Astigmatism: A cylindrical curvature of the cornea that prevents light rays from focusing on one point on the retina. The result is both near and far objects may appear blurry. Astigmatism often occurs in combination with myopia and hyperopia.

Hyperopia (Farsightedness): The focusing point is behind the retina, resulting in difficulty seeing at close distances. A student may see objects well from a distance, but not when objects are near. Hyperopia can result from shortness of the eyeball, a lens that is weak, or a cornea that is relatively flat.

Myopia (Nearsightedness): The image of distant objects is not focused on the retina but rather in front of it, making it appear blurry. The students can see objects that are near, but have difficulty seeing objects from a distance. Myopia can result from an elongated eyeball, a lens that is too strong, or a cornea that is excessively curved.

Eye Conditions

Albinism: Inherited condition resulting in decreased pigment that causes abnormal optic nerve development. In addition to a decreased visual acuity, children with albinism may be sensitive to light. Tinted lenses can relieve light sensitivity, and glasses or low vision aids can help maximize vision.

Amblyopia ("lazy eye"): The suppression of the image of one eye usually due to that eye having a significantly poorer acuity or being turned in/out. Students with amblyopia can have some functional field loss and poor or absent depth perception. Patching the stronger eye to strengthen the weaker eye may be prescribed.

Cataracts: Opacity or cloudiness of the lens. Because light cannot pass through the lens, vision is affected. Some types of cataracts progressively worsen, while others remain unchanged. Cataracts can be found in one eye (unilateral) or both eyes (bilateral). Students with cataracts may have reduced visual acuity, blurred vision, poor color vision, or light sensitivity. Surgery to remove the cataract is often recommended.

Glaucoma: Increased pressure in the eye due to blockage of normal flow of fluid in the eye. The vision of children with glaucoma can fluctuate based on changes in pressure. A child with glaucoma may also have peripheral field loss, poor night vision, and light sensitivity. If not treated, damage to the optic nerve can result.

Nystagmus: Involuntary movement of the eye. This can be horizontal, vertical, circular, or mixed. Because the eyes are moving, a child with nystagmus has difficulty maintaining fixation on objects resulting in reduced visual acuity and fatigue. Nystagmus can be minimized by turning the head or eyes in a certain position, called the "null point." The null point differs from person to person, but is often discovered by the child.

Optic Nerve Atrophy: Damage or degeneration to the optic nerve that carries visual signals to the brain. Vision loss will be dependent on the amount of damage, but may include blurred vision, poor color and night vision, and light sensitivity.

Optic Nerve Hypoplasia: Underdevelopment of the optic nerve in utero, resulting in a small optic nerve and visual impairment. The degree of visual impairment varies significantly, but there is usually an acuity loss. Optic nerve hypoplasia may be associated with other conditions.

Retinitis Pigmentosa (RP): A hereditary, degenerative condition of the retina that results in loss of peripheral vision or "tunnel vision." Initially starts with difficulty in seeing in dimly lit settings and progresses to significant visual loss.

Retinoblastoma: A cancerous tumor of the retina that requires vigorous treatment of all tumors through laser, radiation, and/or chemotherapy. Progression of retinoblastoma may result in enucleation (removal) of the eye. If one eye is removed, the child will not have depth perception.

Retinopathy of Prematurity (ROP): Disruption in the normal development of blood vessels of the retina in premature infants that can result in scarring and detachment of the retina. Children with ROP may have a decreased visual acuity and refractive errors.

Strabismus: A muscle imbalance resulting in the inability of both eyes to look directly at an object at the same time. Types of strabismus include esotropia (an inward turn), exotropia (an outward turn), hypertropia (an upward turn), and hypotropia (a downward turn).

Cortical Visual Impairment

Unlike refractive errors and structural impairments, cortical visual impairment is not caused by any condition of the eye. Rather, it is due to damage to the visual cortex of the brain or the visual pathways that results in the brain not adequately receiving or interpreting visual information.

Children with cortical visual impairment often also have cerebral palsy, seizure disorder, and developmental delays as a result of the damage to the brain. They may exhibit inattention to visual stimuli, preference for touch over vision when exploring objects, and difficulty visually discriminating objects that are placed close together or in front of a visually complex background.

Because this visual impairment is due to the neurological processing of visual information, visual performance may fluctuate slightly or significantly from day to day, or even from moment to moment, depending upon the environment and the seizure activity, motor position, general health, and mood of the child.

Effects of Vision Loss

Vicarious learning is at risk for all students with vision loss. Much of what we learn is by observing and imitating what we see around us. Curious to explore what they see, children move toward objects and people, increasing their knowledge of the world around them. Children without sight are no less curious; however, they require an environment that is aurally and tactually inviting.

In general, the growth and development of children with visual disabilities is no different than their peers; however, the loss of sight does impact a child's learning and behavior in several areas: orientation and mobility, daily living skills, reading and writing, conceptualization and cognitive development, psychosocial development, and vocational choices (Hardman, Drew, & Egan, 2008). The degrees to which these areas of learning and behavior are affected depend on the age of onset, the severity of vision loss, family support, and the type and degree of educational intervention.

Language Development

Because vocabulary acquisition occurs through the integration of visual experiences and words, children with severe vision loss are at a distinct disadvantage in the development of language. Children without sight who live in an environment rich in language may develop vocabulary as a sighted child would; however, they may have little understanding of many words they use in everyday conversation. Figure 11.1 highlights lyrics that may have little meaning for a young child with a vision impairment.

Figure 11.1 "Picture a World" Exercise

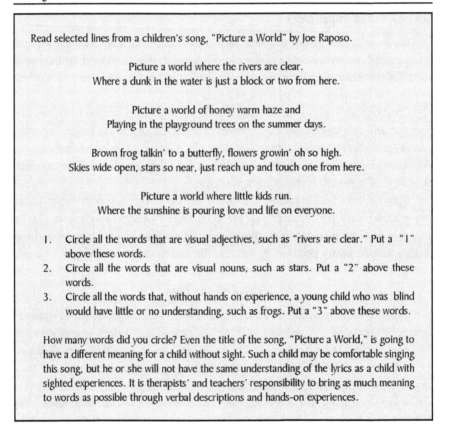

Read selected lines from a children's song, "Picture a World" by Joe Raposo.

Picture a world where the rivers are clear.
Where a dunk in the water is just a block or two from here.

Picture a world of honey warm haze and
Playing in the playground trees on the summer days.

Brown frog talkin' to a butterfly, flowers growin' oh so high.
Skies wide open, stars so near, just reach up and touch one from here.

Picture a world where little kids run.
Where the sunshine is pouring love and life on everyone.

1. Circle all the words that are visual adjectives, such as "rivers are clear." Put a "1" above these words.
2. Circle all the words that are visual nouns, such as stars. Put a "2" above these words.
3. Circle all the words that, without hands on experience, a young child who was blind would have little or no understanding, such as frogs. Put a "3" above these words.

How many words did you circle? Even the title of the song, "Picture a World," is going to have a different meaning for a child without sight. Such a child may be comfortable singing this song, but he or she will not have the same understanding of the lyrics as a child with sighted experiences. It is therapists' and teachers' responsibility to bring as much meaning to words as possible through verbal descriptions and hands-on experiences.

Intellectual Development

Many intellectual tasks, such as determining spatial relationships, require vision. In addition, many geographical and science concepts are more easily understood through visual illustrations, such as graphs and charts. It is not difficult to understand how children with vision disabilities may score low on tests of intellect. However, when children's intellectual abilities are measured on tasks in which vision loss does not interfere, those with and without sight perform similarly. A visual disability does not impair students' intellectual abilities, but they have less information to rely on.

Social Development

Crocker and Orr (1996) found that children with severe vision loss were less likely to initiate social interactions and had fewer opportunities to socialize with other children. Children approach other children because they see them and want to interact. The child without sight must learn to listen for social opportunities and, more importantly, learn to be appropriately assertive in engaging other children to socialize. The inability to use and observe others' use of nonverbal communication can also impair interpersonal interactions. Eye contact, facial expression, gestures, and proximity are all useful in relating to those around us. Children without vision can learn to use various forms of nonverbal communication, but it must be taught through senses other than vision—usually tactual. Children with severe vision loss are no less capable of social relationships, but such relationships are often less available. Therapists and teachers can assist in the social development of children with severe vision loss by providing opportunities in the classroom for interpersonal interactions, and by encouraging and monitoring such interactions.

Academic Development

A number of reports suggest that the academic achievement of many students with severe vision loss is delayed when compared to their sighted peers (Bishop, 2004; Rapp & Rapp, 1992). Such reports must be interpreted with caution due to the different testing conditions that must be used with students who are blind or have low vision. For example, reading large print and Braille takes more time than reading regular print, putting students who use these types of reading adaptations at a disadvantage on timed tests. Beyond testing issues, the general knowledge of students with vision loss may indeed be limited due to such variables as the lack of available reading materials and access to experiences that bring meaning to reading materials. In addition, many students with vision loss lose valuable instructional time due to the lack of necessary classroom, technological, and instructional resources. Therefore, the delay in achievement is often due to numerous variables that are not related to students' intelligence or their potential for academic success.

Educational Approaches/Strategies for Effective Teaching

There are many skills and concepts that children typically learn through vision; therefore, these skills and concepts are never specifically taught. For example, most children learn to use eating utensils by watching their parents use them. The child who cannot observe the use of such utensils must be taught not only how to hold a knife, a fork, and a spoon, but the function of each and the motions that facilitate their use. In other words, children who are blind have much to learn when they enter this world, and most of it must be taught through direct instruction.

Because their ability to learn through imitation is limited, students who are blind or who have low vision learn best through hands-on experiences. These experiences should be frequent and varied enough that children learn to make generalizations and to expect changes in their environment. Young children should be encouraged to explore the world around them. If they must wait for introductions to what is around them, they will surely miss out on much of what they can learn. There are a number of educational tools that can assist children with visual disabilities become more independent in their learning.

Children with little or no vision can benefit greatly from learning Braille. Congenitally blind adults who use Braille have reportedly higher rates of employment, educational levels, and income, and spend more time reading than those who learn to read print (Ryles, 1996). However, as technology has made print materials more accessible through both enlarged print and synthesized speech reading, the use of Braille has declined (Wittenstein, 1994).

Braille

Braille was invented in 1842 by a Frenchman named Louis Braille. It is a tactile system of reading and writing that is still used widely today by persons who are blind or have severe vision loss. The Braille system is based on a cell, a configuration of dots forming two columns of three dots each. Each letter of the alphabet and each punctuation mark are made up of one or more of the possible six dots that make up a cell. There are also contractions or abbreviations for words that are formed in the cells. These same six raised dots are also used to write music.

Most students in the music classroom or music therapy clients learn music by rote and do not read Braille text or Braille music. If the student intends to major in music or become a serious musician, he or she should learn to read Braille music. If students learn music only by rote, they are dependent upon the model, who may or may not play or sing the music correctly, and the students may be reluctant to interpret the music in any way other than the way they heard it. All students, even those who learn music primarily by rote, should be given opportunities to develop as independent musicians.

Large Print

Modern technology, computers, and Xerox machines, in particular, have made large print materials more readily available to students with low vision. Just as important as the size of the print is the contrast between the print and the page, the spacing of letters and lines, as well as the lighting used to read. The American Printing House for the Blind produces books and music for students with low vision.

Many students with low vision can use optical aides to read regular print, allowing them greater access to music materials and music.

It is important to remember that reading Braille or large print generally takes more time to read than standard print. Music educators may want to give students who are blind or have low vision their reading assignments early, or allow them additional time to complete their assignments. Older students should be encouraged to advocate for additional time allowances, and to start assignments early so that they are completed by the given deadline. Developing such skills will be a benefit in college and in the working world.

Assistive Technology

One of the major areas addressed by Universal Design Instruction has been access to the World Wide Web (Rose, Meyer, & Hitchcock, 2005). Any student in today's schools who does not have access to the Internet is at a distinct and severe disadvantage. Great strides have been made in recent years to make the digital materials accessible to students with mobility and vision disabilities. Because much of what posted on the Internet is visually formatted, students who are blind or who have low vision require specialized technologies. The types of adaptive technology available to students with visual impairments generally fall into one of several categories: large print access, speech access, Braille access, scanned material access (Presley & d'Andrea, 2009).

The International Braille and Technology Center for the Blind (IBTC) was established in 1990. It is a comprehensive demonstration and evaluation center complete with nearly every type of speech output and Braille technology, both hardware and software, available in the U.S., Canada, and many other countries as well. The Center includes the full range of assistive technology that students can use to manage information in print or electronic formats—whether they use vision, touch, or hearing to access information. Those technologies most applicable to academic instruction are described briefly below.

Large print and video access. Most Xerox machines and printers can provide large print copies. Computers can also enlarge print to certain size font; however, for those who require greater magnification, there is specialized screen software available, such as inLARGE, ZoomText, and Lunar. Students who need to see text materials in class often use a stand-mounted or hand-held video camera to project a magnified image onto a video monitor or computer/scanner systems. These types of software can also be used to view video material on the Web or played on the computer.

Speech access. Talking word processing programs allow students to hear the letter, word, sentence, or phrase as it is entered into the computer. Pull-down menus also have speech output. Students can use various types of print-to-speech software to access written materials on the Web, to read print materials scanned into the computer, and to read emails or text messages.

Braille access. For students who want written materials translated into Braille, or Braille into text, translation and formatting software programs are available. They are designed to be used with Braille embossers or Braille printers— a printer whose output is Braille instead of print. Braille terminals and keyboards are also available, which allow students to use Braille to read the computer screen and to type word documents.

Scanned material access. There are several types of software, such as Open Book, Expert Reader, and Kurzweill 1000, that use a scanner to take a picture of a page, which it sends it to a computer that translates the picture into understandable text, and then speaks the text aloud or outputs to Braille.

There is important nonverbal information in the classroom that transpires in real time or on videos. Most nonverbal information does not have a text equivalent and therefore must be translated. If a teacher frowns in response to a question, or teachers shake or nod their heads in response to questions, there is no technology that can capture that information. Nonverbal information must be translated verbally. Teachers can translate nonverbal information that occurs in the classroom in real time.

When using videos in the classroom, *Descriptive Video Service* functions much like captioning for the deaf. Visual elements of a performance that are not implied in the dialogue are verbally described to the person with a vision loss. For example, one might give the following visual description of a scene in a play: "Olivia moved across the room—stopping only once to glance in William's direction."

Adaptations to the Music Room or Clinic

Musical technology. Music technology for blind students or musicians falls into two broad categories: software that transcribes print to Braille music or Braille music to print, and software that allows people to produce and manipulate musical sounds. Many music students who are blind do not know Braille music and prefer to learn by rote; however, for those students who do know Braille music, it is advisable to cultivate their musical independence using by transcribing music into Braille.

GOODFEEL® is notation software that is designed to automatically convert several kinds of music files to Braille music. Teachers or therapists do not need to know how to read Braille music to prepare and transcribe music files into Braille music. By combining programs like GOODFEEL® with other traditional music technologies, teachers can scan print music to make Braille copies. They can also edit the music with a program called Lime and produce the Braille copy with GOODFEEL®. These adaptive software programs are available through Dancing Dots–Braille Music Technology, an American company based in Philadelphia that was founded in 1992 to develop and adapt music technology for the blind.

Adapting the music room or clinic. Any student who is blind or who has low vision should be allowed to explore the music room and thus become acquainted with the layout of the room, where music instruments are kept, where he or she will sit, where the music books are shelved, etc. Most children can see when chairs are moved or other changes are made in their environment—the child with visual disabilities should be aptly warned. Some helpful hints for making the music room more accessible are:

1. Talk while writing on the board or while conducting music.
2. Move closer to the student with a visual disability so that he or she can hear easily.
3. Make use of a classmate as a scribe or to provide verbal descriptions of actions in the classroom or on a video.
4. Organize peer partners who will read announcements on the board or lyrics to the music.
5. Use white boards with large black markers, rather than green chalkboards.
6. Provide large print copies of music for students with low vision or recordings of the music if the student is blind.
7. Physically assist students when needed. For example, "Hold the mallets like this" will have no meaning for the student who cannot see "this."
8. Give definitions of words that may be unfamiliar to the student because of the visual nature of the word.
9. Provide music and recordings to the student before such materials are needed in class.
10. Model acceptance and inclusion of the student in all aspects of the music program.

Music Education for Students with Vision Loss

With very little thought, you can probably name several musicians who are blind—Stevie Wonder, Ray Charles, Jose Feliciano, Andrea Bocelli, Ronnie Milsap, George Shearing, Marcus Roberts. Obviously, visual loss does not impair one's ability to become a good musician, even a famous musician. In fact, with the loss of sight, the subsequent development of aural skills is thought by many to enhance one's ability to develop musically (Gougoux et al., 2004). It might not seem strange then that one of the first disability populations to receive music education was children who were blind.

Lowell Mason (1792–1872), considered to be the "father of public school music education," may have been one of the first music educators for students with visual impairments. Mason taught at the Perkins School for the Blind from 1832 to 1836, two years prior to his initiating music education in the Boston schools (Heller & Livingston, 1994). Perkins School for the Blind, Helen Keller's alma mater, was the first school for the blind in the United States and remains one of the most famous schools in the world for the blind. Music at Perkins was considered to be an academic subject as well as a recreational activity for students. As he did in his public school program in music education, Mason taught vocal music, piano, and organ. Nearly all state and private schools for students with visual impairments still include music as an important part of the curriculum (Corn & Bailey, 1991). Many of the programs include instrumental and choral ensembles as well as private lessons in music. Persons with vision loss generally learn to be good listeners, a skill which generalizes well to the study of music.

Although many music students who are blind can easily learn music by listening to others play or sing, it is to their benefit to learn to read Braille music. Reading Braille music allows students to be independent in their music study. Louis Braille, who invented literary Braille, also invented Braille music. Louis Braille was a piano teacher who wanted his students to be able to read music. Both literary Braille and Braille music use the same system of cells containing six raised dots. There are musical scores available in Braille and, given technology and enough time, any score can be transcribed into Braille. The Music Section of the National Library Service for the Blind and Physically Handicapped is the main source for borrowing Braille music in the United States. The National Library Service (NLS) holdings, which include virtually all available Braille scores, offer instrumental and vocal music, popular music, opera librettos, music textbooks, instructional method books, and music periodicals. The National Library Service also has recorded courses for beginning guitar, piano, organ, accordion, recorder, voice, and theory. Loaned materials are sent to borrowers and returned to the library by postage-free mail. The address for NLS appears at the end of this section.

Adapting Music Instruction

Music educators often need some assistance in finding resources for students who are blind. Most school districts have a special education resource teacher for students with visual disabilities. The music educator should identify this resource teacher and ask for help. The resource teacher is often willing and able to provide assistance and, at the very least, serve as a consultant. Resource teachers for students with visual disabilities know literary Braille and will be helpful in transcribing song lyrics or music texts, but most do not know Braille music. However, they are often part of a professional network and can find someone who does know Braille music to transcribe scores, or they can use the translation software described in the earlier section, Assistive Technology.

Various textures for notes, along with verbal descriptions, can provide the student with a tactile translation of printed music—the shapes of notes and symbols, and the linear format of music. The program MusicShop, available through Dancing Dots–Braille Music Technology, displays graphic notations to represent pitch and duration. It uses colored bars of varying lengths instead of traditional music notation. MusicShop relates sound to what music looks like, rather than what it sounds like. Such a graphic display of music would be useful for students who have low vision or a hearing loss.

Graphic or textural information may well transfer later to reading Braille music. Because most music teachers have little time to make materials such as a tactile staff, they often rely on recorded music and have the student learn the music through repeated listening. While time efficient for the teacher, the student learns little about music reading, a skill all music educators should want for their students. The time spent teaching a child to read tactile music or Braille music will reap rewards later in the child's musical development. Students who do use Braille music need lead time to learn their music. Reading Braille music is tedious, slow, and requires memorizing the music.

Many students who are blind will need to learn music by rote, either because they do not know Braille music, or because it is often the most time-efficient way to learn new music. Moss (2009) found that most students participating in instrumental ensembles memorize their music and do not rely on Braille music. There are accompanying advantages and constraints to students using memory as their primary strategy for learning music. One of the constraints is the need for the teacher and student to work ahead of the class. The music must be recorded far enough ahead that the student can memorize the music and be prepared to play or sing in class. Spoken measure numbers or section letters must be recorded as well so that the student can use these markers in rehearsal.

Siligo (2005) offers music educators advice for working with students who have visual impairments in music ensembles. He suggests that teachers encourage students who are blind to learn Braille music. Doing so fosters their musical independence. Along with taking home recordings of the music and working with teachers individually, students with low vision can take advantage of magnifiers, computer printers, and photocopiers to enlarge music, although they will need the music ahead of time to ensure that they are prepared to participate in class.

One of the greatest difficulties for music students who are blind is the use of structured lesson books, such as sight-reading books or technique exercise books. The nature of Braille music reading requires the student to read the music and then memorize it. To memorize an entire sight reading book or technique book would be so time-consuming that few students would be able to accomplish such a task. The music educator can make an assignment from the book so that the student participates, but the teacher should not expect the student to memorize every exercise the sighted student will perform. Because of the difficulties that often occur with transcribing music, many students with vision loss are often comfortable in jazz band where playing by ear and improvisation are valued skills.

Students with a visual disability are often at a disadvantage too if they wish to participate in marching band. Several marching band directors have cleverly invented ways for the student with a visual disability to be attached to the person in front of him or her, or have written arrangements so that the student's section does fewer movements. Choir choreography as well requires inventiveness on the part of the music educator. Choreography is almost always learned through visual imitation. One choir director told his students to be sure Mindy, a student who was blind, knew the choreography. The students rallied around Mindy, and through verbal explanations and physical assistance, she was able to learn the steps as well as the other students—and probably made a few friends as well.

Music stands are often adapted to make music more accessible to the student with low vision. Reading stands with extending arms allow the music to be placed closer to the reader without moving the entire stand. Sometimes an adapted marching lyre can be placed on instruments so the music can be closer to the reader. Instruments that require one hand to hold them and the other to manipulate valves, such as the trumpet, tuba, or trombone, can be mounted on stands so the student who is blind can read Braille music with one hand while he or she plays with the other (McReynolds, 1988).

Verbal explanations and physical assistance are necessary modes of instruction and feedback for students with vision loss. Pointing to a spot in the music, gestures, or visual demonstrations are lost to students who are blind, and generally to those with low vision as well. Head nodding has to be accompanied by phrases such as "you're getting it" or "that's right." In addition, many instructions such as "cross your arms" have no meaning for a student who has never seen arms crossed. In such cases, physical assistance is needed to place the student's arms in position.

Much of the attraction to participating in music programs is the socialization that occurs at rehearsals, performance trips, and just hanging out in the music room before and after school. Music educators can assist in the social development of children with severe vision loss by providing opportunities for interpersonal interactions and encouraging and monitoring such interactions. An astute choir director did much to promote the socialization of Melanie, a student who was blind. On the first day of rehearsal after summer break, he gave the class a few minutes to chat and catch up with each other. As the choir chatted eagerly, he noticed that Melanie sat quietly talking to no one. After bringing the choir back to attention, he said, "I bet most of you do not know how well Melanie knows you. When I point to you, I want you to say "Hello, Melanie." Students who had never exchanged words with Melanie, said "Hello, Melanie" and she quickly and easily stated their names. She had "known" them for years from various classes. The students were then eager to find out if she knew them. "See if she knows me" they asked the choir director. From that rehearsal on, the students greeted Melanie when they saw her and were more open to including her in their conversations. The choir director would have scored no points as a teacher by going home and lamenting over the fact that the students did not include Melanie. He scored many points as a teacher by cleverly teaching the students to include Melanie in their social network.

A number of teachers have written articles (Barss, 1988; Barss, Marrion, & Haroutounian, 1999; Manion, 1986) about teaching music to students with visual disabilities and, without exception, these teachers convey the rewards of such a challenge. The rewards came from finding new ways to teach a concept, from understanding the world from an aural perspective, and from teaching motivated and talented students. Soniya Patel had teachers such as these, and she grew up to be the first blind teacher hired in the state of Tennessee. She has been teaching music for over 12 years to sighted children at Byars Dowdy Elementary School in Lebanon, Tennessee.

Below are several sites that should be useful for music educators teaching students with vision loss:

The National Library Service for the Blind and Physically Handicapped
Library of Congress
1291 Taylor Street, NW
Washington, DC 20011
Telephone: 800-424-8567
Fax: 202-707-0712
Email: nls@loc.gov

National Resource Center for Blind Musicians
Music and Arts Center for Humanity
600 University Avenue
Bridgeport, CT 06601
Telephone: 203-366-3300
Fax: 203-368-2847
Email: info@blindmusicstudent.org

Music Education Network for the Visually Impaired (MENVI)
Southern California Conservatory of Music
MENVI Headquarters
8711 Sunland Boulevard
Sun Valley, CA 91352
Phone: 818-767-6554
Fax: 818-768-6242
Website: http://www.tvimusic.org/SCCM.html

Music Therapy for Students with Vision Loss

Music educators have a long history with students who have vision loss; however, relatively few music therapists serve individuals with vision loss (American Music Therapy Association, 2009; Codding, 2000; Davis, Gfeller, & Thaut, 2008). Music therapists serving this population would benefit greatly from a concerted effort to increase the available resources by those working with individuals who are blind or who have low vision. Many of the resources in print are dated and do not incorporate the modern technologies now available to students and clients who have vision losses. From the existing resources, however, it is clear that various educational and therapeutic objectives for students with vision loss can be addressed through music therapy.

The clients with vision loss with whom music therapists work often have accompanying disabilities such as intellectual disabilities. For clients with vision loss as their primary disability, there are a number of rehabilitation objectives that can be addressed through music therapy. These objectives include the development of listening skills, mobility and orientation skills, daily living skills, social skills, and interpersonal communication skills (Davis et al., 2008; Hunt & Marshall, 2005). According to Codding (2000), music is used to achieve these objectives in several ways: (a) as a structured activity to facilitate learning of academic, motor, social, and verbal behavior; (b) as a stimulus cue or prompt for sound localization and other listening tasks; (c) as a contingency; and (d) as a part of music appreciation and enjoyment.

Listening Skills

Many people believe that when one sense is absent, other senses are naturally enhanced. This assumption is not true. The listening skills of people who are blind are developed just as all listening skills are—through practice. However, there are some data that suggest the earlier the onset of blindness, the more perceptive the individual's listening skills (Gougoux et al., 2004). By virtue of their disability, people who are blind must practice and utilize their listening skills more earnestly than most people. Since much of the information they receive about the world around them is through listening, young children require instruction and experience in developing this skill to its fullest extent (Brown, 1990).

Most music educators and music therapists have taken theory courses in ear training, which is nothing more than structured listening lessons. Teaching the brain to detect minor nuances in musical sounds may well generalize to the recognition of minor nuances in environmental sounds (Heyes, 1980). Learning to discern timbre differences may assist children in learning the difference between male and female voices or an adult and a child's voice. Learning to detect minor changes in loudness may assist in detecting whether a sound source is approaching or retreating. Much of the auditory training information included in the chapter on students with hearing loss can also be applied to young children who are congenitally blind. Of particular importance are the auditory training exercises related to sound localization and sustained attention to sound.

Mobility and Orientation Skills

Orientation is the ability to determine one's position in relation to rest of the environment, and mobility is the ability to move safely and efficiently from one point to another (Heward, 2008). Orientation skills are related to mobility, since persons who are blind must first determine their position in the environment in order to know where they need to go. Orientation and mobility skills are extremely important to the development of a child with vision loss. Because of the need to get around, and thus the subsequent practice that transpires, persons who are blind are generally better than sighted people at using sound to orient themselves and to cue their travel.

Spatial awareness is a necessary skill for determining one's orientation. Chin (1988) found that dance movement instruction significantly improved the spatial awareness of students with visual impairments. Children who are blind must develop freedom of movement and the ability to move with confidence if they are to ambulate comfortably through their environment. The use of music with dance instruction can assist in developing the child's coordination and gross motor skills (Duehl, 1979). Generally, children learn dance steps through imitation. For the child who cannot see someone model the dance steps, verbal descriptions of the dance steps and physical assistance must be used.

Music has been used to teach route travel to adults who have multiple disabilities including blindness. Subjects learned to travel to specific destinations by listening to music broadcast by speakers placed at specific points throughout the building. For example, the cafeteria had special music that played when students were to go to lunch. Mobility and orientation is generally taught through structured exercises and repetition. Using music to highlight environmental landmarks can be enjoyable and efficient. The use of music can also reduce the need for someone to assist students in navigating their environment (Uslan, Malone, & De l'Aune, 1983).

Mobility skills are dependent upon a child's psychomotor development. Infants with vision loss generally lag behind sighted children in motor development. For sighted children, the world meets them halfway. What they see around them motivates them to move. They see objects or people and reach for them. For children who are blind, their ears function as their eyes. Interesting sounds can motivate them to reach out and move. Musical instruments can serve as aural stimuli, motivating the child to reach out. The sound of musical instruments can also be very rewarding to the child who has moved about to find the source of the sound he or she hears (Gourgey, 1998).

Daily Living Skills

Important to life as an independent adult are skills such as cooking, dressing, grooming, financial management, housekeeping, and personal hygiene. These skills, which are taught to all students, must be taught to the student who is blind in alternative ways. Music has long been used to teach daily living skills to children who have intellectual disabilities. The same kind of musical interventions can be employed with children who are blind, but with adaptations made for their lack of sight. For example, the alphabet song has long been used to teach letters. This same song can be used with children who are blind, but Braille letters or other tactile letters need to be substituted for written letters. Songs about hand washing or identifying body parts cannot be taught through visual imitation, but through hands-on experiences.

Social and Interpersonal Communication Skills

Students with severe vision loss are often delayed in the development of social skills. For students without vision, or even limited vision, it is often difficult for them to approach their peers. Most young children observe their peers engaged in various activities and are motivated to join them. Students with little or no vision are often dependent upon others to seek them out. Without equal access to peer activities, they are sometimes isolated and thus lack the opportunities to develop social skills as most children do. Music making and music listening with others is an effective strategy for bringing students with and without vision together. Such activities should be structured and monitored by therapists who understand how to facilitate positive social relationships and to teach social skills such as turn taking, greeting behaviors (shaking hands, introductions), the simulation of eye contact, and table etiquette (Gourgey, 1998; Kern & Wolery, 2001; Kersten, 1981).

Many students without vision have not developed the nonverbal behaviors that assist in interpersonal communication. These nonverbal behaviors include making eye contact, smiling, nodding, leaning in, and using gestures. These behaviors can be taught through structured music activities that introduce the behaviors and provide for the practice of these behaviors. Music therapists can also use contingent music to reward students who use these behaviors appropriately.

Talking about music is one way to for children to practice good communication skills. Flowers and Wang (2002) found that blind children were able to describe music excerpts with approximately the same accuracy as sighted children. Analysis of types of language used showed that sighted children remained consistent in the number of musical elements described across age-groups; however, blind students increased substantially in their descriptions of musical elements at each successive level (kindergarten, primary, upper elementary). Sighted children used significantly more metaphors and emotional descriptors than did blind children. The use of temporal language increased with age, particularly among the blind students, but there were no statistical differences due to visual ability in the study. Describing music, critiquing music, and asking questions about music are all ways to incorporate music learning into the practice of good conversation skills.

For children with a vision loss or any disability, the positive sense of self that comes from developed musical talent does much to enhance their confidence, and, consequently, their willingness to socialize with others. They can also participate in various musical organizations that will allow for rewarding social contacts with their peers. The development of performance skills can do much to enhance any child's sense of self. Many musicians, amateur and professional, have experienced the adulation of others because of their musical skills.

Sensory Stimulation Behaviors That May Accompany Blindness

Students with severe vision loss sometimes engage in stereotypic behaviors that can impair their social and interpersonal relationships. These behaviors are repetitive movements such as body rocking, rubbing or poking the eyes, repetitive finger or hand movements, and head rolling. A common theory that attempts to explain the cause of such behaviors is sensory compensation—the need to compensate for the loss of visual stimulation by engaging in some other form of sensory stimulation. Stereotypic behaviors are socially stigmatizing, and they often discourage classmates from approaching a student who engages in these behaviors. Beyond the social implications, stereotypic behaviors can also interfere with learning. Although elimination is sometimes difficult, contingent music has been shown to significantly reduce stereotypic behaviors in children who exhibit them (Greene, Hoats, & Hornick, 1970; Greenwald, 1978; Kersten, 1981; Smeets, 1972). There are many musical behaviors that are incompatible with stereotypic behaviors. For example, students cannot play a recorder (or at least not very easily) while moving their head in a figure eight, or play a drum while flailing their hands. Musical behaviors should be selected that compete with the stereotypic behaviors a student exhibits.

The contingent use of music can be used to eliminate stereotypic behaviors as well as to reinforce appropriate classroom behaviors. Hill, Bratner, and Spreat (1989) found that contingent music was effective in eliminating noncompliant behaviors in a 17-year-old student who was blind who refused to sit in the classroom. A pressure-sensitive switch was used to deliver music reinforcement when she sat in her seat. The student was able to discriminate among different types of music, and her compliance rates varied accordingly.

Summary

Students with visual disabilities participate frequently in school music organizations but are rarely among the clients seen by school music therapists. However, both music educators and music therapists have much to offer students with visual disabilities. Music educators can assist these students in developing their skills as musicians, and music therapists can do much to help them in developing their social and daily living skills. There is no doubt that loss of vision can present real challenges to students in their daily life; however, music can serve as a valuable tool for overcoming these challenges and can make a valuable contribution to their quality of life.

KEY POINTS FROM THE CHAPTER

Definition of vision loss:
  ♦   IDEA defines vision loss as an impairment in vision that, even with correction, adversely affects a child's educational performance.

- A person is considered legally blind if he or she has 20/200 vision or is able to see objects only within an area of 20 degrees or less.
- Students with low vision or partial sight can read print, although they may depend on optical aids. They use their vision for learning.
- Students who are functionally blind use Braille for reading and writing, but may use functional vision for mobility and other activities of daily living.
- Students who are blind use their tactile and auditory senses for learning and receive no functional input through their sense of vision.
- Vision loss can be congenital or adventitious.

Types of vision loss:
- Astigmatism, hyperopia, and myopia are three types of vision loss.
- Albinism, amblyopia, cataracts, glaucoma, nystagmus, optic nerve atrophy, optic nerve hypoplasia, retinitis pigmentosa, retinoblastoma, retinopathy of prematurity, strabismus, and cortical visual impairment are various eye conditions that may cause vision loss.

Effects of vision loss:
- Students with vision loss are less likely to experience vicarious learning because they cannot observe and imitate others.
- Vision loss impacts children's orientation and mobility, daily living skills, reading and writing, conceptualization and cognitive development, psychosocial development, and vocational choices.
- Children with vision loss may not understand many words used in everyday conversation because they have had no experience with the objects or concepts related to these words.
- Vision affects students' intellectual development because they do not have the benefit of learning through visual illustrations.
- Students with severe vision loss are less likely to initiate social interactions and must be taught nonverbal communication used in interpersonal interactions.
- Students with vision loss may take longer to complete academic tasks because of the adaptations necessary to help them achieve (Braille, large print), or because the resources they need to succeed are not readily available to them.

Educational tools:
- Providing direct instruction and many hands-on experiences helps students with vision loss learn the many concepts that children usually learn through imitation.
- Braille and large print are two educational tools that are used by many successful people with vision loss.

Assistive technology:
- The types of adaptive technology available to students with visual impairments generally fall into one of several categories: large print access, speech access, Braille access, scanned material access.
- The International Braille and Technology Center for the Blind (IBTC) was established in 1990. It is a comprehensive demonstration and evaluation center complete with nearly every type of speech output and Braille technology, both hardware and software, available in the U.S.

Adaptations to the music classroom:
- Dancing Dots–Braille Music Technology is an American company based in Philadelphia that was founded in 1992 to develop and adapt music technology for the blind. Software that translates musical notation to Braille music and Braille music to standard music notation is available.
- Music teachers of students with vision loss should remember to talk while writing on the board or conducting, move closer to students with visual disabilities, have other students help the student with vision loss, use white boards instead of green chalkboards, provide large print copies or recordings of music, physically assist students when needed, give definitions of unfamiliar words of a visual nature, provide materials before needed in class, and model acceptance and inclusion of the student.

Music education for students with vision loss:
- Lowell Mason, considered the "father of public school music education," taught music as an academic subject at the Perkins School for the Blind from 1832–1836. Today, many schools for students with visual impairments continue to include music as part of the curriculum.
- It is beneficial for students with vision loss who wish to be musicians to learn to read Braille music. This allows them to be more independent in their music study.
- Students with vision loss who learn music by rote must be given recordings ahead of time so they can learn the music before the rest of the class.
- With the proper adaptations, students with vision loss can participate in marching band and perform choreography with their school choir. The music teacher must remember to use precise verbal explanations and give much physical assistance during instruction and while giving feedback.
- Music educators should take an active role in ensuring that students with vision loss are included in the social network within their music class or ensemble.

Music therapy for students with vision loss:

♦ Music therapy can be used to help students with vision loss develop their listening skills in order to recognize the nuances of sounds in their environment.

♦ Instruction in dance and movement can help students with vision loss develop confidence to move through space and improve spatial awareness, which is a necessary skill for determining orientation.

♦ Music can be used to teach travel routes and improve mobility in individuals with vision loss.

♦ Music can help teach daily living skills to students with vision loss similar to how it is used to teach children who have intellectual disabilities, but with adaptations made to accommodate their lack of vision.

♦ Musical ensembles can provide a setting for students with vision loss to improve social and interpersonal communication skills. Music activities can also be used to teach and reinforce appropriate nonverbal behaviors.

♦ Contingent music can help decrease the incidence of stereotypic behaviors, including self-stimulating behaviors in which many students with severe vision loss engage.

REFERENCES

American Music Therapy Association. (2009). *Member sourcebook.* Silver Spring, MD: Author.

Barraga, N.C., & Erin, J. (1992). *Visual handicaps and learning* (3rd ed.). Austin, TX: PRO-ED.

Barss, F. (1988). "What's a blindfold?" (Challenge of a blind student). *American Music Teacher, 38,* 24–25.

Barss, F., Marrion, M., & Haroutounian, J. (1999). Learning from Kara: Reflections of three friends. *American Music Teacher, 48,* 15–21.

Bishop, V. E. (2004). *Teaching visually impaired children* (3rd ed.). Springfield, IL: Charles C. Thomas.

Brown, K. R. (1990). Effects of a music-based memory training program on the auditory memory skills of visually impaired individuals (Doctoral dissertation, University of Houston, 1990). *Dissertation Abstracts International, 52*(03), 877A. (UMI No. AAT 9118115)

Chin, D. L. (1988). Dance movement instruction: Effects on spatial awareness in visually impaired elementary students. *Journal of Visual Impairment & Blindness, 82,* 188–192.

Codding, P. A. (2000). Music therapy literature and clinical applications for blind and severely visually impaired persons: 1940–2000. In *Effectiveness of music therapy procedures: Documentation of research and clinical practice* (pp. 159–198). Silver Spring, MD: American Music Therapy Association.

Corn, A. L., & Bailey, G. L. (1991). Profile of music programs at residential schools for blind and visually impaired students. *Journal of Visual Impairment & Blindness, 85,* 379–382.

Crocker, A. D., & Orr, R. R. (1996). Social behaviors of children with visual impairments enrolled in preschool programs. *Exceptional Children, 62,* 451–462.

Davis, W. B., Gfeller, K. E., & Thaut, M. H. (2008). *An introduction to music therapy: Theory and practice* (3rd ed.). Washington, DC: American Music Therapy Association.

Duehl, A. N. (1979). The effect of creative dance movement on large muscle control and balance in congenitally blind children. *Journal of Visual Impairment & Blindness, 73,* 127–133.

Flowers, P. J., & Wang, C. (2002). Matching verbal description to music excerpt: The use of language by blind and sighted children. *Journal of Research in Music Education, 50,* 202–214.

Gougoux, F., Lepore, F., Lassonde, M., Voss, P., Zatorre, R. J., & Belin, R. (2004). Pitch discrimination in the early blind: People blinded in infancy have sharper listening skills than those who lost their sight later. *Nature, 430,* 309.

Gourgey, C. (1998). Music therapy in the treatment of social isolation in visually impaired children. *RE:view, 29*(4), 157–162.

Greene, R. J., Hoats, D. L., & Hornick, A. J. (1970). Music distortion: A new technique for behavior modification. *The Psychological Record, 20,* 107–109.

Greenwald, M. A. (1978). The effectiveness of distorted music versus interrupted music to decrease self stimulatory behavior in profoundly retarded adolescents, *Journal of Music Therapy, 15,* 58–66.

Hardman, M. L, Drew, C. L, & Egan, M. W. (2008). *Human exceptionality: School, community, and family* (9th ed.). Boston: Houghton Mifflin.

Heller, G. N., & Livingston, C. (1994). Lowell Mason (1792–1872) and music for students with disabilities. *Bulletin of Historical Research in Music Education, 16,* 1–16.

Heward, W. L. (2008). *Exceptional children: An introduction to special education* (9th ed.). Upper Saddle River, NJ: Merrill/Prentice Hall.

Heyes, A. D. (1980). Use of musical scales to display distance to objects in an electronic travel aid for the blind. *Perceptual and Motor Skills, 51,* 1015–1020.

Hill, J., Brantner, J., & Spreat, S. (1989). The effect of contingent music on the in-seat behavior of a blind young woman with profound mental retardation. *Education and Treatment of Children, 12,* 165–173.

Hunt, N., & Marshall, K. (2005). *Exceptional children and youth* (4th ed.). Boston: Houghton Mifflin.

Kern, P., & Wolery, M. (2001). Participation of a preschooler with visual impairments on the playground: Effects of musical adaptations and staff development. *Journal of Music Therapy, 38,* 149–164.

Kersten, F. (1981). Music as therapy for the visually impaired. *Music Educators Journal, 67,* 62–65.

Manion, S. (1986). On teaching piano to blind students. *American Music Teacher, 36,* 46–48.

McReynolds, J. C. (1988). Helping visually impaired students succeed in band. *Music Educators Journal, 75,* 36–38.

Moss, F. W. (2009). Quality of experience in mainstreaming and full inclusion of blind and visually impaired high school instrumental music students. *Dissertation Abstracts International, 70*(4-A), 1212.

Presley, I., & D'Andrea, F. M. (2009). *Assistive technology for students who are blind or visually impaired.* New York: AFB Press.

Rapp, D. W., & Rapp, A. J. (1992). A survey of the current status of visually impaired students in secondary mathematics. *Journal of Visual Impairment & Blindness, 86,* 115–117.

Rose, D. H., Meyer, A., & Hitchcock, C. (Eds.). (2005). *The universally designed classroom: Accessible curriculum and digital technologies.* Cambridge, MA: Harvard Education.

Ryles, R. (1996). The impact of Braille reading skills on employment, income, education, and reading habits. *Journal of Visual Impairment & Blindness, 90,* 219–226.

Siligo, W. (2005). Enriching the ensemble experience for students with visual impairments. *Music Educators Journal, 91*(5), 31–36.

Smeets, P. M. (1972). The effects of various sounds and noise levels on stereotyped rocking behavior of blind retardates. *Training School Bulletin, 68,* 226.

Uslan, M., Malone, S., & De l'Aune, W. (1983). Teaching route travel to multiply handicapped blind adults: An auditory approach. *Journal of Visual Impairment & Blindness, 77,* 18–20.

Wittenstein, S. H. (1994). Braille literacy: Preservice training and teachers' attitudes. *Journal of Visual Impairment & Blindness, 88,* 516–524.

Chapter 12

Students with Hearing Loss

CHAPTER OVERVIEW

Hearing is the primary sense through which a child develops speech and language. For most children with normal hearing, speech and language is acquired in a seemingly natural and effortless manner. However, children without adequate hearing are cut off from the richness of sounds that prompt them to respond to others and to eventually imitate the speech they hear. Because hearing loss is a disability that is not readily apparent, its impact on a child's development is often underestimated. Successful communication—the exchange of meaningful information—is central to a child's acquisition of academic and social skills. Communication is the basis of our social and cognitive being; without it, we are cut off from the world. The resulting isolation can affect all aspects of a child's psychological, social, and intellectual development.

There are nearly 80,000 special education students between the ages of 6 and 21 who have a hearing loss (U.S. Department of Education, 2009). There are additional students with a hearing loss who receive no special education services or whose hearing loss has not yet been identified. Most of these students will participate in music classes and some may receive music therapy services. For the teachers and therapists who serve these students, the primary challenge will be to provide a rich and accessible auditory environment that motivates their students to listen, and to develop both communication and music skills.

This chapter includes information on the following topics:
- ♦ Definition and types of hearing loss
- ♦ Effects of hearing loss
- ♦ Educational approaches
- ♦ Assistive technology
- ♦ Adaptations to the music classroom
- ♦ Music education for students with a hearing loss
- ♦ Music therapy for students with a hearing loss

Definitions and Types of Hearing Loss

When we use the term *normal or typical hearing*, we mean hearing that is sufficient to process speech easily. Many children with a mild hearing loss have learned to use nonverbal cues to augment what they hear, such that they appear to have normal hearing. These students' hearing loss is often not detected until they have had a formal hearing test. Learning to use nonverbal cues for communication does not come easily for all children; therefore, even a child with a mild to moderate hearing loss needs some type of assistive listening device, usually a hearing aid, and often some form of educational support services.

Hearing impairment is the disability label used in IDEA to indicate a hearing loss that requires special education and related services. In other words, the hearing loss is so severe that the child's ability to process linguistic information is affected—with or without amplification, and, consequently, the child's educational performance is adversely affected as well. Hearing loss exists on a continuum from mild to profound; however, most special educators distinguish between children who are *deaf* and those who are *hard-of-hearing* (Hardman, Drew, & Egan, 2008; Heward, 2008; Turnbull, Turnbull, & Wehmeyer, 2010).

For students who are *deaf*, the primary means of communication is through the visual channel. Their *residual hearing* or remaining hearing is not sufficient to process speech. These students generally have a hearing loss that is 90 dB or greater (see Table 12.2). Most teachers have the misconception that a student who is deaf has no hearing. Very few individuals have no hearing at all. Most students who are described as deaf have some degree of residual hearing, although it is considered to be nonfunctional for the purposes of processing speech. These students may, however, use their residual hearing to make discriminations about other environmental sounds, including music.

Students who are described as *hard-of-hearing* generally respond to speech and other auditory sounds through the use of their residual hearing and hearing aids. Their ability to process speech for communication purposes varies and is dependent on their auditory and speech perception skills. In addition to students' degree of hearing loss and background in auditory and speech training, the *age of onset*, at what age the hearing loss occurred, is also an important factor in their ability to process speech and develop language. The age of onset will influence greatly the impact of the disability and be a critical variable in determining the services the child will need.

The difference between a *congenital hearing loss* and an *acquired hearing loss* (sometimes referred to as *adventitious loss*) is important. Children who have a congenital hearing loss, a loss that was present at birth, do not have the normal exposure to sounds, especially speech sounds, that other children typically experience. Children with a congenital hearing loss, as well as those who lost their hearing before age 2, are considered to have a *prelingual loss*, which means they lost their hearing before speech development. The implications for such a loss are critical due to the challenges they will face in developing speech and language skills. Children who acquired their hearing loss after age 2 or later in life are considered to have a *postlingual loss*, a loss that followed speech acquisition. Although these children have a distinct advantage, they will need assistance in developing listening skills, conserving their speech, and continuing to develop language.

There are two types of hearing loss based on the anatomical location of the hearing loss. A *conductive hearing* loss refers to a difficulty in conducting or transmitting sound vibrations to the inner ear, thus resulting in a reduction in the loudness of sound. The obstruction may be due to excessive earwax, fluid build up, or parts of the ear such as the eardrum or middle ear bones that do not move properly. Conductive losses can often be corrected through surgery or some other medical intervention. A *sensorineural hearing loss* refers to damage to the auditory nerve, thus resulting in sound that is distorted or unclear being delivered to the brain. This type of hearing loss cannot be treated through corrective surgery, and hearing aids or other types of amplification do not always help the student with a sensorineural hearing loss. Students with both a conductive and sensorineural hearing loss have a *mixed hearing loss.*

Finally, hearing loss may also be described in terms of which ear has the loss. A *unilateral hearing loss* means the loss is in only one ear. A *bilateral hearing loss* indicates that the loss is present in both ears. Most students who receive special services have a hearing loss in both ears, although the loss may be greater in one ear than the other. Students with a hearing loss in only one ear are usually able to develop speech and language normally, although they may have difficulty in determining the location of a sound source or in processing sound in loud or noisy environments, such as the band room. In such environments, sitting with the ear without a loss toward the primary or most important sound source (often the teacher's or director's voice) is generally helpful (Madell & Flexer, 2008; Paul & Whitelaw, 2011).

Terms Related to the Measurement of Hearing

Since music educators and therapists are concerned with the response of the human ear to music stimuli, it is helpful to know those terms that relate to the measurement of hearing (Darrow, 1985a). Sound consists of vibrations that travel in waves, generally through the air. Sound waves can vibrate at different speeds as they travel through the air. The faster the wave vibrates, the higher the pitch. Frequency is the number of vibrations produced per second and is measured in Hertz (Hz). One vibration per second equals 1 Hz. The frequency of a sound is a physical reality, while pitch is our subjective judgment of its frequency. Table 12.1 gives familiar frequency ranges.

Table 12.1 Frequency Ranges

Frequency Range	Hertz
normal hearing	20–20,000 Hz
normal speech	500–2,000 Hz
the piano	27.5–4,186 Hz

The duration of sound has to do with its continuance in time. The aural discrimination of varying lengths of sound is the basis of rhythm perception. Intensity is the amount of energy in a sound wave. Intensity is a quantitative measurement of sound. Loudness is our subjective judgment of this measurement. The intensity of sound is measured in decibels. Zero decibels (0 dB) is the quietest audible sound, while sounds above 120–140 dB can actually cause pain to the ears. Table 12.2 provides some common decibel ranges.

Table 12.2 Common Decibel Ranges

Decibel Levels	Sound Source	Musical Levels
0 dB	just audible sound	
20 dB	soft rustle of leaves	
30 dB	quiet whisper	background music
40 dB	soft speech	p
50 dB	normal conversation	mp
60 dB	loud conversation	mf
80 dB	shouting	f
90 dB	heavy traffic	marching band
100 dB	riveter 35 feet away	
120 dB	jet engine	

Audiology, the science of hearing, has made great strides in the development of instruments that assist in the detection and assessment of hearing loss. Audiologists measure the degree of hearing loss by generating sounds at specific frequencies and intensities on an audiometer, and then measuring an individual's response to these sounds. By viewing these responses displayed graphically on an audiogram, the music educator or therapist can determine the aural accessibility of music stimuli and the degree of amplification required in the clinic or classroom setting.

Fortunately, the medium for music therapists and educators is music, and music is usually more aurally accessible than speech. Music is generally more intense than conversational speech, employs many more frequencies than normal speech, and is composed of notes that are greater in duration than speech sounds. This is why even individuals with severe hearing losses sometimes listen to and enjoy music, yet they may have difficulty in aurally processing speech.

Effects of Hearing Loss

The effects of hearing loss are generally dependent upon the degree of hearing loss. A student's hearing loss is generally referred to as mild (41–55 dB), moderate (56–70 dB), severe (71–90 dB), or profound (91 or greater dB), depending on the student's average hearing level, measured in decibels, throughout the frequencies most important for understanding speech (500–2,000 Hz). Each degree of loss presents unique challenges. Even students with mild or moderate hearing losses, while able to use and understand speech, may feel isolated or awkward because they do not hear everything that is being said or often misunderstand what is being said. Several sources provide helpful references for understanding the effects of differing degrees of hearing loss on communication (Hallahan, Kauffman, & Pullen, 2009; Heward, 2008; Hunt & Marshall, 2005). These effects are described in Table 12.3.

Table 12.3 Effects of Degrees of Hearing Loss on Communication

Degree of Loss	Effect on Communication
Slight loss (27 to 40 dB)	• May have difficulty hearing faint or distant speech • May experience some difficulty with language arts • Has little or no trouble listening to music, but may experience difficulty understanding lyrics
Mild loss (41 to 55 dB)	• Understands conversational speech at a distance of 3 to 5 feet • May miss as much as 50% of conversation if not face-to-face • May have limited vocabulary and speech irregularities • Will need lyric sheet to follow words
Moderate loss (56 to 70 dB)	• Can understand loud conversation only • Will have difficulty in group discussions • Is likely to have impaired speech, limited vocabulary, and difficulty in language use and comprehension • Use of percussion and lower pitched instruments
Severe loss (71 to 90 dB)	• May hear loud voices about 1 foot from ear • May be able to identify environmental sounds • May be able to discriminate vowels, but not consonants • Speech and language likely to be impaired or to deteriorate • Use of drums and lower brass instruments
Profound loss (91 dB or more)	• Is more aware of vibrations than tonal patterns • Relies on vision rather than hearing as primary means of communication • Speech and language likely to be impaired or to deteriorate • Speech and language unlikely to develop spontaneously if loss is prelingual • Musical emphasis on rhythmic elements.

Hearing loss, especially one that is present at birth, has its most consequential effect on a child's development of communication skills, both in terms of spoken language and language comprehension. A hearing loss does not appear to affect children's intellectual development, but may delay their educational achievement in comparison to their peers (Hallahan et al., 2009; Hardman et al., 2008; Heward, 2008; Hunt & Marshall, 2005). Early detection of a hearing loss, appropriate amplification, and intervention can help greatly to reduce the effects of hearing loss.

Language Development

The majority of individuals with a hearing loss are able to use speech as their primary medium for language acquisition. Children with mild and moderate losses develop speech and language in the typical fashion, especially if they were diagnosed early and have had appropriate amplification for hearing speech models. Children with severe and profound hearing losses have a much more difficult time learning to speak and developing language skills. Imagine going to a foreign country and learning the language if you could not hear it well or at all. Children born to deaf parents often have an advantage over children born to hearing parents. Hearing parents generally spend the child's first years learning about deafness, trying to decide what language system to use, and then learning to be proficient at it. Valuable opportunities for early language learning are lost. Children born to deaf parents who use American Sign Language (ASL) start school with communication abilities that are developmentally appropriate to their age. Because of the lack of auditory information most deaf students experience, their greatest academic challenge will be learning to read and write English.

Intellectual Development

Reports from researchers and psychologists indicate that children with hearing losses have cognitive and intellectual abilities that are similar to their peers (Krivitski, McIntosh, Rothlisberg, & Finch, H., 2004; Moores, 2001; Vernon, 2005). Any discrepancies that are evident are attributable to testing biases related to the use of English, a common problem for all second language learners. The scores of deaf children on nonverbal intelligence tests are approximately the same as those of the general school population (Vernon, 2005).

Social Development

Children's social development is heavily dependent upon communication with the world around them. All children are at risk for delayed social development if they do not have access to societal networks at home and at school. The social development of children with hearing losses depends largely on the attitudes of others, and their ability to communicate in a mutually acceptable way with family and peers. Children who are deaf and born to deaf parents are thought to have good self-esteem and social skills due to early communication in the home and presence of other deaf individuals in their daily lives. Students who communicate with sign language are often at risk for isolation in mainstreamed settings, particularly if their only direct communication is with an interpreter, or if there are few other students who sign. It is imperative that parents and siblings learn to sign if a deaf child is to grow up with healthy family ties and the social skills necessary for life as adult. The need for social interaction often leads deaf students to associate primarily with other deaf students. With other deaf peers, they not only are able to communicate comfortably and effortlessly, but they also enjoy similar activities that do not rely on the ability to hear.

Academic Achievement

Unfortunately, students with severe to profound hearing losses often experience deficits in their academic achievement, particularly in reading and writing English. Because the ability to read affects all areas of learning, their achievement in other academic subjects is often depressed as well (Johnson, Liddell, & Erting, 1989). However, recent research indicates the gap between the academic achievement of students who are deaf/hard-of-hearing and students with typical hearing may be narrowing (Antia, Jones, Reed, & Kreimeyer, 2009). Students with deaf parents—or students who demonstrate high rates of class participation, have parents who are involved in their education, or were involved in an early intervention program—fare much better in their academic careers. The goal for educators and therapists is to ensure that all deaf children have the support needed for successful academic achievement.

Educational Approaches

Over the years, various special educational methods and materials have been developed for deaf and hard-of-hearing students—all with the focus on helping children develop language and communications skills. The educational approaches vary in their emphasis on speech communication or sign communication (Paul & Whitelaw, 2011).

The *Oral Approach* is built on the belief that deaf and hard-of-hearing children can learn to talk. The approach advocates the use of speech and speech-reading as the primary means for the transmission of thoughts and ideas with deaf persons. Educators who believe in the Oral Approach philosophy emphasize exclusively the teaching of speech and speech-reading together with amplification and use of the child's residual hearing. Some advocates of the Oral Approach will use *Cued Speech*, a method of supplementing oral communication. It is a system of communication in which eight hand movements supplement the information being spoken. This is not a form of sign language. The hand "cue" is used to indicate, visually, the exact pronunciation of every syllable spoken. With Cued Speech, a person with hearing loss can see all the words a hearing person hears. It is a speech-based method of communication aimed at taking the guesswork out of speech-reading.

The *Manual Approach* includes the use of signs, which are symbolic representations of words made with the hands, and *fingerspelling*, an alternative form of a written alphabet with hand shapes and positions corresponding to the letters of the written alphabet. *Sign languages* are independent languages that have developed specific to the communities in which they originated. There is no universal sign language. For example, American Sign Language is totally different from British Sign Language, even though the oral language for both countries is English.

Most state schools for the deaf use *American Sign Language* (ASL), a natural language with its own grammar and syntax. It is a beautiful and graceful visual-gestural language created by deaf people and used widely in the United States. The signs in ASL are word-like units, which have both concrete and abstract meanings. Signs are made by either one or both hands assuming distinctive shapes in particular locations and executing specified movements. The use of spatial relations, direction, orientation, and movement of the hands, as well as facial expression and body shift, make up the grammar of ASL.

American Sign Language has often been described as a "gestural" language, although hand gestures are only one component of ASL. Facial features such as eyebrow motion and lip-mouth movements are also critical components of its grammatical structure. In addition, ASL makes use of classifiers or hand shapes as well as the space surrounding the signer to describe places and persons not present. ASL shares no grammatical similarities to English and should not be considered in any way to be a broken, defective, or gestural form of English.

Many public school programs employ various combination systems that use both manual and oral communication. The term *simultaneous communication* is used to denote the combined use of speech, signs, and fingerspelling. Receptively, an individual receives the message both by speech-reading what is being said and by reading the signs and fingerspelling simultaneously. There are a number of manually coded English systems that combine signs and fingerspelling with the grammar and syntax of standard English. Sign systems differ from sign language in that they attempt to create visual equivalents of spoken words through manual symbols. There are four major systems in this group: (a) Seeing Essential English, (b) Signing Exact English, (c) Linguistics of Visual English, and (d) Signed English. The use of fingerspelling as the primary mode of communication in combination with spoken English is known as the *Rochester Method,* although this method of communication is rarely used today.

Total Communication is a philosophy that implies acceptance, understanding, and use of all methods of communication to assist the deaf child in acquiring language. Whatever method is most appropriate for a child to develop academically is used for communication. Some educators believe that utilizing any or all forms of communication is unrealistic, and that one form of communication is emphasized at the expense of another.

One approach that has experienced growing interest over the past 20 years is the *Bilingual-Bicultural Approach* (Drasgow, 1998; Hermans, Knoors, Ormel, & Verhoeven, 2008; Mahshie, 1995). Based upon the successful academic achievement of children born to deaf parents and other approaches used with second language learners, some educators have advocated a bilingual-bicultural approach to the education of deaf children. Advocates believe that American Sign Language as a first language can lead to linguistic competence, and that English is better learned as a second language and in the context of bilingual-bicultural instruction. The main obstacle to a bilingual-bicultural approach is finding teachers who are sufficiently fluent in American Sign Language and educated enough about deaf culture such that instruction is truly bilingual and bicultural.

Historically, proponents of the various communication approaches have been at odds. There is increasing consensus that whatever system or method works most successfully for the child should be used to allow for clear and understandable communication.

Deaf Culture

Those who uphold the values of Deaf culture and use ASL take pride in their cultural identity and they describe themselves as "Deaf" with a capital "D." There are others, however, who do not share the language or social ties and thus function more in the hearing world. These individuals are more apt to describe themselves as "deaf" with a lower case "d" or with the term *hard-of-hearing* (Padden & Humphries, 1988).

Culture embodies the beliefs, experiences, and practices of an integrated group of people. These commonalities unify and strengthen the individual members who find understanding from and belonging with others like themselves. Cultural affiliation gives purpose for and insight into the collective values, needs, and ways of achieving group goals (Kaplan, 1996; Padden, 1996; Padden & Humphries, 2006). Through their endeavors, subgroups develop distinct behaviors that are functional for survival within a larger world community. For people who do not hear, to be able to survive in a sound-reliant world, they draw together to engage in a silent society. According to Rutherford (1988), some clear evidence of the Deaf as a distinct community includes a high "endogamous marriage rate," "the existence of a formal societal structure," and "material artifacts" (pp. 134–135). Beyond these characteristics, however, the key feature that defines and maintains virtually all cultures is language. It is through language that people are able to socialize, and thereby they transmit group customs, mores, and expectations. Deaf people thus emerge as a unique group with strong solidarity and identity.

Indeed, what makes Deaf people a cultural group instead of simply a loose organization of people with a similar sensory loss is the fact that their adaptation includes language. An environment created solely by a sensory deprivation does not make a culture. Blind people find themselves in a visual void. This similarity in circumstance certainly provides for a strong group bonding of individuals of similar experience; it does not, however, form a culture. Blind people are vision-impaired members of the variety of Americas' linguistic communities. What does form a culture for Deaf people is the fact that the adaptation to a visual world has by human necessity included a visual language. In the United States this is American Sign Language. (Rutherford, 1988, p. 132)

American Sign Language (ASL) is the native language of people within the Deaf culture (Armstrong, 1999). It originated in the early 19th century through the efforts of Laurent Clerc, a Deaf French educator, and the Reverend Thomas Gallaudet, an American, who saw the need for Deaf education in the United States. It has not been until recently, however, that ASL has gained recognition as an independent, manual/visual language with its own grammar, syntax, and rules. Through the research of William Stokoe in the late 1960s and early 1970s, the myths of ASL being broken English and impeding the development of any language for its users were finally dispelled.

The development of the body of linguistic research related to American Sign Language resulted in an attitudinal shift that moved from viewing deafness as a pathological inability, to identifying it as a cultural difference. Increasingly, people who are Deaf are seen as a linguistic minority within the hearing world (Padden, 1996). They are not defective or impaired people who are intellectually or cognitively inferior to those who do hear.

Most individuals who identify with the American deaf culture are considered to be bilingual. The bilingualism present in the deaf community is a form of minority language bilingualism in which the members of the community acquire and use both the minority language (sign language) and the majority language in its written form and sometimes in its spoken or even signed form. Grosjean (2010) defined bilinguals as those who use two or more languages (or dialects) in their everyday life. Given this definition, most deaf people who sign and who use the majority language (even if only in its written form) in their everyday lives are indeed bilingual. Much like bilingual hearing individuals, bilingual individuals who are deaf are diverse. Depending on their degree of hearing loss, the onset of their hearing loss (prelingually or postlingually), their language of choice, their education, their occupation, and their social networks, they have developed different knowledge and use of their two languages (sign language and the majority language—English), as well as diversity in the skills associated with both languages (production and perception) and production of both languages (written, spoken, signed) (Grosjean, 2010).

Past misconceptions about the language and the abilities of those who are Deaf built many barriers and obstacles to mutual understanding and interaction between Deaf and hearing communities. These misconceptions and the resulting barriers have had an impact on the educational and political experiences of the Deaf. They feel that traditionally hearing educators and leaders have made decisions about the teaching practices and social position of those who are Deaf without consideration for the special needs and views of the group itself. As a result, people have felt compelled to advance their group's acceptance within the hearing world to gain respect and rights. They have made great strides in exerting their issues by educating the public about their language, social and political organizations, and rich legacy of Deaf folklore, art, and literature (Padden & Humphries, 2006).

Music and Deaf Culture

Music in Deaf culture has a long and varied history (Darrow & Heller, 1985; Sheldon, 1997). In respect for the Deaf community, it is important to discuss the role of music in a cultural context (Darrow & Loomis, 1999). This respect means expanding the conventional constructs through which music involvement is traditionally defined. The adaptability of music makes it accessible to people who are Deaf, especially given that most Deaf and hard-of-hearing students have residual hearing. Therefore, there are certain frequencies, timbres, and intensities of music that can be auditorily detected. Further, music becomes visual and tactile.

There are certain aspects of music participation that are particularly meaningful to students who have hearing losses. In the performances of others and their own, students with hearing losses can perceive musical vibrations, rhythms, movement, and expression. Some individuals can make meaningful discriminations about pitch (Darrow, 1992). There are other referential features of music, such as emotion and imagery that can be detected even by listeners with little hearing (Darrow, 2006; Darrow & Novak, 2007).

Many children enjoy music and learn about popular artists from their peers and siblings (Darrow, 2000). In spite of music's attractiveness to many Deaf and hard-of-hearing young people, research indicates however, that it is erroneous to assume that all individuals who are Deaf value music (Darrow, 1993). Some individuals reject music as a hearing value, find no use for it in their lives, or feel no sense of loss because of music's absence. These findings have implications for music therapy and education practices with children who are Deaf. Music therapists and educators must recognize and understand their students' place within or outside of Deaf culture.

There are numerous individuals with hearing losses who have found careers in musical performance. The most notable perhaps is Evelyn Glennie, a world-renown concertizing percussionist who has a profound hearing loss. Other well-known musicians with hearing loss include Peter Townsend, rock guitarist; Foxy Brown, rap artist; Johnny Ray, American singer and song writer; and Ludwig van Beethoven, composer. In addition, there are many lesser known instrumentalists, singers, rock band musicians, and dancers, who are also Deaf. When individuals are wired neurologically to be musical, they usually find a way to express their talents, regardless of their hearing status. Modern technology can do much to help them access musical sounds.

Assistive Technology

Nearly every child with a hearing loss can benefit from assistive listening devices or other forms of supportive technology. The assistive listening device used most often by children with hearing losses is a *hearing aid.* A hearing aid is an amplification device and, as such, makes sounds louder. There are various kinds of hearing aids that can be worn over the ear, in the ear, and on the body. The music therapist or music educator should check to make sure a child's hearing aid is working when he or she is in the classroom or clinic. Hearing aids make sounds louder, not necessarily clearer; however, modern digital hearing aids are matched to a child's hearing loss by amplifying some frequencies and not others, thus making sounds much clearer than early hearing aids. Nevertheless, hearing aids do not provide a child with normal hearing (Madel & Flexer, 2008).

With group listening devices, such as an *FM loop system,* a radio link is established between the teacher and the child. FM systems are the most flexible and durable of all large group assistive listening devices and therefore are very popular in school systems. The teacher wears a microphone and the child wears a receiver. These types of listening devices amplify only the teacher's voice, consequently reducing the interference of other ambient noise in the environment. These devices are particularly useful in the music room, because the microphone can worn by the teacher but also placed next to the stereo for music listening activities, or next to an instrument that is being played.

Other technologies that have improved the life of persons with hearing losses are instant messaging used with email services, video calling software such as *Skype*, closed captioning, alert devices, and cochlear implants. TDDs are telephones with small screens that display a typed message. Both parties must have a TDD. If one party does not have a TDD, he or she can use a relay service. The caller (deaf or hearing) contacts the relay center using a TDD or voice. The relay operator then dials the number and transmits the message using a TDD (to the party who is deaf) or voice (to the party who is hearing). The popularity of instant messaging has made TDDs nearly obsolete.

Closed captioning has had a great impact on the leisure time activities of persons with a hearing loss. Since July 1, 1993, all television sets 13 inches or larger must be closed-caption ready. That is, they can be set to display captioning for all programs that are closed-captioned. Unfortunately, not all programs on television are closed captioned, but the number is increasing every year. Many news shows are now real-time captioned, making persons who are deaf aware of current events and emergency announcements as they are broadcast. Closed captioning also has benefits for all children and adults learning to speak and read English.

Alert devices are used by individuals who are deaf to signal the doorbell, a telephone ringing, the alarm clock, a baby crying, or fire alarm. A sound sensitive switch is attached to a flashing light or vibrator to provide a visual or tactile signal. Some adults use hearing ear dogs to alert them to sound—much like persons who are blind use seeing eye dogs.

Another increasingly used technological device is the *cochlear implant.* The cochlear implant (CI) is an assistive hearing device designed for persons with severe-to-profound losses, typically bilateral, who receive little to no benefit from conventional hearing aids. In the United States, as of April 2009, roughly 25,500 children have been implanted with CIs (National Institutes of Deafness and Other Communication Disorders, 2010). The implant consists of an external portion that sits behind the ear and a second portion that is surgically placed under the skin. The CI is different than a hearing aid, which amplifies sounds. Instead, the CI bypasses damaged structures in the inner ear and directly stimulates the fibers or hairs in the cochlea. An implant does not restore normal hearing, but rather provides a useful representation of sounds in the environment to help persons who are deaf interpret the sounds and speech they hear.

A cochlear implant consists of four parts: (a) a microphone for picking up sounds, (b) a speech processor to select and arrange sounds picked up by the microphone, (c) a transmitter and receiver/stimulator to receive sounds from the speech processor and convert them into electric impulses, and (d) electrodes to collect the impulses from the stimulator and send them to the brain. Cochlear implants, coupled with intensive post-implantation training, can help young children to acquire speech and language. Most children who receive implants are between 2 and 6 years old, although recent trends are toward earlier implantation (Gfeller, Driscoll, Kenworthy, & Van Voorst, in press).

A cochlear implant requires both major surgery and important, time-consuming training to learn or relearn auditory skills, such as the interpretation and identification of sounds. The decision to implant a child should not be made hastily or haphazardly. Some people within the deaf community regard the use of cochlear implants as an attempt to make children who are deaf like hearing children, or to erode membership in the Deaf culture. The use of any type of assistive technology is a value-based decision that children who are deaf and their parents must make for themselves. Exploring all options and working with a team of various hearing-related professionals can be beneficial in making decisions regarding the best assistive listening device and educational placement for children who are deaf.

Cochlear Implants and Music Listening

Cochlear implants have performed well and hold great promise for the future in helping CI recipients understand speech. Significant challenges exist for those individuals listening to music. Many post-lingual CI recipients find that, after implementation, changes in pitch and timbre and other aspects of music make music listening less enjoyable and less satisfactory than when they listened to music before implantation. Gfeller (2001) suggests that some of the more satisfied music listeners are those recipients who acknowledge that music doesn't sound like it did before their hearing loss, but they have learned to enjoy music in a new and different way. In addition, adult recipients compare music to memories of music through their residual hearing, but implanted children have always heard music through a device designed to transmit speech and, therefore, may be less critical of the sounds they hear.

Looi and She (2010) developed and administered the University of Canterbury Music Listening Questionnaire (UCMLQ) to 100 adult CI recipients. From the resulting data, they found that CI users are more likely to spend more time listening to music if they enjoy it; the longer they listen, the more they enjoy listening to music; and that, in general, CI users prefer to listen to:

- low frequency instruments rather than high frequency instruments,
- individual instruments (i.e., guitar) rather than families of instruments (i.e., brass),
- fewer rather than more performers,
- country and western rather than pop/rock/jazz/classical, and
- slower rather than faster music.

Looi and She concluded that incorporating familiar songs and the above factors into a music training program appears to be a reasonable starting point. They also recommend using adaptive procedures that include pairing visual and auditory cues. In addition to these general suggestions, Gfeller et al. (in press) and Gfeller (n.d.) offer useful tips for music teachers and therapists working with young children who have cochlear implants. These suggestions were gleaned from conversations with many CI recipients, as well as from research on systematic training.

Choose the listening environment carefully.

- Music will generally sound more pleasant in a quiet room without echo.
- Some children will like to use earphones or direct connection to the CI sound processor. Other people prefer using speakers. Whatever the choice, use sound equipment of good quality.
- Reduce sounds from other sources (hallways, air conditioners, etc.).

Choose music selections carefully.

- Familiar songs that have numerous repetitions of musical patterns or words can be easier to understand.
- Find out which musical sounds, instruments, and styles are most pleasant through trial and error.

- Begin singing a cappella.
  - » Add instruments after establishing basic vocabulary and concepts.
- Judiciously incorporate background music.
  - » Turn off music when giving instructions.
  - » Keep background accompaniment relatively quiet in relation to the melody line.

Prepare for movement activities.

- Avoid damage to the external parts of the CI during movement activities.
  - » Avoid large motions that can cause the cord connecting the magnet and processor to be pulled.
  - » Adjust the use of manipulables (streamers, sticks, etc) to avoid entanglement .
- Provide physical assistance for children whose hearing impairment affects their balance.
- Select movements that foster practice of target speech sounds.
  - » For example, use songs about body parts, songs about spatial relations, "put your right hand in, put your right hand out," etc.

Be strategic and realistic about listening.

- Listening practice should be broken up into short, but frequent sessions. Brief practices distributed over time can be much more effective than one or two long practice sessions.
- Start out by simply paying attention to the rhythm, and then gradually focus attention on other aspects.

Make the musical sounds as good as possible.

- Keep the volume at a moderate level.
- Some people find that digital music recording formats, such as CDs, MP3s and other digital music players, are easier to understand.
- Use quality instruments.
- Provide copies of the lyrics when listening to songs.

Broaden music listening goals.

- Remember that music is more than just notes. It is a social activity that brings children together. Teachers can enjoy the planning and preparation of a music event, and focus on the social aspect.
- If children become overwhelmed, think about taking a silence break. Turn down/off the music until they are "ready" for more listening.
- Sometimes listening to vocal music can be a challenging and interesting way to improve speech perception.

Understand implant maintenance and troubleshooting.

- Learn the specifics of volume and sensitivity control for the particular processor your students will be wearing.
- Familiarize yourself with the technology as it changes in your classes.

A substantial body of research exists on music perception and cochlear implant users, primarily due to Kate Gfeller, F. Wendell Miller Professor at The University of Iowa. Gfeller has long been involved in applied research and clinical protocols for aural rehabilitation of children and adults who wear cochlear implants (Gfeller, Christ, Knutson, Witt, & Mehr, 2003; Gfeller, Knutson, Woodworth, Witt, & DeBus, 1998; Gfeller, Mehr, & Witt, 2001; Gfeller et al., 2007; Gfeller, Witt, Spencer, Stordahl, & Tomblin, 2000; Gfeller, Woodworth, Robin, Witt, & Knutson, 1997).

Adaptations to the Music Classroom

There are two primary aspects of the music classroom setting for which adaptations should be made in order to meet the needs of children who are deaf or hard-of-hearing. The purpose of these adaptations is to facilitate communication. Aspects of the classroom that require adaptations are the physical environment and interpersonal communication. Below are suggested adaptations to the physical environment in addition to those listed above for cochlear implant users, which are good for all students with hearing loss.

Adaptations to the Physical Environment:

1. The clinical setting should have good lighting for speechreading.
2. Clinic room fixtures such as draperies, carpeting, and upholstery can be used to absorb unnecessary noise.
3. Seating should be in a circle for group activities.
4. If the children who are deaf/hard-of-hearing wear hearing aids, they should be positioned with their hearing aids toward the teacher.
5. The speaker's face must be clearly seen. Music teachers who sit at a piano should be careful not to obstruct their face.
6. Optimal speechreading distance should be kept at 6 feet.
7. If necessary, additional assistive communication devices such as microphones, visual aids, tactile aids, sign language interpreters, and appropriate technological aids should be added to the physical environment.

Adaptations in Interpersonal Communication:
One-to-One Communication

1. Get the student's attention before speaking: a tap on the shoulder, a wave, or other visual sign of soliciting attention.

2. Speak slowly and clearly, but exaggeration and over-emphasis of words distorts lip movements, making speechreading more difficult. Speechreading is a skill not all deaf persons are able to acquire. Only about 1/3 to 1/4 of all speech is visible on the lips, and even the best speechreaders can't read everything, although they can pick up contextual clues to fill in some of the gaps.

3. Look directly at the person when you speak. Even a slight turn of the head can obscure the deaf person's view. Other distracting factors affecting communication include mustaches obscuring the lips, smoking, chewing gum, and putting your hand in front of your face.

4. Don't be embarrassed about communicating via paper and pencil. Getting the message across is more important than the medium used.

5. Try to maintain eye contact with the deaf person. Eye contact helps convey the feeling of direct communication. If an interpreter is present, continue to talk directly to the deaf person who can turn to the interpreter if the need arises.

6. If you are having some difficulty getting an idea across, try to rephrase a thought or restate a sentence, rather than repeating exactly the same words. Sometimes a particular group of lip movements is difficult to speechread.

7. Use pantomime, body language, and facial expression to help communicate.

Using an Interpreter

The role of an interpreter is to facilitate communication between the teacher or therapist and the student. Interpreters are simply the conduit for transmitting information; they should not be asked to interject opinions or to instruct the student who is deaf or hard-of-hearing. There are several rules for using interpreters in the classroom:

1. Speak directly to the student as you would speak to any student. Do not ask the interpreter to tell or ask the student information, such as "Ask Susan if she did her homework."

2. Maintain eye contact and interact face-to-face with the student, not the interpreter. The best place for the interpreter is to the teacher's side or slightly behind him or her.

3. It is the interpreter's responsibility to interpret sounds, such as sudden noises, especially emergency alarms, or anything that is said in the classroom environment. Do not say anything to the interpreter or about the student that you do not want interpreted.

Group Situations and Meetings

1. Seat the student who is deaf near the speaker where he or she can see the speaker's face.

2. Try to avoid standing in front of a light source, such as window. The bright background and shadows created on the face make it almost impossible to speechread.

3. Aid the student who is deaf in following a lecture, movie, or video by providing a brief outline or script printout.

4. In a training situation, try to provide new vocabulary in advance. It is almost impossible to speechread unfamiliar words.

5. Use visual aids. They can be a tremendous help to students who are deaf. Vision is their primary channel for receiving information. Make full use of overhead projectors, chalkboards, films, diagrams, charts, and other visual media where appropriate.

6. Try to avoid unnecessary pacing and speaking while writing on the chalkboard or lecturing. It is difficult to speechread a person in motion and impossible from the side or from the back.

7. Slow down the pace of communication slightly. This often helps to facilitate understanding. Many speakers tend to talk too fast. Try to allow a little extra time for the student who is deaf to assimilate the information and respond.

8. Make sure the student who is deaf is not left out when vital information is presented. Write out any changes in meeting times, special arrangements, or additional instructions. Allow extra time when pointing out the location of materials, referring to manuals and other media, because the student must look, then return attention for further instruction.

9. Repeat questions or statements that are spoken by others in the room who may not be in the student's visual field. Students who are deaf are cut off from whatever they cannot see. Since it is often necessary to know the question in order to fully understand the answer, questions or statements from other students should be repeated by the teacher for the benefit of all students in the classroom.

(National Technical Institute for the Deaf, n.d.)

Music Education for Students with a Hearing Loss

Some people believe that to be musical, one must have good hearing; however, many students with hearing losses are indeed musical. The degree of interest in music among such students varies, as it does among those with typical hearing (Darrow, 1993; Gfeller et al., 2000). Many deaf and hard-of-hearing students enjoy participating in musical activities, and their education in the arts should not be forfeited for entirely nonmusical goals (Birkenshaw-Fleming, 1990; Darrow, 2000). Musical objectives for deaf and hard-of-hearing students can follow those that are often outlined for typical hearing students. Objectives should include various forms of music participation:

1. Listening to music
2. Singing
3. Playing instruments
4. Moving to music
5. Creating music
6. Reading music

Music education objectives might also include knowledge about masterpieces of music and the elements of music: rhythm, melody, harmony, form, and expression. Traditional approaches to teaching music concepts can be employed with deaf and hard-of-hearing students (Ford, 1990; Robbins & Robbins, 1980, 1990; Schatz, 1990). Because of their visual and movement components, music educators have indicated that Orff and Kodaly approaches are particularly useful (Darrow & Gfeller, 1991). Students with hearing losses are at a distinct disadvantage if they are taught music solely through listening. Gfeller (2001) gives special attention to the aural rehabilitation of music listening for cochlear implant recipients. Regardless of the type of hearing device used, most students with hearing losses learn best through active participation in music making. Learning music through performing, reading, and writing music is essential for the student with hearing losses. Additional adaptive strategies include the use of visual and tactile aids. Almost any aural concept can be represented in some visual way. The music educator can use kinesthetic movement, such as having students outline the movement of a melody with their hands. Contemporary gaming is particularly useful for including students who have hearing losses. Musical games such as *Donkey Konga* and *Guitar Hero* are not dependent upon players' auditory stills, but rather on their visual processing skills and digital dexterity—both strengths of students with hearing losses. Research indicates that in such games, students who are deaf and hard-of-hearing perform as well as students with typical hearing (Darrow & Novak, 2009).

Special attention should also be given to amplification of music stimuli (Dalgarno, 1990; Geers, Hojan, & Hojan-Jezierska, 1997), the quality of recording equipment and instruments, the familiarity and complexity of the music material (Gfeller, Christ, et al., 2003), as well as the suggestions given earlier for adaptation of the physical and communication environment. Every individual, regardless of hearing status, deserves the right to participate in the musical arts and, as a result, experience a part of our culture. Some deaf individuals do not consider music a part of deaf culture and, consequently, look upon musical study as a "hearing value." Many members of the deaf community, however, do find music to be an important part of their lives (Darrow, 1993).

Adapting Musical Instruction

In teaching music, the music educator must be aware of the use of music with this population as it relates to students' individual strengths and preferences (Darrow, 1991; Gfeller, Knutson, et al., 1998; Gfeller, Woodworth, et al., 1997). Some students prefer listening to instrumental music than to vocal music because access is not dependent upon speech perception skills. Other students, eager to participate in the popular music culture, prefer vocal music and will work hard to follow the lyrics of contemporary artists as they listen. Still other students are not interested in listening to music to all, but prefer to respond to music in physical ways, such as playing instruments or moving to music.

Specific strategies for music training have been employed with persons who have hearing loss, such as:

- computerized music training programs used with those who have had cochlear implants (Gfeller, Witt, Kim, et al., 1999; Gfeller, Witt, Stordahl, et al., 2001);
- training using vibrotactile stimuli (Darrow, 1992; Darrow & Goll, 1989);
- training using frequency adjustments of the musical stimuli (Darrow, 1990a).

Additional adaptations can be made based on generalizations from the research in music perception and performance of deaf and hard-of-hearing individuals (Darrow, 1979, 1984, 1987b, 1989a; Darrow & Cohen, 1991; Gfeller & Lansing, 1991, 1992). By reading the research and reviewing these characteristics, the music therapist can make the appropriate adaptations in teaching music to students who are deaf or hard-of-hearing. Following are some of the implications for teaching derived from research on music and individuals with hearing losses:

1. Rhythmic abilities tend to be stronger than pitch-related abilities.
2. Discrimination of or production of rhythmic patterns is more difficult than beat reproduction.
3. Music stimuli must be presented at appropriate level of amplification.
4. Tactile perception can, in part, compensate for auditory deficits.
5. Visual cues, such as tapping the beat, are particularly helpful.
6. Music skills may be delayed rather than deviant.
7. Pitch discriminations can be made more easily in lower frequency ranges.
8. Pitch discrimination skills can be developed with training.
9. Discrimination skills may be misjudged because of language problems, which interfere with students' ability to describe what is heard.
10. The vocal range of students with hearing losses is often lower and more limited.
11. Students with hearing losses can benefit both musically and academically from participation in music activities.

12. Students with hearing losses are often more responsive to the rhythmic aspects of music than the tonal aspects.

13. Students with hearing losses may require greater exposure, both in duration and intensity, to music stimuli than do typical hearing students in order to meet educational and therapeutic objectives.

14. Sustaining instruments may provide more useful aural feedback than do percussive instruments.

15. Use of moderate tempi assists in greater rhythm performance accuracy.

16. Students with hearing losses may perform more accurately by reading standard music notation than by relying on the ear to imitate or learn by rote.

17. Students with hearing losses can improve their vocal intonation, both in singing and in speaking, by participating in vocal activity.

18. The vocal range of song literature should be taken into consideration with singers who have hearing losses.

19. Students with hearing losses are capable of improvements in ear training, as are typical hearing students.

20. Vibrotactile stimuli are a useful supplemental tool in the music instruction of students with hearing losses.

21. As with typical hearing students, students with hearing losses can develop an ear more sensitive to sound over time.

22. Students with hearing losses can benefit from instruction in the use of musical vocabulary.

23. Students with hearing losses exhibit certain musical preferences in regard to sound, source, intensity, and listening conditions.

24. Amplification and sound quality of the musical media should be given particular attention when instructing students with hearing losses.

25. Music instruction can assist in the development of a number of nonmusical behaviors such as speech production, listening, language, social, and academic skills.

Interpreting Songs into Sign

Interpreting songs into sign is a popular activity for deaf and hard-of-hearing as well as typical hearing students. Darrow and Gfeller (1991) surveyed public school music educators teaching deaf and hard-of-hearing students and found that signing songs is a frequent activity in the music classroom. With increasing adoption of the total communication philosophy, students in deaf education programs are finding song signing to be a useful means of sharing cultural values and performing popular music. Signing songs, however, should not be simply "finger play." Many of the elements of music and expressive aspects of music can be illustrated through the signing of music: rhythm, tempo, changes in tempo, style, texture, tone color (male signers for male voices, etc.), form, and dynamics. Careful attention should also be given to the art of interpreting songs into sign. The signing should be as meticulously executed as the singing of the songs. The following guidelines will assist in interpreting songs into sign (Darrow, 1987a):

1. Signs used for song interpretation can reflect volume, pitch (though rarely used), rhythm, and mood, as well as the lexical content by a variety of uses of body language, facial expression, space, and manner of execution.
2. Incorporating rhythm into signs is the most important factor distinguishing musical from nonmusical signing. Signing is paced to match the rhythm of the words.
3. Signs are drawn out or accelerated depending on the duration of the sung word.
4. Fingerspelling is rarely used.
5. Instrumental sections or humming requires the creative uses of mime. The viewer should be aware of what is happening in the music at all times.
6. Figurative language or symbolism requires creativity on the part of the signer.
7. Many times a single sign can reflect an entire phrase in a song.
8. Musical signing should transmit emotion as vividly as the audible song.
9. Some interpreters suggest that signs move upward as the melody moves upward, and as the melody moves downward, so should the signs. This adds very little to the performance for the deaf audience.
10. For sections marked forte, signs should be larger and executed with more force than sections marked piano.
11. Crescendos can also be expressed by gradually making signs larger and more intense. Decrescendos likewise should be expressed by gradually making signs smaller and more gently.
12. Signs should also follow the phrasing of the song, flowing one into the next with a slight pause at the end of the phrase.
13. The song style, whether it be classical, folk, rock, country, or pop, can be interpreted through the rhythm of signs, facial expression, body language, and, though unrelated to the signs, the dress of the signer.
14. When groups are performing in sign, special attention should be given to ensemble work. Signs should be synchronized: all hands moving in unison, all signs executed the same way, all signs made in the same amount of space.
15. Signs, like voices, should also blend. No individual signer should stand out among the group. Practice with a mirror or videotape.
16. Use a deaf individual as your "sign master." Acknowledge him or her in the program.
17. Sign performers should wear solid colors.

Music educators often find that teaching deaf and hard-of-hearing students can be both challenging (Darrow, 1999) and rewarding (Burgess, 1997; Johns, 2001; Kaiser & Johnson, 2000; Vassallo, 1997). The music education of students with hearing loss has a substantial history (Darrow & Heller, 1985; Sheldon, 1997). Many students with hearing loss continue their public school music education into college (Darrow & Loomis, 1993). Some students with hearing loss even go on to major in music and become music teachers (Darrow, 2010).

Music Therapy for Students with a Hearing Loss

The term *therapy* usually implies the remedial treatment of a disease or other physical or mental disorder. Members of the deaf community have made great strides in recent years to depathologize their disability. Deafness is no longer viewed as a medical condition, a deficit in need of treatment. The only true deficit related to deafness is being cut off from the usual means of acquiring and transmitting language. As a result, most deaf individuals communicate manually rather than orally. They regard this alternative form of communication as their only "difference." The loss of hearing, however, has many implications for the development of communication skills. Consequently, music therapy remains a viable educational intervention for children with hearing losses. The range of goals targeted for this population are linguistic, behavioral, academic, motor skills, social interaction skills, and self-concept. Clearly, the most important goals are those related to the child's linguistic development, since linguistic skills have important implications for the attainment of all other goals.

> [T]he main focus of educational programs for deaf children is the acquisition of English. Whereas some educators have recently argued that this rigid focus on English is unhealthy and that more attention should be given to learning history, science, math, etc.—through any available means of communication—it is still generally true that the majority of a deaf child's time and energy in school is spent on developing skills in English. (Baker-Shenk & Cokely, 1991, p. 63)

With the focused training of English literacy being the critical chore in deaf education, music therapy serves as a motivating and engaging method of successfully achieving linguistic objectives. Through music therapy, academic goals can be incorporated into activities related to language development. The design of these applications can be further influenced by the needs and priorities of the individual student, as discussed in the section on Deaf culture. Therefore, the linguistic objectives for deaf and hard-of-hearing children fit into two distinct categories: developing aural-oral English literacy, and learning English as a second language through American Sign Language. Spoken language objectives for music therapy with students who have significant hearing losses are related to communication: (a) auditory training, (b) language development, and (c) speech production and perception. For deaf and hard-of-hearing students learning English as a second language though American Sign Language, objectives will be directed toward auditory training, primarily for information related to the environment and safety—not speech acquisition, and toward England language concepts.

Auditory Training

The goal of auditory training is to teach the complex task of listening. The ability of individuals to use their hearing for the purpose of listening varies. Good hearing does not necessarily ensure skilled listening; conversely, poor hearing does not necessarily indicate an inability to listen. Listening is a mental process; hearing is a physical process. It is the function of the ear to collect auditory stimuli and deliver them to the brain, at which time the brain takes over and hearing becomes listening (Darrow, 1990b). The development of good listening skills allows students with hearing losses to use their residual hearing to the maximum extent possible. When students with hearing losses learn to interpret the sounds around them, they also increase the rate and quality of their social and communicative development.

Training the ear to listen requires: (a) analysis of the desired auditory task, (b) the structuring of successive approximations to the desired goal, and (c) regular and systematic evaluation of the client's auditory skill level. Auditory training should consist of sequential listening exercises. Nearly all auditory tasks can be broken down into four very basic levels of aural processing (Madell & Flexer, 2008). These levels of aural processing follow, as well as ways of integrating music to determine a child's present level.

1. Detection—the listener determines the presence or absence, initiation or termination of music stimuli.
2. Discrimination—the listener perceives differences in music stimuli (such as fast and slow, high and low, music versus speech).
3. Identification—the listener appropriately applies labels (such as forte or piano, woodwind or brass) to music stimuli.
4. Comprehension—the listener makes critical judgments regarding music stimuli (such as judgments concerning form, harmony, or texture; or the comprehension of song lyrics).

Most students with hearing losses develop detection and discrimination skills through normal interaction with the environment. It is the third and fourth levels of auditory processing—identification and comprehension—that require the attention of the music therapist.

There are a number of other listening behaviors that are subsumed within these four basic levels of auditory processing. These additional listening behaviors are prerequisites to auditory comprehension. In 1977, Derek Saunders developed a hierarchy of auditory processing still used today, This hierarchy can assist the music therapist in developing sequential listening objectives for a wide range of clients. The hierarchy was developed with the processing of the speech signal in mind; however, music applications can be made and are given in each of the hierarchical steps. Speech and music contain many common properties, though perhaps identified by different names. In music, reference is made to intonation, tempo, accent, and rhythm. Speech counterparts are speech inflection, rate, stress, and speech rhythm.

Once again, proficiency at the first four levels of the hierarchy is usually acquired naturally; however, musical activities and games can be structured to practice these fundamental listening behaviors (Darrow, 1985b). The remaining six levels of auditory processing should provide a guide for music listening experiences.

1. *Awareness of acoustic stimuli*—Is the child aware that music is in the environment?
2. *Localization*—Can the child identify the location of the musical sound source? Can the child identify which child is playing the instrument?
3. *Attention*—Can the client attend to the music over time? Can the child take a step each time he or she hears the beat of a drum?
4. *Discrimination between speech and nonspeech*—Can the child discriminate between music and nonmusic sounds? Can the child discriminate between a person speaking and a person singing?
5. *Auditory discrimination*—Can the child discriminate between the timbre of different instruments or the entrance and exit of specific instruments within the total music context (figure/ground discrimination)? Can the child determine if it is a man or woman singing, or a boy or a girl?
6. *Suprasegmental discrimination*—Can the child make discriminations about the expressive qualities of the music (dynamics, tempo, phrasing)?
7. *Segmental discrimination*—Can the child make discriminations about changes in pitch? Can the child discriminate individual words in the context of a song?
8. *Auditory memory*—Can the child remember what instruments were heard? Can the child remember facts about the lyrics? Who was the song about?
9. *Auditory sequential memory*—Can the child remember in what order instruments were heard? Can the child remember the sequence of events in a song?
10. *Auditory synthesis*—Can the child make critical judgments regarding form, texture, harmony? Can the child answer questions about the song lyrics, or the story told in a song?

Songs are particularly useful in developing auditory attending skills and word recognition (Darrow & Gfeller, 1986). For example, give students cards with individual words that appear in a song, and ask them to hold up the words when they hear them in the song. Another example is to give students the lyrics of a song with selected words replaced with a blank. Then ask students to fill in the blanks as they listen to the song. Students must attend to the lyrics as they hear them and discriminate the words that are missing on their lyric sheets. Filling in the words also requires that they sound out and attempt to spell the missing words.

There are various views regarding a child's ability to generalize music listening skills to linguistic use; however, teaching a child to develop a focused and analytical attention to sound will undoubtedly transfer to the development of good listening habits, regardless of the source of sound stimuli. Although we can do little to improve students' ability to hear, we can do much to improve their ability to listen. Our goal is to increase the amount of information they receive through the sense of hearing. We do this by teaching them to interpret the sounds they hear. Listening, like any other skill, must be practiced through regular, sequential listening exercises. The ear is a valuable listening device, and music, a powerful medium through which listening skills can be taught, practiced, and rewarded.

Language Acquisition and Development

Language is the means by which people communicate. Native languages are generally learned auditorily, with ease, and over a relatively short period of time. Aural exposure to language is the most important component in the development of communication skills. Without adequate aural exposure to language, children who are deaf essentially learn a "foreign" language with only the assistance of nonverbal cues such as facial expression, body language, and small movements of the lips—on which approximately only one third of all speech is visible. It is understandable that without alternative forms of communication such as sign language, children who are deaf are at a tremendous disadvantage during the process of language development. Even children with mild hearing losses often experience difficulty with the fine discriminations that must be made in comprehending language (Paul & Whitelaw, 2011).

Other more subtle forms of language, such as sarcasm and play-on-words, are dependent on the aural processing of speech. Many verbal behaviors are also learned auditorily; some of these include social customs such as "please" and "thank you," use of compliments, and avoidance of inappropriate questions. Young children are generally able to comprehend various words or phrases long before they are able to use them appropriately, demonstrating the importance of exposure as an antecedent to expression. Every professional involved in the habilitation of young children who are deaf, including music therapists, should have among their objectives the acquisition and development of language.

The two fundamental components of language with which the music therapist is most likely to work are vocabulary knowledge and word-class usage (Gfeller & Darrow, 1987). Receptive and expressive skills, as well as reading and writing skills, should be employed as a part of instructional strategies. In order to foster language development to the fullest extent possible, methods of achieving these goals should not be confined solely to lesson objectives, but to every procedure employed in the music therapy setting. The music therapist can make most interactions an opportunity for learning language (Rickard, Robbins, & Robbins, 1990).

For young children who are deaf, the most important language objective will be the increased and appropriate use of vocabulary. Developing vocabulary skills is not as simple as defining words. Word meaning in a single context measures only one component of vocabulary knowledge. Words often have multiple meanings and serve separate language functions. Children who are deaf tend to know fewer words and use them in a singular context (Davis & Hardick, 1981). A child who is deaf may know the word *kid* in its noun form—a child or young goat—but not in its verb, adverb, or adjective form. It is the therapist's task to introduce vocabulary words, their multiple meanings, and their proper use in as many circumstances as possible: in song texts, song writing, informal conversation, and contrived situations. The therapist's choice of target words should be made in consultation with the child's classroom teacher or professionals who specialize in the language development of children who are deaf.

Children who are deaf may also experience difficulty with word-class usage. Children with a moderate degree of residual hearing tend to use most word classes adequately with the exception of adverbs, pronouns, and auxiliaries. Children with minimal residual hearing use fewer words in all classes than children with no hearing loss. A characteristic of most children's language is a tendency to overuse nouns and articles, thus the speculation that a hearing loss interferes with the function of words as well as understanding of their meaning (Davis & Hardick, 1981; Paul & Whitelaw, 2008). The music therapist must attempt to provide good models of word usage, opportunities for varied word use, and corrective feedback. Again, this can be accomplished through the study of song texts, informal conversation, or contrived situations. Additional approaches are activities such as song writing, song signing, and small group ensembles where communication is essential (Gfeller, 1987, 1990).

Properties of music, such as rhythm, accents, tempo, and repetition, help to organize the language of music. These same features support the structure of the English language, and teaching children songs to sign can be useful for practicing syntax, vocabulary, and idioms. Songs also facilitate some of the strategies Diaz-Rico and Weed (1995) emphasize that teachers should employ in order to help students build communicative competence: repetition, memorization, formulaic expressions, elaboration, monitoring one's own errors, appealing for assistance, requesting clarification, and role playing.

Songs are also useful in developing language skills, particularly vocabulary development and word class use. Songs can have highlighted words that students must define and for which they select an appropriate synonym. Another example is to give students the lyrics of a song with selected words replaced with a blank. Then ask students to fill in the blanks with the correct class of word, such as verb, adjective, adverb, noun, etc. Students can choose from a response set, or write any word from the correct word class. Teachers can also identify use of idioms, simile, symbolism, contractions, slang, etc.

The creative role of music therapists working with children who are deaf not only demands originality in designing goal-directed applications, but it also challenges theapists to draw on a multitude of instructional resources, not limited to musical materials. Instruments may be used, but additional visual and tactile aids must be incorporated, such as picture files, charts and posters, slides, printed material, and costumes (Diaz-Rico & Weed, 1995). These materials can complement the musical structure of the session and serve to facilitate comprehension and to reinforce participation.

As the students' knowledge of English improves, they will have more expertise in conveying English concepts through music. Evidence of their literacy can take the form of written songs, or it can be displayed by role playing the literal and the intended meanings of English idioms through dance. For example, the phrase "let the cat out of the bag" can be performed first in a literal scene with one dancer opening an imaginary bag and letting out another character who dances like a cat. In a second scene, other dancers can convey the concept when one person tells another a secret.

Speech Production and Perception

Speech production is acquired and controlled through the auditory system. Children learn to speak by imitating the sounds of others. The degree to which these sounds are available to a child who is deaf will directly influence the quality of speech production and the ability to receive the speech signal. The aspects of speech that are most severely affected by a hearing loss are phonation, rhythm, and articulation. Children who are deaf often do not associate breath control with the power source needed for fluid speech; consequently, they may breathe in the middle of words or phrases. Errors of rhythm constitute one of the most problematic aspects of the speech of a child who is deaf. The speech is generally slower, the syllables prolonged, and stress placed on inappropriate syllables. Speech intelligibility varies widely among children who are deaf; however, even individuals with very little hearing are capable of developing intelligible speech.

Hearing one's own voice allows the speaker the aural feedback necessary to self-correct pronunciation of words, adjust vocal inflection, and imitate speech rhythm. Children who are deaf are dependent on corrective feedback and instruction in remedial strategies. The music therapist can provide assistance in both of these areas. Music therapy objectives may include, though are not limited to, the following: vocal intonation, vocal quality, speech fluency, and speech intelligibility. In speech, the melodic elements such as rhythm, intonation, rate, and stress are referred to as the prosodic features of speech. These prosodic features convey important contextual information. Music activities such as singing can aid in the recognition and development of these melodic aspects of speech (Darrow & Starmer, 1986; Gfeller, 1986). Appropriate procedures include free vocalization, vocal imitation, rhythmic vocalization, and work on vocal phrasing and dynamics. Traditional music activities such as pitch-matching practice, singing songs and vocal exercises, and following notated melodic contours are also helpful (Bang, 1977).

The remediation of poor vocal quality can also be enhanced through traditional music activities. A breathy quality can be alleviated by vocalise that exercise the diaphragm; a nasal quality can be minimized by incorporating vocal exercises that utilize the head voice. The volume of a client's voice can be monitored during music therapy by teaching and practicing the use of expressive terms such as *piano* and *forte, decrescendo* and *crescendo.*

Speech fluency and articulation are not as easily influenced by the use of music therapy techniques. Speech fluency can be improved by the rhythmic chanting and singing of syllables, syllable combinations, words, word combinations, phrases, and, finally, complete sentences. Articulatory problems constitute the greatest challenge for speech and music therapists. Problems with articulation usually involve sound omissions, such as final consonants; substitutions, such as "thoup" instead of "soup"; interjections, such as "boyee" instead of "boy"; and mispronunciation of sounds, such as "sh," "th," or "s." The music therapist can carefully select songs that focus on specific speech sounds or words. The therapist should also maintain a record of the number of intelligible words in a given song (Darrow, 1989b). Consultation with the client's speech therapist can be extremely helpful in selecting appropriate and realistic objectives. In addition to directed music activities, feedback regarding a client's speech intelligibility should be given by the music therapist during everyday interactions in the clinical setting. Traditional assessments used in speech therapy can also be of use to the music therapist (Darrow, Gfeller, Gorsuch, & Thomas, 2000; Gfeller & Baumann, 1988).

Summary

The sensory and cultural differences of many students who are deaf or hard-of-hearing provide unique challenges for the music therapist and music educator. For deaf and hard-of-hearing students, music may not always be an auditory experience, though music can, most assuredly, be a tactual, visual, social, and esthetic experience for these students. By adapting music so it can be experienced through other senses, the music therapist and educator utilize alternative pathways to further the academic and musical growth of students with hearing losses. Many music educators and therapists find that such pathways lead to truly enjoyable and enriching experiences for themselves as well as for their students.

KEY POINTS FROM THE CHAPTER

Definition and types of hearing loss:
   ♦ According to IDEA, a hearing impairment is a hearing loss so severe that it impacts a student's ability to process linguistic information and academic performance, requiring special education and related services.

♦ Students who are deaf may have some residual hearing but generally are not able to use it for processing speech. These students use the visual channel to communicate.

♦ Students who are hard-of-hearing generally respond to speech using residual hearing and hearing aids.

♦ Hearing loss may be congenital (present at birth) or adventitious (acquired).

♦ Prelingual hearing loss occurs before age 2, while postlingual hearing loss occurs after age 2.

♦ A conductive hearing loss means there is a difficulty transmitting sound vibrations to the inner ear, while a sensorineural hearing loss refers to damage to the auditory nerve. A mixed hearing loss includes both conductive and sensorineural hearing loss.

♦ Hearing loss may be unilateral (present in one ear) or bilateral (present in both ears).

♦ Frequency, measured in Hertz (Hz), is the number of sound wave vibrations produced per second. Intensity of sound is measured in decibels (dB). These measurements are used by audiologists to determine the degree of a person's hearing loss.

Effects of hearing loss:

♦ Whether a hearing loss is slight (27 to 40 dB), mild (41 to 55 dB), moderate (56 to 70 dB), severe (71 to 90 dB), or profound (91 dB) determines to what degree hearing loss affects an individual.

♦ Language development is seriously affected by hearing loss, especially if the hearing loss is present at birth.

♦ While intellectual development is apparently not affected by hearing loss, educational achievement may be impacted due to testing biases.

♦ The social development of students with hearing loss is at risk if they are not able to readily communicate with those around them, both at school and at home.

♦ Students with severe to profound hearing loss often experience delays in academic achievement.

Educational approaches:

♦ The Oral Approach advocates the use of speech and speechreading, along with amplification and use of residual hearing. Some proponents of this approach also support the use of cued speech to supplement oral communication.

♦ The Manual Approach makes use of signs and fingerspelling to communicate thoughts and ideas.

♦ American Sign Language is a distinct language with its own grammar and syntax. It is used widely by deaf people in the United States.

- Simultaneous communication is the combined use of speech, signs, and fingerspelling.
- The Rochester method is the use of fingerspelling in combination with spoken English, although this method is rarely used today.
- Total communication uses whatever methods are most appropriate for a student to succeed academically.
- The Bilingual-Bicultural Approach teaches American Sign Language as a first language and English as a second language.
- Many people who are deaf and use ASL consider themselves part of a Deaf (with a capital "D") culture, which embodies the beliefs, experiences, and practices of people who are deaf.
- Music has a part in Deaf culture, although some people who are deaf reject music as a hearing value.

Assistive technology:
- Hearing aids amplify sounds and are commonly used by children with hearing losses.
- An FM loop system is a radio link between a microphone worn by the teacher and a receiver worn by the child, amplifying only the teacher's voice.
- Telecommunication devices for the deaf (TDD) are telephones with screens that display typed messages.
- All modern televisions are required to have a closed captioning feature, although not all television programs are closed captioned.
- Cochlear implants can help restore the hearing of individuals with sensorineural hearing loss.

Adaptations to the music classroom:
- Adaptations should be made to the physical environment and within interpersonal communication to help students with hearing loss succeed in the music classroom.

Music education for students with a hearing loss:
- Many students with hearing loss enjoy participating in musical activities.
- It is imperative that music educators be familiar with the research on the musical strengths and preferences of students with hearing loss so that the teacher can employ adaptive instructional strategies.
- Interpreting songs into sign is a popular activity for classes that include students with hearing loss as well as typical hearing students. When signing songs, careful attention must be given to the execution of the signs.

Music therapy for students with a hearing loss:
- Music can be used in auditory training to help students learn to maximize their residual hearing by listening carefully.

- ◆ Language development, especially vocabulary knowledge and word usage, is an area in which music therapy can be used to help students with hearing loss.
- ◆ Music therapy can help improve the speech production of students with hearing loss, including vocal intonation, vocal quality, speech fluency, and speech intelligibility.

Note: Parts of this chapter were taken from articles or chapters on the same topic by the author.

REFERENCES

Antia, S. D., Jones, P. B., Reed, S., Kreimeyer, K. H. (2009). Academic and progress of deaf and hard-of-hearing students in general education classrooms. *Journal of Deaf Studies and Deaf Education, 14*(3), 292–311.

Armstrong, D. F. (1999). *Original signs: Gesture, sign and the sources of language.* Washington, DC: Gallaudet University Press.

Baker-Shenk, C., & Cokely, D. (1991). *American Sign Language: A teacher's resource text on grammar and culture.* Washington, DC: Gallaudet University Press.

Bang, C. (1977). A music event. Hicksville, NY: M. Hohner.

Birkenshaw-Fleming, L. (1990). Music can make a difference. In A. A. Darrow (Ed.), *Proceedings from the Second National Conference on Music and the Hearing Impaired at Gallaudet University* (pp. 14–20). Lawrence, KS: The University of Kansas.

Burgess, S. F. (1997). But I don't know anything about music for the hearing impaired. *Early Childhood Connections, 3,* 35–37.

Dalgarno, G. (1990). Technology to obtain the best musical sound for hearing impaired listeners. In A. A. Darrow (Ed.), *Proceedings from the Second National Conference on Music and the Hearing Impaired at Gallaudet University* (pp. 43–59). Lawrence, KS: The University of Kansas.

Darrow, A. A. (1979). The beat reproduction response of subjects with normal and impaired hearing: An empirical comparison. *Journal of Music Therapy, 16,* 6–11.

Darrow, A. A. (1984). A comparison of rhythmic responsiveness in normal and hearing impaired children and an investigation of the relationship of rhythmic responsiveness to the suprasegmental aspects of speech perception. *Journal of Music Therapy, 21,* 48–66.

Darrow, A. A. (1985a). Music for the deaf. *Music Educator's Journal, 71*(6), 33–35.

Darrow, A. A. (1985b). The use of music in auditory training [Videotape]. Lawrence, KS: The University of Kansas.

Darrow, A. A. (1987a). Exploring the art of sign and song. *Music Educator's Journal, 74*(1), 32–35.

Darrow, A. A. (1987b). An investigative study: The effect of hearing impairment on music aptitude. *Journal of Music Therapy, 24,* 88–96.

Darrow, A. A. (1989a). Music and the hearing impaired: A review of the research with implications for music educators. *Update: Applications of Research in Music Education, 7*(2), 10–12.

Darrow, A. A. (1989b). Music therapy with the hearing impaired. *Music Therapy Perspectives, 6,* 61–70.

Darrow, A. A. (1990a). The effect of frequency adjustment on the vocal reproduction accuracy of hearing impaired children. *Journal of Music Therapy, 27,* 24–33.

Darrow, A. A. (1990b). The role of hearing in understanding music. *Music Educator's Journal, 77*(4), 24–27.

Darrow, A. A. (1991). An assessment and comparison of hearing impaired children's preference for timbre and musical instruments. *Journal of Music Therapy, 28,* 48–59.

Darrow, A. A. (1992). The effect of vibrotactile stimuli on the recognition of pitch change by hearing impaired children. *Journal of Music Therapy, 29,* 103–112.

Darrow, A. A. (1993). The role of music in Deaf culture: Implications for music educators. *Journal of Research in Music Education, 41*(2), 93–110.

Darrow, A. A. (1999). Music educators' perceptions regarding the inclusion of students with severe disabilities in music classrooms. *Journal of Music Therapy, 36,* 254–273.

Darrow, A. A. (2000). *Conversations with deaf children about music.* Paper presented at the American Music Therapy Association Conference, St. Louis, MO.

Darrow, A. A. (2006). The perception of emotion in music by deaf and hard-of-hearing children. *Journal of Music Therapy, 43*(1), 2–15.

Darrow, A. A. (2010). *Interviews with music teachers and music students who have a hearing loss.* Unpublished manuscript, Florida State University, Tallahassee, FL.

Darrow, A. A., & Cohen, N. (1991). The effect of programmed pitch practice and private instruction on the vocal reproduction accuracy of hearing impaired children: Two case studies. In K. Bruscia (Ed.), *Case studies in music therapy* (pp. 191–204). Philadelphia: Barcelona.

Darrow, A. A., & Gfeller, K. (1986). Music therapy with children who are deaf and hard-of-hearing. In C. E. Furman (Ed.), *Effectiveness of music therapy procedures: Documentation of research and clinical practice* (pp. 230–266). Silver Spring, MD: American Music Therapy Association.

Darrow, A. A., & Gfeller, K. (1991). A study of public school music programs mainstreaming hearing impaired students. *Journal of Music Therapy, 28,* 23–39.

Darrow, A. A., Gfeller, K., Gorsuch, A., & Thomas, K. (2000). Music therapy with children who are deaf and hard of hearing. In *Effectiveness of music therapy procedures: Documentation of research and clinical practice* (2nd ed., pp. 135–157). Silver Spring, MD: American Music Therapy Association.

Darrow, A. A., & Goll, H. (1989). The effect of vibrotactile stimuli via the SOMATRON™ on the identification of rhythmic concepts by hearing impaired children. *Journal of Music Therapy, 26,* 115–124.

Darrow, A. A., & Heller, G. N. (1985). William Wolcott Turner and David Ely Bartlett: Early advocates of music education for the hearing impaired. *Journal of Research in Music Education, 33,* 269–279.

Darrow, A. A., & Loomis, D. (1993). *A study of Gallaudet University music students.* Paper presented at the North America Joint Music Therapy Conference, Toronto, Canada.

Darrow, A. A., & Loomis, D. (1999). Music and deaf culture: Images from the media and their interpretation by deaf and hearing students. *Journal of Music Therapy, 36,* 88–109.

Darrow, A. A., & Novak, J. (2007). The effect of vision and hearing loss on listener's perception of referential meaning in music. *Journal of Music Therapy, 44,* 57–73.

Darrow, A. A., & Novak, J. (2009, April). *Musical gaming: Crossing the cultural divide between Deaf and hearing.* International Symposium on Research in Music Behavior, St. Augustine, FL.

Darrow, A. A., & Starmer, G. J. (1986). The effect of vocal training on the intonation and rate of hearing impaired children's speech: A pilot study. *Journal of Music Therapy, 23,* 194–201.

Davis, J. M., & Hardick, E. J. (1981). *Rehabilitative audiology for children and adults.* New York: John Wiley & Sons.

Diaz-Rico, L. T., & Weed, K. Z. (1995). *The crosscultural, language and academic development handbook: A complete K–12 reference guide.* Needham Heights, MA: Allyn & Bacon.

Drasgow, E. (1998). American Sign Language as a pathway to linguistic competence. *Exceptional Children, 64,* 329–342.

Ford, T. A. (1990). Development of rhythmic concepts and skills. In A. A. Darrow (Ed.), *Proceedings from the Second National Conference on Music and the Hearing Impaired at Gallaudet University* (pp. 21–30). Lawrence, KS: The University of Kansas.

Geers, W., Hojan, E., & Hojan-Jezierska, D. (1997). Fitting of hearing aids with loudness scaling of music and environmental sounds. *Applied Acoustics, 51,* 199–201.

Gfeller, K. E. (1986). Music as a remedial tool for improving speech rhythm in the hearing-impaired: Clinical and research considerations. *MEH Bulletin, 2,* 3–19.

Gfeller, K. E. (1987). Songwriting as a tool for reading and language remediation. *Music Therapy, 6*(2), 28–38.

Gfeller, K. E. (1990). A cognitive-linguistic approach to language development for preschool children with hearing impairments. *Music Therapy Perspectives, 8*, 47–51.

Gfeller, K. E. (2000). Accommodating children who use cochlear implants in the music therapy or educational setting. *Music Therapy Perspectives, 18*(2), 122–130.

Gfeller, K. (2001). Aural rehabilitation of music listening for adult cochlear implant recipients: Addressing learner characteristics. *Music Therapy Perspectives, 19*(2), 88–95.

Gfeller, K. E. (2007). Music therapy and hearing loss: A 30-year retrospective. *Music Therapy Perspectives, 20*(2), 100–107.

Gfeller, K. (n.d.). *Music and implants: Piecing the puzzle together.* Retrieved May 14, 2010, from http://www.cochlearamericas.com/PDFs/Music_and_CI.pdf

Gfeller, K., & Baumann, A. (1988). Assessment procedures for music therapy with hearing impaired children: Language development. *Journal of Music Therapy, 25*, 192–205.

Gfeller, K., Christ, A., Knutson, J. F., Witt, S., & Mehr, M. (2003). The effects of familiarity and complexity on appraisal of complex songs by cochlear implant recipients and normal hearing adults. *Journal of Music Therapy, 60*(2), 78–112.

Gfeller, K., & Darrow, A. A. (1987). Music as a remedial tool in the language education of hearing impaired children. *The Arts in Psychotherapy, 14*, 229–235.

Gfeller, K., Driscoll, V., Kenworthy, M., & Van Voorst, T. (in press). Music therapy for preschool cochlear implant recipients. *Music Therapy Perspectives.*

Gfeller, K., Knutson, J. F., Woodworth, G., Witt, S., & DeBus, B. (1998). Timbral recognition and appraisal by adult cochlear implant users and normally hearing adults. *Journal of the American Academy of Audiology, 9*, 1–19.

Gfeller, K., & Lansing, C. R. (1991). Melodic, rhythmic, and timbral perception of adult cochlear implant users. *Journal of Speech and Hearing Research, 34*, 916–920.

Gfeller, K., & Lansing, C. R. (1992). Musical perception of cochlear implant users as measured by the primary measures of music audiation: An item analysis. *Journal of Music Therapy, 29*, 18–39.

Gfeller, K., Mehr, M., & Witt, S. (2001). Aural rehabilitation of music perception and enjoyment of adult cochlear implant users. *Journal of the Academy of Rehabilitative Audiology, 34*, 17–27.

Gfeller, K., Turner, C., Oleson, J., Zhang, X., Gantz, B., Froman, R., et al. (2007). Accuracy of cochlear implant recipients on pitch perception, melody recognition, and speech reception in noise. *Ear and Hearing, 28*(3), 412.

Gfeller, K., Witt, S., Spencer, L., Stordahl, J., & Tomblin, J. B. (2000). Musical involvement and enjoyment of children who use cochlear implants. *The Volta Review, 100*, 213–233.

Gfeller, K., Witt, S., Stordahl, J., Mehr, M., & Woodworth, G. (2001). The effects of training on melody recognition and appraisal by adult cochlear implant recipients. *Journal of the Academy of Rehabilitative Audiology, 33*, 115–138.

Gfeller, K., Woodworth, G., Robin, D. A., Witt, S., & Knutson, J. F. (1997). Perceptions of rhythmic and sequential pitch patterns by normally hearing adults and adult cochlear implant users. *Ear and Hearing, 18*, 252–260.

Gfeller, K. E., Witt, S. A., Kim, K.-H., Adamek, M., & Coffman, D. (1999). A computerized music training program for adult cochlear implant recipients. *Journal of the Academy of Rehabilitative Audiology, 32*, 11–27.

Grosjean, F. (2010). Bilingualism, biculturalism, and deafness. *International Journal of Bilingual Education and Bilingualism, 13*, 133–145.

Hallahan, D. P., Kauffman, J. M., & Pullen, P. C. (2009). *Exceptional learners: An introduction to special education* (11th ed.). Boston: Allyn & Bacon.

Hardman, M. L, Drew, C. L, & Egan, M. W. (2008). *Human exceptionality: School, community, and family* (9th edition). Boston: Houghton Mifflin.

Hermans, D., Knoors, H., Ormel, E., & Verhoeven, L. (2008). The relationship between reading and signing skills of deaf children in bilingual education programs. *Journal of Deaf Studies and Deaf Education, 13*, 518–530.

Heward, W. L. (2008). *Exceptional children: An introduction to special education* (9th ed.). Upper Saddle River, NJ: Merrill/Prentice Hall.

Hunt, N., & Marshall, K. (2005). *Exceptional children and youth: An introduction to special education.* Boston: Houghton Mifflin.

Johns, E. (2001). Introducing music to the hearing-impaired. *Teaching Music, 8*(6), 36–40.

Johnson, R. E., Liddell, S. K., & Erting, C. J. (1989). Unlocking the curriculum: Principles for achieving success in deaf education. *Gallaudet Research Institute Working Papers* (89-3). Washington, DC: Gallaudet University. Retrieved July 4, 2010, from http://eric.ed.gov/PDFS/ED316978.pdf

Kaiser, K., & Johnson, K. (2000). The effect of an interactive experience on music majors' perceptions of music for deaf students. *Journal of Music Therapy, 37*, 222–234.

Kaplan, H. (1996). The nature of deaf culture: Implications for speech and hearing professionals. *Journal of Academy of Rehabilitative Audiology, 29*, 71–83.

Krivitski, E. C., McIntosh, D. E., Rothlisberg, B., & Finch, H. (2004). Profile analysis of deaf children using the Universal Nonverbal Intelligence Test. *Journal of Psychoeducational Assessment, 22*, 338–350.

Looi, V., & She, J. (2010). Music perception of cochlear implant users: A questionnaire, and its implications for a music training program. *International Journal of Audiology, 49*, 116–128.

Madell, J., & Flexer, C. (2008). *Pediatric audiology: Diagnosis, technology, and management.* New York: Thieme Medical.

Mahshie, S. N. (1995). *Educating deaf children bilingually.* Washington, DC: Gallaudet University Press.

Moores, D. F. (2001). *Educating the deaf: Psychology, principles, and practices* (5th ed.). Boston: Houghton Mifflin.

National Institutes of Deafness and Other Communication Disorders. (2010). *Cochlear implants.* Retrieved May 13, 2010, from http://www.nidcd.nih.gov/health/hearing/coch.asp

National Technical Institute for the Deaf. (n.d.). *Tips for communication.* Rochester, NY: Author.

Padden, C. (1996). *From the cultural to the bicultural: The modern deaf community.* New York: Cambridge University Press.

Padden, C., & Humphries, T. (1988). *Deaf in America: Voices from a culture.* Cambridge, MA: Harvard University Press.

Padden, C., & Humphries, T. (2006). *Inside deaf culture.* Cambridge, MA: Harvard University Press.

Paul, P. V., & Whitelaw, G. M. (2011). *Hearing and deafness: An introduction for health and educational professionals.* Sudbury, MA: Jones and Bartlett.

Rickard, P., Robbins, C., & Robbins, C. (1990). Experiences in developing a creative language arts program. In A. A. Darrow (Ed.), *Proceedings from the Second National Conference on Music and the Hearing Impaired at Gallaudet University* (pp. 11–13). Lawrence, KS: The University of Kansas.

Robbins, C., & Robbins, C. (1980). *Music for the hearing impaired: A resource manual and curriculum guide.* St. Louis, MO: Magnamusic-Baton.

Robbins, C., & Robbins, C. (1990). Musical activities with young deaf children. In A. A. Darrow (Ed.), *Proceedings from the Second National Conference on Music and the Hearing Impaired at Gallaudet University* (pp. 8–10). Lawrence, KS: The University of Kansas.

Rutherford, S. D. (1988). The culture of American Deaf people. *Sign Language Studies, 59*, 109–147.

Saunders, D. A. (1977). *Auditory perception of speech.* Englewood Cliffs, NJ: Prentice Hall.

Schatz, V. (1990). Using percussion to teach music concepts and enhance music and movement experiences. In A. A. Darrow (Ed.), *Proceedings from the Second National Conference on Music and the Hearing Impaired at Gallaudet University* (pp. 85–92). Lawrence, KS: The University of Kansas.

Sheldon, D. A. (1997). The Illinois School for the Deaf band: A historical perspective. *Journal of Research in Music Education, 45*, 580–600.

Turnbull, A., Turnbull, R., & Wehmeyer, M. (2010). *Exceptional lives: Special education in today's schools* (6th ed.). Upper Saddle River, NJ: Merrill.

U.S. Department of Education, National Center for Education Statistics. (2009). *Digest of Education Statistics, 2008* (NCES 2009-020) (Chapter 2).

Vassallo, L. (1997). The creative arts: Tool to deaf pride and hearing friends. *Perspectives in Education and Deafness, 15*(3), 12–14.

Vernon, M. (2005). Fifty years of research on the intelligence of deaf and hard-of-hearing children: A review of literature and discussion of implications. *Journal of Deaf Studies and Deaf Education, 10*, 225–231.

Chapter 13

Students with Physical Disabilities

CHAPTER OVERVIEW

Students with physical disabilities exhibit a wide range of characteristics and individual differences. Some physical disabilities are congenital; others are adventitious, thus requiring students to make emotional as well as physical adjustments. Physical disabilities typically restrict movement, and movement is central to many children's activities. Therefore, the social life of children with physical disabilities is often restricted as well. Most physical disabilities are also visible, and children rarely want to look different than their peers. The music classroom can be a positive and nurturing environment for children with physical disabilities. Music educators and music therapists have much to offer these students in the areas of emotional, social, and musical development, as well as in physical rehabilitation.

Many individuals with physical disabilities have no accompanying cognitive impairments; consequently, they are often the primary advocates for all persons with disabilities. Their advocacy has resulted in the passage of important antidiscrimination and entitlement laws for persons with disabilities. Because most physical disabilities are readily apparent, individuals with such conditions have a long history of social discrimination, stigmatization, and prejudice (Longmore, 2003). Though conditions for persons with physical disabilities have greatly improved since the passage of the Americans with Disabilities Act, many adults are still underemployed and experience difficulty in accessing and funding physical assistance services (O'Brien, 2001). As educators, we must teach students to advocate for themselves, and we must provide them with the skills to do so.

There are nearly 70,000 special education students between the ages of 6 and 21 who have physical disabilities, and another 142,00 with multiple disabilities that often include physical disabilities (U.S. Department of Education, 2009). There are additional students who have

---

physical disabilities that accompany their primary disabilities, such as those with traumatic brain injuries. Most students with physical disabilities will participate in music classes, and those with the most severe disabilities will typically receive music therapy services. For the teachers and therapists who serve these students, the primary challenge will be to adapt instructional strategies to a diverse population of students.

This chapter includes information on the following topics:
♦   Definitions of physical disabilities
♦   Types of physical disabilities
♦   Factors influencing the impact of physical disabilities
♦   Educational implications
♦   Assistive technology
♦   Music education for students with physical disabilities
♦   Music therapy for students with physical disabilities

Definitions of Physical Disabilities

There are two terms that are often used interchangeably: *physical disabilities* and *orthopedic impairments.* IDEA (2004) uses the term *orthopedic impairments* to refer to impairments caused by congenital anomaly (e.g., abbreviated limbs), impairments caused by disease (e.g., rheumatoid arthritis), and acquired impairments (e.g., spinal cord injuries). Most practitioners in the fields of special education, music education, and music therapy refer to such impairments as *physical disabilities.* Regardless of the terminology, the group of students represented by these classifications varies widely.

Types of Physical Disabilities

All types of physical disabilities or types of paralysis can be classified by the extremities involved. These general classifications include:
•   Hemiplegia – one side of the body is involved.
•   Diplegia – the legs are more involved than the arms.
•   Monoplegia – only one limb is involved.
•   Paraplegia – only the legs are involved.
•   Quadriplegia – all four limbs are involved.

There are two broad types of physical disabilities: neurological conditions and musculoskeletal conditions. A *neurological condition* is one that affects the central nervous system, either the brain or the spinal cord. Damage to the brain or spinal cord can be mild—resulting in minimal disability, or severe—resulting in dependency in all areas of daily living. Causes of neurological impairments are generally classified as *traumatic* or *nontraumatic*. Those causes due to accidents or abuse are considered traumatic, and those causes due to disease or congenital malformations are considered nontraumatic. The most common neurological conditions among school-aged children are cerebral palsy, seizure disorders, spina bifida, spinal cord injuries, and traumatic brain injury (covered in Chapter 8).

Musculoskeletal conditions are those that occur due to disease or defects to the muscles or bones. Such disabilities involve the arms, legs, joints, or spine. Students with these disabilities are not neurologically impaired, although the resulting physical limitations may be similar. Like neurological impairments, the causes are *congenital* (appearing at birth) or *adventitious* (occurring after birth). The most common musculoskeletal conditions seen in school-aged children are muscular dystrophy, amputations, and juvenile rheumatoid arthritis.

Neurological Conditions

Cerebral palsy, the most common physical disability among school-aged children, generally results from injury to the brain before or during birth. However, children can be diagnosed up to age 6 with brain damage due to external causes such as lack of oxygen or encephalitis (Hunt & Marshall, 2005). Cerebral palsy is characterized by lack of muscular control that affects a child's ability to move or maintain balance. The child's muscles and the nerves that connect them to the spinal cord are intact; however, the impairment occurs due to the injury that impedes the signal to the brain to control these nerves and muscles (Turnbull, Turnbull, & Wehmeyer, 2010). Cerebral palsy is most often characterized by motor dysfunctions or movement patterns. Depending on where the insult to the brain occurs, one or more of the following movement patterns will be exhibited: spasticity, athetosis, or ataxia. By far, the most common motor dysfunction is *spasticity*. Spasticity involves contraction or tightness of one or more muscle groups causing limited movement. *Athetosis* involves abrupt, twisting, involuntary movements. *Ataxia*, which is represented in only 1 to 10% of cases of cerebral palsy, results in poor balance and hand use (United Cerebral Palsy Association, 2010). Children with cerebral palsy may also have mixed motor dysfunction resulting in any combination of the above movement patterns.

Seizure disorders are the result of abnormal discharges of electrical energy in the brain. Anyone can have a seizure, but repeated seizures are generally referred to as *epilepsy* (Epilepsy Foundation, 2010). Many children with cerebral palsy have epilepsy, as well as other children who have had brain injuries or infections and illnesses affecting the brain. There are two types of seizures: *grand mal seizures* and *petit mal seizures*. Sixty percent of all individuals with seizure disorders have grand mal seizures. Grand mal seizures involve the whole body, generally last a few minutes, and frequently result in loss of consciousness. Most people experience a warning called an *aura*. An aura may be a certain sensation, smell, or visual effect.

The progression of a seizures goes from a stiffening of the body, heavy or irregular breathing, drooling, to large jerking motions followed by disorientation and fatigue. Petit mal seizures, in contrast, often go unnoticed. Petit mal seizures are characterized by rapid eye blinking or inattentive staring. Children who experience petit mal seizures often develop grand mal seizures as they grow older. Medication and surgery have proven beneficial to individuals who experience seizures. Medication can affect a child's alertness in the music classroom or stamina for certain physical activities.

If a student has a grand mal seizure in the music classroom, there is little to be done except to ease the child to the floor, place the child on his or her side to keep the airway open and clear, and wait for the movements to subside. After the movements have subsided, the child should be allowed to rest until he or she feels ready to return to normal classroom activity. Educating other students in the classroom about seizures can prevent the stigmatization that often accompanies seizure disorders.

Spina bifida is characterized by an abnormal opening in the spinal column. The spine is made up of small bones or vertebrae that typically cover and protect the spinal column. In the case of spina bifida, the spinal column did not close completely during prenatal development, resulting in the protrusion of the spinal cord at the opening. If the defect is at the base of the spine, the damage or paralysis may be minimal; however, if the damage is higher, greater loss of function can result. Spina bifida occulta is the most common form of spina bifida. Only a small portion of the vertebrae is missing, usually in the lower spine, and the spinal cord or its covering does not protrude. Most people do not even know they have this form of spina bifida until they are x-rayed for other reasons. There are no resulting disabilities. Meningocele spina bifida is a more serious form in which the covering of the spinal cord, though not the spinal cord itself, protrudes from the opening. This type of spina bifida is generally not disabling. Myelomeningocele spina bifida is the most serious form in which the spinal cord along with the covering protrudes at the opening. This form of spina bifida generally results in lower limb paralysis and an inability to control bladder or bowel (Spina Bifida Association of America, 2010).

Spinal cord injuries (SCI) result in loss of mobility or feeling. The causes of most spinal cord injuries are trauma, such as diving or car accidents, and gun shot wounds. The effects of SCI depend on the type of injury and the level of the injury. SCI can be classified as complete or incomplete. A complete injury means that there is no function below the level of the injury, that is, no sensation and no voluntary movement. A complete injury also means that both sides of the body are equally affected. With an incomplete injury there is some functioning below the level of the injury; the person may be able to move one limb more than another or have some sensation in the affected limbs.

The degree of disability depends upon the site of the spinal injury. The first 8 vertebrae are the cervical vertebrae, and breaks in these vertebrae usually result in quadriplegia. Persons having an injury above the 4th vertebrae (C-4 level) may also require a ventilator to breathe. The next 12 vertebrae are the thoracic vertebrae, and breaks in these vertebrae usually result in paraplegia. Persons with SCI may also experience urinary tract infections, respiratory problems, and, because of their immobility, pressure sores. Pressure sores can become infected and, if left untreated, can result in death.

Musculoskeletal Conditions

Muscular dystrophy is not a singular disability, but a group of nine hereditary muscular disorders that vary in age of onset, the muscles involved, and the rate of progression (Turnbull et al., 2010). These disorders are considered neuromuscular conditions in which the voluntary muscles of the body become progressively weak. The most common muscular dystrophy, and the one diagnosed most often in children is *Duchenne* muscular dystrophy. It is genetically transmitted and primarily affects boys. It is usually diagnosed before the child begins school. The incidence is generally considered to be 1 in approximately 3,000 births (National Institute on Neurological Disorders and Strokes, 2010). The life expectancy of children with Duchenne muscular dystrophy is in the early 20s (Muscular Dystrophy Association, 2010). Muscle weakness eventually progresses to the muscles supporting the heart and lungs, and thus results in respiratory disease that is most often the cause of death. Adjustment to the disability and quality of life issues should be a part of these children's curriculum planning.

Amputations or *congenital malformations* result in absent or abbreviated limbs. Other types congenital malformations are curvature of the spine or a clubfoot. These types of malformations can be corrected with surgery. Many congenital malformations have no known cause. Others are the result of medications or drugs ingested by the mother during pregnancy, or illnesses such as rubella incurred by the mother during pregnancy. The degree of disability or need for special education services is dependent upon the severity of the loss. Many students with such disabilities attend regular classes and have learned to accommodate their disability without any specialized equipment. Some children born without arms become adept at using their feet with the same facility that others use their hands—even learning to play instruments with their feet or residual limbs.

Osteogenesis imperfecta (OI), also known as the "brittle bone" disorder, is a genetic disorder characterized by bones that break easily, often for little or no apparent reason. There are four types of OI based on the severity of the disorder. Type I is the most common and mildest form of OI. Most fractures occur before the child reaches puberty. Children with Type I OI generally have loose joints and low muscle tone, and are normal or near-normal in stature. More severe forms of OI, Types II–IV, often result in smaller stature, hearing loss, more fractures, bone deformity, and curvature of the spine. Despite numerous fractures and restricted activity, most children with OI attend school with their peers and require little if any accommodations. Music therapy is directed toward physical exercise to promote muscle and bone strength, which helps to prevent fractures.

Achondroplasia is the most common form of skeletal dysplasia—conditions where bones do not grow and develop normally. *Achondroplastic dwarfism* is characterized by an average-size trunk, short arms and legs, and a slightly enlarged head and prominent forehead. Children with dwarfism typically grow to be about 4 feet in height. They are disabled only by their height, although some may have surgery to correct leg curvatures.

Juvenile rheumatoid arthritis is a condition of the joints and the most common arthritis in children. Its effect on the joints can range from mild to severe. JRA can result in joint inflammation, joint contracture (stiff or bent joint), joint damage, and/or changes in joint growth. Other symptoms may include joint stiffness and weakness in muscles and other soft tissues around involved joints. A rheumatologist, a physician who specializes in the diagnosis and treatment of arthritis and arthritis-related conditions, makes a diagnosis based on symptoms. There are no specific tests for JRA. There are three major types of JRA. The specific type of JRA is based on the number of limbs affected, and thus severity. Pauciarticular JRA affects four or fewer joints; polyarticular JRA affects five or more joints; and systemic onset JRA affects at least one joint but results in the inflammation of internal organs as well. JRA can affect a student's mobility, strength, and endurance, and thus their ability to participate in some school activities. Most children have no difficulty participating in music, although instruments may need to be adapted based on the child's range of motion and degree of discomfort.

Factors Influencing the Impact of Physical Disabilities

Some physical disabilities have little impact on a child's ability to perform in school, while others may severely impact their academic, social, or emotional development. Perrin et al. (1993) proposed 13 dimensions that help to determine the impact of a child's physical disability:
1. Duration of the disability
2. Age of onset
3. Limitation of age-appropriate activities
4. Visibility of the disability
5. Length of expected survival
6. Degree of mobility
7. Degree of physical functioning
8. Cognitive abilities
9. Emotional or social implications
10. Sensory functioning
11. Communication functioning
12. Course of the disability (stable or progressive)
13. Unpredictability of the disability

Of these 13 dimensions, there are several that have implications for the provision of music therapy services. Depending on the age of onset, or a child's physical, cognitive, and communication functioning, he or she may be eligible for music therapy services as part of his or her IEP. Children will likely attend regular music classes with their peers if their disability is not severe and results primarily in mobility limitations.

Regardless of any other factors, the severity and visibility of the disability will likely have implications for the child's emotional and/or social development. Bugental (2003) found that visible disabilities are less acceptable to others than are those that cannot be readily observed—such as learning disabilities or hearing loss. In a landmark text, *Physical Disability: A Psychological Approach,* Beatrice Wright (1983) reported that, in social interactions between persons with and without a physical disability, those without a disability exhibited the following behaviors: terminated conversations more quickly, smiled less, showed more signs of discomfort or restlessness, made less eye contact, and maintained greater physical distance. Strong family and social support can do much to mitigate the impact of teasing or rejection by others. Teachers and therapists must also be vigilant about fostering and monitoring the acceptance of students with physical disabilities. They must first, however, examine their own attitudes towards individuals with disabilities.

Society places a great deal of importance on physical appearance and athleticism. How the public perceives individuals with physical disabilities has important implications for their social and psychological well-being, as well as their opportunities for employment. Antidiscrimination laws, such as the Americans with Disabilities Act passed in 1990, have helped bring individuals with physical disabilities into the mainstream of society. Unfortunately, there are no laws that can protect individuals with physical disabilities from being pitied, feared, or rejected. Teachers and therapists working with children who have physical disabilities are encouraged to embrace the "people first" philosophy—and to encourage their students to do likewise. Figure 13.1 is a self-evaluation that can help you determine your degree of comfort with people who have physical disabilities.

Figure 13.1. Attitudes Toward Persons with a Disability: Self-Evaluation

Using the following scale, rate your level of comfort with the following scenario.
   5 = very comfortable
   4 = somewhat comfortable
   3 = don't know
   2 = somewhat uncomfortable
   1 = very comfortable

> *Madison is a bright young individual, who graduated in the top 5% of his/her class with a degree in psychology. Madison has a bright future as a researcher, is attractive and has a great sense of humor. Madison also has cerebral palsy, uses a wheelchair, and has speech that is sometimes difficult to understand.*

How comfortable would you be with...
1.   hiring Madison for a job meeting the public?
2.   Madison as your closest friend?
3.   Madison as your only child?
4.   Madison as your brother or sister?
5.   Madison as your parent?
6.   Madison as your co-worker?
7.   Madison as your neighbor?
8.   dating Madison?
9.   marrying Madison?
10. your child dating or marrying Madison?

Educational Implications

Children with physical disabilities benefit greatly from early intervention programs. Physical therapy, occupational therapy, speech therapy, if needed, and music therapy are often critical components of an early intervention program. Therapeutic goals include attention to gross motor skills such as sitting, standing, and walking—all of which have implications for a child's mobility. Fine motor skills, such as pointing and grasping, will have important implications for the development of basic communication and academic skills. Early intervention strategies that address both gross and fine motor skills will also play an important role in the development of a child's social and daily living skills.

The educational needs of students with physical disabilities vary greatly—even among those with the same condition. Students who are limited only in their physical abilities will likely have the same curriculum and educational goals as their peers. However, these students may need additional instruction in the use of adaptive equipment and in the management of their daily living activities. Students with cognitive disabilities in addition to their physical disabilities will need further curricular support in academic areas.

Students with the most profound disabilities will have additional educational goals that address their transition into community life. These goals are generally related to physical independence and future employment after high school. Music therapists' goals and objectives for such students may include transition goals; however, it is unlikely that music educators will address any of these goals in the music classroom, although they may want to work with students on developing important leisure skills such as listening to music and accessing public music events.

Assistive Technology

Recent technological advancements in general have done much to improve the quality of life for all persons with a physical disability. Assistive technology includes any device that substitutes for or enhances a student's physical functioning. The term assistive technology encompasses a broad range of aids, from simple homemade devices such as Velcro handgrips for musical instruments, to sophisticated voice synthesizers and communication boards for students who are unable to speak. The Individuals with Disabilities Education Act (IDEA) considers assistive technology to be any piece of equipment or product that increases, maintains, or improves the functional capabilities of individuals with disabilities. School districts may need to provide the following services to a student with physical disabilities:

- Evaluate the student's technology needs
- Acquire the necessary technology
- Coordinate technology use with other therapies and interventions
- Provide training for the individual, the individual's family, and the school staff in the effective use of the technology

There are three broad uses of assistive technology for students with disabilities: (a) independent living, (b) alternative or augmented communication, and (c) instructional aid. Independent living aids are any device that allows a person to live independently. These devices include, but are not limited to, the following: wheelchairs; walkers; prosthetics; lowered light switches, sinks, and shelving; grab bars installed in a bathroom; adapted hand controls for an automobile; and a "reacher" to pick up things when a person can't bend or has limited range of motion. Alternative or augmented communication devices are any aids that assist an individual with communication, such as picture boards, speech synthesizers, head pointers, or portable keyboards. Instructional aids are any device that assists a student in the learning environment. Some examples are text-to-speech computer software, digital recorders, page turners, page grips, keyboard modifications, or touch screens. Many of the aforementioned assistive devices are useful in the music classroom. School districts often hire rehabilitation engineers who individualize adaptations for students' specific needs. Music educators and music therapists can seek their assistance in making adaptations to musical instruments and other classroom materials.

Music Education for Students with Physical Disabilities

Students with physical disabilities generally attend regular music education classes. As music educators, we are fortunate that most music activities are highly flexible and can be adapted easily for students with physical limitations. These students learn music as other students do, through singing, listening, playing, moving, reading, and creating; however, in order for them to participate fully in music making, certain accommodations may be needed. Students' physical disabilities may necessitate

284 Music in Special Education

adjustments to the physical environment, classroom seating arrangements, and selected musical instruments. Other necessary adaptations may include the use of special music devices or switches, as well as the careful selection of appropriate instruments and musical goals.

Adaptations to the Music Classroom

Adapting the environment. The music classroom can be an inviting or intimidating environment for students with physical disabilities. Several simple adaptations can help make the room more appealing and accessible for students who use wheelchairs or other mobility devices. The room may need desks or tables that are adjustable to accommodate wheelchairs. If chairs are typically used for instruction, students can simply use their wheelchairs, and others can easily transfer from walkers or crutches to the classroom chairs. The room itself may need entry ramps and wider aisles so those who use wheelchairs can move around easily. Shelving for instrument storage can be set at a height that all students can reach. Other accommodations may need to be made for students who use assistive technology for instructional purposes. For example, students who use a computer or speech synthesizer in class may need to sit near an electrical outlet.

Adapting instruments. The main adaptations that will be made for students with physical disabilities will be those to classroom instruments. Many adaptations can be made inexpensively and simply (Clark & Chadwick, 1978). Occupational therapists or rehabilitation engineers are also excellent resources for ideas that can be used to customize instruments for students with special needs. West Music (http://www.westmusic.com/) is a good source for purchasing commercially available adapted instruments. Common adaptations to classroom instruments are touch-sensitive pads, Velcro straps, large knobs, stands to hold instruments, and color-coded systems. McCord and Fitzgerald (2006) offer useful advice for music educators and music therapists teaching instrumental music to students with various cognitive and physical disabilities. They provide suggestions for common adaptations for teaching each of the instrument families: woodwind, brass, percussion, and strings, and for music reading, music playing, and music writing.

Selecting instruments. There are a number of principles to guide you when selecting instruments for students with physical disabilities. These principles can assist you in determining the instruments best suited to meet selected therapeutic and educational goals, as well as instruments that can accommodate students' physical limitations. In Figure 13.2, Jennifer Jones, MT-BC, outlines a number of useful guidelines for selecting instruments.

Figure 13.2 Guidelines for Selecting Instruments

---

1. Musical considerations are foremost and include ensuring that the instrument...
- contributes meaningfully to the ensemble or piece.
- has dynamic output that can be adequately achieved by the player's physical abilities.
- possesses a timbre that complements the music.
- is motivating to play, thus encouraging persistence to mastery in the player.
- has a reasonable repertoire, and there is an instructor available should the student wish to pursue study.

---

2. Physical considerations are pivotal to selecting instruments, including examination of the...
- size and weight of the instrument in relation to student's strength and stamina.
- accessibility of the classroom storage areas, tables, keyboard instruments, and classroom instruments.
- mallet size—initially using short mallets with "chubby" grips.
- child's ability to hold the instrument.

Velcro straps can be used to secure some instruments to a child's wrist. Heavier instruments may be supported by commercially available or customized stands. Instruments can also be purchased in smaller sizes, such as 1/2 or 3/4 size guitars and violins. Some instruments can also be purchased in lighter materials, such as plastic versus wood.

---

3. Cognitive considerations may also be necessary. Students may ...
- be more successful learning to play an instrument by rote rather than by reading music.
- be more successful playing rhythm rather than melody.
- need to focus so much of their attention on the motor skills required to play the instrument that they find it difficult to watch the conductor or to read their music.
- have difficulty coordinating the use of both hands, particularly if each hand completes a different motor task (e.g., holding a drum in hand and striking with the other).
- have access to only one side of the body and/or experience difficult crossing midline.

Instructional methods to compensate for the challenge of focusing attention on motor tasks and reading notated music include: (a) selecting instruments that typically perform repeated patterns, (b) having the student play a steady beat, and (c) having the student memorize the part.

---

4. Sensory implications require an understanding of students':
- preference for high and low frequencies.
- preference for certain textures.
- tolerance of loud sounds and vibrations.

Adding sandpaper, satin fabric, glossy sealers, or felt may alter the texture of some instruments; however, the effect on the acoustical properties must be evaluated. For example, felt can be placed on the handle of a maraca without comprising the sound, but felt on a drum's head will muffle the tone.

Instruments selected after thorough assessment of musical, physical, cognitive, and sensory aspects can promote joyful music making for students with and without physical disabilities.

Instruments for one-handed players. Many students with physical disabilities will have use of only one hand. A number of instruments, and some music, can be adapted for one-hand playing. There have been some well-known pianists who acquired injuries and have consequently performed selected repertoire for one hand. There is music available for left- or right-handed pianists, but most of it is for advanced players since the melody and accompaniment are combined for the one hand. However, digital keyboards can be adapted easily so that beginning musicians can play relatively sophisticated music using single-finger chords, background tracks, or various rhythm tracks. Students can also work in pairs, one to control the sounds, one to play the keyboard. Music for one-handed pianists can be found at http://pianoeducation.org/pnoonhnd.html.

Valves on most brass instruments are played primarily using only one hand, making them an ideal instrument for students who have partial paralysis or a missing limb. It is possible to play left-handed; however, instruments are typically played right-handed. The French horn, typically keyed with the left hand, can also be switched to the right hand. Although only one hand is involved in playing the valves, the other hand is important in supporting and positioning the instrument, as well as in creating certain sound effects. Stands can be used to support the instruments.

A number of wind instruments have been adapted for players with limited use of the second hand. Students with childhood rheumatoid arthritis can have an instrument adapted so it can accommodate their limited range of motion. These adaptations usually involve extensions to the keys or molding the end of the instrument back toward the player. Recorders can be adapted for one-handed playing by adding keys to cover the holes normally closed by the missing hand. Stringed instruments can be adapted for playing with the bow in the left hand and also for bowing with a prosthetic device. Some innovative music educators have devised their own adaptations, such as using an airbed pump to enable a child with cystic fibrosis to play a recorder. The air valve is attached to the recorder and pumped with the foot.

Incorporating the Use of Music Technology

Contemporary technology has done much to make music more accessible for students with physical disabilities. Listening to music, playing music, and creating music are all accessible to such students, thus enhancing their music learning experiences. Technology also assists in individualizing instruction that is needed for some students. In addition, using a contemporary medium that is readily accessible and commonplace makes adaptive music making less stigmatizing for students with physical disabilities. The digital age has made all instruments accessible even to students with the most limiting disabilities (Miranda & Wanderley, 2006). Technology is a powerful tool that can transform traditional music methods as well as generate new creative methods of music instruction.

There are numerous commercially available software programs that are useful to students with physical disabilities. Even students who use mouth sticks to operate their computers can use these programs effectively. Examples of such software are *Garage Band, Music Mania, Band-in-a-Box, Finale, Soundedit 16, Rock Rap 'n Roll, Music Ace,* and *Making Music.* McCord (2001) offers a list of common recommendations that may appear in the students' IEP that underscores the importance of using technology in the music classroom:

- Use of multisensory learning approaches
- Instruction delivered in more than one mode of learning
- Haptic, hands-on, or kinesthetic learning activities
- Modified curriculum
- Small-group learning structure
- Individualized instruction
- Use of computer as an aid to learning (p. 31)

There is a wide range of computer software and hardware available to support the accessibility of music instruction for students with physical disabilities. Many school districts have computer specialists on staff who can help to adapt or create music software and hardware. Below is a short list of some of the equipment available commercially that you may want to consider:

- *Soundbeam* gets its name because any movements within the "beam" trigger musical sounds or phrases. The beam can vary in length from 35cm to 6m so that the smallest movements of a finger, head, or foot can trigger, at a distance and without physical contact, sequences of sounds from sound modules, samplers, or keyboards. In the commercial literature, the Soundbeam is described as "invisible expanding keyboard in space." Information can be found at http://www.soundbeam.co.uk/
- *Kaoss Pad* is a processor that allows the student to control and manipulate sounds using a touch-sensitive pad. The touch-sensitive pad provides greater access to students with limited use of their hands. Information can be found at http://www.zzounds.com/
- *Fruity Loops* is electronic music creation software made by Cakewalk. It is available in two versions. Fruity Loops requires advanced mouse skills, but it provides a creative musical outlet for those who cannot play traditional musical instruments. Information can found at http://www.hitsquad.com/
- *The Tactile Musical MIDI Mate* is a device that allows people with physical disabilities to play music independently with using a textured panel. The MIDI Mate consists of eight different tactile squares, adapted switch inputs, a Musical Instrument Digital Interface (MIDI) connection for connecting to electronic keyboards, and a removable cartridge containing a microprocessor with software to play music. Information can found at http://www.tecsol.com.au/MidiMate.htm
- *Fractunes* is a music program that generates on-screen colored images that change in direct response to the notes that are played. Music signals are created by an Omnichord and an electronic piano keyboard. As the

player touches these highly responsive instruments, a sensitive cause-effect relationship is established. Compositions can also be imported from notation software to be played back, creating changing visual images. Information can be found at http://www.soundonsound.com/

- *Super Switch Ensemble: Access to Music* is a music performance program designed specifically for individuals with special needs. It includes over 100 songs and activities that can be used for music making as well as the facilitation of motor, cognitive, and social development. Switch Ensemble allows groups of students with varying abilities to play music together. Information can be found at http://www.switchintime.com/

- *Musical Toys* is produced by Technical Solutions Australia for young children with physical disabilities. The toys incorporate lights and colors to encourage fine motor manipulation: Sunshine Symphony, Musical Snail, Musical Monkey, Musical Blocks, Musical Cow. Information can be found at http://www.tecsol.com.au/MusicalToys.htm

- *Musical Floor Mat* is also produced by Technical Solutions Australia for students who want to make music and have the ability to make only large gross motor movements. Such a floor mat can be used to motivate ambulatory movements during physical therapy. Information can be found at http://www.tecsol.com.au/MusicFloor.htm

- *Instrument holding devices* for various classroom instruments are produced by A Day's Work. The holding devices are particularly useful for students with limited physical abilities. Using such devices impedes fatigue and facilitates manipulation of the instrument. Information can be found at http://www.adaysworkmusiceducation.com/#Instrumentsandaids

Participation in Musical Ensembles

As stated in the opening of this chapter, students with physical disabilities are often restricted in their activities, particularly in many types of sports activities and some arts activities such as dance and theater. The music classroom should be one place where all students can participate fully. Musical ensembles offer opportunities for social participation as well as musical experiences. Students with physical disabilities must often endure unwarranted pity and overprotection. It is important for music educators to highlight their strengths and minimize their differences. When students must work together for a common goal and collectively experience success, individual differences are overlooked more easily. The astute ensemble director monitors all social interactions within his or her musical organization and intercedes when necessary. When students with physical disabilities are carefully integrated in musical ensembles, their social experiences are broadened and their sense of self strengthened.

It may seem that choral ensembles are the most logical placement for students with physical disabilities; however, the child's musical interests should be the foremost concern. Although fewer adaptations may need to be made in the choral environment, adaptations made in instrumental ensembles often provide the greatest rewards. "Mainstreaming Stories" illustrates the benefits of including students who, at first, may seem to present challenges too great to overcome.

Mainstreaming Stories

A student in Wichita, Kansas, signed up for high school orchestra. He had always wanted to play a string instrument. When the student came to class, the director was surprised to find that he could not read music, but perhaps was even more surprised to find that he could move neither his arms nor legs. The director called a friend, a music therapist, and she sent him information on a client who had used a computer with a mouth stick to compose music. The orchestra director went to work and set up a workstation in one of the practice rooms. The student came to class every day and worked through a music reading program on the computer. After finishing the program, he told the director he would like to learn something about arranging music for strings. The director gave him several books to read and a number of scores to study. The student, who was, as it turned out, very musical, wrote a beautiful suite for string ensemble. The high school orchestra premiered the suite on its spring concert. At the conclusion of the piece, the orchestra invited the composer to come on stage and be recognized by the audience and his peers. This student was not participating as other students were; nevertheless, he was making a meaningful contribution to the ensemble. His director found a way to adapt the curriculum such that this student's talents were not lost.

Another young student longed to play the trumpet, even though she was born without arms. Her grandfather and father built a cast iron stand that held her trumpet, and, with cables that ran from the valves, she learned to play with her feet. She played trumpet throughout high school, playing a solo at contest her senior year.

Marla loved playing the clarinet in band, but she had never been able to march with the band in parades or during the halftime shows at football games. Her friend Bill had many friends in band and, consequently, had always wanted to play in band, but had never had the opportunity to learn an instrument. They conspired and determined a way to realize their dreams. Bill suited up in the band uniform he had always wanted to wear and pushed Marla in her wheelchair among the other clarinetists in the New Year's Day parade.

These stories highlight the joys of teaching music to students with physical disabilities. How fortunate that this orchestra director, grandfather and father, and friend found a way for these students to succeed and to experience the joy of making music. All students deserve the opportunity to participate in music and to interact with other students who share their love of music.

Music Therapy for Students with Physical Disabilities

The primary goal of music therapists working with students who have physical disabilities will be to address the student's mobility and physical functioning. Many students with physical disabilities, however, have accompanying cognitive disabilities that affect other important skills necessary for academic success. Music therapists may choose to address the student's primary disability or both cognitive and physical disabilities. As always, a music therapist should consult with the student's special education teacher, physical therapist, and IEP to determine priorities for therapeutic programming.

Another important consideration is the nature of the student's disability. Some disabilities require special attention to the way students are moved, physically positioned, or transferred from a wheelchair to the floor or a chair. The nature of physical disabilities varies from child to child, even among those with the same disability; therefore, it is important for music therapists to be in contact with a child's teacher or therapist to determine any special instructions relevant to the child's physical well-being and safety.

Another important consideration is the development of the disability. Some disabilities are progressive, such as muscular dystrophy, whereas others are responsive to habilitative and rehabilitative interventions. Knowing and understanding a child's diagnosis will provide the music therapist with information important to the nature and developmental course of the disability. A clear understanding of the disability in general, and of the child's functioning level will allow the music therapist to program realistic IEP goals and objectives.

Additional knowledge that is imperative to programming music therapy goals for students with physical disabilities is the typical development of children's gross and fine motor skills. Information important to therapeutic programming for all children, including those with physical disabilities, is the normal development of cognitive, social, and emotional behaviors. Knowing developmental milestones allows for the programming of treatment goals that move students forward in a developmentally appropriate manner (Thaut, Mertel, & Leins, 2008).

Although cognitive, social, emotional, or daily living skills may also be addressed with students who have physical disabilities, the primary goal will be the development of motor skills. Music therapy has a long history in rehabilitation programs for individuals with physical disabilities (Gilliland, 1951; Josepha, 1964). Music has been successful in aiding children and adolescents in the development, maintenance, or restoration of their physical functioning. Music has been found to effectively enhance various aspects of physical performance (Schwartz, Fernhall, & Plowman, 1990). Because of music's versatility, it can be used to meet numerous goals related to one's physical health. Live or recorded music can be used for the following purposes.

Motivate physical movements. All of us have heard music that makes us want to move or dance. Most health clubs use music to motivate patrons to continue moving, to divert their attention from any discomfort they may be experiencing, and to reduce boredom. Music has been used in various physical therapy programs to stimulate physical activity as well. Live music is generally preferred, so it can be used to match the client's motions in tempo, style, and rhythm (Boldt, 1996; Copeland & Franks, 1991). Tam et al. (2007) suggest that music is the ideal motivator for clients to move during occupational and physical therapies. The perception of pain is often associated with physical exercise and physical therapy. Past research has shown music's ability to mask the perception of pain, and without pain, clients are more motivated to exercise (Mitchell & McDonald, 2006).

There are musical elements that also contribute to the benefits of exercise as well as to clients' commitment to an exercise regime. The selection of music is generally based on the music's tempo and style. Tempo is the most important musical element associated with exercise (Wininger & Pargman, 2003). In order to strengthen students' exercise compliance, the tempo of music should be matched to an individual's functional abilities and to the purpose of the exercise. Rhythmic durations of music influence the length and range of individuals' physical movements. Various researchers have found that the use of music during exercise results in a higher recovery heart rate, longer periods of exercise, greater breath capacity, general physical function, and commitment to exercise (Beckett, 1990; Hagen, Armstrong-Esther, & Sandilands, 2003; Johnson, Otto, & Clair; 2001; McBride, Graydon, Sidani, & Hall, 1999).

Synchronize selected movements. Music has long been used to synchronize the movements of dancers and skaters. It has also been effective in synchronizing the movements of persons with cerebral palsy and those who have had strokes or other physically disabling conditions (Hurt, Rice, McIntosh, & Thaut, 1998; Staum, 1983; Thaut, McIntosh, & Rice, 1997). The auditory perception of rhythm is neurologically connected to the timing of physical movement. Rhythm has the ability to facilitate sensorimotor skills by organizing the temporal organization of motor responses.

Structure exercises or exercise routines. The rhythmic structure and form of music provide natural cues for organizing exercise movements and physical routines (Beisman, 1967; MacNay, 1995). Carefully selected music can set the pace and duration of physical therapy sessions or exercise routines. Music also provides a positive and enjoyable atmosphere for exercise—which is, for many children, an undesirable activity.

Promote adherence to a physical exercise program. Because of music's ability to entertain and its popularity among members of any age group, it has been used effectively to promote adherence to physical exercise programs (Johnson et al., 2001). Music can make exercise repetitions seem less tedious and monotonous.

Develop and maintain muscle function. Music can be used to accompany exercises that work specific muscles, or carefully selected instruments that require the use of specific muscle groups can be used (Safranek, Koshland, & Raymond, 1982; Sears 1957; Thaut, Schleiffers, & Davis, 1991). Music can also be used to facilitate muscular movements that aid in strengthening the muscles (Pearce, 1981).

Increase fine and gross motor coordination and control. Students are often highly motivated to work on physical precision in order to play a desired instrument. Eye-hand coordination is required to read music and play simultaneously, and to play many instruments that require gross and fine motor movements. The use of rhythmic auditory stimuli (RAS) has been shown to improve the control of ambulation in individuals with uneven or arrhythmic gait patterns (Staum, 1983) and the temporal muscular control in children with gross motor dysfunction (Thaut, 1985; Thaut, McIntosh, McIntosh, & Hoemberg, 2001).

Facilitate relaxation during exercise. Relaxation is an important part of increasing limb range of motion and developing limb or digital flexibility. It is especially important when working with children who have cerebral palsy and others who have difficulties with spasticity. Music has been especially effective when used in conjunction with standard relaxation exercises (Scartelli, 1984).

Distract one from the pain experienced during strenuous physical exercise. Music has long been used as an effective form of audio-analgesia. It is used to mask pain or to distract one from pain during physical activity (Boutcher & Trenske, 1990; MacNay, 1995; Maslar, 1986; Nelson & Finch, 1963; Rider, 1985).

Instrument Playing as a Form of Physical Therapy

In addition to the use of live or recorded music, the playing of musical instruments can be carefully structured to improve arm or manual strength and dexterity. Instruments can be purposefully selected so children experience improvement in:

- range of motion—by carefully placing instruments so that the child must reach for them;
- hand grasp strength—by gradually increasing the weight of instruments the child must hold to play;
- hand dexterity—by increasing the complexity of the manual manipulation required to play the instrument; and
- digital flexibility—by using instruments, such as keyboards, that require the use of individual fingers.

In order to determine appropriate objectives and assessments, the music therapist may wish to consult with the school's occupational therapist—the person most often responsible for working on a student's manual strength and dexterity. Effective collaboration and co-treatment among members of the therapy team can be particularly beneficial for students involved in a physical therapy program.

Neurologic Music Therapy

Neurologic Music Therapy (NMT) is the therapeutic application of music to cognitive, sensory, and motor dysfunction due to neurologic disruptions in the human nervous system (Thaut, 1999a). Clair, Pasiali, and LaGasse (2008) provide a list and introductory description of the therapeutic mechanisms and goals of NMT. The therapeutic mechanisms employed include sensorimotor integration, rhythmic entrainment, auditory feedback, and patterned information processing, particularly that which deals with sound. NMT sensorimotor training, which is most applicable to the populations discussed in this chapter, is used to remediate gait disorders, improve posture, and facilitate upper extremity movement. The standardized techniques used for such applications are Rhythmic Auditory Stimulation (RAS), Patterned Sensory Enhancement (PSE), and Therapeutic Instrumental Music Playing (TIMP) (Thaut, 1999b).

Careful consideration should be taken when attempting to utilize NMT strategies with children. Consultation with a physical therapist or other professionals familiar with childhood neurological development is strongly urged. There are important considerations music therapists should take into account when they are working with children who have physical disabilities and when planning to use strategies outlined in NMT. Clair et al. (2008) and Hurt-Thaut and Johnson (2003) outline these considerations:

- Neurological development in children is different from neurologic development in adults.
- Children who are acquiring motor skills may require different strategies than those who are relearning these skills. The NMT protocol designed for rehabilitation may not transfer to the developmental model.
- Children have different abilities in motor entrainment than adults.
- Children under 5 years of age do not generally match an external stimulus, therefore making the ability to effectively utilize a technique such as RAS unlikely. Indeed, children under 5 often cannot identify the steady beat in musical stimuli, so, for these children, matching that beat motorically would be impossible.

Researchers have found that some NMT strategies are effective with children, such as RAS (Hurt et al., 1998; Kwak, 2000). While RAS and other NMT techniques have been shown to be effective with children, careful consideration of the child's developmental level is necessary to effective treatment.

Rhythmic Auditory Stimulation (RAS) is a technique used to facilitate rhythmic movement. An individual's gait, or walk, is typically smooth and rhythmic. In working with a client to develop a rhythmic gait, music can be used as an external time cue to regulate the body's movement in time. A metronomic beat, matched to a client's gait parameters, is embedded in background music. The client then listens to the music while practicing gait-training exercises. The rhythmic cue organizes motor responses, making them more even and rhythmic, and eventually improves functional motor movement.

Much of the research addressing the effectiveness of RAS has been carried out with older adults as participants, but when the physical disability is due to neurologic disorders, logical transfers can be made to teens with similar therapeutic objectives. Researchers have found that gait performance during functional in-home tasks can be improved using RAS (Nieuwboer et al., 2007; Rochester et al., 2005). Other researchers have found that RAS was effective in reducing knee tremors (Kenyon & Thaut, 2000), improved gait in children with cerebral palsy (Kwak, 2000), and in gait disorders due to spinal cord injuries (de l'Etoile, 2008). Otaga (2006) found that RAS increased participants' walking distance, velocity, and stride length, a common therapeutic objective for children with cerebral palsy.

Patterned Sensory Enhancement (PSE) is a technique using rhythmic, melodic, harmonic, and dynamic-acoustical elements of music to provide temporal, spatial, and force patterns to structure and cue functional movements (Thaut, 1999a). PSE involves individual musical patterns in which (a) the rhythm structures the *timing* of the movement, (b) the duration guides the *range* of motion, (c) the pitch indicates the *direction* of the movement, and (d) the dynamics and harmony indicate the *degree of force* to be used in the movement. The musical patterns are then incorporated into a sequence of motions that form functional movement patterns—such as hand grasp.

Therapeutic Instrumental Music Playing (TIMP) is the use of musical instrument playing to facilitate engagement in physical exercise and to simulate functional movement patterns in motor therapy (Clair et al., 2008). Similar to purposes cited previously in this chapter, music instruments are selected and positioned to increase range of motion, to enhance endurance and strength, and to improve digital dexterity and coordination. The instrumental music to be played is structured to meet objectives specific to a client's needs.

The use of music to improve the functional movements of persons with physical disabilities has a long and established history (Gilliland, 1951; Josepha, 1964; Staum, 1983; Whitall, McCombe-Waller, Silver, & Macko, 2000). A number of researchers have documented the use of Neurologic Music Therapy in particular; consequently, the utility of music therapy in rehabilitative medicine is well recognized and respected among medical professionals (Thaut, Kenyon, Hurt, McIntosh, & Hoemberg, 2002; Thaut, McIntosh, Prassas, & Rice, 1993; Thaut, McIntosh, Rice, Miller, Rathbun, & Brault, 1996; Thaut, Miltner, Lange, Hurt, & Hoemberg, 1999).

Summary

Students with physical disabilities need to develop as much independence as possible. The music educator or therapist should monitor students' physical abilities carefully and provide assistance only when obviously needed or requested. He or she should also cultivate an atmosphere of acceptance in the classroom. Students with disabilities often have fewer opportunities to interact socially with their peers. Involving students with physical disabilities in music education activities and organizations can increase their opportunities for socialization. Musical ensembles are an excellent forum to develop peer relationships, develop social skills, and provide opportunities for cooperation and working together as a group. Group music therapy sessions can also provide opportunities for students with physical disabilities to socialize with others as well as to have opportunities for self-expression. The adaptability of music is well suited to meet the many needs of this diverse population.

KEY POINTS FROM THE CHAPTER

Definition and classification of physical disabilities:
- ◆ IDEA (2004) uses the term *orthopedic impairments* to refer to impairments caused by congenital anomaly (e.g., abbreviated limbs), impairments caused by disease (e.g., rheumatoid arthritis), and acquired impairments (e.g., spinal cord injuries).
- ◆ All types of physical disabilities or types of paralysis can be classified by the extremities involved. These general classifications include hemiplegia, diplegia, monoplegia, paraplegia, and quadriplegia.
- ◆ There are two broad types of physical disabilities: neurological conditions and musculoskeletal conditions.

Types of physical disabilities:
- ◆ Examples of neurological conditions found among school children include cerebral palsy, seizure disorders, spina bifida, and spinal cord injuries.
- ◆ Examples of musculoskeletal conditions found among school children include muscular dystrophy, amputations or congenital malformations, osteogenesis imperfecta, achondroplasia, and juvenile rheumatoid arthritis.

Factors influencing the impact of physical disabilities:
- ◆ Perrin et al. (1993) proposed 13 dimensions that help to determine the impact of a child's physical disability. Several factors that are particularly important are visibility of the disability, severity of the disability, and age of onset.

Educational implications:
- ◆ The educational needs of students with physical disabilities vary greatly—even among those with the same condition. Students who are limited only in their physical abilities will likely have the same curriculum and educational goals as their peers. However, these students may need additional instruction in the use of adaptive equipment and in the management of their daily living activities.

Assistive technology:
♦ Recent technological advancements in general have done much to improve the quality of life for all persons with a physical disability. Assistive technology includes any device that substitutes for or enhances a student's physical functioning.
♦ There are three broad uses of assistive technology for students with disabilities:
♦ independent living, (b) alternative or augmented communication, and (c) instructional aid.

Music education for students with physical disabilities:
♦ There are several types of adaptations that can be made to the music classroom. These adaptations can greatly facilitate the participation of students with disabilities.
  » Adapting the environment
  » Adapting instruments
  » Selecting instruments
♦ A number of instruments, and some music, can be adapted for one-hand playing.
♦ There is a wide range of computer software and hardware available to support the accessibility of music instruction.
♦ Musical ensembles offer opportunities for social participation as well as musical development.

Music therapy for students with physical disabilities:
♦ Music can be used to meet numerous goals related to one's physical health. Live or recorded music can be used to:
  » motivate physical movements
  » synchronize selected movements
  » structure exercises or exercise routines
  » promote adherence to a physical exercise program
  » develop and maintain muscle function
  » increase fine and gross motor coordination and control
  » facilitate relaxation during exercise
  » distract one from the pain experienced during strenuous physical exercise
♦ In addition to the use of live or recorded music, the playing of musical instruments can be carefully structured to improve arm or manual strength and dexterity. Instruments can be purposefully selected so children experience improvement in:
  » range of motion
  » hand grasp strength
  » hand dexterity

»   digital flexibility
♦ Neurologic Music Therapy (NMT) is the therapeutic application of music to cognitive, sensory, and motor dysfunction due to neurologic disruptions in the human nervous system (Thaut, 1999a). The standardized techniques used for such applications are:

»   Rhythmic Auditory Stimulation (RAS)
»   Patterned Sensory Enhancement (PSE)
»   Therapeutic Instrumental Music Playing (TIMP)

♦ Careful consideration should be taken when attempting to utilize NMT strategies with children. Consultation with a physical therapist or others familiar with childhood neurological development is strongly urged.

Conclusion:

♦ Students with physical disabilities need to develop as much independence as possible.
♦ Monitor students' physical abilities carefully and provide assistance only when obviously needed or requested.
♦ Cultivate an atmosphere of acceptance in the classroom.
♦ Involving students with physical disabilities in music education activities and organizations, as well as group music therapy sessions, can provide opportunities for socialization and self-expression.

REFERENCES

Beckett, A. (1990). The effects of music on exercise as determined by physiological recovery heart rates and distance. *Journal of Music Therapy, 27*, 126–136.

Beisman, G. L. (1967). Effect of rhythmic accompaniment upon learning of fundamental motor skills. *Research Quarterly, 38*, 172–176.

Boldt, S. (1996). The effects of music therapy on motivation, psychological well-being, physical comfort, and exercise endurance of bone marrow transplant patients. *Journal of Music Therapy, 33*, 164–188.

Boutcher, S. H., & Trenske, M. (1990). The effects of sensory deprivation and music on perceived exertion and affect during exercise. *Journal of Sport and Exercise Psychology, 12*, 167–176.

Bugental, D. B. (2003). *Thriving in the face of childhood adversity.* New York: Psychology Press.

Clair, A. A., Pasiali, V., & LaGasse, B. (2008). Neurologic music therapy. In A. A. Darrow (Ed.), *Introduction to approaches in music therapy* (pp. 153–171). Silver Spring, MD: American Music Therapy Association.

Clark, C., & Chadwick, D. (1978). *Clinically adapted instruments for the multiply handicapped.* Westford, MA: Modulations.

Copeland, B. L., & Franks, B. D. (1991). Effects of types and intensities of background music on treadmill endurance. *Journal of Sports Medicine and Physical Fitness, 31*, 100–103.

de l' Etoile, S. K. (2008). The effect of rhythmic auditory stimulation on the gait parameters of patients with incomplete spinal cord injury: An exploratory study. *International Journal of Rehabilitation Research, 31*(2), 155.

Epilepsy Foundation. (2010). Retrieved from http://www.epilepsyfoundation.org/

Gilliland, E. G. (1951). Prescriptions set to music—Musical instruments in orthopedic therapy. *Exceptional Children, 18*, 68–70.

Hagen, B., Armstrong-Esther, C., & Sandilands, M. (2003). On a happier note: Validation of musical exercise for older persons in long-term care settings. *International Journal of Nursing Studies, 40*(4), 347–357.

Hunt, N., & Marshall, K. (2005). *Exceptional children and youth* (4th ed.). Boston: Houghton Mifflin.

Hurt, C. P., Rice, R. R., McIntosh, G., & Thaut, M. H. (1998). Rhythmic auditory stimulation in gait training for patients with traumatic brain injury. *Journal of Music Therapy, 35*, 228–241.

Hurt-Thaut, C. P., & Johnson, S. (2003). Neurologic music therapy with children: Scientific foundations and clinical application. In S. Robb (Ed.), *Music therapy in pediatric healthcare: Research and evidence-based practice* (pp. 81–100). Silver Spring, MD: American Music Therapy Association.

Individuals with Disabilities Education Improvement Act of 2004, 20 U.S.C. § 1400 *et seq.* (1990). (Session law # P.L. 101-476).

Johnson, G., Otto, D., & Clair, A. A. (2001). The effect of instrumental and vocal music on adherence to a physical rehabilitation exercise program with persons who are elderly. *Journal of Music Therapy 38*, 82–96.

Josepha, M. (1964). Therapeutic value of instrumental performance for severely handicapped children. *Journal of Music Therapy, 1*, 73–79.

Kenyon, G. P., & Thaut, M. H. (2000). A measure of kinematic limb instability modulation by rhythmic auditory stimulation. *Journal of Biomechanics, 33*, 1319–1323.

Kwak, E. E. (2000). *Effect of rhythmic auditory stimulation on gait performance in children with spastic cerebral palsy.* Unpublished master's thesis, University of Kansas, Lawrence.

Longmore, P. K. (2003). *Why I burned my book and other essays on disability.* Philadelphia: Temple University Press.

MacNay, S. K. (1995). The influence of preferred music on the perceived exertion, mood, and time estimation scores of patients participating in a cardiac rehabilitation exercise program. *Music Therapy Perspectives, 13*, 91–96.

Maslar, P. M. (1986). The effect of music on the reduction of pain: A review of the literature. *The Arts in Psychotherapy, 13*, 215–219.

McBride, S., Graydon, J., Sidani, S., & Hall, L. (1999). The therapeutic use of music for dyspnea and anxiety in patients with COPD who live at home. *Journal of Holistic Nursing, 17*(3), 229–250.

McCord, K. (2001). Music software for special needs. *Music Educators Journal, 87*(4), 30–35, 65.

McCord, K., & Fitzgerald, M. (2006). Children with disabilities playing musical instruments. *Music Educators Journal, 92*(4), 46–53.

Miranda, E. R., & Wanderley, M. M. (2006). *New digital musical instruments: Control and interaction beyond the keyboard.* Middleton, WI: A-R Editions.

Mitchell, L. K., & McDonald, R. A. R. (2006). An experimental investigation of the effects of preferred and relaxing music listening on pain perception. *Journal of Music Therapy, 43*, 295–316.

Muscular Dystrophy Association (MDA). (2010). Retrieved from http://www.mdausa.org/

Nelson, D. O., & Finch, L. W. (1963). Effects of audio-analgesia on gross motor performance involving acute fatigue. *Research Quarterly, 33*, 588–592.

National Institute on Neurological Disorders and Strokes (NINDS). (2010). Retrieved from http://www.ninds.nih.gov/disorders/md/md.htm

Nieuwboer, A., Kwakkel, G., Rochester, L., Jones, D., van Wegen, E., Willems, A., et al. (2007). Cueing training in the home improves gait-related mobility in Parkinson's disease: The RESCUE trail. *Journal of Neurology, Neurosurgery and Psychiatry, 78*, 134–140.

O'Brien, R. (2001). *Crippled justice: The history of modern disability policy in the workplace.* Chicago: The University of Chicago.

Ogata, M. (2006). *The effect of rhythmic auditory stimulation on walking distance in the frail elderly.* Unpublished master's thesis. University of Kansas, Lawrence.

Perrin, E. C., Newacheck, P., Pless, B., Drotar, D., Gortmaker, S. L., Leventhal, J., Perrin, J. M., Stein, R. E. K., Walker, D. K., & Weitzman, M. (1993). Issues involved in the definition and classification of chronic health conditions. *Pediatrics, 91*, 787–793.

Pearce, K. A. (1981). Effects of different types of music on physical strength. *Perceptual and Motor Skills, 53,* 351–352.

Rider, M. (1985). Entrainment mechanisms involved in pain reduction, muscle relaxation, and music-mediated imagery. *Journal of Music Therapy, 22,* 183–192.

Rochester, L., Hetherington, V., Jones, D., Nieuwboer, A., Willems, A. M., Kwakkel, G., & Van Wegen, E. (2005). The effect of external rhythmic cues (auditory and visual) on walking during a functional task in homes of people with Parkinson's disease. *Archives of Physical Medicine & Rehabilitation, 86,* 999–1006.

Safranek, M. G., Koshland, G. F., & Raymond, G. (1982). The influence of auditory rhythm on muscle activity. *Physical Therapy, 2,* 161–168.

Scartelli, J. (1984). The effect of the EMG biofeedback and sedative music only on frontalis muscle relaxation ability. *Journal of Music Therapy, 21,* 67–78.

Schwartz, S. E., Fernhall, B., & Plowman, S. A. (1990). Effects of music on exercise performance. *Journal of Cardiopulmonary Rehabilitation, 10,* 312–316.

Sears, W. W. (1957). The effect of music on muscle tonus. In E. T. Gaston (Ed.), *Music therapy* (pp. 199–205). Lawrence, KS: Allen Press.

Spina Bifida Association of America (SBAA). (2010). Retrieved from http://www.sbaa.org/

Staum, M. J. (1983). Music and rhythmic stimuli in the rehabilitation of gait disorders. *Journal of Music Therapy, 20,* 69–87.

Tam, C., Schwellnus, H., Eaton, C., Hamdani, Y., Lamont, A., & Chau, T. (2007). Movement-to-music technology: A play and music experience for children with physical disabilities. *Occupational Therapy International, 14*(2), 99–112.

Thaut, M. H. (1985). The use of auditory rhythm and rhythmic speech to aid temporal muscular control in children with gross motor dysfunction. *Journal of Music Therapy, 22*(3), 108–128.

Thaut, M. H. (1999a). Music therapy in neurological rehabilitation. In W. B. Davis, K. E. Gfeller, & M. H. Thaut (Eds.), *An introduction to music therapy: Theory and practice* (2nd ed., pp. 221–247). Dubuque, IA: McGraw-Hill.

Thaut, M. H. (1999b). *Training manual of Neurologic Music Therapy.* Ft. Collins, CO: Colorado State University: Center for Biomedical Research in Music.

Thaut, M. H., Kenyon, G. P., Hurt, C. P., McIntosh, G. C., & Hoemberg, V. (2002). Kinematic optimization of spatiotemporal patterns in paretic arm training with stroke patients. *Neuropsychologia, 40,* 1073–1081.

Thaut, M. H., McIntosh, K. H., McIntosh, G. C., & Hoemberg, V. (2001). Auditory rhythmicity enhances movement and speech motor control in patients with Parkinson's disease. *Functional Neurology, 16,* 163–172.

Thaut, M. H., McIntosh, G. C., Prassas, S. G., & Rice, R. R. (1993). The effect of auditory rhythmic cuing on stride and EMG patterns in hemiparetic gait of stroke patients. *Journal of Neurologic Rehabilitation, 7,* 9–16.

Thaut, M. H., McIntosh, G. C., & Rice, R. R. (1997). Rhythmic facilitation of gait training in hemiparetic stroke rehabilitation. *Journal of Neurological Sciences, 151,* 207–212.

Thaut, M. H., McIntosh, G. C., Rice, R. R., Miller, R. A., Rathbun, J., & Brault, J. M. (1996). Rhythmic auditory stimulation in gait training of Parkinson's disease patients. *Movement Disorders, 11,* 193–200.

Thaut, M. H., Mertel, K., & Leins, A. K. (2008). Music therapy for children and adults with physical disabilities. In W. B. Davis, K. E. Gfeller, & M. H. Thaut (Eds.), *An introduction to music therapy theory and practice* (pp. 143–180). Silver Spring, MD: American Music Therapy Association.

Thaut, M. H., Miltner, R., Lange, H. L., Hurt, C. P., & Hoemberg, V. (1999). Velocity modulation and rhythmic synchronization of gait in Huntington's disease. *Movement Disorders, 14,* 808–819.

Thaut, M. H., Schleiffers, S., & Davis, W. (1991). Analysis of EMG activity in biceps and triceps muscle in an upper extremity gross motor task under the influence of auditory rhythm. *Journal of Music Therapy, 28,* 64–88.

Turnbull, A., Turnbull, R., & Wehmeyer, M. (2010). *Exceptional lives: Special education in today's schools* (6th ed.). Upper Saddle River, NJ: Merrill.

United Cerebral Palsy Association. (UCPA). (2010). Retrieved from http://www.upca.org/

U.S. Department of Education, National Center for Education Statistics. (2009). *Digest of Education Statistics, 2008* (NCES 2009-020) (Chapter 2).

Whitall, J., McCombe-Waller, S., Silver, K. H., & Macko, R. F. (2000). Repetitive bilateral arm training with rhythmic auditory cueing improves motor function in chronic hemiparetic stroke. *Stroke, 31,* 2390–2395.

Wininger, S. R., & Pargman, D. (2003). Assessment of factors associated with exercise enjoyment. *Journal of Music Therapy, 40*(1), 57–73.

Wright, B. A. (1983). *Physical disability: A psychosocial approach* (2nd ed.). New York: Harper & Row.

Part III

Students with Disabilities:
Research, Band, and Family

Chapter 14

A Content Analysis of the Research Literature on Music Therapy with School-Aged Clients[1]

CHAPTER OVERVIEW

Evidence-based practice in education and therapy refers to the use of research and scientific studies as a basis for determining the best practices. The term *best practices* is generally regarded—as implied by the word best—to be a superior or innovative practice that has been shown to bring about the most desirable results for clients or students. *Webster's New Millennium™ Dictionary of English* (2008) defines best practice as a practice that is most appropriate under the circumstances, especially as considered acceptable or regulated in business; a technique or methodology that, through experience and research, has reliably led to a desired or optimum result. The basic premise of evidence-based practice or best practices is to provide transparency and to assure administrators, parents, and other concerned individuals that educational and therapeutic techniques and interventions will provide the best possible outcomes. The use of evidence-based practices requires that music educators and music therapists read their professional journals—particularly research journals, understand the results of the research as it is reported, and attempt to implement the findings into their teaching and therapy practices.

Jellison (2000) defines music research in special education as "the study of music behaviors of disabled children and youth (infant through 21), including the study of the functional use of music to reach nonmusical learning outcomes" (p. 201). Research in special education has documented music-related outcomes with students who have a variety of special needs. Research in this area contains both musical and nonmusical goals (Darrow, Colwell, & Kim, 2002). This chapter is an overview and content analysis of the research pertaining to therapeutic nonmusical goals.

---

[1] Guest Contributing Author, Sarah B. Klein, MM, MT-BC, Music Therapist, Abilitations Children's Therapy & Wellness Center, Raleigh, North Carolina.

This chapter includes information on the following topics:
- ♦ Content analysis as a research method
- ♦ Procedures for literature search, review, and analysis
- ♦ Criteria for including studies
- ♦ Content analysis of the research literature on music therapy with school-aged clients
  - » Sources cited
  - » Populations included
  - » Total number of participants
  - » Presentation of music
  - » Effectiveness of intervention
  - » Types of interventions and procedures
- ♦ Discussion of the literature

Content Analysis as a Research Method

Numerous studies carried out with various populations have demonstrated the efficacy of music therapy with school-aged children. However, to review this group of studies as a whole is a demanding task. One way researchers have addressed this challenge has been through content analysis. By charting and evaluating the characteristics of a group of studies, content analyses present a comprehensive overview of trends in the literature. Although rarely performed in the field of music therapy, content analyses may be of value to music therapists seeking effective interventions for use in practice as well as to researchers wishing to identify appropriate areas for exploration.

Traditionally, a content analysis is a research method used in the social sciences to study social trends by empirically analyzing frequencies of words or concepts in a body of text. As demonstrated by Jellison (2000) and Yarbrough (1984), content analyses may also be used to determine trends in areas of research by applying content analysis methodology to a group of studies. Jellison found trends in the literature by analyzing, categorizing, and quantifying 148 data-based articles pertinent to music and children and youth with disabilities. Categories for analysis included disability or description of participants, population age range, inclusive or special education context, method of data collection, opportunity for generalization, behaviors observed, function of music, research mode, number of participants, populations and/or independent variables, and dependent variables. Yarbrough's content analysis examined all 658 articles published in the *Journal of Research in Music Education* from 1953 through 1983. The study explored frequencies and percentages of "(a) articles based on dissertations and theses and (b) articles using historical, philosophical, experimental, descriptive, and behavioral research methodologies"

(p. 213). As evidenced by these two articles, content analyses have been effective in highlighting trends in music education and music therapy research as well as in indicating common practices in these fields. The versatility of content analysis methodology enables its application to a wide range of disciplines; consequently, there are many approaches to completing a content analysis. Independent of the methodological approach taken, the purpose of a content analysis remains consistent: to reduce a large amount of textual information "to more relevant, manageable bits of data" (Weber, 1990, p. 5).

Procedure for Literature Search, Review, and Analysis

A three-step procedure was followed to complete the content analysis. First, inclusion criteria were selected and a thorough literature search was performed to locate all possible studies for inclusion. The search included both published literature and unpublished theses and dissertations. Second, each study was analyzed, categorized, and coded for the following 10 categories: type of source, total number of participants, population, and age range of participants (Table 14.1); research design, duration of study, and presentation of music (Table 14.2); and therapeutic objective and method of evaluation, intervention strategies, and level of effectiveness (Table 14.3). Finally, study characteristics were analyzed for demographic and procedural trends in the literature (Table 14.4) and conclusions were drawn.

Two sources were consulted as starting points for related studies: Jellison's (2000) chapter on disabled children and youth presented research from 1975–1999; Standley's (1996) meta-analysis on the effects of contingent music presented research from 1970–1993 done in a variety of settings, including public schools. Additional studies were found by conducting hand searches for the *Journal of Music Therapy* and the *Journal of Research in Music Education*. Sources were also found through online database searches using Education Resources Information Center (ERIC), The American Psychological Association (PsychINFO), and Dissertation Abstracts, and by consulting the reference sections of included literature. The literature search located 64 studies that met criteria for inclusion in the content analysis.

Criteria for Including Studies

Studies qualified for inclusion if they (a) utilized experimental methods and contained empirical data; (b) were reported in English and dated 1975 through 2009; (c) utilized at least two school-age participants with one or more exceptionalities; (d) took place in an educational setting; (e) used music as a structure, prompt/cue, or contingency; and (f) used a therapeutic non-music objective as the dependent variable. Single-subject case studies were excluded from this content analysis. Following Jellison's (2000) example, the literature review began with studies published in 1975 to reflect the enactment of The Education for All Handicapped Children Act (P.L. 94-142).

Content Analysis of the Research Literature on Music Therapy with School-Aged Clients

The present content analysis incorporates research done with various school-aged populations, each with unique responses to music therapy; therefore, this chapter will provide an introduction to a number of exceptionalities served in school settings, as well as evidence of music therapy's effectiveness with each population. Exceptionalities included in this literature review are the majority of populations served under IDEA: developmental delays, intellectual disabilities, autism, emotional and behavioral disorders, specific learning disabilities, speech and language impairments, sensory impairments, and orthopedic impairments. Though officially listed as an "other health impairment" on the National Dissemination Center for Children with Disabilities website (2009), for the purposes of this paper, children with attention deficit hyperactivity disorder (ADHD) will be grouped with individuals who have behavioral disorders, since many of the symptoms of the two diagnoses overlap. Due to a lack of relevant school-based research, three populations listed under IDEA will not be included in the review of literature: deaf-blindness, traumatic brain injury, and other health impairment (excluding ADHD).

Sixty-four studies that matched the criteria for inclusion were organized according to 10 categories: type of source, total number of participants, population, and age range of participants are presented in Table 14.1; research design, duration of study, and presentation of music are presented in Table 14.2; therapeutic objective and method of evaluation, intervention strategies, and level of effectiveness are presented in Table 14.3. The characteristics presented in Tables 14.1–14.3 are further summarized in Table 14.4, which outlines the frequencies and percentages of major characteristics that define this group of studies.

Table 14.1 Content Analysis on Type of Source, Total Number of Participants, Population, and Age Range
(see key of abbreviations at end of table)

Author (Date)	Type of Source	Total Participants	Population	Age Range
Ayres (1987)	Published (JMT)	5	ID	6–11
Benson, Lovett, & Kroeber (1997)	Published (JCEP)	48	SLD	7–9
Bottari & Evans (1982)	Published (JSP)	24	SLD	9–11
Braithwaite & Sigafoos (1998)	Published (JMT)	5	DD	3–4
Brownell (2002)	Published (JMT)	4	ASD	6–9
Bryan, Sullivan-Burstein, & Mathur (1998)	Published (JLD)	96	SLD	12–13
Buday (1995)	Published (JMT)	10	ASD	4–9
Burleson, Center, & Reeves (1989)	Published (JMT)	4	EBD with autism or schizophrenia	5–9
Cassity (1981)	Published (JMT)	13	Physical disabilities	9–13
Chou (2008)	Unpublished (T)	5	ASD	2–4

Table 14.1 Content Analysis on Type of Source, Total Number of Participants, Population, and Age Range
(see key of abbreviations at end of table)

Author (Date)	Type of Source	Total Participants	Population	Age Range
Claussen & Thaut (1997)	Published (CJMT)	21	SLD	9–11
Copans-Astrand (2000)	Unpublished (T)	40	Various	7–12
Cripe (1986)	Published (JMT)	8	ADD	6–8
D'Arcangelis (1978)	Unpublished (T)	23	EBD	average = 12.09 yr
Darrow & Starmer (1986)	Published (JMT)	22	HI	9–12
DeBedout & Worden (2006)	Published (JMT)	17	ID	5–13
de Mers (2007)	Unpublished (T)	3	ASD & DD	5–6
Dorow (1975)	Published (JMT)	3	ID	9–15
Dorow (1976)	Published (JMT)	17	ID	average = 20 yr
Edgerton (1994)	Unpublished (T)	11	ASD	6–9
Eidson (1989)	Published (JMT)	25	EBD	11–16
Gfeller (1983)	Published (JMT)	60	SLD	9–11
Greenwald (1978)	Published (JMT)	4	ID	7–22
Gregoire (1984)	Published (JMT)	17	ID	6–11
Haines (1989)	Published (MT)	19	EBD	11–16
Hairston (1990)	Published (JMT)	8	ASD & ID	average = 8 yr 10 m
Harding & Ballard (1982)	Published (JMT)	3	EI	3–5
Holloway (1980)	Published (JMT)	8	ID	8–18
Hoskins (1988)	Published (JMT)	16	DD & ID	2–5
Jellison, Brooks, & Huck (1984)	Published (JRME)	100	ID	8–15
Karper (1979)	Published (PMS)	71	ID	10–12
Katagiri (2009)	Published (JMT)	12	ASD	9–15
Kennedy & Scott (2005)	Published (JMT)	34	ESL	10–12
Lim (2007)	Unpublished (D)	50	ASD	3–5
Madsen, Smith, & Feeman (1988)	Published (JMT)	48	Various	K & 4th–5th grades
McCarty, McElfresh, Rice, & Wilson (1978)	Published (JMT)	38	EBD	3–14
Meyers (1973)	Unpublished (T)	4	ASD	3–5
Michel, Parker, Giokas, & Werner (1982)	Published (JMT)	66	Remedial reading	7th–9th grades
Miller (1977)	Published (AJMD)	30	ID	9–14
Montello & Coons (1998)	Published (JMT)	16	EBD and SLD	11–14
Murphy, Doughty, & Nunes (1979)	Published (MR)	6	ID	14–19
Myers (1979)	Published (JMT)	18	ID	7–11
Register (2001)	Published (JMT)	50	EI	4–5
Register, Darrow, Standley & Swedberg (2007)	Published (JMT)	41	SLD	2nd grade
Reitman (2005)	Unpublished (D)	14	ASD	3–5
Rickson (2006)	Published (JMT)	13	ADHD	11–16

Table 14.1 Content Analysis on Type of Source, Total Number of Participants, Population, and Age Range
(see key of abbreviations at end of table)

Author (Date)	Type of Source	Total Participants	Population	Age Range
Rickson & Watkins (2003)	Published (JMT)	15	EBD & ADHD	11–15
Robb (2003)	Published (JMT)	6	EI for visual impairments	4–6
Rogers-Wallgren, French, & Ben-Ezra (1992)	Published (PMS)	12	ID	10–18
Roskam (1979) (First released as dissertation in 1977)	Published (JMT)	36	SLD	6–9
Ross (1997)	Unpublished (T)	3	Speech & Language	3–5
Rowley (2006)	Unpublished (D)	45	Head Start	3–6
Schmidt, Franklin, & Edwards (1976)	Published (PR)	3	ASD	7–10
Shehan (1981)	Published (JMT)	16	SLD	7–10
Soraci, Deckner, McDaniel, & Blanton (1982)	Published (JMT)	11	ID	5–10
Spencer (1988)	Published (JMT)	27	ID	16–40
Spudic & Somervill (1978)	Published (ETMR)	36	ID	11–18
Staum (1983)	Published (JMT)	25 (9 children)	Gait disorders	5–19 + adults
Sussman (2009)	Published (JMT)	9	DD	2–6
Thaut (1985)	Published (JMT)	24	Gross motor dysfunction	6–8
Windwer (1981)	Published (JRME)	13	Hyperactive	5–8
Wolfe (1980)	Published (JMT)	12	Cerebral palsy	3–37
Wolfe (1982)	Published (JMT)	84	Hyperactive	3rd grade
Wolfe & Hom (1993)	Published (JMT)	10	Head Start	5

KEY:

Type of Source:
T = Thesis
D = Dissertation
AJMB = *American Journal on Mental Deficiency*
CJMT = *Canadian Journal of Music Therapy*
CTMR = *Education and Training of the Mentally Retarded*
JCEP = *Journal of Experimental Child Psychology*
JLD = *Journal of Learning Disabilities*
JMT = *Journal of Music Therapy*
JRME = *Journal of Research in Music Education*
JSP = *Journal of School Psychology*
MR = Mental Retardation
MT = Music Therapy
PMS - Perceptual and Motor Skills
PR = *Psychological Reports*

Population:
ASD = Autism Spectrum Disorder
DD = Developmental Disabilities
EBD = Emotional/Behavioral Disorder
EI = Early Intervention
ESL = English as a Second Language
HI = Hearing Impairments
ID = Intellectual Disability
SLD = Specific Learning Disability

Age range:
K = Kindergarten
yr = years
m = months

Table 14.2 Content Analysis on Research Design, Duration of Study, and Presentation of Music
(see key of abbreviations at end of table)

Author (Date)	Research Design	Duration of Study	Presentation of Music
Ayres (1987)	Ss as Con	26 sessions	Recorded
Benson et al. (1997)	Exp/Con	3 sessions	Live
Bottari & Evans (1982)	Ss as Con	2 sessions	Recorded
Braithwaite & Sigafoos (1998)	Ss as Con	27 sessions	Live
Brownell (2002)	Ss as Con	20 sessions	Live
Bryan et al. (1998)	Exp/Con	1 session	Recorded
Buday (1995)	Ss as Con	8 sessions	Recorded
Burleson et al. (1989)	Ss as Con	8 sessions	Recorded
Cassity (1981)	Ss as Con	18 sessions	Live
Chou (2008)	Ss as Con	14 sessions	Live
Claussen & Thaut (1997)	Exp/Con	2 days	Recorded
Copans-Astrand (2000)	Exp/Con	14 sessions	Both
Cripe (1986)	Ss as Con	2 sessions	Recorded
D'Arcangelis (1978)	Exp/Con	14 sessions	Both
Darrow & Starmer (1986)	Ss as Con	16 sessions	Live
DeBedout & Worden (2006)	Ss as Con	1 session	Both
de Mers (2007)	Ss as Con	up to 23 sessions	Both
Dorow (1975)	Ss as Con	25–38 sessions	Recorded
Dorow (1976)	Ss as Con	20 sessions	Recorded
Edgerton (1994)	Ss as Con	10 sessions	Live
Eidson (1989)	Exp/Con	10 sessions	Live
Gfeller (1983)	Exp/Con	3 sessions	Recorded
Greenwald (1978)	Ss as Con	42 sessions	Recorded
Gregoire (1984)	Ss as Con	6 days	Recorded
Haines (1989)	Exp/Con	12 sessions	Both
Hairston (1990)	Combination	25 sessions	Live
Harding & Ballard (1982)	Ss as Con	38 sessions	Live
Holloway (1980)	Ss as Con	10 sessions	Both
Hoskins (1988)	Ss as Con	30 sessions	Live
Jellison et al. (1984)	Exp/Con	up to 6 sessions	Live as structure; Recorded as reinforcement
Karper (1979)	Exp/Con	6 sessions	Recorded
Katagiri (2009)	Ss as Con	8 sessions	Both
Kennedy & Scott (2005)	Exp/Con	12 sessions	Both
Lim (2007)	Exp/Con	6 sessions	Recorded
Madsen et al. (1988)	Exp/Con	16 sessions	Recorded
McCarty et al. (1978)	Ss as Con	29 days	Recorded
Meyers (1973)	Ss as Con	20 sessions	Live

Table 14.2 Content Analysis on Research Design, Duration of Study, and Presentation of Music
(see key of abbreviations at end of table)

Author (Date)	Research Design	Duration of Study	Presentation of Music
Michel et al. (1982)	Ss as Con & Exp/Con	4 sessions	Recorded
Miller (1977)	Exp/Con	26 sessions	Recorded
Montello & Coons (1998)	Exp/Con & Ss as Con	4 months	Both
Murphy et al. (1979)	Ss as Con	15 sessions	Recorded
Myers (1979)	Ss as Con	1 session	Recorded
Register (2001)	Exp/Con	1 school year	Live
Register et al. (2007)	Exp/Con	12 sessions	Both
Reitman (2005)	Ss as Con	8 sessions	Both
Rickson (2006)	Exp/Con & multiple contrasting treatment	16 sessions	Live
Rickson & Watkins (2003)	Exp/Con	16 sessions	Both
Robb (2003)	Ss as Con	4 sessions	Live
Rogers-Wallgren et al. (1992)	Exp/Con	30 sessions	Recorded
Roskam (1979)	Exp/Con	3 months, 2 hrs/week	Live
Ross (1997)	Ss as Con	5 months	Live
Rowley (2006)	Ss as Con	16 weeks	Live
Schmidt et al. (1976)	Ss as Con	20 sessions	Live
Shehan (1981)	Ss as Con	20 mins. per subject	Recorded
Soraci et al. (1982)	Ss as Con	4 sessions	Recorded
Spencer (1988)	Exp/Con	20 sessions	Live (control = music listening)
Spudic & Somervill (1978)	Ss as Con	3 sessions	Recorded
Staum (1983)	Ss as Con	4 sessions	Recorded
Sussman (2009)	Ss as Con	4 sessions	Live
Thaut (1985)	Exp/Con	3 sessions	Recorded
Windwer (1981)	Ss as Con	9 classes	Recorded
Wolfe (1980)	Ss as Con	32–57 sessions	Recorded
Wolfe (1982)	Combination	3 months total; 3 testings per subject	Recorded
Wolfe & Hom (1993)	Ss as Con	6 teaching sessions; 3 sessions/week until Ss reached criteria	Live

KEY:

Research Design:
Exp = Experimental Group
Con = Control Group
Ss as Con = Subjects as Own Control

Table 14.3 Content Analysis on Objective and Evaluation, Intervention Strategies, and Effectiveness
(see key of abbreviations at end of table)

Author (Date)	Objective & Evaluation	Intervention Strategies	Effectiveness
Ayres (1987)	Improved oral functions during eating aeb an Oral Functions in Feeding Evaluation and increase in elapsed feeding times	Non-contingent background music played during feeding	Not effective for elapsed feeding times; 4.2% mean increase in oral functioning
Benson et al. (1997)	Transfer of learning to increase reading skills aeb correct application of invariant reading patterns	Reading and non-reading (music) training	Not effective for Ss with SLD in transferring patterns from music to reading
Bottari & Evans	Improved retention of verbal material aeb recall and recognition scores of verbal material contained in song lyrics	Lyrics sung with and without instrumental musical accompaniment and lyrics spoken with and without instrumental accompaniment	Sung lyrics significantly effective in increasing recall for Ss with strong visual-spatial skills ($p < .05$)
Braithwaite & Sigafoos (1998)	Increased communication responsiveness aeb percentage of opportunities with appropriate communication	Social vs. musical antecedents for greeting, naming objects, and requesting materials	Effective for 3 out of 5 Ss (level of significance not given)
Brownell (2002)	Increase in targeted behavior aeb frequency of occurrence for 1 hour following intervention	Singing social stories about targeted behavior	Significantly effective ($p < .05$); singing more effective than contact control (reading social stories) for 1 out of 4 Ss
Bryan et al. (1998)	Increased social-information processing skills aeb responses to questions about a social problem	Self-induced positive affect, music-induced positive affect, music-induced negative affect, and neutral affect	Happy music significantly effective in engendering positive interpretations, but also resulted in more embellishments ($p < .05$)
Buday (1995)	Increased imitation of signed and spoken words aeb number of words signed/spoken	Signs taught with music and speech vs. signs taught with rhythm and speech	Significantly effective for both signed words ($p < .05$) and spoken words ($p < .02$)
Burleson et al. (1989)	Increase in accuracy of task performance aeb on color-coded sorting task	Background music (George Winston's "December")	Significantly effective ($p < .062$)
Cassity (1981)	Increased peer acceptance of an individual aeb Ss's affective rankings of peers	Piano performance at the end of group MT sessions	Significantly effective ($p < .025$)
Chou (2008)	Increased social-communicative behaviors aeb frequency of eye contact, vocalization/ verbalization, and gesture imitation	Small-group music therapy using singing, choice making, sign language, and books	Effective for gestural imitation, but no significant differences between music and non-music conditions
Claussen & Thaut (1997)	Increased mathematical retention aeb number of multiplication problems solved	Familiar music as a mnemonic device during rehearsal of multiplication tables	Significantly effective ($p < .05$)
Copans-Astrand (2000)	Improved reading skills aeb scores on STAR and K-TEA reading tests	Rhythm-based Orff-Schulwerk MT	Significantly effective ($p < .05$)

Table 14.3 Content Analysis on Objective and Evaluation, Intervention Strategies, and Effectiveness
(see key of abbreviations at end of table)

Author (Date)	Objective & Evaluation	Intervention Strategies	Effectiveness
Cripe (1986)	Decreased activity level and increased attention span aeb number of motor activities and length of time attending to a task	Background instrumental rock music during free play and during maze and coloring activities	Significantly effective for decreased activity level ($p < .05$); not effective for increased attention span
D'Arcangelis (1978)	Increased musical growth aeb Colwell's Music Achievement Tests and increased self-esteem aeb Piers-Harris Children's Self Concept Scale	Music education vs. music therapy approaches; both approaches used singing, music listening, playing instruments, improvising, moving to music, and reading charts	Effective, but no significant differences between approaches
Darrow & Starmer (1986)	Improved speech aeb Visi-Pitch analysis speech for fundamental frequency, frequency range, speech rate, and intonation differences between statements and questions	30-minute vocal training classes that included equal amounts of singing and vocal exercises	Significant reduction of fundamental frequency ($p < .01$) and a significant increase in frequency range ($p < .05$)
DeBedout & Worden (2006)	Increased motivation aeb videotaped observation of limb and head movement, vocal sound, and facial expression change	Presence of music therapist vs. use of switch-activated toys and recorded music	Continuous guitar significantly effective ($p < .1$); continuous guitar and "activated" guitar significantly effective ($p < .05$)
de Mers (2007)	Increased prosocial behavior aeb occurrences of hitting, screaming, and asking during free play following MT	Small-group MT sessions targeting hitting, screaming, and asking behaviors; used songs, movement activities, instrumental activities, and games	Moderately effective (level of significance not given); anecdotal support of effectiveness
Dorow (1975)	Increased imitative behavior aeb Ss's completion of trained individual tasks	Training and testing of imitative behaviors with verbal approval, music, and food as contingencies	Significantly effective (level of significance not given); most effective when all 3 reinforcers were used
Dorow (1976)	Improved mathematical and music listening skills aeb scores on math and music listening skills tests	Televised music lessons contingent on correctly answering a math problem	Significantly effective ($p < .05$)
Edgerton (1994)	Increased communication aeb the Checklist of Communicative Responses/Acts Score Sheet (CRASS)	Improvisational MT based on the Nordoff and Robbins Creative MT approach	Significantly effective ($p < .01$)
Eidson (1989)	Generalization of interpersonal skills from MT sessions to the classroom aeb videotaped observation of behaviors	Group MT sessions structured to target selected behaviors and a token economy with performance in a music video as a reward	Significantly effective
Gfeller (1983)	Improved short-term memory aeb recall of multiplication tables	Musical rehearsal of multiplication tables and the addition of modeling and cuing to rehearsal	Significantly effective only when modeling and cueing were used ($p < .0001$)

Table 14.3 Content Analysis on Objective and Evaluation, Intervention Strategies, and Effectiveness
(see key of abbreviations at end of table)

Author (Date)	Objective & Evaluation	Intervention Strategies	Effectiveness
Greenwald (1978)	Decreased self-stimulatory behaviors aeb duration of inappropriate behavior during 11-minute sessions	Contingent music/distorted music and contingent music/silence, with music listening contingent on appropriate behavior	Not effective
Gregoire (1984)	Effectiveness in task performance aeb amount of correctly matched numbers (1–20)	Listening to a story illustrated on a felt board, a rest period paired with relaxing music, and a 5-minute number matching task	Not effective
Haines (1989)	Increased self-esteem aeb the Coopersmith Self-Esteem Inventory	Group music therapy focused on creative, expressive activities	Anecdotal significance only
Hairston (1990)	Behavioral, communicative, social, and academic development aeb SWAN and DTORF data and percent of time spent in appropriate behaviors	Group music and art therapy sessions; music therapy made use of singing and rhythm instrument playing	Significantly effective for time spent observing teacher, appropriate play, and acceptance of physical contact ($p < .05$)
Harding & Ballard (1982)	Increase in spontaneous speech aeb appropriate verbal responses to questions, initiation of verbal interaction, verbalization during story retelling, and on-task behavior	Music activities aimed at developing spontaneous speech (sung nursery rhymes, finger play songs, "Old MacDonald Had a Farm," and rhythmically told stories), and preferred songs and instruments as a contingency	Effective (level of significance not given)
Holloway (1980)	Increase in preacademic and motor skills aeb accuracy of targeted behaviors	Contingent music listening and instrument playing as reinforcement for correct responses	Nonsignificantly effective
Hoskins (1988)	Increase in verbal response and improvement of expressive language abilities aeb performance on standardized speech test	Group music activities structured to increase expressive language skills through antiphonal singing using picture cards	Significantly effective for melodic test ($p < .05$); non-significantly effective for spoken test
Jellison et al (1984)	Increased positive interactions and acceptance of students with ID aeb observations of social interaction type and quality	Small cooperative group work and rock music listening contingent on cooperation	Significantly effective for 3rd, 4th, and 6th grades, but not 5th ($p < .05$)
Karper (1979)	Learning of a novel motor skill using a soccer ball aeb score (total number of successful attempts)	Popular or classical background music during practice sessions	Not effective
Katagiri (2009)	Increased understanding of emotions (happiness, sadness, anger, and fear) aeb recognition of facial expressions, identification of situation-based emotions, and Ss ability to encode facial expressions	Verbal instruction, verbal instruction with background music representing emotions, and singing songs about emotions	All conditions significantly effective ($p < .05$); background music was the most effective intervention

Table 14.3 Content Analysis on Objective and Evaluation, Intervention Strategies, and Effectiveness
(see key of abbreviations at end of table)

Author (Date)	Objective & Evaluation	Intervention Strategies	Effectiveness
Kennedy & Scott (2005)	Improved use of the English language aeb scores on the Story Retelling Inventory and Speaking Checklist	Group music therapy structured to target ESL objectives through music listening, singing, writing, musical games, movement, rhythmic training, sign language, and lyric analysis	Significantly effective ($p < .01$)
Lim (2007)	Improved speech production aeb Verbal Production Evaluation Scale measurements of semantics, phonology, pragmatics, and prosody of 36 target words	Developmental speech-language training through music; used a music video containing songs and pictures of the 36 target words	Significantly effective, but no significant difference between conditions (music training and speech training) ($p < .05$)
Madsen et al. (1988)	Learning of academic skills aeb scores on a Basic Skills Assessment; improved attitude aeb a Likert-type attitudinal assessment	Cross-age tutoring using music as a teaching aid and as a contingency for older students' participation	Significantly and anecdotally effective
McCarty et al. (1978)	Decreased inappropriate bus behavior aeb duration of time of each incident of fighting or out-of-seat behavior	Preferred music listening contingent on appropriate bus behavior	Significantly effective (level of significance not given)
Meyers (1973)	Improved speech aeb number of personal pronouns used in a 15-minute period	MT sessions targeting usage of personal pronouns; used singing and movement	Significantly effective for 2 out of 4 Ss (level of significance not given)
Michel et al. (1982)	Improved vocabulary scores	Dichotic presentation of vocabulary words and definitions in one ear and music in the other	Significantly effective as demonstrated by one sub-study ($p < .05$)
Miller (1977)	Increased arithmetic performance aeb number of correct computations	Tokens earned for correct arithmetic computations and redeemed for music listening, either preferred or non-preferred	Significantly effective ($p < .005$); music preference did not result in significant differences
Montello & Coons (1998)	Increased prosocial behaviors aeb homeroom teachers' ratings of attention, motivation, and hostility	Active, rhythm-based group MT vs. passive, listening-based group MT	Significantly effective ($p < .1$); most effective for group B (passive followed by active MT) ($p < .024$)
Murphy et al. (1979)	Increase in upright head positioning monitored by a photo-electric relay system	Response-contingent presentation of music	Effective aeb increases in percent of time Ss maintained erect head positioning
Myers (1979)	Word retention aeb recall scores for a paired-associate task	Presentation of words as a list, story, and song	Not effective
Register (2001)	Improved prereading and writing skills aeb scores on the Print Awareness Test for Logos, the Print Awareness Test of Word Identification, and the Print Concepts Checklist	Group music therapy targeting writing skills and reading/book concepts; used books, word and letter cards, charts, and other visuals, as well as illustration assignments	Both control and treatment MT sessions were significantly effective; treatment resulted in significantly higher scores in logo identification and word recognition ($p < .05$)

Table 14.3 Content Analysis on Objective and Evaluation, Intervention Strategies, and Effectiveness
(see key of abbreviations at end of table)

Author (Date)	Objective & Evaluation	Intervention Strategies	Effectiveness
Register et al. (2007)	Improved reading skills aeb scores on the vocabulary and reading comprehension subtests of the Gates-MacGinitie Reading Test for 2nd grade	Intensive short-term music curriculum targeting reading comprehension and vocabulary skills	Significantly effective ($p < .05$)
Reitman (2005)	Increased joint attention aeb PDDBI scores and video analysis of joint attention behaviors	MT sessions targeting joint attention; used songs, imitation activities, instrument play, and movement activities	Significantly effective ($p = .02$) according to video analysis; 7 out of 10 Ss improved significantly
Rickson (2006)	Decreased motor impulsivity aeb Synchronized Tapping Task and parent and teacher versions of Conners' Global Index Restless-Impulsive (R-I) Scale and Conners' DSM-IV Hyperactive-Impulsive (H-I) Scale	Instructional vs. improvisational MT approaches; used percussion ensemble activities	Significantly effective compared to no-contact control ($p < .05$; $p = .004$ on STT); instructional approach resulted in slightly improved scores overall
Rickson & Watkins (2003)	Increased prosocial behaviors aeb scores on parent and teacher versions of the Developmental Behavior Checklist	Group MT sessions; used music listening, singing, active rhythm-based activities, instrument play, and group song writing	Anecdotal significance only
Robb (2003)	Increase in attentive behavior and group participation aeb observation of attentive behavior, facing central speaker, following one-step directions, manipulating objects according to function, and remaining seated	Music and play-based group MT; music sessions used singing, instrument play, and movement	Significantly effective for attentive behavior ($p = .002$); nonsignificantly effective for group participation behaviors
Rogers-Wallgren et al. (1992)	Increased independence in physical fitness performance aeb percent task score	Verbal praise plus music or vibratory reinforcement following each step of a 7-step task analysis of independent performance	Not effective
Roskam (1979)	Increased auditory awareness and improved reading skills aeb scores on test of reading recognition, reading comprehension, spelling, nonverbal auditory awareness, and verbal auditory awareness	Prescriptive music therapy, language development activities, and a combination of both	Nonsignificantly effective
Ross (1997)	Improved speech patterns aeb videotaped observations of frequency of accurately uttered bilabial sounds	Singing songs targeting the sounds /M/, /P/, and /B/	2 out of 3 students demonstrated improvement during intervention; all 3 demonstrated improvement during follow-up
Rowley (2006)	Increase in appropriate behavior aeb Behavioral Objective Sequence ratings by Head Start teachers	Group music therapy sessions targeting behavioral objectives	Significantly effective; most effective with ages 5–6

Table 14.3 Content Analysis on Objective and Evaluation, Intervention Strategies, and Effectiveness
(see key of abbreviations at end of table)

Author (Date)	Objective & Evaluation	Intervention Strategies	Effectiveness
Schmidt et al. (1976)	Increased appropriate and decreased inappropriate behaviors aeb frequency of positive and negative behaviors and overt responses to music	Individual and small-group MT sessions under 2 conditions: reinforcement and shaping, and differential reinforcement; used familiar songs	Effective (level of significance not given); more improvement during individual sessions
Shehan (1981)	Retention of words aeb number of correctly recalled words in a paired-associate learning task	Presentation of word pairs in music, verbal, music/visual, and verbal/visual formats	Significant differences between modes of presentation (p < .01), with greatest recall resulting from verbal/visual and musical/visual modes
Soraci et al. (1982)	Decreased stereotypic behaviors aeb frequency of the following behaviors: rocking, idiosyncratic stereotypic behaviors, vocalizations, rhythmic behaviors, and fidgeting	Listening to 4 different rates of a rhythmic musical soundtrack ("Soul Sacrifice" by Santana, played at 78, 45, 33, and 16 rpm)	Rocking significantly lower at 16 rpm (p < .05); vocalizations significantly lower at 16 and 78 rpm (p < .01); rhythmic behaviors significantly lower at 33 rpm (p < .05)
Spencer (1988)	Increased ability to follow directions aeb number of directions performed correctly	Group MT sessions using instrumental activities, movement activities, or music listening	Movement activities were significantly effective (p < .025)
Spudic & Somervill (1978)	Decrease in distractibility and increase in academic performance aeb observer ratings of activity levels and accuracy of arithmetic task	Calming or exciting background music during performance of arithmetic problems	Not effective
Staum (1983)	Rehabilitation of gait disorders aeb timed deviations between footfalls, cadence inconsistencies, and observer ratings	Individually determined music and rhythmic percussive sounds used to accompany walking	Significantly effective
Sussman (2009)	Increased peer awareness aeb duration of sustained attention toward peers and frequency of alternating attention from peer to peer	Musical vs. nonmusical passed object (rain stick vs. baton filled with glitter) and guitar music vs. no music during passing	Significantly effective (p < .05); the most effective condition had no music during the passing of a musical object
Thaut (1985)	Improved temporal muscular control aeb graphic recordings of voltage coded sensor signals attached to hands and feet	Presentation and fading of auditory rhythm and rhythmic speech during movement sequence	Significantly effective (p < .05) with rhythmic stimuli; not effective after fading
Windwer (1981)	Decreased level of activity aeb scores on the Motor Activity Rating Scale	A 7-minute instrumental tape of an ascending music progression cycle as background music during art class	Not effective; resulted in significant increases in activity level (p < .05)
Wolfe (1980)	Increase in erect head positioning as monitored by a mercury switch relay mechanism	Automated interrupted music as a contingency (music/silence vs. music/tone)	Effective for 4 out of 12 participants
Wolfe (1982)	Improved task performance aeb total number of letters marked through and level of movement aeb frequency of bodily movements	Continuous background music and contingent interruption and presentation of music during task	Not effective

Table 14.3 Content Analysis on Objective and Evaluation, Intervention Strategies, and Effectiveness
(see key of abbreviations at end of table)

Author (Date)	Objective & Evaluation	Intervention Strategies	Effectiveness
Wolfe & Hom (1993)	Retention of sequential verbal information aeb number of trials needed to recall telephone numbers	Telephone numbers taught to familiar and unfamiliar melodies, through speech, and with or without contingent music	Significantly effective for familiar melody condition (p < .04); contingency was not effective
KEY			
Miscellaneous:			
aeb = as evidenced by			
MT = Music Therapy			

Table 14.4 Frequency of Occurrence of Sources Cited, Populations, Total Number of Participants, Presentation of Music, and Effectiveness of Intervention (1975–2009)

Category	Frequency	Percentage of Total
Total Number of Studies Reviewed	64	100
Age range of children and youth: 2–22 years		
Sources Cited		
Journal of Music Therapy	41	64.1
Thesis or Dissertation	10	15.6
Journal of Research in Music Education	2	3.1
Perceptual and Motor Skills	2	3.1
American Journal on Mental Deficiency	1	1.6
Canadian Journal of Music Therapy	1	1.6
Education and Training of the Mentally Retarded	1	1.6
Journal of Experimental Child Psychology	1	1.6
Journal of Learning Disabilities	1	1.6
Journal of School Psychology	1	1.6
Mental Retardation	1	1.6
Music Therapy	1	1.6
Psychological Reports	1	1.6
Total	64	100
Populations		
Intellectual disability	17	26.6
Autism spectrum disorder	11	17.2
Specific learning disabilities and remedial reading	10	15.6
Emotional/behavioral disorders	7	10.9
ADD/ADHD	5	7.8
Developmental disabilities	5	7.8
Early Intervention and Head Start programs	5	7.8

Table 14.4 Frequency of Occurrence of Sources Cited, Populations, Total Number of Participants, Presentation of Music, and Effectiveness of Intervention (1975–2009)

Category	Frequency	Percentage of Total
Physical disabilities/orthopedic impairments	4	6.3
Various	2	3.1
English as a second language	1	1.6
Hearing impairments	1	1.6
Speech and language impairments	1	1.6
Visual impairments	1	1.6
Total Number of Participants		
2–5	12	18.8
6–10	8	12.5
11–15	25	39.1
26–50	13	20.3
51–100	6	9.4
Total	64	100
Presentation of Music		
Recorded	29	45.3
Live	22	34.4
Both	13	20.3
Total	64	100
Effectiveness of Intervention		
Significantly effective for at least one objective or group	40	62.5
Effective (level of significance not given)	9	14.3
Non-significantly effective (or effective for less than 50% of the total number of participants)	4	6.3
Anecdotal significance only	2	3.2
Not effective	9	14.3
Total	64	100

Note. The total for the "Populations" category does not equal the total number of studies due to the involvement of more than one type of exceptionality in some studies.

Sources Cited

The published articles included in this content analysis came from 12 different peer-reviewed journals, with almost two thirds (41 studies; 64.1%) from the *Journal of Music Therapy*. The next most frequent category was unpublished theses and dissertations, which contributed 10 studies (15.6%). Two journals each contributed two articles; these were the *Journal of Research in Music Education* (3.1%) and *Perceptual and Motor Skills* (3.1%). Other journals that offered an article for inclusion dealt with subjects such as specific disabilities, child and school psychology, and music therapy.

Populations

The most commonly researched population was that of individuals with intellectual disabilities, constituting more than a quarter of the total number of included articles (17 studies; 26.6%). The second largest category included students with autism spectrum disorders (11 studies; 17.2%), followed by specific learning disabilities and remedial reading groups (10 studies; 15.6%). Seven studies explored the use of music therapy with individuals who had emotional and behavioral disorders (10.9%). Attention deficit disorder and attention deficit hyperactivity disorder, developmental disabilities, and early intervention or Head Start programs each constituted 5 studies (7.8%). Only 4 articles used participants with physical disabilities (6.3%). Two studies reported including participants with a variety of exceptionalities (3.1%). Finally, there were four categories that offered 1 study each: English as a second language (1.6%), hearing impairments (1.6%), speech and language impairment (1.6%), and visual impairments (1.6%). It should be noted that these percentages total more than 100% due to the involvement of more than one type of exceptionality in some studies.

Total Number of Participants

Results of a frequency count of the number of participants included in each study showed that, of the 64 studies examined, 12 had between 2 and 5 participants (18.8%), 8 had between 6 and 10 participants (12.5%), 25 had between 11 and 25 participants (39.1%), 13 had between 26 and 50 participants (20.3%), and 6 had between 51 and 100 participants (9.4%). These numbers demonstrate that the majority of research in this area included between 11 and 25 participants, while studies that included more than 50 constituted only 9.4% of the total.

Presentation of Music

In analyzing how researchers presented music to participants, it was found that most used recorded music (29 studies; 45.3%); however, live presentation was only slightly less common (22 studies; 34.4%). Thirteen studies used both live and recorded music at some point in the design (20.3%). For example, Jellison, Brooks, and Huck (1984) used live music as a structure and recorded rock music for listening as a contingency. It is important to clarify that, while Spencer's (1988) study had a recorded music component, it was counted in the live presentation category given that the recorded music served as a control condition.

Effectiveness of Intervention

Studies were separated into the following categories regarding effectiveness: those that were reported to be significantly effective for at least one objective or group (40 studies; 62.5%); those that were reportedly effective, but did not mention a level of significance (9 studies, 14.3%); those that were effective, though not significantly so or effective for less than half of the total number of participants (4 studies; 6.3%); those that reported effectiveness anecdotally, but did not offer statistical significance (2 studies; 3.2%); and those that were not effective (9 studies; 14.3%). These data are represented in Figure 14.1.

Figure 14.1 Percentage of Studies Reporting Each Level of Effectiveness

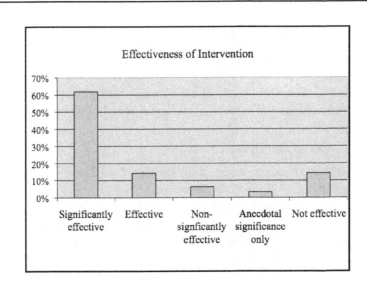

Types of Interventions and Procedures

Specific interventions and procedures are listed in Table 14.3, under the category "Intervention Strategies." To determine the effectiveness of the interventions, effectiveness data were taken from the results section of each study.

Almost two thirds of the 64 studies that met criteria for inclusion (62.5%) reported that music therapy was significantly effective in accomplishing non-musical objectives. Most of these indicated a level of significance below .05, although in one study, a slightly higher level of significance ($p < .062$) was obtained (Burleson, Center, & Reeves, 1989). These 40 articles reported having used a variety of methods that included vocal, instrumental, and movement activities; music listening as a contingency; and music listening as structure or cue (background music, mood-inducing music, and music as a mnemonic device or instructional tool).

Nine studies (14.3%) reported that music interventions were effective, but did not include a level of significance. Many of these employed group or individual music therapy sessions that involved activities such as singing, sign language with music, music listening, instrument play, movement to music, and musical games (Chou, 2008; D'Arcangelis, 1978; de Mers, 2007; Harding & Ballard, 1982; Meyers, 1973; Ross, 1997; Schmidt, Franklin, & Edwards, 1976). Other interventions included musical antecedents for greeting, naming objects, and requesting materials (Braithwaite & Sigafoos, 1998) and music listening as a contingency (Harding & Ballard, 1982; Murphy, Doughty, & Nunes, 1979).

Four studies (6.3%) found music therapy to be nonsignificantly effective or effective for less than 50% of participants. Half of these used music listening and/or instrument play as a reward for demonstrating a targeted behavior (Holloway, 1980; Wolfe, 1982). Ayres' (1987) procedure utilized noncontingent background music to accompany feeding times. In Roskam's (1979) study, music was used as a structure by providing prescriptive music therapy in combination with language development activities.

Of the two studies (3.2%) that reported anecdotal significance only, both used group music therapy as the intervention. One curriculum focused on creative, expressive activities (Haines, 1989), and the other used music listening, singing, rhythm-based activities, instrument play, and group song writing (Rickson & Watkins, 2003).

There was wide variety among nine studies (14.3%) that were found not to be effective (Benson, Lovett, & Kroeber, 1997; Greenwald, 1978; Gregoire, 1984; Karper, 1979; Myers, 1979, Rogers-Wallgren, French, & Ben-Ezra, 1992; Spudic & Somervill, 1978; Windwer, 1981; Wolfe, 1982). Some used music as a contingency, rewarding participants with music listening for movement in the targeted direction. Other researchers presented background music during practice of a skill or during involvement with a non-musical activity. Music was used as a structure in Myers' (1979) procedure, in which a group of paired-associate words was presented as a list, story, or song, and in Benson, Lovett, and Kroeber's (1997) investigation of students' abilities to transfer learning of invariant reading patterns from a musical context to a textual context.

In summary, music interventions were varied and included both music making and music listening. Procedures varied greatly, but could be categorized as having used music as a structure, prompt/cue, or contingency. There were no clear trends in interventions that produced significant results versus those that were found not to be effective; all groupings of effectiveness utilized a variety of interventions.

Implications for Practice

The results of the present study indicate that the majority of music therapy interventions used with individuals who have varying exceptionalities has been significantly effective. Since both peer-reviewed and unpublished literature were reviewed, it can be assumed that this finding is unbiased and can therefore be presented in support of music therapy programs offered in schools. By making this information available to school administrators, music therapists may enhance the level of support for their programs, thereby creating and maintaining opportunities for students to benefit from music therapy services.

Findings may also be used to inspire additional research. This content analysis outlines trends in the literature and comprehensively describes 64 studies that have been carried out with school-aged populations. This information may assist practitioners in developing research inquiries and designs. As more literature is accumulated, music therapy's reputation as an evidence-based practice will continue to grow.

Finally, the descriptions of intervention strategies provided in Table 14.3 may be of particular interest to music therapists practicing in the schools. This table may inspire therapists to expand their repertoire of activities and interventions. Perhaps by being exposed to new approaches, students may experience accelerated progress towards goals and objectives. This table also lists level of effectiveness directly beside intervention strategies, permitting therapists to assess how successfully strategies have been employed by other music therapists. Looking at this information together, music therapists may be aided in creating a strong program and addressing students' needs as efficaciously as possible.

Suggestions for Future Research

As demonstrated by the present content analysis, most of the studies examining the use of music therapy with school-aged individuals have involved participants with intellectual disabilities. Exceptionalities that have been moderately represented in the current literature are autism spectrum disorders and specific learning disabilities. There is a dearth of literature involving individuals with emotional and behavior disorders; ADD/ADHD; developmental disabilities; early intervention needs; physical disabilities; hearing, speech and language, or visual impairments; and those learning English as a second language. Future researchers may wish to further investigate music therapy practices with these underrepresented populations. It would also be useful to replicate studies presented in this paper in order to gain greater understanding of the efficacy of specific interventions. Despite environmental constraints, it is important that researchers attempt to include as many participants as possible.

This content analysis demonstrated that music therapy was effective in 62.5% of the studies included. The criteria for inclusion were broad in order to present an expansive and unbiased account of the current literature. It is likely that by refining criteria to include only studies with specific characteristics (e.g., live music interventions, one-disability population, a smaller age range), results would be different. It would be beneficial to perform such an investigation to better understand what specific music therapy approaches are the most effective.

As illustrated in this chapter, a content analysis collects and summarizes findings from a large group of literature. Another methodology that performs this function is a meta-analysis. Meta-analysis is a statistical procedure used to integrate data from a number of related studies with the intention of generalizing the results. Data from each study are subjected to statistical analysis to determine effect sizes. From a comparison of effect sizes across multiple variables, conclusions can be drawn (Glass, McGaw, & Smith, 1981). Music therapy researchers have begun to use meta-analysis as a way of determining the overall efficacy of various interventions. Standley contributed the first meta-analysis in the field of music therapy in 1986, and since then 11 more such studies have been issued. The data presented in the present content analysis could be further analyzed through the process of meta-analysis. This undertaking would require the calculation of effect sizes for those studies that reported results in a format conducive to replicated data analysis. Such information could further support the work of music therapists in schools and justify to administrators the importance of funding music therapy as a related and/or district-wide service.

Conclusions

This content analysis assessed the efficacy of music therapy approaches targeted to reach non-musical objectives with school-aged children who have varying exceptionalities. The procedure involved organizing the results reported in 64 independent studies, both published and unpublished. A variety of strategies were found to be effective; these included background music, mood-inducing music, music as a mnemonic device or instructional tool, musical antecedents, and music as a contingency or structure. Activities included singing, playing instruments, moving to music, listening to music, songwriting, using sign language with music, and musical games. Through an analysis of reported results, it was demonstrated that nearly two thirds of the included studies were significantly effective in helping participants reach targeted objectives. Such positive results support the use of music therapy in schools to address the educational objectives of children and youth with special needs.

The value of music therapy stems from its universal appeal and versatility. Music activities can be adapted to engage a wide range of individuals, regardless of their ages, abilities, or musical preferences. Music can be used to address cognitive, academic, social, emotional, physical, communication, and behavioral goals through a medium that many students enjoy and find motivating. Through continued research, music therapists will gain a greater understanding of the effectiveness of specific music therapy approaches. Such findings will increase and enhance the learning opportunities available to students with varying exceptionalities.

REFERENCES

Ayres, B. R. (1987). The effects of a music stimulus environment versus regular cafeteria environment during therapeutic feeding. *Journal of Music Therapy, 24*(1), 14–26.

Benson, N. J., Lovett, M. W., & Kroeber, C. L. (1997). Training and transfer-of-learning effects in disabled and normal readers: Evidence of specific deficits. *Journal of Experimental Child Psychology, 64*(3), 343–366.

Bottari, S. S., & Evans, J. R. (1982). Effects of musical context, type of vocal presentation, and time on the verbal retention abilities of visual-spatially oriented and verbally oriented learning disabled children. *The Journal of School Psychology, 20*(4), 329–338.

Braithwaite, M., & Sigafoos, J. (1998). Effects of social versus musical antecedents on communication responsiveness in five children with developmental disabilities. *Journal of Music Therapy, 35*(2), 88–104.

Brownell, M. D. (2002). Musically adapted social stories to modify behaviors in students with autism: Four case studies. *Journal of Music Therapy, 39*(2), 117–144.

Bryan, T., Sullivan-Burstein, K., & Mathur, S. (1998). The influence of affect on social-information processing. *Journal of Learning Disabilities, 31*(5), 418–426.

Buday, E. M. (1995). The effects of signed and spoken words taught with music on sign and speech limitation by children with autism. *Journal of Music Therapy, 32*(3), 189–202.

Burleson, S. J., Center, D. B., & Reeves, H. (1989). The effect of background music on task performance in psychotic children. *Journal of Music Therapy, 26*(4), 198–205.

Cassity, M. D. (1981). The influence of a socially valued skill on peer acceptance in a music therapy group. *Journal of Music Therapy, 18*(3), 148–154.

Chou, Y. (2008). *The effect of music therapy and peer-mediated interventions on social-communicative responses of children with autism spectrum disorders.* Unpublished master's thesis, University of Kansas.

Claussen, D. W., & Thaut, M. H. (1997). Music as a mnemonic device for children with learning disabilities. *Canadian Journal of Music Therapy, 5,* 55–66.

Copans-Astrand, D. (2000). *The effect of rhythm-based Orff-Schulwerk music therapy on the reading skills of students in varying exceptionalities classes.* Unpublished master's thesis, Florida State University, Tallahassee.

Cripe, F. F. (1986). Rock music as therapy for children with attention deficit disorder: An exploratory study. *Journal of Music Therapy, 23*(1), 30–37.

D'Arcangelis, J. B. (1978). *Music therapy versus music education: The effect of two approaches on severely emotionally impaired children's musical growth and self esteem development.* Unpublished master's thesis, Western Michigan University, Kalamazoo.

Darrow, A. A., Colwell, C., & Kim, J. (2002). Research on mainstreaming: Implications for music therapists. In B. Wilson (Ed.), *Models of music therapy intervention in the school settings: From institutions to inclusion* (pp. 27–47). Silver Spring, MD: American Music Therapy Association.

Darrow, A. A., & Starmer, G. J. (1986). The effect of vocal training on the intonation and rate of hearing impaired children's speech: A pilot study. *Journal of Music Therapy, 23*(4), 194–201.

DeBedout, J. K., & Worden, M. C. (2006). Motivators for children with severe intellectual disabilities in the self-contained classroom: A movement analysis. *Journal of Music Therapy, 43*(2), 123–135.

de Mers, C. L. (2007). *Effects of music therapy on prosocial behavior of students with autism and developmental disabilities.* Unpublished master's thesis, University of Nevada, Las Vegas.

Dorow, L. G. (1975). Conditioning music and approval as new reinforcers for imitative behavior with the severely retarded. *Journal of Music Therapy, 12*(1), 30–39.

Dorow, L. G. (1976). Televised music lessons as educational reinforcement for correct mathematical responses with the educable mentally retarded. *Journal of Music Therapy, 13*(2), 77–86.

Edgerton, C. L. (1994). The effect of improvisational music therapy on the communicative behaviors of autistic children. *Journal of Music Therapy, 31*(1), 31–62.

Eidson, C. E., Jr. (1989). The effect of behavioral music therapy on the generalization of interpersonal skills from sessions to the classroom by emotionally handicapped middle school students. *Journal of Music Therapy, 26*(4), 206–221.

Gfeller, K. C. (1983). Musical mnemonics as an aid to retention with normal and learning disabled students. *Journal of Music Therapy, 20*(4), 179–189.

Glass, G. V., McGaw, B., & Smith, M. L. (1981). *Meta-analysis in social research.* Beverly Hills, CA: Sage.

Greenwald, A. M. (1978). The effectiveness of distorted music versus interrupted music to decrease self-stimulating behavior in profoundly retarded adolescents. *Journal of Music Therapy, 15*(2), 58–66.

Gregoire, M. (1984). Music as a prior condition to task performance. *Journal of Music Therapy, 21*(3), 133–145.

Haines, J. H. (1989). The effects of music therapy on the self-esteem of emotionally-disturbed adolescents. *Music Therapy, 8*(1), 78–91.

Hairston, M. J. P. (1990). Analysis of responses of mentally retarded autistic and mentally retarded nonautistic children to art therapy and music therapy. *Journal of Music Therapy, 27*(3), 137–150.

Harding, C., & Ballard, K. D. (1982). The effectiveness of music as stimulus and a contingent reward in promoting the spontaneous speech of three physically-handicapped children. *Journal of Music Therapy, 19*(2), 86–101.

Holloway, M. S. (1980). A comparison of passive and active music reinforcement to increase preacademic and motor skills in severely retarded children and adolescents. *Journal of Music Therapy, 17*(2), 58–69.

Hoskins, C. (1988). Use of music to increase verbal response and improve expressive language abilities of preschool language delayed children. *Journal of Music Therapy, 25*(2), 73–84.

Jellison, J. A. (2000). *A content analysis of music research with disabled children and youth* (1975–1999): Applications in special education. In *Effectiveness of music therapy procedures: Documentation of research and clinical practice* (3rd ed., pp. 199–264). Silver Spring, MD: American Music Therapy Association.

Jellison, J. A., Brooks, B., & Huck, A. M. (1984). Structuring small groups and music reinforcement to facilitate positive interactions and acceptance of severely handicapped students in the regular music classroom. *Journal of Research in Music Education, 32*(4), 243–264.

Karper, W. B. (1979). Effects of music on learning a motor skill by handicapped and non-handicapped boys. *Perceptual & Motor Skills, 49*(3), 734.

Katagiri, J. (2009). The effect of background music and song texts on the emotional understanding of children with autism. *Journal of Music Therapy, 46*(1), 15–31.

Kennedy, R., & Scott, A. (2005). A pilot study: The effects of music therapy interventions on middle school students' ESL skills. *Journal of Music Therapy, 42*(4), 244–261.

Lim, H. A. (2007). *The effect of "developmental speech-language training through music" on speech production in children with autism spectrum disorders.* Unpublished doctoral dissertation, University of Miami.

Madsen, C. K., Smith, D. S., & Feeman, C. C. (1988). The use of music in cross-age tutoring with special education students. *Journal of Music Therapy, 25*(3), 135–144.

McCarty, B. C., McElfresh, C. T., Rice, S. V., & Wilson, S. J. (1978). The effect of contingent background music on inappropriate bus behavior. *Journal of Music Therapy, 15*(3), 150–156.

Meyers, M. L. (1973). *Teaching speech to autistic children through a program of specific music therapy.* Unpublished master's thesis, Newark State College.

Michel, D. M., Parker, P., Giokas, D., & Werner, J. (1982). Music therapy and remedial reading: Six studies testing specialized hemispheric processing. *Journal of Music Therapy, 19*(4), 219–229.

Miller, D. M. (1977). Effects of music-listening contingencies on arithmetic performance and music preference of EMR children. *American Journal of Mental Deficiency, 81*(4), 371–378.

Montello, L. M., & Coons, E. E. (1998). Effects of active versus passive group music therapy on preadolescents with emotional, learning, and behavioral disorders. *Journal of Music Therapy, 35*(1), 49–67.

Murphy, R., Doughty, N., & Nunes, D. (1979). Multielement designs: An alternative to reversal and multiple baseline evaluation strategies. *Mental Retardation, 17*(1), 23–27.

Myers, E. G. (1979). The effect of music on retention in a paired-associate task with EMR children. *Journal of Music Therapy, 16*(4), 190–198.

National Dissemination Center for Children with Disabilities. (2009). *Categories of disability under IDEA law.* Retrieved November 2, 2009, from http://www.nichcy.org/Disabilities/Categories/Pages/Default.aspx

Register, D. (2001). The effects of an early intervention music curriculum on prereading/writing. *Journal of Music Therapy, 38*(3), 239–248.

Register, D., Darrow, A. A., Standley, J., & Swedberg, O. (2007). The use of music to enhance reading skills of second grade students and students with reading disabilities. *Journal of Music Therapy, 44*(1), 23–37.

Reitman, M. R. (2005). *Effectiveness of music therapy interventions on joint attention in children diagnosed with autism: A pilot study.* Unpublished doctoral dissertation, Carlos Albizu University.

Rickson, D. J. (2006). Instructional and improvisational models of music therapy with adolescents who have attention deficit hyperactivity disorder (ADHD): A comparison of the effects of motor impulsivity. *Journal of Music Therapy, 43*(1), 39–62.

Rickson, D. J., & Watkins, W. G. (2003). Music therapy to promote prosocial behaviors in aggressive adolescent boys—A pilot study. *Journal of Music Therapy, 40*(4), 283–301.

Robb, S. L. (2003). Music interventions and group participation skills of preschoolers with visual impairments: Raising questions about music, arousal, and attention. *Journal of Music Therapy, 40*(4), 266–282.

Rogers-Wallgren, J. L., French, R., & Ben-Ezra, V. (1992). Use of reinforcement to increase independence in physical fitness performance of profoundly mentally retarded youth. *Perceptual and Motor Skills, 75*(3), 975–982.

Roskam, K. (1979). Music therapy as an aid for increasing auditory awareness and improving reading skill. *Journal of Music Therapy, 16*(1), 31–42.

Ross, S. Y. (1997). *Effects of singing on speech patterns of children with expressive language delays.* Unpublished master's thesis, Texas Woman's University, Denton.

Rowley, T. (2006). *The effect of music therapy as a behavior intervention for preschoolers in a Head Start program.* Unpublished doctoral dissertation, Ball State University, Muncie, IN.

Schmidt, D. C., Franklin, R., & Edwards, J. S. (1976). Reinforcement of autistic children's responses to music. *Psychological Reports, 39*(2), 571–577.

Shehan, P. K. (1981). A comparison of mediation strategies in paired associate learning for children with learning disabilities. *Journal of Music Therapy, 18*(3), 120–127.

Soraci, S., Jr., Deckner, C. W., McDaniel, C., & Blanton, R. L. (1982). The relationship between rate of rhythmicity and the stereotypic behaviors of abnormal children. *Journal of Music Therapy, 19*(1), 46–54.

Spencer, S. L. (1988). The efficiency of instrumental and movement activities in developing mentally retarded adolescents' ability to follow directions. *Journal of Music Therapy, 25*(1), 44–50.

Spudic, T. J., & Somervill, J. W. (1978). The effects of musical stimulation on distractibility and activity level among retarded subjects. *Education & Training of the Mentally Retarded, 13*(4), 362–366.

Standley, J. M. (1986). Music research in medical/dental treatment: Meta-analysis and clinical applications. *Journal of Music Therapy, 23*(2), 56–122.

Standley, J. M. (1996). A meta-analysis of the effects of music as reinforcement for education/therapy objectives. *Journal of Research in Music Education, 44*(2), 105–133.

Staum, M. J. (1983). Music and rhythmic stimuli in the rehabilitation of gait disorders. *Journal of Music Therapy, 20*(2), 69–87.

Sussman, J. E. (2009). The effect of music on peer awareness in preschool age children with developmental disabilities. *Journal of Music Therapy, 46*(1), 53–68.

Thaut, M. H. (1985). The use of auditory rhythm and rhythmic speech to aid temporal muscular control in children with gross motor dysfunction. *Journal of Music Therapy, 22*(3), 108–128.

Weber, R. P. (1990). *Basic content analysis* (2nd ed.) Newbury Park, CA: Sage.

Webster's New Millennium™ Dictionary of English. (2008). Preview Edition (v 0.9.7). Lexico.

Windwer, C. M. (1981). An ascending music stimulus program and hyperactive children. *Journal of Research in Music Education, 29*(3), 173–181.

Wolfe, D. E. (1980). The effect of automated interrupted music on head posturing of cerebral palsied individuals. *Journal of Music Therapy, 17*(4), 184–206.

Wolfe, D. E. (1982). The effect of interrupted and continuous music on bodily movement and task performance of third grade students. *Journal of Music Therapy, 19*(2), 74–85.

Wolfe, D. E., & Hom, C. (1993). Use of melodies as structural prompts for learning and retention of sequential verbal information by preschool students. *Journal of Music Therapy, 30*(2), 100–118.

Yarbrough, C. (1984). A content analysis of the Journal of Research in Music Education, 1953–1983. *Journal of Research in Music Education, 32*(4), 213–222.

Chapter 15

Including Students with Disabilities in Beginning Band[1]

CHAPTER OVERVIEW

Over 6 million students with disabilities receive services under IDEA each year in the U.S (Data Accountability Center, 2007). This number accounts only for students with disabilities who are eligible under IDEA and does not account for the thousands of students each year who have disabilities and qualify for accommodations under Section 504 of the Rehabilitation Act. Music educators who teach performing music areas, such as beginning band, will most likely have students with many of these disabilities in their classes. Unfortunately, most band directors receive very little training to prepare them to work effectively with these students.

This chapter provides information about some of the common characteristics found within the most prevalent disabilities among school-aged children. Based around these characteristics, instructional strategies and adaptations are provided to assist band directors in their work with students with disabilities. Examples are provided for adaptations specific to brass instruments, and these adaptations can be generalized to other band instruments.

This chapter includes information on the following topics:
- ♦ Students with disabilities in band: Common limitations
- ♦ Beginning band curricular and instructional issues
- ♦ Instructional strategies to support students' success

Background

As stated by the Music Teachers National Association (MTNA), "competent music teachers have knowledge and understanding of students' physical, social, and cognitive growth and past musical experiences. They assimilate this knowledge to

---

[1] Guest Contributing Author, Kristin Webster, MA, MT-BC

develop a course of study and to prepare instruction that meets the needs of each student while cultivating positive and productive relationships" (MTNA, 2010). In 2000, Colwell and Thompson surveyed 171 universities to examine the special education courses offered to undergraduate music education majors. The researchers found that approximately a quarter of the schools surveyed did not offer any special education course that could be taken by music education majors. Of the schools that did offer courses on special education, 86% required music education majors to take at least one course in special education. This means that many music educators did not have opportunities during their education to take even a general course on the needs of students with disabilities. Results also indicated that the schools that offered a music therapy program were more likely to offer special education courses specific to the music classroom (Colwell & Thompson, 2000). Therefore, those universities without music-specific special education courses available to their students do not offer courses tailored to discuss strategies for working with students with special needs in a band setting. As a result, many band directors have limited understanding of the specific needs of students with disabilities.

Over two decades ago, researchers found that educational preparation and instructional support for mainstreaming were limited in regards to coursework pertinent to mainstreamed students, the level of participation in placement procedures, and in-service educational support (Gfeller, Darrow, & Hedden, 1990). A more recent study conducted indicated that band directors continue to receive little information on placement procedures and few participate in IEP meetings. In fact, in those instances where information was provided in advance regarding a team meeting, only 58% of the band directors surveyed participated in the meetings due to lack of understanding of information or inability to make arrangements to schedule in order to attend (Scott, 2007).

As a result of limited coursework related to students with disabilities and inclusion band, there is a strong need for information regarding the types of disabilities that one might encounter, and ways in which one can best prepare the classroom, materials, and instructional strategies to meet the needs of these students. Much of the current research regarding these issues is limited to suggestions based on an individual teacher's experiences or case studies. This information is helpful in some circumstances, but there continues to be a need for more information on adaptations and modifications in a band setting. Band directors have expressed concerns regarding support (from teachers, paraprofessionals, and parents), instructional methods presented in band method books, and environmental and behavioral challenges within the classroom. Since band is a performance area, some band directors may be concerned that including students with disabilities may compromise the instruction and aesthetic experiences of other students in the band. With proper training and experience, band directors can develop strategies to support the specific needs of students with disabilities while also making band a successful experience for everyone.

Students with Disabilities in Band: Common Limitations

Prevalent Disorders and Common Characteristics

It is possible that a student with any of the 13 diagnoses listed in IDEA could participate in beginning band. The previous chapters in part two of this book describe the primary characteristics of students with the most prevalent disabilities that one might find in schools. In addition, each chapter highlights possible adaptations for successful inclusion in music classes. These adaptations may be useful in general music classes as well as performing music classes such as band and choir. As stated in Chapter 1, some of the most prevalent disabilities found in schools are specific learning disabilities (LD), speech and language disorders (SLD), mental retardation (MR), and emotional disturbance (EBD). According to experts in the field, the most prevalent disorders found specifically within band settings are consistent with those previously mentioned, with the addition of autism spectrum disorder (ASD) and attention deficit hyperactivity disorder (ADHD).

It is often the case that band directors are not provided with information regarding diagnosis or treatment plans for students with disabilities enrolled in band. At a minimum, all music educators should have basic information about the various disabilities. Each disability category presents with primary characteristics that are typically observed in students with that diagnosis. Not all students with the same diagnosis have the exact same needs or abilities, and there is overlap of students' needs and abilities between diagnosis categories. Some of the areas of limitation can be seen in students without disabilities, and instructional adaptations may be helpful for them as well.

Rather than thinking in terms of disability category alone, the tables below present areas of limitations that students with various disabilities might manifest related to cognitive, language and communication, social/emotional, and physical functioning in band. This information can assist the band director in indentifying some of the potential strengths and limitations of his or her students. These lists are not exhaustive, nor should they be interpreted as implying that every individual with one of the specified disabilities will display all of the characteristics listed. Instead, they are a compilation of characteristics often displayed by individuals with the specified disabilities. It is also important to note that typically developing students may exhibit any of the difficulties listed below, but their limitations are likely to be less pervasive. When thinking about disability characteristics, those related to a disability are usually different from typical development in terms of intensity, frequency, and duration. For example, a typically developing student might have trouble attending to the band director on any given day, but a student with ADHD might always have trouble focusing on the teacher and need frequent reminders about behaviors in band.

The skills that may be important for students to successfully participate in band have been separated into cognitive skills (ability to perceive, process, and comprehend information), language and communication skills, social or behavioral skills, and physical skills. The checks within the charts indicate problems associated with specific diagnoses. These were determined through review of diagnostic criteria from a variety of published sources (all of which are cited at the end of each section).

Students with Cognitive Limitations

Among the disabilities previously mentioned, there are several characteristics that may inhibit a student's ability to comprehend and essentially learn how to read music or play an instrument. A student with a learning disability, for example, may present with challenges specific to reading and math, short- or long-term memory, generalization, processing or comprehension, and problem solving. Students with ADHD may exhibit difficulties with following directions, decision making, or following through on tasks or instructions; become easily distracted; display a lack of motivation; and have difficulty with problem solving. An individual with an intellectual disability may exhibit short- or long-term memory deficits; difficulty with reading or math, generalization, decision making, following directions, or problem solving; as well as a lack of motivation. Individuals with ASD might display cognitive deficits similar to individuals with intellectual disabilities. They might also have decreased verbal comprehension and difficulty following through with instructions. On the other hand, some students with Asperger's syndrome (an ASD diagnosis) have high intelligence. Students with emotional or behavior disorders could also experience difficulty following through with instructions and could be easily distracted, as well as appear irresponsible and lose track of personal belongings (such as their instrument or music). Students with any of these disabilities may also experience difficulty sustaining attention (Adamek & Darrow, 2005; American Psychiatric Association, 2000; Davis, Gfeller, & Thaut, 2009; Hallahan, Kauffman, & Pullen, 2009; Turnbull, Turnbull, & Wehmeyer, 2010). Table 15.1 displays the most common characteristics found across all of the five of the most prevalent disorders.

Table 15.1 Cognitive Limitations by Disability Category

Cognitive Skills Limitations	LD	ADHD	MR	ASD	EBD
Reading and Math	X		X		
Short-Term Memory	X	X	X		
Problem Solving	X	X	X		
Generalization	X		X	X	
Following Directions	X	X	X	X	X
Sustaining Attention	X	X	X	X	X
Motivation	X	X	X		X

Students with Language and Communication Limitations

Many students with disabilities have difficulties related to language and communication, and they may be limited in their ability to express themselves and to understand what others are saying to them (see Table 15.2) (Hallahan et al., 2009). There are two aspects of language that can hinder an individual's ability to communicate effectively: receptive language and expressive language. Receptive language involves decoding or understanding messages in communication, and expressive language refers to encoding or sending messages in communication. In a band setting, students may appear to have difficulty following directions, which could be due to a lack of understanding, or they may display outbursts or unusual behavior because they are unable to effectively communicate their wants or needs. Students with a learning disability, ASD, intellectual disability, and an emotional or behavior disorder may have difficulties with expressive or receptive language skills. Students with ASD may also have difficulty producing spontaneous, intelligible speech. Students with ADHD may have difficulty monitoring their speech, for example, speaking out of turn or raising their hand to ask a question (American Association on Intellectual and Developmental Disabilities [AAIDD], 2010; Adamek & Darrow, 2005; American Psychiatric Association, 2000; Davis et al., 2008).

Table 15.2 Language and Communication Limitations by Disability Category

Language and Communication Limitations	LD	ADHD	MR	ASD	EBD
Spontaneous Speech				X	
Monitoring Speech		X		X	
Using Language Correctly				X	
Receptive Language Skills— Understanding and Following Directions	X		X	X	
Expressive Language Skills— Communicating Thoughts, Wants, or Needs	X		X	X	X

Students with Social and Behavioral Limitations

Band class can provide many opportunities for social interaction for students, and students with social and behavioral limitations might have problems that need to be addressed (see Table 15.3). Students may exhibit disruptive behaviors, such as difficulty remaining in one's seat, hyperactivity within the body or speech, and potentially physical aggression. Specifically, students with ADHD and EBD may have difficulty sitting still or remaining seated, as a result of hyperactivity and problems with focus of attention. Students with EBD may be physically aggressive at times. Students with intellectual disabilities may act out when frustrated, and they may have difficulty waiting their turn and building friendships with others. Individuals with learning disabilities may have difficulty understanding the perceptions of others or modeling other's behaviors, and they may become frustrated easily. Students with ASD have social skill deficits resulting in difficulty understanding the perceptions of others, building and maintaining relationships or friendships, waiting their turn, or maintaining eye contact, and they may be physically aggressive with peers or adults typically due to their inability to express wants and needs (Adamek & Darrow, 2005; American Psychiatric Association, 2000; Davis et al., 2008; Turnbull et al., 2010).

Table 15.3 Social/Behavioral Limitations by Disability Category

Social/Behavioral Limitations	LD	ADHD	MR	ASD	EBD
Understanding Social Cues	X		X	X	X
Hyperactive		X			X
Physically Aggressive				X	X
Staying in Seat/Sitting Still		X	X		X
Understanding Perceptions of Others	X	X	X	X	X
Building and Maintaining Friendship		X	X	X	X
Attending to the Director		X	X	X	X
Frustrates Easily	X	X	X	X	X

Students with Physical Functioning Limitations

Limitations in physical and motor functioning can have a big impact on a student's ability to hold and play an instrument (see Table 15.4). Fine motor skills, more specifically coordination and finger dexterity, can hinder a student's ability to push down valves or keys on an instrument. Gross motor skills, such as balance, may also be limited, resulting in difficulty picking up, holding, and potentially playing the instrument. Individuals with intellectual disabilities, ASD, LD, and ADHD may experience difficulties with these tasks. Students with ASD may also have sensory integration deficits, resulting in hyper- or hypo-responsive sensory perceptions specific to tactile touch or other sensory input, as well as restrictive, repetitive, or stereotyped patterns of behavior. Students with ADHD may experience difficulty controlling motor behavior. Individuals with EBD do not typically display physical limitations; however, a decrease in physical well-being as a result of depression or motivation is possible (Hallahan et al., 2009).

Table 15.4 Physical Limitations by Disability Category

Physical Limitations	LD	ADHD	MR	ASD	EBD
Fine Motor Skills	X		X	X	
Gross Motor Skills	X		X	X	
Coordination	X	X	X	X	
Balance			X	X	
Endurance			X		
Control of Motor Behavior		X			
Physical Well-Being			X		X
Hyper-Responsive or Hypo-Responsive to Touch				X	

Beginning Band Curricular and Instructional Issues

Beginning Band Curriculum

It is important to identify the curriculum and skills focused on in beginning band before identifying the areas in which adaptations or modifications can be made to assist students with disabilities. Many resources identify specific goal areas and specific music skills that are typically the focus of beginning band curricula (Colwell & Hewitt, 2011; Duke & Byo, 2003; Music Educators National Conference (MENC), 1996; Ramsey, 2001). Although the sequence and approach may differ across texts, the primary skills for teaching music through performance in beginning band include:

- Tone quality
  - » Posture, breath support, embouchure, tone production
- Technical training
  - » Holding the instrument, ear training and listening skills, slurring, articulation, fingerings, note reading, signs and symbols of music, counting rhythms, maintain a steady pulse, vibrato, and practicing
- Music-making skills
  - » Scales, arpeggios, slurs, phrasing, tuning the instrument, playing alone and in small and large ensembles
- Experiencing music and making discriminating choices in music
  - » Listening and describing music, aural discriminations of music styles, form, improvisation, and evaluation
- Instilling values, knowledge, and skills
  - » Music history (instruments, instrumentation, culture, the arts)

Band method books also include specific information related to learning the instrument, the basics of technical training, and terms and skills involved in reading music. As an example, Table 15.5 delineates some of the curricular areas and skills covered in beginning band, specific to brass instruments. The beginning band curriculum requires that a student utilize a combination of cognitive, communication, social/emotional, and physical skills in order for the student to realize success in band.

Table 15.5 Elements of Beginning Band Curriculum

Learning the Instrument		
• Parts of the instrument • Inserting the mouthpiece • Assembly • Lubricating the hand slide and tuning slide	• Oiling the rotary valve • Caring for the valves and valve casings • Applying oil to valves • Caring for slides	• Applying slide grease • Cleaning water keys • Cleaning the mouthpiece • Caring for the exterior of the instrument • Storing the instrument
Basics of Technical Training		

	• Posture
	• Breathing and airstream
	  - Producing the essential tone
	  - Embouchure
	  - Buzzing
	• Mouthpiece placement
	• Reading fingering/slide chart
	• Understanding positions	

Reading Music		

• Note names
  - Musical alphabet
  - Spaces-Lines
• Staff
• Key signature
• Flat/Sharp/Natural
• Time signatures: 4/4, 3/4, 2/4
• Bar lines
• Double bar
• Measure
• Breath mark
	• Rhythm
	  - Whole note/rest, half note/ rest, quarter note/rest, eighth note/ rest, dotted notes
	• Form
	  - Round
	• Common time
	• Cut time
	• Ledger lines
	• Repeat sign
	• Fermata
		• Tie
		• Phrase
		• Solo/soli/tutti
		• Slurs
		• Pick-up notes
		• First and second endings
		• Harmony
		• Dynamics
		• Tempo markings
		• Accent

Instrument Selection

There are many things to consider when helping students select an instrument. No matter what the ability level, there will always be instruments that are more suitable or appropriate for each student due to aspects such as instrument size, or embouchure and breath support required to play the instrument. Duke and Byo (2003) believe that some instruments, specifically flute, clarinet, alto saxophone, trumpet, trombone, and euphonium and baritone, are the most appropriate starting instruments for beginning band students. They recommend excluding French horn, tuba, double reed instruments, and percussion for at least the first year, due to the complexity or sheer size of these instruments. Some other considerations that should be made when assisting a student in choosing an instrument include caring for the instrument, properly holding the instrument, and producing a quality sound on the instrument. While these issues are important for all students, the following section provides ideas to support the needs of students with disabilities who may encounter additional challenges.

Caring for the Instrument

Caring for an instrument involves cleaning (both the exterior and interior), oiling, and proper storage. Students who have difficulties with problem solving, following directions, asking for help when needed, motivation to complete difficult tasks, frustration, fine and gross motor skills, or coordination may have additional challenges when caring for their instruments. For these students, one suggestion may be to select instruments that require less regular cleaning. For example, brass instruments that require more oiling and valve care do not require the daily interior and exterior cleaning that woodwind instruments do in order to avoid build-up or rust. Band directors may also want to provide students with supplemental handouts or worksheets on the steps that should be completed after practicing each day, or they may train paraprofessionals and parents in the importance in instrument care so they can assist students in proper instrument care. Some students may benefit from a reinforcement contract that specifies the tasks involved in cleaning the instrument, with a scheduled reward for completion of the tasks.

Posture, Playing, and Quality of Sound

In order to begin to learn the instrument, students need to be able to hold the instrument properly to create a quality sound. Students' behavior and physical issues, such as remaining seated, fine and gross motor skills, coordination, balance, endurance, and control over physical movements should all be considered. Sometimes the instrument itself can provide the structure needed to help the student focus attention and remain seated. For example, for a student who experiences difficulty sitting still or remaining seated, a sousaphone with a sousaphone stand could be helpful. The size and nature of the instrument and stand may keep students focused and in one place for an extended period of time, making it harder for easily distracted students to get up and move around, as well as keeping their hands busy to prevent them from distracting students around them (McCord, 2006). If a student has use of only one hand or if fine motor skills are impaired in one or both hands, a brass instrument may be a better choice over a woodwind instrument. Brass instruments require only one hand to push the valves or move the slide, whereas woodwinds require both hands (Mixon, 2005). It has also been suggested that valved brass instruments such as the trumpet, baritone, valved trombones, and tubas are the most appropriate choices for students with intellectual disabilities, because they have fewer fingerings to learn and remember (Zdzinski, 2001). For those students with physical needs, an instrument stand could be purchased to accommodate for holding the instrument with the opposite hand. An instrument stand may be a good option for students with difficulty controlling their motor movements, or with challenges with muscle strength or coordination. See the section on "Additional Resources for Band Directors" at the end of this chapter for more information on instrument stands and other useful resources.

Another thing to keep in mind when selecting an instrument is the skill required to produce a good sound on the instrument. Posture, breath support, and oral-muscular abilities are critical aspects of producing good tone quality on a wind instrument. Using brass instruments as an example, the size of a trumpet or euphonium mouthpiece compared to a French horn or tuba mouthpiece is quite different. Some instruments take more breath support than others, and some instruments may require more oral-muscle control than others. As previously mentioned, it might be most appropriate to introduce students to the trumpet, trombone, or euphonium first, and then switch to a French horn or tuba once they have learned how to form the correct embouchure needed to play or have developed a more highly trained ear (Duke & Byo, 2003).

Instructional Strategies to Support Students' Success

For a variety of reasons, many band directors do not feel equipped to include students with disabilities into the band. Some band directors may feel that every student should be able to perform at a certain level of difficulty in order to be in their band. It is no secret that there is a high level of competiveness and pride that many directors feel they must uphold, and by writing in fingerings or simplifying the rhythm on a student's parts, directors may feel as though they are lowering their standards. Although some band directors may have concerns about including students with disabilities in the band, they cannot exclude students from their classrooms on the basis of disability. On the other hand, if a select ensemble requires an audition and a specific music skill level to participate, the student with disabilities must have the opportunity to audition, but it is not mandated that the student be included if he or she does not meet the playing requirements. Band directors who utilize some of the adaptations provided below may feel more confident when working with students who have a variety of learning needs, and they may be more accepting of these students' participation in band.

Universal Design for Learning

Band directors may become overwhelmed when considering the variety of students' limitations listed in the previous tables. It can be intimidating to think about all the time and effort that must be put forth in order to meet the needs of a student with disabilities in a band setting. However, as discussed in the section on Universal Design for Learning in Chapter 4, efforts taken to make the classroom environment and instructional method and materials more accessible for students with disabilities can ultimately create a more accessible learning experience for all students in the classroom. Band directors might consider regularly utilizing principles of UDL, such as varying the ways that information is delivered to students as well as varying how students can respond to demonstrate understanding. This approach may ultimately foster increased student engagement throughout the band with all students.

Adaptations Specific to Students' Cognitive Limitations

The most common characteristics previously mentioned among students with LD, ADHD, ASD, MR, and EBD include difficulties with:
- Reading and math
- Problem solving
- Generalization
- Short-term memory
- Following directions
- Sustaining attention
- Motivation

General Instructional Strategies

Instructional strategies can be designed using UDL principles, or they can be created specifically for a student's special needs. Suggestions specific to cognitive limitations that may be applied prior to utilizing more specific adaptations are provided below.

- Reading and math difficulties:
  » Provide a hands-on approach, such as tapping the rhythm on the student's hand/shoulder/leg.
  » Have the entire class sing, chant, or clap the rhythm before playing it on their instruments.
- Difficulty following directions:
  » Provide the entire class with a written form of the daily rehearsal schedule, including page or exercise numbers.
  » Set clear expectations by posting classroom "rules" in various locations around the room, as well as in the students' folder.
- Short-term memory difficulties:
  » Create a form to write assignments on, or write directly in students' assignment book, as well as verbally communicate homework assignments with the student.
  » Utilize the school's website for posting assignments, if possible.

» Provide students with a fingering or slide chart to keep on their stand.

» Write in fingerings, or have an aide work with students on writing in their fingerings.

» Provide students with small chart of note names, note values, key signatures, etc.

- Problem solving:

» Investigate signs or behaviors and common phrases students often use if they are frustrated or upset in an attempt to identify when students may need help.

Of the strategies for instruction described in Chapter 4, adaptations to participation, input, and difficulty may all be appropriate to support students' ability to learn to read music and play an instrument. Sample adaptations specific to students' cognitive limitations are listed below.

Participation

For individuals with difficulties in reading or math, partial participation may be a good option, in that it would allow a student to still be involved in playing with the group, while doing so at a lesser degree of difficulty. Band directors can modify the student's part, such as changing eighth-note rhythms to quarter- or half-note rhythms, while still finding ways to work with that student on areas of difficulty. Or a student might be able to learn only some of the songs on the concert, so he or she would participate only in the rehearsal and performance of those songs.

Input

Students may experience difficulty generalizing information from their other classes into the band room. They might have difficulty following classroom rules, or they might have difficulty following directions if the expectations have not been made clear. Since some students will have problems processing information, the band director might use a multimodal approach when presenting information. For students who are visual learners, posting the classroom rules in numerous locations around the room or providing them with a hard copy on their stand may be helpful. For auditory learners, band directors can present the rules in a simple and fun song that the entire class could sing together. For individuals with difficulties in math or reading skills, a more handson approach might be beneficial. A band director could have the class march around the room, or even clap their hands or pat their knees to internalize and learn a new rhythm. Duke and Byo (2003) suggest directors first sing rhythms (using "ta" or "da"), then have the students imitate the beat while conducting with their hands. By using a simple recurring pulse (conducting patterns are not necessary), students have a visual representation of the rhythm to help them internalize the rhythm and the beat. Once students have mastered singing through an exercise while conducting, directors can have students practice their fingerings while still singing, finally playing the rhythm on their instruments once they have mastered the rhythm of the exercise.

For individuals with ADHD, sustaining attention is often a challenge. A simple adaptation can be made to decrease distractions and increase the level of attention by covering up or deleting pictures or images on the page if they do not serve an educational purpose. The use of highlighters to identify new information or sharps, flats, or fingerings can also be helpful. One could also use bold or colored print on specific terminology or within notation. It is important to use color or a color-coding system in a structured, consistent, and purposeful manner (de l'Etoile, 2005). Lastly, for individuals with short-term memory deficits, mnemonic devices can be useful for recalling information. A simple example of this is teaching the names of the spaced notes of the treble clef as FACE and the names of the lined notes by memorizing the phrase Every Good Boy Does Fine (de l'Etoile, 2005). Many of these suggestions can be developed as UDL approaches for use by the entire class, or they may be individualized for the needs of a specific student.

Difficulty

There are multiple ways in which adapting the skill level, the type of problem, or the rules on how a student may approach a task can be utilized in a band setting to address cognitive limitations. Students with limited problem-solving skills, lack of motivation, and low frustration tolerance may give up easily on tasks that are too difficult. To address this issue, band directors might decrease the amount of homework or questions on a quiz or test in a manner that best reflects each individual's level of functioning. Or, they might adapt the music by decreasing the complexity of the rhythms or melodic lines.

> Kate, a young girl with an intellectual disability, plays the euphonium in her 5th grade band. Kate thoroughly enjoys being in band; however, she has some limitations in short-term memory and is struggling to keep up with learning new, more challenging rhythmic patterns. In working on some of the difficulties Kate is experiencing in remembering note names and fingerings, Kate's director assists her in developing a few mnemonic devices to help her recall this information. By working on it together and allowing Kate to come up with her own ideas, the strategies become more personalized and thus easier for her to remember. Kate's director also works with her after class on learning and counting more difficult rhythmic patterns, while also adapting her part to play in class so that she may participate with success at the degree most appropriate for her current level of development.

Adaptations Specific to Students' Language and Communication Limitations

Students with language and communication limitations face many challenges in the band when interpreting what others are saying to them or when they try to express themselves. Limitations to be focused on within this section include:

- Spontaneous speech
- Monitoring speech
- Using language correctly
- Receptive language skills
- Expressive language skills

General Instructional Strategies

The following list provides ideas for instructional strategies that a band director might utilize to support students' language and communication needs, prior to making more specified adaptations with one individual student in mind.

- Difficulty monitoring speech:
  » Implement a behavior plan for the entire class in which students earn reinforcements for raising their hand to ask/answer questions.
- Receptive communication difficulties:
  » Provide directions and assignments to students in more than one form of communication (multimodal approach), such as auditory (speaking), visual (written form of directions), and gestural (physically showing student the fingering or slide position).
- Expressive communication difficulties:
  » Communicate with other teachers or paraprofessionals who interact with the student on a daily basis to become familiar with phrases or terminology the student commonly uses and understands. Band directors may also gain access to visual aids that the student uses to communicate
  » Before or after class, ask students how they are doing or if they need help with anything, rather than expecting them to ask their question during class, in front of their peer group.

Students with language and communication limitations will have difficulty in the areas of receiving information and expressing themselves. Adaptations related to input, peer support, and output may be needed to support the students' needs.

Input

As mentioned in the previous section, presenting information to students through a number of different forms of communication may be helpful for students with language comprehension deficits. Duke and Byo (2003) suggest teaching beginner band students through rote, taking away the music (which can be distracting if the goal at hand is to teach correct embouchure), and demonstrating for students who then watch, listen, and echo back what was heard. Another way to present information such as note names or rhythms to students is to create flash cards with pitch and rhythm patterns extracted from exercises written on them to reinforce music reading skills (Zdzinski, 2001). Band directors could also work with students on writing in fingerings, slide positions, or note names above notes. The process of writing them in together, rather than just doing it for the student, can be good practice, and many students experience success and less frustration from having that extra information in front of them. For higher functioning students, one could simply provide students with a fingering chart that can be kept on their stand to use as a reference (McCord, 2006). Below is an example of another modification that can be made to the delivery of instructions for students with receptive language limitations.

> *Matthew is a young man with a learning disability, who has communication deficits specific to receptive language skills. Matthew's band director, Mr. Seidel, has begun to notice that he often plays the wrong exercise numbers during warm-ups or plays from the wrong page throughout rehearsal. In speaking with Matthew's special education teacher, Mr. Seidel learns that Matthew often needs directions provided to him in writing and that check lists have been helpful in keeping him on-task. Mr. Seidel begins typing up a schedule for Matthew for each rehearsal, as well as writing it on the board for the entire class. Once an exercise or activity is finished, Matthew crosses off that item on his list. Mr. Seidel also assigns one of the students seated next to Matthew to work with him on checking his schedule, getting out his materials, and crossing off each item throughout the rehearsal.*

Peer Support

Music educators should identify strong students in their class who will possibly be good friends for a special student who may need help. Finding those students who can act as a buddy to a student with a disability will not only benefit the child with special needs, but will acknowledge the individual talents of the typically developing child as well. It is important to foster those relationships, especially in a band where students are working together as a team to create music (Hammel, 2004).

Output

Band directors may need to adapt how students can respond to instruction. If a student has a limited vocabulary or lack of spontaneous speech, for example, this might involve the use of word cards, simple sign language, or, in some cases, the use of communication devices in order to ask or answer questions. Band directors could also utilize the musical skills they have at their disposal as a mode of communication (for example, call-and-response rhythmic patterns or melody lines). In order to demonstrate their knowledge, students could play a rhythm or scale on their instrument rather than notating it for a quiz or test.

Adaptations Specific to Students' Social and Behavioral Limitations

There are many social and behavior limitations associated with these prevalent disabilities. Some of the most commonly exhibited limitations are listed below. Since students work together to create music, band is a naturally social environment where social skills are utilized every day.

- Understanding social cues
- Hyperactive
- Physically aggressive
- Remaining seated
- Understanding the perceptions of others
- Building and maintaining friendships
- Attending to the director
- Easily frustrated

General Instructional Strategies

Band directors deal with social and behavioral issues in band every day since all student need redirection, positive reinforcement, and reminders some of the time. The strategies listed below can be useful with students who display behavioral or social problems in band.

- Difficulty sustaining attention or displaying hyperactivity:
  - » Allow for partial participation (give students a break from class or allow them to participate for only half of the class period).
  - » Assign other musical tasks for students to do if they need a break (fingerings or slide position flash cards, computer programs to work on theory, etc.).
  - » Prepare multiple exercises and have the entire group move on to something different.
- Difficulty remaining seated:
  - » Allow students to get up and move around at a specific time (for example, after 15 minutes of actively participating).
  - » Implement a behavioral plan in which students receive some form of positive reinforcement for remaining seated for a specified amount of time.
  - » Experiment with moving around sections of the band. Students will get a different visual and auditory vantage point in relation to other sections and to the director. Who says percussion always need to be in the back or flutes always have to be in the front?
- Lack of motivation
  - » Provide positive reinforcement of some form for students upon completion of assignments or practicing.

»   Modify the number of hours students are expected to practice each week.

•   Frustrates easily

»   Allow students more time to complete assignments or quizzes/tests, or provide additional support from peers when needed.

Provided below are more specific adaptations regarding participation, difficulty, and time strategies.

Participation

Partial participation could again be an appropriate option for students who experience difficulty remaining seated and staying on-task due to hyperactivity or other possible causes. If a student is able to remain on-task and focused for 30 of the 50 minutes of class, the band director could excuse the student from rehearsal to go to a practice room (possibly with a paraprofessional or peer buddy), use the computer to practice music theory, or return to the classroom to work fingerings or note name worksheets. The band director thus gives the student the opportunity to have a successful experience. It is important to note that when students are excused from rehearsal, they are encouraged to continue working on music skills, not to pass out papers or go back to the classroom and have free time. In certain cases, a 5-minute break may be all it takes for the student to regain focus and return to rehearsal.

Difficulty

Many beginning band students become frustrated at some point throughout the learning process. In an attempt to be proactive in identifying circumstances or behaviors that can result in feelings of frustration or aggression for the student, band directors can seek the advice of paraprofessionals and teachers to learn as much as possible about students and what techniques or phrases may help defuse the situation. Band directors might use a prearranged signal or word to notify the student when his or her behavior is inappropriate. This unobtrusive approach gives the student an opportunity to modify behavior and get back on track, often before other students in the class are aware of any problems (Hammel, 2004). In situations where students are unable to perform at the same level as their peers, band directors can make modifications or adaptations to music or assignments, which will reduce negative responses and contribute to a more successful experience.

Time

For many students with disabilities, the amount of time needed for comprehension or learning a new skill is longer than what is expected of a typically developing student. However, when given that extra time to think about what they are being asked before answering, or to finish an assignment or test, they may be fully capable of meeting expectations. This approach is especially useful when working with students who frustrate easily due to learning problems. Band directors may know the student well enough to understand how much time is needed for comprehension, or they may talk with the classroom teacher to arrange for additional time, which may be needed to help the student learn or develop a new skill.

> *Everett is a young boy with ADHD who recently joined the 5th grade band, wanting to play a brass instrument. The band director has been informed that Everett can usually remain on task for about 25 minutes, after which he often becomes distracted or disruptive to his peers, has difficulty remaining seated, and is easily agitated. In helping Everett select an instrument, the band director has suggested he try the tuba. She will have him start on the sousaphone, utilizing the sousaphone stand, which will limit his hyperactivity. The band director recognizes that after 30 minutes Everett can no longer remain on task and participate without distracting his peers. At this point, Everett goes to the practice room or back to his classroom to practice note names, rhythms, and fingerings on a computer or with a peer buddy.*

Adaptations Specific to Students' Physical Limitations

Certainly physical skills are important for playing instruments, and the selection of an appropriate instrument is a primary concern. Students with physical limitations who are learning to play an instrument may have problems in the following areas:

- Fine motor skills
- Gross motor skills
- Coordination
- Balance
- Endurance
- Control of motor behavior
- Hyper- and hypo-responsive to touch

Band directors need to make sure that their room is accessible for students who have mobility limitations, such as those who use a wheelchair. Risers and stairs can create barriers that need to be addressed. Schools must have accessibility options for students with physical disabilities, and the school administrator may need to assist in having the physical space in the band room modified. Other students with physical limitations may need more than modifications to the room. The following ideas and sample adaptations related to varying participation and varying difficulty levels can be utilized to support the students' success in band.

Participation

Physical limitations such as limited endurance may restrict a student's ability to participate in rehearsal for the entire length of class. This may also reduce the amount of practice time feasible for the student. Students with ASD who are hyper-responsive to touch or sound might not be able to participate for the full class period and may need to be excused to avoid overstimulation. They may also be unable to process loud sounds in band, which can result in unusual behavior, acting out, or other distress. Band directors need to be aware of variations in students' behavior and make the necessary adaptations in the interest of the student.

Difficulty

The level of difficulty within the music may need to be adapted or modified for students with fine or gross motor deficits. Fast rhythms or melodic lines with multiple notes typically require the arms, hands, fingers, and possibly tongue to move quickly, which may take longer for students with physical limitations to master, or it may not even be an appropriate expectation. For students with motor deficits or coordination and balance issues, having a stand may ease the difficulty in properly holding the instrument and thus assist them in playing more accurately.

> Rachel, a young girl with autism spectrum disorder, plays the trombone in her 5th grade band. Among other things, Rachel has physical limitations specific to coordination, balance, and fine and gross motor skills. Rachel originally wanted to play the clarinet; however, her band director suggested she could experience more success on the trombone, as moving the slide requires fewer fine motor skills than pushing down the keys on a clarinet. After a few weeks, Rachel's director noticed that she still was experiencing some difficulty holding the instrument properly and coordinating the slide. He discussed his concerns with her parents, who were more than willing to make the accommodations necessary for Rachel to continue playing in band. With their permission, Rachel's director ordered a trombone stand for her that would allow her to position the trombone at the appropriate height and angle, eliminating the coordination and balance issues she was previously experiencing. With the assistance of this stand, Rachel can now concentrate on learning slide positions, along with the rest of her trombone section.

Adaptations to Curriculum and Strategies within Method Books

Many of the current method books used in beginner band programs were not written with students with disabilities in mind. As a result, some of the ways in which the material is presented can make learning to read music even more challenging for these individuals. Below are some simple adaptations for method books, and the curriculum as a whole, specific to the characteristics, behaviors, and needs of students with the most prevalent disorders.

For individuals with limitations in cognitive functioning, skills such as learning to read music and count rhythms, memorizing and remembering fingerings or slide positions, and maintaining the motivation necessary to learn how to read music can be a challenge. There are many ways to adapt instructional materials like method books to help support the learning needs of students.

- *Write in rhythms, note names, or fingerings, or provide a chart that students can use when needed.* For some band directors, this may not seem like a good option because the student is not being forced to learn the material. However, one should keep in mind that it might not be developmentally appropriate to expect some students to memorize this information. By taking the time to write in the information, or assigning the student to write it with help from another person, the band director can potentially save time during rehearsal, reducing frustration for the student and allowing him or her to feel more independent and successful.

- *Provide supplemental materials to enhance the material in the method books.* Many of the method books present material at a fast pace, and the number of exercises provided to practice a specific rhythmic pattern may not provide enough repetition for students with disabilities. Band directors can utilize other resources, or develop simple exercises specific to that individual's needs, in order to help them master the skill.

- *Utilize individualized practice sheets or contracts to increase motivation.* This may help some students who are easily frustrated and lack the motivation necessary to learn to play an instrument and read music. At the beginning of the school year, the band director can write and sign a contract with the student in which the student agrees to practice every week. Then, depending upon the needs of the student, the band director and student could meet on a weekly, biweekly, or monthly basis to determine what the student should be practicing, how often, and for how long. There should be a place for the student's parent or caregiver to sign, as well as a place for the student to sign, acknowledging that he or she has completed the work. For some students, a form of reinforcement may be helpful in motivating them to practice their music. It is important to discuss this with students, selecting a reward that is, in fact, reinforcing to them. Depending on the students, this could be something they receive on a monthly or weekly basis. In addition, this method can also help the band director recognize where the students' strengths and weaknesses are over time and better assist the students through the learning process.

- *Eliminate distractions on the pages of the method books.* For students who have difficulty sustaining attention and become distracted easily, there may be aspects of the material itself that are distracting. For example, many method books include small pictures of animals or scenery, as well as decorated pages with multiple colors or fonts that serve no greater purpose than to make the page look interesting. A simple way to eliminate distractions such as these is to photocopy the page in black and white, covering up the pictures. Once a copy has been made, the band director could use colors or symbols in a purposeful way to help students remember the key signature or fingerings on the page by highlighting every sharp in yellow, every flat in green, and so on. Another way to eliminate distractions within the music is to cover everything on the page, leaving only the exercise or line currently being worked on visible to the student.

Many of these adaptations could easily be applied to an entire classroom, which could increase the likelihood of success not only for an individual with special needs in a band setting, but for all the students in band as well.

Collaboration

As discussed in previous chapters, it is extremely important for all music educators, and in this case band directors, to develop open lines of communication with teachers and parents in an attempt gather as much information as possible about a student with a disability enrolled in band. By gathering information on the student's strengths and weaknesses, as well as current instructional and behavioral approaches being used with each student, one can increase the likelihood of successful inclusion in a band setting. This process could be done through meetings or e-mail exchanges with the general or special education teachers, observation, or requesting and utilizing the student's IEP. In the case that a band director is not able to meet with other teachers or observe the student in another setting, a phone call meeting or e-mail exchange is still a good option. Collaboration with teachers, paraprofessionals, and parents will help the student to be more successful in band and at home when practicing. These individuals know the students well and they can help the student generalize information among the home, classroom, and band. Refer to the section on "Working with Other Teachers and Paraprofessionals" in Chapter 4 for strategies and suggestions when meeting with and working with other educators.

If the school or school district has a music therapist on staff, the band director can consult with him or her to discuss strategies that support the student's learning needs. The music therapist can offer information on the student or disability; tips or suggestions on how to gather additional information; and adaptations or modifications to the instruments, classroom environment, or instructional strategies and curriculum. In some cases, it may also be appropriate for the music therapist to accompany the student to band or to provide individual adapted lessons.

Once band directors have gathered information on the individuals with disabilities in their bands, they can move forward in making the accommodations necessary for those students to be successful. With the help of a music therapist or other educators in the building, they can begin to organize their classroom, adapt or modify the curriculum and expectations placed upon each student, assist the students with disabilities in choosing the most appropriate instrument, set expectations and become familiar and comfortable with behavior plans, and, if necessary, prepare the other students within the band as to what they can expect and ways they can help these students to be as successful as possible.

KEY POINTS FROM THE SECTION

Inclusion in a band setting:
- ◆ Music educators who teach performing music areas, such as beginning band, will most likely have students with many of these disabilities in their classes. Unfortunately, most band directors receive very little training to prepare them to work effectively with these students.
- ◆ The greatest concerns among band directors regarding the inclusion of students with disabilities in band include lack of resources available on this topic, support (from teachers, paraprofessionals, and parents), instructional methods presented in band method books, environmental and behavioral challenges within the classroom, and decreased instructional and aesthetic experiences of other students in the band.
- ◆ According to experts in the field, the most prevalent disorders in band include learning disabilities, attention deficit hyperactivity disorder, intellectual disabilities, autism spectrum disorder, and emotional and behavioral disorders.

Common characteristics:
- ◆ Among the most prevalent disorders, the following are identified as the most common characteristics likely to impact a student's level of success within a band setting:
  - » Cognitive limitations
  - » Language and communication limitations
  - » Social and behavioral limitations
  - » Physical limitations

Beginning band curriculum:
- ◆ Tone quality
  - » Posture, breath support, embouchure, tone production
- ◆ Technical training
  - » Holding the instrument, ear training and listening skills, slurring, articulation, fingerings, note reading, signs and symbols of music, counting rhythms, maintain a steady pulse, vibrato, and practicing

- ◆ Music-making skills
  - » Scales, arpeggios, slurs, phrasing, tuning the instrument, playing alone and in small and large ensembles
- ◆ Experiencing music and making discriminating choices in music
  - » Listening and describing music, aural discriminations of music styles, form, improvisation, and evaluation
- ◆ Instilling values, knowledge, and skills
  - » Music history (instruments, instrumentation, culture, the arts)

Selecting an instrument:

- ◆ Keep in mind students' strengths and weaknesses, as well as the challenges involved with each instrument (holding the instrument, posture, producing a quality sound)
- ◆ Specifics related to caring for an instrument

Adaptations:

- ◆ Considerations such as making materials and information more readily understood and accessible, the way students respond to and demonstrate an understanding of information, and the students' level of engagement can and should all be applied in a band setting when utilizing principles of UDL.
- ◆ Band directors should begin by implementing instructional strategies useful for an entire class, and then specify the cognitive, language, social/emotional, or physical adaptations based on the students' needs.

Additional resources for band directors:

- ◆ Ergobrass has a website containing a variety of different brass instrument stands for both adults and children.
  - » www.ergobrass.com
- ◆ Music Racer has a website with free music theory "games" for students to practice music terms, note names, and fingerings. This is a great tool to use with students who may not be capable of staying in rehearsal the entire class period. Instead of sending them back to their classroom or giving them chores that do not improve their knowledge of their instrument, allow them to play a game while continuing to learn!
  - » www.musicracer.com

REFERENCES

Adamek, M. S., & Darrow, A. A. (2005). *Music in special education.* Silver Spring, MD: American Music Therapy Association.

American Association on Intellectual and Developmental Disabilities (AAIDD). (2010). *Frequently asked questions on intellectual disability and the AAIDD definition.* Retrieved May 14, 2010, from http://www.aamr.org/content_185.cfm

American Psychiatric Association. (2000). *Diagnostic and statistical manual of mental disorders* (4th ed., text revision). Washington, DC: Author.

Colwell, C. M., & Thompson, L. K. (2000). "Inclusion" of information on mainstreaming in undergraduate music education curricula. *Journal of Music Therapy, 37*, 205–221.

Colwell, R. J., & Hewitt, M. P. (2011). *The teaching of instrumental music* (4th ed.). Boston: Prentice Hall.

Data Accountability Center. (2007). *Individuals with Disabilities Education Act (IDEA) data: Part B data and notes.* Retrieved April 6, 2010, from https://www.ideadata.org/PartBData.asp

Davis, W. B., Gfeller, K. E., & Thaut, M. H. (2008). *An introduction to music therapy: Theory and practice.* Silver Spring, MD: American Music Therapy Association.

de l'Etoile, S. K. (2005). Teaching music to special learners: Children with disruptive behavior disorders. *Music Educators Journal, 91*(5), 37–43.

Duke, R. A., & Byo, J. L. (2003). *The habits of musicianship: A radical approach to beginning band.* The Center of Music Learning. Retrieved May 13, 2010, from http://cml.music.utexas.edu/Habits/HabitsOpener.htm

Gfeller, K., Darrow, A., & Hedden, S. (1990). Perceived effectiveness of mainstreaming in Iowa and Kansas schools. *Journal of Research in Music Education, 38*, 90–101.

Hallahan, D. P., Kauffman, J. M., & Pullen, P. C. (2009). *Exceptional learners: An introduction to special education.* New York: Pearson.

Hammel, A. M. (2004). Inclusion strategies that work. *Music Educators Journal, 90*(5), 33–37.

McCord, K. (2006). Children with disabilities playing musical instruments. *Music Educators Journal, 92*(4), 46–52.

Mixon, K. (2005). Special learners: Including exceptional students in your instrumental music program. *Teaching Music, 13*(3), 30–34.

Music Educators National Conference (MENC). (1996). *Performance standards for music, grades preK-12.* Reston, VA: Author.

Music Teachers National Association (MTNA). (2010). *Professional certification standards: What a nationally certified teacher of music should know and be able to do.* Retrieved May 13, 2010, from http://www.mtnacertification.org/Standards/tabid/126/Default.aspx

Ramsey, D. S. (2001). Beginning band—goals and objectives: Teaching music through performance in band—beginning band. In R. Miles & T. Dvorak (Eds.), *Teaching music through performance in beginning band.* Chicago: GIA.

Scott, L. P. (2007). Talking with music teachers about inclusion: Perceptions, opinions and experiences. *Journal of Music Therapy, 44*, 38–56.

Turnbull, A., Turnbull, R., & Wehmeyer, M. (2010). *Exceptional lives: Special education in today's schools* (6th ed.). Upper Saddle River, NJ: Merrill.

Zdzinski, S. F. (2001). Instrumental music for special learners. *Music Educators Journal, 87*(4), 27-29, 63.

Chapter 16

Family and Disability

CHAPTER OVERVIEW

The family is a universal social institution. It is the primary communal unit of American society. Though the composition of American families may vary, their functions are similar. The two primary functions of families are to foster the relationship betweens two adults, and to bring children into the world. Other child-related functions of the family are to socialize children and to acquaint them to the rules that govern social order. Additional functions of the family are to provide emotional security and economic support to its members (Horwitz, 2005). Emotional security is generally garnered through attachment bonds. The attachment between parent and child is important to the psychosocial well-being of the child, and it serves as the foundation for other relationship attachments throughout the child's life (Hartup, 1989). Relationship attachments are characterized by reciprocity—that is, they are mutually beneficial to both parties. If the relationship is marked by undue dependency, the strength of the relationship is at risk. Like emotional security, economic support is important to family functioning and can be subject to circumstantial stress.

The role of music in family life can take many forms. Music can serve as the cornerstone of the family—such as famously in the Osmond and Jackson families, or simply as a shared activity where family members sing or play together, or as a passive activity where music is played in the home. The role music takes in family life is dependent upon the musical experiences of family members and upon the value placed on music by family members. Much has been written about the importance of music in child development (Campbell, 2001) and, as a result, many parents now place a higher value on music in their children's lives. Numerous programs such as *Kindermusik* (www.kindermusik.com) and the *Musikgarten* (www.musikgarten.org) have been created to support the development of children and the integration of music in their lives. Most classes are offered to parents and their infants, toddlers, and young children. In addition to the field of music education, the music therapy profession has also become more involved in the lives of families. Many parents of children with disabilities have found that music therapy serves their children in ways no other form of therapy can do. Professionals in both fields have found that music can make important contributions to family quality of life.

This chapter includes information on the following topics:
- ◆   The culture of families
- ◆   Family Systems Approach
- ◆   The impact of disability on the family
- ◆   The role of the family in special education
- ◆   Special music education and the family
- ◆   Music therapy and the family
- ◆   Case study: The Turnbull family

The Culture of Families

The United States Census Bureau (2008) considers a family to be a group of two or more people related by marriage, birth, or adoption and residing together. Culture is generally considered to be the shared values, traditions, and beliefs of a group of people. Family culture, then, is the unique way in which a family group forms itself in terms of size, structure, rules, roles, customs, communication style, problem-solving approaches, habits, activities, beliefs, and values. The racial or ethnic background of a family may strongly influence family culture, and yet some families may disregard the cultural norms of their ethnic or racial group in favor of the dominant culture group in which they live. Some families include extended family members, and others do not. Some families are loud, while others are quiet. Some families are openly demonstrative, while others are reserved. Some families discuss everything from politics to sex, while other families discuss only those issues that relate to family functioning. Families are different, and every family has its own unique culture. Culture is about legitimate and important differences. It is these differences that mark a culture. Most families have both strengths and weaknesses.

Characteristics of healthy and functioning families are consistent rules, limits, expectations, affection, a clearly identified hierarchy, open communication, and mutual acceptance (Peterson, 2000). Every family has a power structure. Power in the family context is considered to be who assigns tasks, makes financial decisions, arranges activities, etc. In a healthy family, it is the parents who hold the greatest power; though one parent may yield more power than the other. Family governance can also be shared among family members. Communication among all family members is of utmost importance to family relationships, though some family members may have more personal communication with certain family members, or special ways of communicating with others. Consistency regarding behavioral expectations, displays of affection, and family roles is important to the security of all family members. Family culture provides the framework that directs these relationship practices.

Family Systems Approach

Various professionals who work with families often borrow a framework used by sociologists to study and understand family life. Family Systems Approach is a way of working with families that emphasizes the interdependency of family members rather than focusing on individuals in isolation from the family. This approach underlies the most influential forms of contemporary family work. The family is viewed as an interrelated social system with unique characteristics and needs. The approach is based on the assumption that experiences affecting one family member will affect all family members and the overall functions of the family (Turnbull & Turnbull, 2001). Other assumptions are that the behaviors of a family member cannot be understood without understanding the family as whole, and that environment plays an interactive and important role in the understanding the family.

Several concepts are important to the Family Systems Approach: feedback, interdependence of parts, wholeness, and multiple levels. Feedback that promotes change is positive feedback, while negative feedback is that which maintains the status quo or impedes change. Interdependence of parts suggests that change in any part of the family system also changes other parts of the system. The concept of wholeness suggests that understanding a family's dynamics necessitates knowing all of its members. In addition, the family has multiple levels. It exists as a part of larger outside suprasystems, and has multiple subsystems within (Klein & White, 1996).

Propositions of the Family Systems Approach relate to change and to the embedment of systems. The first proposition is that systems are frequently resistant to change. Family members may be resistant to change regarding their roles, power, or place within the family system. Change is inevitable in families: people marry, people die, people move, people become ill. Family growth requires change. For example, adult children do not expect to be treated by their parents as they were when they were young children. Patterson (2002) stated, "Improved functioning or growth occurs when a system is challenged just enough to encourage the development of new capabilities, but not so much that the system is overwhelmed by the demands" (p. 239).

The second proposition of Family Systems Approach is closely related to the concept of wholeness. All suprasystems and subsystems of the family are interrelated. The larger constellation of family must then be given consideration in order to gain proper perspective of an individual member. When change occurs in families, it does not occur in isolation or in relation to only one family member. If a child marries, the parents must adjust to living without the child in the home, and adjust to a new family member. If a family member becomes critically ill, other members of the family are affected, personally and often financially and socially. The interrelatedness of family systems contributes to the concept of family wholeness.

The Impact of Disability on the Family

Given the assumptions, concepts, and propositions of the Family Systems Approach, it is likely that the disability of a child—whether congenital or acquired, will have a considerable impact on the family unit. Disability does not just happen to the child—it happens to the whole family. Disability affects families in different ways, depending on the type and severity of disability, the age of the child with a disability, and the functional health of the family. Disability can change the life course of a family and of some family members. How the family responds to a disability and resultant challenges also affect the life and development of the child with a disability. Some families are able to cope with and adapt well to a disability. Families may even become closer and stronger due to a disability; however, other families often struggle and eventually collapse. There are numerous programs and resources for the parents of children with disabilities, but these resources are often difficult to navigate and to coordinate.

When presented with the news their child has a disability, parents often respond in predictable ways. Their first reaction is frequently shock, followed by disappointment, guilt, and fear. Most parental fantasies do not include having a child a disability. Parents have rehearsed ideas of what their child will be like, look like, and grow to be as an adult. When they learn their child has a disability, they often have to adapt these ideas and adopt new ones. Some parents experience guilt, wondering what they did or didn't do that may have contributed to the birth of a child with a disability. They may also experience fear, wondering how well they will parent a child with disability, how they will deal with possible financial expenses, how they will secure appropriate educational services, or how their child will affect their personal and social relationships and those of the child's siblings. In later years, they may fear for the well-being of their child upon their death. Many parents soon resolve these fears and find that their child indeed fulfills many of their initial dreams.

The nature and degree of disability, as well as of demands associated with the disability, all affect how a family will respond. Sensory disabilities, such as hearing loss, may affect communication within the family. Vision loss or other physical disabilities may affect how the family environment is structured. Cognitive disabilities may impact the degree of responsibility that must be assumed for the family member with a disability. Some children's disabilities will affect where their families must live in order to secure appropriate educational services for them. The needs of children with disabilities can place personal and financial stress on families, change the roles of family members, and affect goals of the family. In spite of or because of these implications for family life, families with disabilities often survive and thrive.

Hanson (2003) documented families' lives 25 years after the birth of a child with Down Syndrome. In spite of many challenges, families reported that the children with Down Syndrome had been the source of many positive contributions to their families. Nevertheless, Cohen and Petrescu-Prahova (2006) reported that children with disabilities aged 5–15 were more likely to live with single parents (usually mothers) than children without disabilities. If family members have their needs met, enjoy their life together, and have opportunities to pursue and achieve goals that are meaningful to them as individuals, the quality of family remains intact (Park, Turnbull, & Turnbull, 2002).

The Role of the Family in Special Education

Going to public schools was not possible for many children with disabilities during most of the 20th century. Before P.L. 94-142 was passed in 1975, public schools educated approximately 1 in 5 children with disabilities (Winzer, 1993). Most children with disabilities were denied access to their neighborhood schools and were educated in segregated institutions, if they were educated at all. Parents of children with disabilities paid the same taxes their neighbors paid, but they were unable to send their children to the public schools supported by those taxes. Many public school administrators believed their schools' facilities and faculty were inadequate to provide services to students with disabilities and, in most cases, they were correct. More disturbing, though, was the fact that many school officials also doubted the value of education for such students (Stainback, Stainback, & Bunch, 1989).

There were state schools for students who were deaf or blind, and some state schools for students with developmental disabilities. Children left home to attend and to live in dormitories at these schools, often at the age of only 4 or 5 years old. In larger metropolitan areas, some parents were able to find a private school that would accept their child; however, they often had to pay an expensive tuition fee and drive their child many miles to school each day. It is not difficult to understand then why some parents, particularly those of children with severe disabilities, felt the best placement for their child was in a state residential institution, a facility where they believed their child would be cared for and would receive educational training. Unfortunately though, many of these children lived a life of mere existence in such institutions. Today there are laws that protect the educational rights of children with disabilities, and the rights of their parents to play an active role in their education.

Most children with disabilities require some degree of special education services, and parents play an important role in determining those services. Parents have the right to be informed about their children's educational needs and what services will be provided to meet their children's needs. Children with parents who are actively involved in their education have the greatest likelihood of benefiting from their school experiences.

Parents and/or caregivers play a particularly integral role in early intervention programs for children with disabilities. They are responsible for securing or providing much of the special training their children require prior to entry into preschool. Up to preschool, families participate in the Individualized Family Service Plan (IFSP) process. The IFSP addresses a child's functional and educational needs with particular attention to the role of the family or primary caregiver. If parents are employed, a child's primary caregiver can receive training, along with the parents, in early interventions designed to prepare the child for school. After children enter preschool, they receive an Individualized Education Plan (IEP); however, parents continue to play a critical role in the educational services provided to their children up to the age of 21 (Berry, 2009).

IDEA has outlined specific components of the Individualized Family Service Plan. These components are found in Figure 16.1.

Figure 16.1 Required Components of the IFSP

1. Child's levels of development—physical, cognitive, communication, social, emotional—based on objective criteria
2. Family's resources, priorities, and concerns; strengths and weaknesses of the child
3. Services necessary to meet the needs of the child and family, including services from education, health, and social service agencies as well as informal networks and resources
4. Specific early intervention services based on peer-reviewed research
5. The projected dates for initiation and duration of each service across agencies, and the frequency, intensity, location, and structure of each service
6. Natural environments in which early intervention services will be provided, including a statement justifying the use of settings other than "natural environments"
7. Name of the service coordinator from the profession most immediately relevant to the infant's or toddler's or family's needs who will be responsible for the implementation of the plan, including transition services
8. Steps to be taken to support the transition of the toddler with a disability to preschool or other appropriate services

(IDEA 2004, P.L. 108-446, § 636[d])

As discussed in Chapter 6, the IEP is the parents' primary conduit to their child's school program. Parents have certain legal rights and safeguards pertaining to their involvement in the IEP process. IDEA granted parents the following rights in the education of their children (see Figure 16.2).

Figure 16.2. Parental Rights in the IEP Process

1.	To give consent in writing before the child is initially evaluated
2.	To give consent in writing before the child is initially placed in a special education program
3.	To request an independent education evaluation if parents feel the school's evaluation is inappropriate
4.	To request an evaluation at public expense if parents disagree with the school's evaluation
5.	To participate on the committee that considers the evaluation of, placement of, and programming for the child
6.	To inspect and review educational records and challenge information believed to be inaccurate, misleading, or in violation of the privacy or other rights of the child
7.	To request a copy of information from the child's educational record
8.	To request a hearing concerning the school's proposal or refusal to initiate or change the identification, evaluation, or placement of the child or the provision of a free and appropriate public education

(Hardman, Drew, & Egan, 2006)

Special Music Education and the Family

All children have the right to learn about music and to make music. Children with disabilities frequently want to take music lessons as their siblings do; however, it may be difficult for their parents to find private teachers who feel capable of giving lessons to children who present cognitive, physical, or behavioral challenges. Rarely do private music teachers have any formal training in working with children who have disabilities, and, as a result, their teaching methods are most often developed through trial and error. Fortunately, many private music teachers have shared their experiences and provided a type of peer education by publishing articles in professional journals (Barss, Marrion, & Haroutounian, & Benham, 1999; Gougoux, Lepore, Lassonde, Voss, Zatorre, & Belin, 2004).

Beyond training, the primary difference between the practices of public school music educators and private music teachers is their legal obligation to teach students with disabilities. Private music teachers may consider it their moral obligation to teach students with disabilities; however, they may also choose their students, and, if they wish, exclude certain students. Private music teachers who are willing to give piano lessons or other types of lessons to children with disabilities will likely find many parents who are interested in their services.

Nearly all children enjoy performing. Children with disabilities, like all children, should have the opportunity to learn to sing or play an instrument and to experience the thrill of an appreciative audience. The litmus test for a private teacher should be that a child's performance does not highlight his or her disability, but rather abilities. Some children will require adapted music lessons, which may take the form of adapted music scores or musical instruments. Music notation can be enlarged or color-coded, or have note names written in. Most instruments may be physically adapted to suit a child's disability. Keyboards can also be color-coded or have note names adhered to the keys. The music teacher and parents should accept whatever adaptations the child needs to be musically successful. There are various music curricula and instruments that have been adapted especially for children with disabilities. Many of these products can be purchased through West Music (http://www.westmusic.com/).

All young musicians benefit from the support of their parents. Children with disabilities will likely progress more rapidly in their music study if parents participate in their lessons and assist them with practice. Such collaborations may also provide opportunities for parents and children to perform together, and thus spend quality time enjoying a shared interest. It is important, however, for a teacher and parents to be in agreement regarding the musical goals for a child with a disability.

Musical Goals for Students with Disabilities

The special music educator and private music teacher are both concerned with children's musical growth and development. Music educators specialize in the acquisition of musical knowledge, skills, and appreciation. Private music teachers are generally concerned with skill development only, that is, learning to sing or to play an instrument. Both differ from music therapists, who use music primarily to achieve non-music goals, such as academic, physical, social, or emotional goals. Musical goals for children with disabilities are similar to, though not limited to, those for children without disabilities. MENC: The National Association for Music Education has outlined nine content standards, called the National Standards for Music Education (MENC, 1994):

1. Singing, alone and with others, a varied repertoire of music
2. Performing on instruments, alone and with others, a varied repertoire of music
3. Improvising melodies, variations, and accompaniments
4. Composing and arranging music within specified guidelines
5. Reading and notating music
6. Listening to, analyzing, and describing music
7. Evaluating music and music performances
8. Understanding relationships between music, the other arts, and disciplines outside the arts
9. Understanding music in relation to history and culture

Parents of children with disabilities may have additional non-musical goals for their child's participation in music. Many of these goals follow Merriam's (1964) functions of music in society: music as a means of emotional expression, entertainment, communication, physical response, and integration into society.

Beyond these non-musical goals, however, children with disabilities may wish to become musicians who can engage in music making throughout their lives. There are a number of active musicians with disabilities who may serve to inspire or to serve as role models for young children with disabilities.

Musicians with Disabilities

- Evelyn Glennie is likely the most famous musician with a profound hearing loss. She is a percussionist who has performed all over the world. She learned to tune the timpani by blowing into the head of the instrument and feeling the vibrations against her cheeks. She also feels sounds in various parts of her body and uses those sensations to play various other percussion instruments. She paved the way for many other young musicians with hearing losses.
- Cherisse Miller has a B.A. degree in piano performance from the University of South Carolina. Her hearing loss is 60–70 percent in each ear.
- Yew Choong Cheong studied piano at the University of West Virginia. His hearing loss is severe enough that he cannot use a telephone.
- Catherine Hetherington also has a hearing loss and was awarded a Master's of Music with Distinction from the Scottish Royal Academy of Music.
- There are many well-known musicians who are blind—Stevie Wonder, Ray Charles, Jose Feliciano, Andrea Bocelli, Ronnie Milsap, George Shearing, and Marcus Roberts.
- Patrick Hughes, who plays in the University of Louisville marching band, is blind and has severe physical disabilities as well.
- What can be more daunting than the loss of fingers for a pianist, the absence of a hand for a violinist, or the absence of arms for a guitarist? Yet, in spite of incredible odds, these three individuals have found a way to make music: Hee Ah Lee, Tony Melendez, and Adrian Anantawan.
- Many persons with severe physical disabilities are judged by their appearance. Others often assume that cognitive disabilities accompany their physical disabilities. Such has been the case for Thomas Quasthoff, born with serious birth defects caused by his mother's exposure during pregnancy to the drug thalidomide. He is a bass-baritone and is generally regarded as one of the finest singers of his generation.

Not all young musicians with disabilities will wish to become performers as adults. There are many non-musical goals that can be achieved through music as well. Music therapy has much to offer children with disabilities, their siblings, and their parents. Music therapists who specialize in work with families address goals that are important to family cohesiveness and socialization.

Music Therapy and the Family

Music can play an important role in facilitating children's integration into the family unit, beginning with their birth. Research has long supported the use of music to ease the pain of labor delivery (Clark, McCorkle, & Williams, 1981; Hanser, Larson, & O'Connell, 1983). Music can be beneficial to the newborn as well, and to premature infants in particular. Standley (1991) advocated the use of music in the pacification/stimulation of the premature infant. Music can calm the baby by masking aversive sounds often heard in neonatal units, as well as provide the aural and cognitive stimulation needed for neurological development. Pacification and stimulation of the infant are the primary functions of music in neonatal care, although music can serve typical developing infants as well. Music can:

- *act as an attention-focusing stimulus.* Music can distract the infant from aversive sounds, or act as a stimulus to regulate steady breathing.
- *be a distraction stimulus to divert attention from pain.* Music in the environment, particularly preferred music, is difficult to ignore. Actively engaging in music listening can decrease an infant's perception of pain.
- *act as a conditioned stimulus for relaxation.* Preferred music and music with specific characteristics, such as a slow tempo and a steady beat, can induce relaxation and often sleep.
- *decrease tension and anxiety.* Music accompanied with guided imagery can often decrease tension and anxiety associated with childbirth, as well as an anxiety due to changes in an infant's environment.
- *be used as a structural aid to breathing.* Appropriately paced music can reinforce and support breathing patterns conducive to relaxation.
- *provide a stimulus for pleasure response.* Most mothers and fathers enjoy some genre of music; consequently, it can be used to evoke a positive emotional state.

(Music Therapy Association of British Columbia, 2010)

Beyond infant pacification and stimulation, music can be used to assist in creating a bond between child and parent. Many parents do not know how to play with a young child, particular a child with severe disabilities. Playing musical games and instruments are ways parents can engage in meaningful interactions with their child. A music therapist can assist them in selecting developmentally appropriate games and instruments. Young children with severe disabilities often require critical care and frequent attention. Parents need to spend time with their child in a way that is positive, enjoyable, and stimulating. Parents who simply listen to their preferred music while rocking and swaying their child to sleep will find that the task is more enjoyable, that time passes more quickly, and that doing so assists in building a positive bond between them and their child.

Many parents are at a loss as to what activities they can share with a child who has a serious disability. Not all parents are musicians nor feel comfortable actively making music, but all parents and children can listen to music—in the home, in the car, or in the community. Nearly all families can enjoy children's concerts in the community. Many libraries and books stores have special musical events for young children. Music programs such as *Musikgarten* and *Kindermusik* provide more formalized musical experiences for parents and children.

Five Broad Family Goals for Music Therapists

Music therapy goals for families, much like those in IEPs or IFSPs, should be made in consultation with the parents. Consultation between parents and the music therapist is important for several reasons: most parents want to be involved with their child's life, a child's development is enhanced when parents and professionals work together, and, finally, it is the law. Music therapists may need to make parents aware of the services they can provide to the family. Many parents are unaware of music therapy services outside of the school system. Possible family goals for music therapists are:

1. *To provide services to the child with a disability.* These services can be provided to the child alone, or to siblings as well. Much like parents, brothers and sisters often do not know how to engage in meaningful experiences with a child who has a severe disability. Through carefully selected music activities, the music therapist can nurture the sibling bond and provide entertaining as well as educational experiences for both the siblings and the child with a disability.

2. *To provide training on the uses of music to families or individual family members.* After a family assessment of needs, the music therapist can train family members in ways to use music to address specific concerns, such a child's poor sleep habits (music used for relaxation), noncompliance to rules (music used as a contingency), or compliance with painful medical procedures (music used as a distraction).

3. *To enhance the care-giving capacity of the family.* The music therapist can inform the parents about ways they can use music to promote meaningful and positive family interactions, such as family sing-a-longs, songs and musical games to use in the car while traveling, songs to use while changing diapers, or other care duties.

4. *To give parents and other family members respite from the demands of caring for a child with a disability.* Music therapists are trained to work with and to care for children with a disability; therefore, when music therapists provide respite care for a family, their role can be more than just supervision of the child. They can provide educational and well as therapeutic sessions for the child.

5. *To improve the family quality of life.* The music therapist can address family issues related to stress, problem behaviors, socialization, spirituality, and life transitions.

In addition, there are five questions all music therapists should ask parents when they begin to work with a family that has a child with a disability.

1. What are the skill areas that concern you most on your child's IEP?
2. What is the behavior at home that you feel most needs improvement?
3. What is the most difficult problem you face in parenting your child?
4. What are your hopes, dreams, and expectations for your child?
5. What are your expectations of me as your child's music therapist?

Asking these questions demonstrates respect for the parents and their wishes for their child. Many professionals are quick to judge parents and often assume that they know what is best for a child. Respecting parents' knowledge about their child will greatly enhance the therapeutic and professional relationships a music therapist has with both the child and the parents. Parents need support from professionals. They are often burdened with numerous concerns that relate directly to a child's disability. These concerns can be characterized as the "al" list:

Financial	Physical	Custodial
Educational	Psychological	Transitional
Emotional	Occupational	Behavioral
Social	Residential	Familial
Medical	Marital	Spiritual

Many parents who have children with disabilities find ways to be personally empowered, to enjoy the positive aspects of parenting a child with a disability, and to overcome the many risk factors associated with having a child who has a disability. Model parents are informed, loving, and involved in their child's life. They engage in self-care. They know when to ask for help from others. Ann and Rud Turnbull walked the walk as model parents of a child with several severe disabilities. As directors of the Beach Center on Disability at The University of Kansas, they have enabled many other parents to achieve the utmost quality of life for their child and for their families.

Case Study: The Turnbull Family

This case study is taken from articles written by Rud and Ann Turnbull, parents of J.T. Turnbull, and is used with permission (Beach Center on Disability, 2010; Turnbull & Turnbull, 1999).

> *J.T. Turnbull was a handsome young man. When J.T. was an infant, he received the label of low-moderate mental retardation. In his*

adolescence, he acquired the label of autism. As an adult, he acquired the labels of bipolar disorder and obsessive-compulsive disorder. When he was at the stable point of his bipolar cycle, J.T. was cheerful, relational with others, and able to make decisions. He derived genuine pleasure from his many activities. When he slipped from that stable state into depression, he became sad, socially aloof, and nearly incapable of making a decision. And when he accelerated into the opposite polarity, he became excessively cheerful, often silly and baby-like; he engaged in extensive self-talk rather than interacting with others, had difficulty sleeping, and was unyieldingly insistent on having his own way. One of his parents' greatest challenges was to choreograph and calibrate his supports in light of his rapidly changing moods and anxiety levels, which varied not just week-to-week, but sometimes as often as hour-to-hour. As well-known scholars in the field of special education, his parents understood his cognitive disability, but it was the bipolarity and the OCD that baffled them. J.T.'s most challenging behavior came when his mood cycle was in a depressed state and his anxiety cycle was at a high level. The combination of low mood and high anxiety appeared to lead to the OCD behaviors, with the worst one being absolute "fixation" on hair. During these occasions, J.T. frequently engaged in repetitive verbalizations about hair, attempts to touch hair, and aggressively pulling others' hair.

J.T.'s vocabulary was limited, partly the result of his difficulty in processing sounds. A music therapist worked with J.T., teaching him to process sounds in ways he enjoyed. Speech therapy also helped J.T. with his articulation and his use of an augmented email program produced by Ablelink (www.ablelinktech.com) to communicate with his sisters and friends, who were part of his life but lived far away. Ultimately, music therapy enabled him to make known what he wanted and to socialize with others. It advanced his self-determination and his integration into the community. But music therapy was more than therapy. It was also a source of great joy. When J.T. sang, strummed a guitar, or kept rhythm with drums or bongos, he experienced an outlet for his emotions. Music was able to elevate his spirit and moods. He learned the songs that he was able to sing with his family and friends at nearly every social event in his life. Music was a key to J.T.'s soul and to the hearts of those who entered his life. His favorite song was, "Annie's Song," by John Denver: "Come, let me love you, let me give my heart to you . . . come, love me again." Those words express the reciprocity that existed in J.T.'s life—the mutuality that acknowledged his positive contributions to others even as they made positive contributions to him.

He closed all of his parties with this song, with his fellow party-goers singing along, often with joyful tears in their eyes.

There were two major foci to J.T.'s involvement with music therapy: decreasing problem behaviors and increasing overall quality of life. Because of the ease with which J.T. memorized song lyrics, it became natural to use this modality to impart important information by changing lyrics to familiar songs or creating new songs. The lyrics might include a simple task analysis of what J.T. was or was not supposed to be doing in a given situation. Some problem behaviors that were addressed through song included pouring mouthwash down the sink—remedied by singing the Beatles' "Let It Be," getting up in the morning—remedied by singing The Everly Brothers' "Wake Up, Little Suzie," and hair pulling—remedied by original lyrics that J.T. helped to create.

To increase J.T.'s quality of life, his music therapist increased the breadth of J.T.'s relationship with music. One of J.T.'s greatest accomplishments was learning to play the guitar. With minimal cueing, J.T. was able to play simple folk songs on his guitar and sing simultaneously. Singing and playing provided the opportunity for success in a medium in which he felt intense pride. Singing and playing was also used as a basis for interactions with his friends. As one of the most capable individuals in his group music therapy sessions, J.T. was able to put his musical facility to work as a model and a leader, a position he was not frequently afforded in other groups.

Though music played a role in nearly every aspect of J.T.'s life, music's most important role was to facilitate J.T.'s integration into the Turnbull family life. Unable to have deep and meaningful conversations with family members, J.T. was able to communicate with them through song. When his younger sister was born, he welcomed her into the family by singing "K-k-k-Katy, Beautiful Katy." He was able to participate in his other sister's wedding by singing "Once in Love with Amy (always in love with Amy)," thus reminding everyone why they were there. J.T. was particularly close to his maternal grandfather. At his grandfather's passing, J.T. stood with other family members at his bedside and led them in singing "Swing Low, Sweet Chariot." J.T. was also able to participate in the spiritual life of his family by singing his favorite hymns, often motivating other family members to sing with his same great gusto. At family birthdays, it was J.T. who made the toast to the honored member with "Happy Birthday." Until his unexpected death at age 41, J.T. used music to bring joy into the lives of everyone he knew, most importantly his parents and sisters.

Conclusions

Music can play a therapeutic and/or an education role in the family with a disability. Both roles serve to integrate the child with a disability more completely into the family unit. By playing and singing together, music can also serve as a leisure activity for the family. All families need time for leisure. Children with disabilities often have physical and/or cognitive limitations that prevent them from participating in many traditional leisure activities. Music's universal appeal and adaptability make it a desirable leisure activity for families. Participation can be active or passive, depending on the talents, preferences, or abilities of family members.

Finally, the music therapist or music educator can serve as a family advocate by helping to transition the child with a disability from the home and into community life. Music therapists can do much to assist in the societal assimilation of a child with a disability. They can do so by directing the child and family to opportunities for positive community interactions. As a family advocate, they can encourage the continued musical, social and interpersonal growth of the child and family by presenting opportunities for music making in the community. Community ensembles, church choirs, open mic night at various venues, and civic concerts are opportunities for music making and/or listening that are generally open to all individuals, and are activities that families can participate in together regardless of musical skills or disabilities. Participation in such organizations or performance events may make the transition from school to community life more rewarding and less threatening for children with disabilities, and indeed for the entire family.

KEY POINTS FROM THE CHAPTER

♦ Music can make important contributions to family quality of life.
♦ Music can serve as the cornerstone of a family, or play an active or passive role in the family.
♦ The role music takes in family life is dependent upon the musical experiences of family members, and upon the value placed on music by family members.
♦ Families are different, and every family has its own unique culture.
♦ Family culture is the unique way in which a family group forms itself in terms of size, structure, rules, roles, customs, communication style, problem-solving approaches, habits, activities, beliefs, and values.
♦ Characteristics of healthy and functioning families are consistent rules, limits, expectations, affection, a clearly identified hierarchy, open communication, and mutual acceptance.
♦ Every family has a power structure and, in a healthy family, it is the parents who hold the greatest power.
♦ Family Systems Approach is a way of working with families that emphasizes the interdependency of family members, rather than focusing on individuals in isolation from the family.

◆ Concepts important to the Family Systems Approach are feedback, interdependence of parts, wholeness, and multiple levels.

◆ Propositions of the Family Systems Approach relate to change and to the concept of wholeness.

◆ Disability does not just happen to the child—it happens to the whole family.

◆ Disability affects families in different ways, depending on the type and severity of disability, the age of the child with a disability, and the functional health of the family.

◆ Disability can change the life course of a family and of some family members.

◆ The nature and degree of disability, as well as of demands associated with the disability, all affect how a family will respond.

◆ Children with parents who are actively involved in their education have the greatest likelihood of benefiting from their school experiences.

◆ Parents and/or caregivers play a particularly integral role in early intervention.

◆ The IFSP or IEP is the parents' primary conduit to their child's school program for children with disabilities.

◆ Children with disabilities, like all children, should have the opportunity to learn to sing or play an instrument, and to experience the thrill of an appreciative audience.

◆ The litmus test for a private teacher should be that a child's performance does not highlight his or her disability, but rather abilities.

◆ Musical goals for children with disabilities are similar to, though not limited to, those for children without disabilities.

◆ Music therapy can play an important role in facilitating children's integration into the family unit.

◆ There are five broad goals for music therapists working with families:

   1. To provide services to the child with a disability.

   2. To provide training on the uses of music to families or individual family members.

   3. To enhance the care-giving capacity of the family; the music therapist can inform the parents about ways they can use music.

   4. To give parents and other family members respite from the demands of caring for a child with a disability.

   5. To improve the family quality of life.

REFERENCES

Barss, F., Marrion, M., Haroutounian, J., & Benham, K. (1999). Learning from Kara: Reflections of three friends. *American Music Teacher, 48,* 15–21.

Beach Center on Disability. (2010, April 15). *Real story: J.T. Turnbull—Putting it all together for a life that belongs to the person.* Retrieved from http://www.beachcenter.org/resource_library/beach_resource_detail_page.aspx?i ntResourceID=1751&JScript=1

Berry, J. O. (2009). *Lifespan perspectives on the family and disability.* Austin, TX: Pro-Ed.

Campbell, D. (2001). *The Mozart Effect: Tapping the power of music to heal the body, strengthen the mind, and unlock the creative spirit.* New York: Harper Collins.

Clark, M. E., McCorkle, R. R., & Williams, S. B. (1981). Music therapy assisted labor and delivery. *Journal of Music Therapy, 28,* 88–100.

Cohen, P., & Petrescu-Prahova, M. (2006). Gendered living arrangements among children with disabilities. *Journal of Marriage and Family, 68,* 630–638.

Gougoux, F., Lepore, F., Lassonde, M., Voss, P., Zatorre, R. J., & Belin, R. (2004). Pitch discrimination in the early blind: People blinded in infancy have sharper listening skills than those who lost their sight later. *Nature, 430,* 309.

Hanser, S., Larson, S. C., & O'Connell, A. S. (1983). The effect of music on relaxation of expectant mothers during labor. *Journal of Music Therapy, 20,* 50–58.

Hanson, M. J. (2003). Twenty-five years after early intervention: A follow-up of children with Down syndrome and their families. *Infants and Young Children, 16,* 354–365.

Hardman, M. L., Drew, C. J., & Egan, M. W. (2006). *Human exceptionality: School, community and family* (8th ed.). Boston: Allyn & Bacon.

Hartup, W. W. (1989). Social relationships and their developmental significance. *American Psychologist, 44,* 120–126.

Horwitz, S. (2005). The functions of the family in the great society. *Cambridge Journal of Economics, 29,* 669–684.

Individuals with Disabilities Education Improvement Act of 2004, 20 U.S.C. § 1400 *et seq.* (1990). (Session law # P.L. 101-476).

Klein, D. M., & White, J. M. (1996). *Family theories: An introduction.* Thousand Oaks, CA: Sage.

MENC: National Association of Music Education. (1994). *National Standards for Music Education.* Reston, VA: Music Educators National Conference

Merriam, A. P. (1964). *The anthropology of music.* Evanston, IL: Northwestern University Press.

Music Therapy Association of British Columbia. (2010). *Childbirth and neonatal care.* Retrieved July 4, 2010, from http://www.mtabc.com/page.php?55

Park, J., Turnbull, A. P., & Turnbull, H. R. (2002). Impacts of poverty on quality of life in families of children with disabilities. *Exceptional Children, 68,* 151–170.

Patterson, J. M. (2002). Understanding family resilience. *Journal of Clinical Psychology, 58,* 233–246.

Peterson, G. (2000). *Making healthy families.* Berkeley, CA: Shadow and Light.

Stainback, W., Stainback, S., & Bunch, G. (1989). Introduction and historical background. In S. Stainback, W. Stainback, & M. Forest (Eds.), *Educating all students in the mainstream of regular education* (pp. 3–14). Baltimore: Paul H. Brookes.

Standley, J. M. (1991). The role of music in pacification/stimulation of premature infants with low birth weights. *Music Therapy Perspectives, 9,* 19–25.

Turnbull, A. P., & Turnbull, H. R. (1999). Comprehensive lifestyle support for adults with challenging behavior: From rhetoric to reality. *Education and Training in Mental Retardation and Developmental Disabilities, 34,* 373–394.

Turnbull, A. P., & Turnbull, H. R. (2001). *Families, professionals and exceptionality: Collaborating for empowerment* (4th ed.). Upper Saddle River, NJ: Prentice Hall.

Turnbull, A. P., Turnbull, H. R., Erwin, E. J., & Soodak, L. C. (2006). *Families, professionals, and exceptionality: Positive outcomes through partnership and trust* (5th ed.). Upper Saddle River, NJ: Prentice Hall.

United States Census Bureau. (2008). *Current population survey (CPS)—Definitions and explanations.* Population Division Fertility and Family Statistics Branch. Retrieved March 24, 2009, from www.census.gov/population/www/cps/cpsdef.html

Winzer, M. (1993). *The history of special education: From isolation to integration.* Washington, DC: Gallaudet University Press.

Appendix

Acronyms and Abbreviations in Special Education

AAMD – American Association on Mental Deficiency

AB – Adaptive Behavior

ABA – Applied Behavior Analysis

ABS – Adaptive Behavior Scale

ACC – Augmentative and Alternative Communication

ACR – Annual Case Review

ADA – Average Daily Attendance

ADA – Americans with Disabilities Act

ADD – Attention Deficit Disorder

ADHD – Attention Deficit Hyperactivity Disorder

AFB – American Foundation for the Blind

APE – Adaptive Physical Education

APHB – American Printing House for the Blind

ARC – Association for Retarded Citizens

ASDC – American Society for Deaf Children

ASHA – American Speech-Language-Hearing Association

ASL – American Sign Language

AT – Assistive Technology

ATTIC – Assistive Technology Training and Information Center

AU – Autism

CA – Chronological Age

CARF – Commission on Accreditation of Rehabilitation Facilities

CASE – Council of Administrators of Special Education

CCC – Case Conference Committee

CD – Communication Disorder

CEC – Council for Exceptional Children

CEO – Chief Executive Officer

CF – Cystic Fibrosis

CHINS – Child in Need of Services

CIC – Clean Intermittent Catheterization

CIPYC – Center for Innovative Practices for Young Children

CMHC – Community Mental Health Center

CO-OP – Cooperative (Special Education Cooperative)

CP – Cerebral Palsy

CPIP – Collaborative Parent Involvement Project

CR – Compliance Review

CRO – Central Reimbursement Office

CSPD – Comprehensive System of Personnel Development

CSSO – Chief State School Officer

D & E – Diagnosis and Evaluation

DAS – Division of Assistance to States, U.S. Department of Education

DB – Deaf and Blind

DD – Developmental Disability

DFC – Division of Family and Children

DMH – Division of Mental Health

DOE – Department of Education

DPP – Division of Personnel Preparation, U.S. Department of Education

DSE – Director of Special Education or Division of Special Education

DSI – Dual Sensory Impairment

EC – Early Childhood

EDGAR – Education Department General Administrative Regulations, U.S. Department of Education

EEG – Electroencephalogram

EEOC – Equal Employment Opportunity Commission

EH – Emotional Handicap

EHA-B – Education for the Handicapped Act, Part B (now IDEA)

EKG – Electrocardiogram

EPC – Educational Planning Committee

ESEA – Elementary and Secondary Education Act

ESY – Extended School Year

FAPE – Free and Appropriate Public Education

FAS – Fetal Alcohol Syndrome

FBA – Functional Behavioral Analysis

FERPA – Family Educational Rights and Privacy Act of 1974 (P.L. 93–380)

FRCD – Family Resource Center on Disabilities

FS – First Steps

FSSA – Family and Social Services Administration

GPC – Governor's Planning Council

HB – Homebound

HHS – Health and Human Services (U.S. Department)

HI – Hearing Impairment

ICF – Intermediate Care Facility

ICFMR – Intermediate Care Facility for Mentally Retarded

IDEA-B/H – Individuals with Disabilities Education Act, Part B or Part H

IEP – Individualized Education Program (or Plan)

IFSP – Individualized Family Service Plan

IHP – Individualized Habilitation Program (or Plan)

IMC – Instructional Materials Center

IPP – Individual Program Plan

IQ – Intelligence Quotient (score on intelligence test)

IRP – Individual Rehabilitation Plan (or Program)

IRS – Internal Revenue Service

ISDD – Institute for the Study of Developmental Disabilities

ITP – Individualized Transition Plan

LCC – Local Coordinating Committee (or Council)

LD – Learning Disability

LDA – Learning Disability Association

LEA – Local Education Agency

LEIA – Local Early Intervention Agency

LPCC – Local Planning and Coordinating Council

LRE – Least Restrictive Environment

MCR – Multi-Categorical Resource

MD – Muscular Dystrophy

MDR – Manifestation Determination Review

MH – Mental Handicap

MH – Multiple Handicap

MIMH – Mild Mental Handicap

MOMH – Moderate Mental Handicap

NARIC – National Rehabilitation Information Center

NASDSE – National Association of State Directors of Special Education

NCLB – No Child Left Behind

NICHCY – National Information Center for Children and Youth with Disabilities (now National Dissemination Center for Children with Disabilities)

NMT – Neurologic Music Therapy

NORD – National Organization for Rare Diseases

OCR – Office for Civil Rights

OFSS – Office of Family and Social Services

OHI – Other Health Impairment

OI – Orthopedic Impairment

OSEP– Office of Special Education Programs, U.S. Department of Education

OSERS – Office of Special Education and Rehabilitation Services, U.S. Department of Education

OT – Occupational Therapy or Occupational Therapist

P & A – Protection and Advocacy

PAC – Parent Advisory Council

PBS – Positive Behavioral Support

PE – Physical Education

P.L. – Public Law

PSE – Patterned Sensory Enhancement

PT – Physical Therapy or Physical Therapist

PTI – Parent Training and Information (Centers)

PVE – Pre-Vocational Education

RAS – Rhythmic Auditory Stimulation

RFP – Request for Proposal

ROM – Range of Motion

RP – Retinitis Pigmentosa

RRC – Regional Resource Center

RS – Related Services

RTI – Response to Intervention

SBVTE – State Board of Vocational Technical Education

SEA – State Education Agency

SED – Special Education Director

SEP – Special Education Programs (office of OSERS)

SIB – Self-Injurious Behavior

SIP – State Improvement Plan

S/LP – Speech/Language/Hearing Pathologist

SMH – Severe Mental Handicap

SOP/SSP – State Operated Program/State Supported Program

SPOE – Systems Point of Entry

SPP – State Performance Plan

SSDI – Social Security Disability Income

SSI – Supplemental Security Income

TADS – Technical Assistance Development System

TAPP – Technical Assistance to Parents Program

TBI – Traumatic Brain Injury

TDD – Telephone Device for the Deaf

TIMP – Therapeutic Instrumental Music Playing

TTY – Tele-typewriter

UCP – United Cerebral Palsy (Association)

UTS – Unified Training System

VI – Visual Impairment

Terms and Definitions

Accessible: Modified or designed so that persons with limited mobility (in wheelchairs or with crutches, for example) can move into and around the structure or building.

Achievement Test: A test that measures progress in school subject areas such as reading, spelling, and math. Examples of this type of test are the Wide Range Achievement Test (WRAT) and the Peabody Individual Achievement Test (PIAT).

Adaptive Behavior: How a person fits in socially and emotionally with other people of similar age and cultural background and in a variety of situations.

Advocacy: A program or situation in which agencies or individuals speak or act on behalf of the interests of themselves or other individuals or groups.

Annual Case Review (also called "Case Conference"): Law requires that a student's special education program be reviewed each year. A review involves an updating of the student's progress and planning his/her IEP for the coming year.

Annual Goals: These describe the educational performance to be achieved by a student by the end of the school year.

Aptitude Test: A test to measure an individual's ability to learn in a particular area, such as music, mechanics, etc.

Assessment: The process of testing and observing the child in order to understand the nature, personality, learning style, and abilities of the child to help make decisions about the kind of educational programming required.

At-risk: Term used to describe children who are considered likely to have difficulties in school because of home-life circumstances, medical difficulties at birth, or other factors, and who may need early intervention services to prevent further difficulties.

Attention Span: The extent to which a person can concentrate on a single task.

Audiologist: A specialist who has studied the science of hearing and is concerned with studying the nature of hearing, preventing hearing loss, administering hearing tests to detect possible hearing loss, and giving information to people about hearing aids, training programs, or medical treatment.

Auditory Association: The ability to relate to concepts presented orally (i.e., "If a ball is round, a block is _____.")

Auditory Closure: The ability to fill in the missing parts that are left out of an auditory presentation (i.e., "Banan__.")

Auditory Discrimination: The identification of likenesses and differences between sounds.

Auditory Perception: The ability to receive sounds accurately and to understand what they mean when combined into words.

Auditory Sequential Memory: The ability to remember what one hears in the specific order or sequence it was presented, which may affect a person's ability to follow oral directions.

Behavior Management/Modification: A method for changing specific human behaviors that emphasizes regular encouragement or discouragement of behaviors that can be seen, and for observing what happens both before and after the behavior.

Behavioral Objectives: Objectives that are written to describe what a child will be able to do as a result of some planned instructions. Behavioral objectives are usually interpreted as objectives that can be measured in some definitive or quantitative way.

Case Conference: The meeting held to discuss evaluation results, determine if there is a need of special services, and plan for the student's educational future by developing the IEP.

Case Management/Service Coordination: Activities carried out by a case manager that may include coordination and assistance to families or individuals to gain access to appropriate services. The term service coordination may be used in place of the term case management.

Central Directory: A system that is managed and maintained in one central location for keeping track of services, resources, and experts that provide assistance to individuals with disabilities and their families.

Cerebral Dominance: The control of activities by the brain with one side (hemisphere) usually considered consistently in control over the other. The left side controls language in most people and is thought to be the dominant side.

Chronological Age: A person's actual age by the calendar, usually given by year and month, such as CA=6.7 (6 years, 7 months).

Cognition: The act or process of knowing; the various thinking skills and processes are considered cognitive skills.

Complainable Issue: An issue arising from a violation or suspected violation of Article 7, for example, the school denying related services for a student. A complainable issue is not directly related to identification, evaluation, or placement of a student.

Complaint: The action taken to notify the state education agency that special education regulations are not being followed. A complaint triggers an investigation of the suspected problem.

Conceptual Disorder: A disturbance in the thinking process and in cognitive activities or, a disturbance in the ability to form concepts.

Confidentiality: Refers to being careful and using good judgment in reporting only the information about the child that is relevant when disclosing personal information to school personnel, social workers, friends, etc.

Congenital: A condition existing from birth.

Consent: Refers to being fully informed and agreeing to a proposed plan of educational evaluation and/or placement. Parental consent in education has three basic parts:

1) the parent is fully informed;

2) the parent agrees in writing; and

3) consent is given voluntarily.

Criterion Referenced Testing: Measures that answer the question, "What can this student do?" not "How does this student perform compared to other students?" Individual performance is compared to an acceptable standard (criterion).

Culturally Appropriate Assessment: Assessment tools and methods that are "fair" to the student in the sense that they are given in his native language; given and interpreted with reference to the child's age, socioeconomic status, and cultural background; given by trained persons; and appropriate, even if the child has a physical, mental, speech, or sensory disability. This has come to mean an assessment must be fair to students of all language and cultural backgrounds.

Decoding: Ability to interpret sounds or symbols into ideas.

Developmental Delay or Lag: A measurable delay means that a significant difference exists between the child's age-expected level of development (adjusted for prematurity, if applicable) and the child's current level of functioning.

Developmental Disability: A severe, chronic disability of a person that is a result of a mental or physical impairment, or combination of a mental or physical impairment, that appears before the person is 22 years of age, which is likely to continue throughout that person's lifetime and which substantially limits that person's ability to function in three or more major life activities.

Diagnostic Services: The services necessary to identify the presence of a disability, its cause, and complications, and to determine the extent to which the disability is likely to limit the individual's daily living and working activity.

Diagnostic Tests: Assessments and evaluations used to find specific strengths and weaknesses in a developmental learning skill or academic subject.

Directionality: The relationship of an object or point in space to another object in space. Difficulty in this developmental skill may result in left-right confusion in reading and writing.

Distractibility: Attention that moves rapidly from one thing to another, giving unusual, fleeting attention to trivial sights and sounds, and having very little ability to concentrate.

Down Syndrome: A developmental disability, one of the most common causes of mental retardation, caused by specific chromosomal abnormalities.

Due Process: A legal term that assures that persons with disabilities have the right to challenge any decision made on their behalf.

Dysfunction: Poor or impaired ability to perform or function in a particular way, usually as a result of delayed development.

Early Intervention: Programs and services provided to infants and children with disabilities during the years of most rapid growth and development, the years from birth to age 5.

Educational Surrogate Parent (ESP): A person who has received training and acquired the knowledge and skills to substitute for the natural parent when a student's parent or guardian is not known or when the student is a ward (CHINS) of the Division of Family and Children (formerly Department of Public Welfare). The function of the educational surrogate parent is to serve as an advocate and represent the student's educational needs and interests in the special education process in place of the natural parent(s).

Evaluation: The process of collecting and interpreting information about a child. An evaluation consists of a variety of tests, observations, and background information and is done by a group of qualified people called a "multidisciplinary team."

Expressive Language: Skills required to produce language for communication with other individuals. Speaking and writing are expressive language skills. Sign language is also considered an expressive language skill.

Family Assessment: The ongoing process used to identify the family's strengths and needs related to the development of the child.

FAPE (Free and Appropriate Public Education): By federal law, every disabled child is entitled to an education that meets his individual needs, whether in a public school setting or in a private school, at public expense, if a public program is not available or appropriate.

Figure-ground (auditory): The ability to listen (focus auditorially) to specific sounds when there is a lot of background noise and to ignore background noise, for example, in the classroom.

Figure-ground (visual): The ability to see (focus visually) specific forms or figures of a visual field and ignore background forms and figures, for example, to find a picture or hidden figure.

Fine Motor Coordination (eye/hand): Purposeful, coordinated movements of the hand and eye to achieve specific movements, such as writing, sorting, sewing, etc.

Free, Appropriate Public Education (FAPE): An educational program designed to meet the individual needs of a student with a disability at no cost to the parent or child, provided by or through the public schools.

Functional Education: Instruction about basic skills needed in everyday life.

Goal: The level of ability accepted as reasonable and/or desirable for a specific student at a specific time; the "end result" expected at a certain point in time, for example, the student will be able to write his name by the end of the first semester.

Grade Equivalent: The score a student obtains on an achievement test, translated into a standard score, which allows the individual student's score to be compared to the typical score for students in his grade level. A "grade equivalent" score of 6.0 means the score that the average beginning sixth grader makes; a "grade equivalent" score of 6.3 means the score that the average student who has been in sixth grade for 3 months makes.

Gross Motor Coordination (leg/arm): Movement that involves balance, coordination, and large muscle activity as needed for walking, running, skipping, jumping, and other physical activities.

Health Impaired: Describes students who have persistent medical or health problems, such as heart conditions, epilepsy, diabetes, etc., that adversely affect their educational performance.

Hearable Issue: An issue relating to the initiation, the change, or the denial of identification, evaluation, or educational placement of a child. A hearing can be seen as an "appeal" of case conference disagreements.

Hyperactivity: Overactive, either in unplanned or planned body activities, for example, the child is in a constant state of motion.

Hypoactivity: Lethargy or extreme lack of movement, that is, the opposite of hyperactivity.

IEP (Individualized Education Program): A written statement, developed by the assessment team (school administrator, child's special education teacher, child's general education teacher(s), parent(s), child's district professional(s), and child) translating the child's evaluation and information into a practical plan for instruction and delivery of services.

Impartial Hearing Officer: A fair, unbiased person appointed by the state to preside over a due process hearing.

Impulsive: Acting (upon impulse) without thought or consideration of the outcome or consequences of an action.

Inclusion/Mainstreaming: Strategies and processes that educators, therapists, principals, families, and students use to include students/classmates with disabilities in general education classes and activities and in society as a whole.

Independent Evaluation: An evaluation conducted by a qualified agency or individual who is not employed by or under contract with the public school system.

Independent Living: Carrying on day-to-day living functions either with personal attendant care services or without direct supervision.

Individualized Education Program (IEP): The written educational plan for the student in special education with goals and objectives to be learned. Each student has his/her own IEP.

Individualized Family Service Plan (IFSP): A written plan for each infant or toddler receiving early intervention services that includes goals for the family and a transition plan for the child into services for children above the age of 3.

Informal Assessment: Assessment procedures such as classroom observations, interviewing, or teacher-made tests that have not usually been tried out with large groups of people and that do not necessarily have a standard set of instructions for their use and interpretation.

Intelligence Quotient (IQ): A measurement of thinking (cognitive) ability for comparing an individual with others in the same age group.

ITP (Individualized Transition Plan): A yearly plan designed for every child receiving special education services from age 14 on, which supports that child's growth from one stage of his/her educational placement to the next, that is, from high school to post-high school activities. This plan is centered around the child and his/her desires for the future. Several factors are routinely addressed in the ITP: vocational interests, educational plans, and cultural and social concerns.

Kinesthetic Method: A method of teaching reading or remediating reading disorders by having the student trace the outline of the words, thereby using muscle movement to reinforce and supplement auditory and visual stimuli.

Language, Expressive: Speaking and writing.

Language, Receptive: Listening and reading.

Least Restrictive Environment (LRE): One of the principles of normalization, it requires that people with disabilities receive services and support in environments that do not limit their life activities unnecessarily. For example, students with disabilities should be educated in ways that meet their needs and least limit their opportunities to be near and interact with other students.

Mainstreaming/Inclusion: Strategies and processes that educators, therapists, principals, families, and students use to include students/classmates with disabilities in general education classes and activities and in society as a whole.

Mediation: A formal intervention process between parents and school systems to achieve reconciliation, settlement, or compromise.

Modality: The pathway through which an individual receives information and learns. This may be auditory, visual, or tactile-kinesthetic (listening, seeing, or touching, etc.).

Multidisciplinary Team (M-team): The people who gather information through the assessment and evaluation process and who are trained in a variety of specialized areas and disciplines. Parents are a part of this team, along with therapists, psychologists, and teachers, and they bring their very specialized perspective of their child to the team.

Multisensory Approach: The use of many modalities or avenues of input at the same time to teach; the student will see, hear, smell, and touch an object or perform a particular task using his/her eyes, eyes, nose, and hands.

Neurologists: Medical doctors who specialize in diseases of the nervous system. They diagnose and may treat patients who are thought to have physical causes for mental disturbances.

Norms: Information, provided by the test-maker, about "normal" or typical performance on the test. Individual test scores can be compared to the typical score made by other persons in the same age group or grade level.

Objectives: Small, measurable steps of learning that help a student reach a goal, for example, learning to hold a pencil before learning to write.

Occupational Therapy (OT): Services provided by, or under the supervision of, an occupational therapist to evaluate and train a person to use gross and fine motor skills and self-care skills, and to use sensory and perceptual motor integration with the intent of strengthening the person's ability to function as independently as possible.

Operations: Processes involved in thinking:

- cognition—comprehension or understanding
- memory—retention and recall of information
- convergent thinking—bringing together of known facts
- divergent thinking—use of knowledge in new ways
- evaluation—critical thinking

Paraprofessionals: Individuals who work under the supervision or direction of licensed teachers or related services personnel to assist in areas that relate to personal, social, and instructional needs. The term includes, but is not limited to, instructional or program assistants, school bus monitors, interpreters, notetakers, and job coaches.

Parent Involvement: Parents have the right and responsibility to participate with the schools in special education planning and decisions. Federal and state regulations support parent involvement.

Payor of Last Resort: Funding source to be used for services that an eligible child needs but is not entitled to under any other federal, state, local, or private source.

Perception: The process of organizing or interpreting information received through the senses, such as auditory or visual thoughts, ideas, or impressions; a level of learning that can be described as existing in the mind.

Perceptual–motor: A term describing the use of the various channels of perception with motor activity or movement. Channels of perception include visual, auditory, tactile, and kinesthetic (seeing, hearing, touching).

Perseverance: The tendency to continue an activity once it has been started and to be unable to change or stop the activity, even though it is acknowledged to have become inappropriate.

Phonetics: Study of all the speech sounds in the language and how these sounds are produced.

Phonics: Use of phonetics in the teaching of reading. Relating the sound (phoneme) of the language with the equivalent written symbol.

Physical Therapy (PT): Services provided by, or under the supervision of, a physical therapist to evaluate individual developmental levels, functional abilities, reflex levels, range of motion, muscle strengths, perceptual motor levels, and respiratory function, and to provide therapy in identified areas of need.

Placement: The services and classes chosen by the case conference committee that will provide the most appropriate program for the student. The IEP is the planning document used to describe all the details of the student's program or placement.

Procedural Safeguards: The steps taken to ensure that a person's legal rights are not denied (see "Complaint," "Due Process").

Psychiatrist: Medical doctor who specializes in mental illness. Psychiatrists counsel patients, diagnose mental illness, and prescribe drugs.

Psychologist: A person trained in dealing with the study of mental processes and human behavior (not to be confused with a psychiatrist, who is a medical doctor).

Psychometrist: A psychologist who specializes in administering and evaluating psychological tests, including intelligence, aptitude, and interests tests.

Psychomotor: Refers to muscle responses, including development of fine-motor small muscles (cutting, etc.) and large muscles (walking, jumping, etc.).

Receptive Language: The ability to understand language that is spoken or written by others and received by the individual; receptive language skills include listening, reading, and understanding signs and finger spelling.

Referral: The process of directing a person to another person or service agency that can provide needed services. Referral is also the term used to start the educational evaluation process.

Regulations: Statements that clarify the laws that are passed by Congress or the state legislature. Regulations are written and issued by departments within the executive branch of government; the regulations for P.L. 101-476 Individuals with Disabilities Education Act, which were enacted by the U.S. Congress, were written by the U.S. Department of Education.

Rehabilitation: The process of helping a person who has a disability learn or relearn the skills needed for daily living and work activities.

Related Services: Developmental, corrective, and other supportive services as are required to assist a child with a disability to benefit from special education; these include services such as transportation, physical therapy, occupational therapy, audiology, etc.

Resource Room: A room within a school where a specially trained teacher gives help in specified subjects to students who need extra help. This special assistance is usually provided for students who have learning disabilities in an "LD Resource Room," where the teacher has a small number of students and can give individual help to each one.

Resource Specialist Teacher (RST): A credentialed teacher with advanced training in special education. The resource specialist can do the following: offer educational assessment of students, provide individual and small group instruction, develop instructional materials and teaching techniques for the classroom teacher, assess pupil progress, and coordinate recommendations in the student's IEP with parents and teachers.

Self-concept: A person's idea of and feelings about himself/herself.

Sensorimotor: Relating to both senses and movement and the combination of the input of sensations and the output of motor activity. Motor activity reflects what is happening to the sensory organs, such as visual, auditory, tactile, and kinesthetic sensations.

Sequencing: The ability to put things in the correct order. Sequential memory is the ability to remember, in order, what has been heard, seen, or read.

Service Coordination: Activities carried out by a service coordinator that may include management and assistance to families or individuals to gain access to appropriate services. The term *case management* may be used in place of the term *service coordination.*

Social Perception: The ability to understand the meaning of behavior in situations and appropriately relate such understanding to one's own behavior.

Social Worker: A person from a service agency, such as a nursing home or group home, involved with helping an individual and/or family deal with specific problems and needs (e.g., social, emotional, financial, etc.).

Soft Neurological Signs: Nervous system disorders that are mild or swift and difficult to detect, as contrasted with the gross or obvious neurological abnormalities.

Spatial Orientation: The ability to organize space in terms of the individual relating his physical self to the environment with reference to distance, size, position, and direction.

Special Education (Sp. Ed.; S.E.): Instruction designed for one person's needs, specially planned to satisfy or address the needs of a person with a disability.

Specific Learning Disability (SLD): Refers to problems in academic functioning, such as writing, spelling, doing math, or reading, which cannot be explained by ability, vision, hearing, or health impairments.

Speech/Language Therapy: The process of correcting speech and/or language problems or working to improve a person's ability to use speech or language. A specially trained speech therapist or pathologist teaches on a one-to-one or small group basis.

Spina Bifida: A congenital disability; an opening in the spine that causes nerves within the spine to be damaged. There may be differing degrees of paralysis in the lower part of the body.

Standardized Test: Any one of a variety of tests given to a student or group of students using uniform conditions, with the same instructions, time limits, etc. Tests are designed by sampling performance of other students, using results as a "norm" for judging achievement.

State Plan: A plan in which each state writes out, in detail, how it will provide services to comply with federal law in order to receive federal funds. The state plan is required under P.L. 101-476 (formerly P.L. 94-142). Copies are available upon request from the Indiana Department of Education.

Supported Employment: Paid employment in community settings for persons with severe disabilities who need ongoing support to perform their work. Support can include on-the-job training, transportation, or supervision.

Tactile Perception: The ability to interpret and give meaning to sensory stimuli that are experienced through the sense of touch.

TBI: Traumatic Brain Injury.

Total Communication: The combined use of finger spelling, sign language, speech, and lip reading to communicate with persons who have a hearing impairment.

Transition Plan, Individualized (ITP): A yearly plan designed for every child receiving special education services from age 14 on, which supports that child's growth from one stage of his/her educational placement to the next, that is, from high school to post-high school activities. This plan is centered around the child and his/her desires for the future. Several factors are routinely addressed in the ITP: vocational interests, educational plans, and cultural and social concerns.

Transition Services: Services provided during the period between preschool and school, school and adult services, or any other period where careful planning is needed to ensure the smooth transfer of records and information and the continuity of programming from one setting to another. The term commonly refers primarily to planning during high school for adult services.

Visual Discrimination: The ability to recognize small differences between similar and slightly different forms or shapes, as in alphabet letters p, d, or q.

Visual Motor Coordination: The ability to coordinate vision with the movements of the body or parts of the body.

Visual Perception: The identification, organization, and interpretation of stimuli received by the individual through vision/eyesight.

Visual Reception: The ability to gain meaning from visual stimuli.

Vocational Education: An educational program that provides training in daily living skills, occupational skills for paid or unpaid employment, and/or career preparation for students in post-secondary programs.

VR: Vocational Rehabilitation (or VOC Rehab).

Index

T

U

V

W

Z